THE LIBRARY OF HO

MY PRIVATE WAR

The Library of Holocaust Testimonies

My Lost World by Sara Rosen
From Dachau to Dunkirk by Fred Pelican
Breathe Deeply, My Son by Henry Wermuth
My Private War by Jacob Gerstenfeld-Maltiel

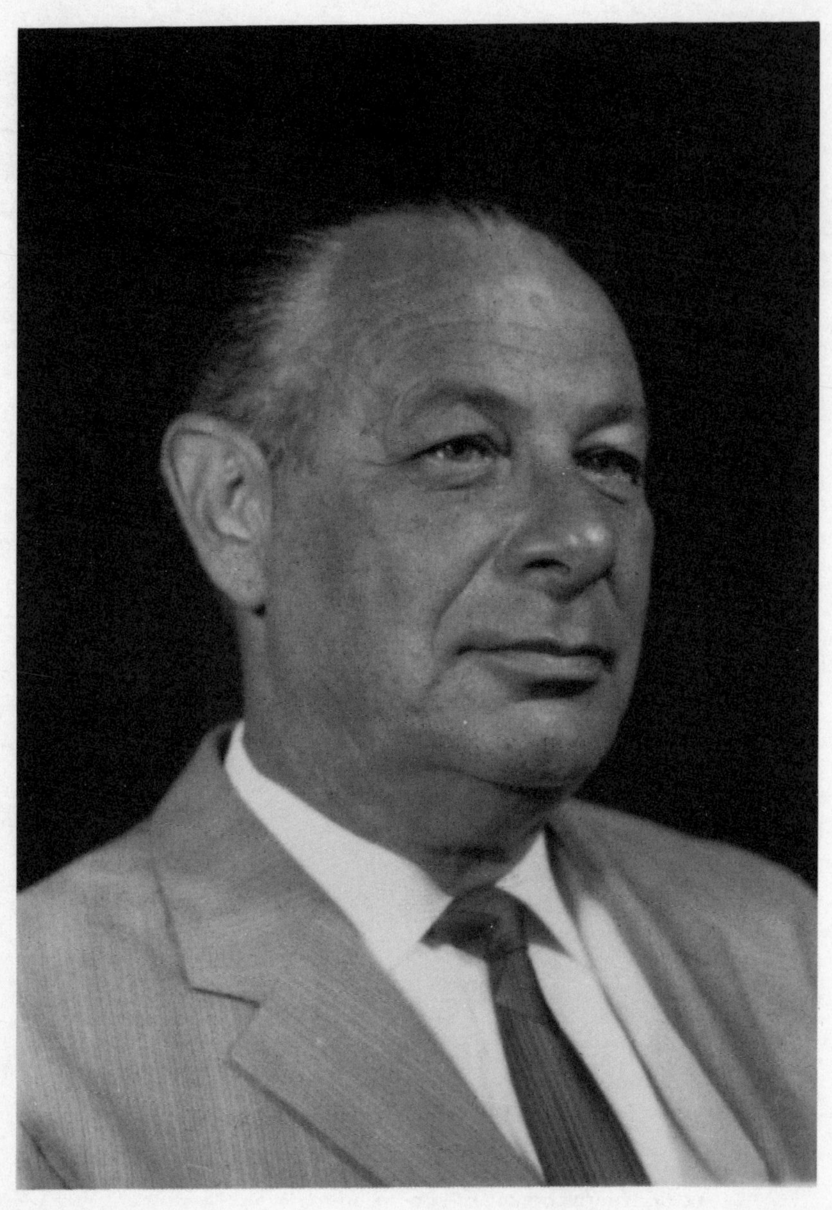

MY PRIVATE WAR

One Man's Struggle to Survive the Soviets and the Nazis

Jacob Gerstenfeld-Maltiel

VALLENTINE MITCHELL

First published in 1993 in Great Britain by
VALLENTINE MITCHELL & CO. LTD.
Gainsborough House, Gainsborough Road,
London E11 1RS, England

and in the United States of America by
VALLENTINE MITCHELL
c/o International Specialized Book Services, Inc.
5602 N.E. Hassalo Street, Portland, Oregon 97213

British Library Cataloguing in Publication Data

Gerstenfeld-Maltiel, Jacob
My Private War: One Man's Struggle to
Survive the Soviets and the Nazis. –
(Library of Holocaust Testimonies)
I. Title II. Series
940.54

ISBN 0-85303-260-2

Library of Congress Cataloging-in-Publication Data

Maltiel-Gerstenfeld, Jacob.
My private war : one man's struggle to survive the Soviets and the Nazis / Jacob Gerstenfeld-Maltiel.
p. cm. — (The Library of Holocaust Testimonies)
ISBN 0-85303-260-2
1. Jews—Ukraine—L'vov—Persecutions. 2. Holocaust, Jewish (1939–1945)—Ukraine—L'vov—Personal narratives. 3. Maltiel-Gerstenfeld, Jacob. 4. L'vov (Ukraine)—Ethnic relations.
I. Title. II. Series.
DS135.R93L8954 1993
940.53'18'0948817—sc20 92-34654
CIP

Typeset by Regent Typesetting, London

Printed and bound in the United Kingdom by
Watkiss Studios Limited, Holme Court, Biggleswade, Beds.

Contents

CONTENTS

The Library of Holocaust Testimonies

It is greatly to the credit of Frank Cass that this series of survivors' testimonies is being published in Britain. The need for such a series has long been apparent here, where many survivors made their homes.

Since the end of the war in 1945 the terrible events of the Nazi destruction of European Jewry have cast a pall over our time. Six million Jews were murdered within a short period; the few survivors have had to carry in their memories whatever remains of the knowledge of Jewish life in more than a dozen countries, in several thousand towns, in tens of thousands of villages, and in innumerable families. The precious gift of recollection has been the sole memorial for millions of people whose lives were suddenly and brutally cut off.

For many years, individual survivors have published their testimonies. But many more have been reluctant to do so, often because they could not believe that they would find a publisher for their efforts.

In my own work over the past two decades, I have been approached by many survivors who had set down their memories in writing, but who did not know how to have them published. I realized what a considerable emotional strain the writing down of such hellish memories had been. I also realized, as I read many dozens of such accounts, how important each account was, in its own way, in recounting aspects of the story that had not been told before, and adding to our understanding of the wide range of human suffering, struggle and aspiration.

With so many people and so many places involved, including many hundreds of camps, it was inevitable that the historians and students of the Holocaust should find it difficult at times to grasp the scale and range of the events. The publication of memoirs is therefore an indispensable part of the extension of knowledge, and of public awareness of the crimes that had been committed against a whole people.

Martin Gilbert
Merton College
Oxford

Introduction

And I alone have escaped to tell the tale

Job 1, 16

Who walked through Poland's day of carnage
And was a Jew from the dead arisen
Made wiser by the death which he survived
Must feed the flames like an apostle

Stanislaw Lec

Every Jew who came through the nightmare of the *Shoah* did so as the result of a unique and miraculous set of circumstances. This was certainly true of Jacob Gerstenfeld-Maltiel. Born in Lvov in 1907 into a prosperous and acculturated Jewish family, he studied law at Lvov University between 1926 and 1932, working subsequently in an insurance company and a bank in Warsaw. When the war broke out, he fled eastward to Lvov, where he experienced the 21 months of Soviet occupation, as he describes in the first section of these memoirs. His account of Soviet rule, written like the whole of his testimony in the last months of 1943 and early 1944, has both immediacy and credibility.

Gerstenfeld was not sympathetic to communism and was well aware of the brutal and terroristic character of the Soviet system. He describes in some detail the all-pervasive propaganda and totalitarian aspirations of the new regime, as well as its use of deportation as a means of eliminating its opponents. But he also shows how the new rulers' incompetence and slovenliness enabled a resourceful individual to survive and even to prosper. Gerstenfeld's main worry seems to have been that he would be too successful within the new regime and might, as a consequence, lose any chance of remaining within the European world, which he believed at the outset of the war would soon re-establish itself.

It was this unwillingness to enmesh himself in the Soviet system that led him to refuse a promotion to a senior book-keeping post in the Urals. Certainly, in Gerstenfeld's account, the Soviet system was characterized by its long-term goal of creating a new socialist man and was prepared to employ whatever means were necessary to achieve this end. In his experience, however, its violence was different in scale, and perhaps in quality, from what was meted out by the Nazis to the population of Lvov, in particular, to its Jewish community swollen by the war to nearly 160,000 people.

Although the Lvov ghetto was the third largest in Nazi-occupied Europe, relatively little has been written about it. Lvov, before the First World War the capital of the Austrian province of Galicia, had been the third largest city in pre-war Poland, with a population of over 350,000. Predominantly Polish, but situated in the mainly Ukrainian eastern part of the province, it had in 1939 a Jewish population of nearly 110,000. The number of Ukrainians in the city is more difficult to determine because of the desire of the Polish census-takers to inflate the size of the Polish population, but they probably accounted for between 10 and 15 per cent of its population. Certainly Lvov was one of the main centres of the Ukrainian national movement, the seat of the Greek Catholic Metropolitan, Archbishop Andrei Sheptytsky, and the headquarters of the main Ukrainian political parties in Poland, like the Ukrainian National Democratic Union (UNDO), with their extensive system of co-operatives and highly developed daily and weekly press.

Lvov was also a major Jewish centre. Jewish emancipation had been achieved under Habsburg rule in the 1860s and had been followed by the acculturation and assimilation of much of the Jewish elite. Lvov was, indeed, the home of the first reformed synagogue on the Polish lands, where services were shortened, accompanied by an organ and a sermon was preached, first in German and then, from 1903 on, in Polish. This transition from German to Polish as the language of the Jewish elite was an index of the success of Polonization as pursued by the autonomous Polish-controlled governments of Galicia which ruled the province from the 1860s.

With the development in the province in the 1880s and 1890s of modern political anti-semitism, there was a measure of disillusionment with the view that assimilation to the Polish nation would "solve" the Jewish problem. This led to the emergence of a vigorous and well-established Zionist movement. Certainly the pattern of Jewish social and political life in Lvov differed significantly from that in the major Jewish centres in Russian Poland, Warsaw, Lodz and Vilna. German and Polish were widely spoken within the community, and politically Zionism was much stronger than its rivals, Jewish socialism and neo-orthodoxy. The number of Jews who could "pass" as Poles and even as Germans was much higher than in Warsaw and elsewhere in Russian Poland, as emerges constantly in Gerstenfeld's narrative. The establishment of an independent Polish state had led to the centralization of political and cultural life in the capital, Warsaw. This phenomenon also affected the Jewish life, but on the eve of the Second World War, Lvov was still a major centre of Jewish activity. The community maintained three Jewish secondary schools with Polish as the language of instruction, a Hebrew college and a great many *hederim*. It was still, as it had long been, the home of a large number of Jewish publishers and supported three daily Jewish newspapers, two in Polish and one in Yiddish.

The character of Nazi policy towards the Jews of Lvov did not differ significantly from their behaviour elsewhere in occupied Poland. The only difference was that, as in Vilna and in Bialystok, the period between the imposition of Nazi rule in June 1941 and the adoption of the policy of mass murder was rather brief. This accounts for a number of specific features of the Lvov situation: the constant incitement by the Nazis of vicious anti-Jewish violence and the late establishment (September 1942) of a ghetto physically separated from the rest of the city. For the rest, the nature of Nazi rule in Lvov was very similar to that in other large Polish towns such as Warsaw and Lodz. Here Gerstenfeld's account is a significant contribution to our understanding of how the policy of genocide was carried out. He stresses that the success of Nazi policy depended on deception – the Nazis took great pains to convince the Jews that their goal was not mass murder, but deportation to the East or even beyond Europe. Jewish experience made this deception credible. The Jews had undergone a long history of persecution and had survived it largely by waiting for the outbreak of anti-Jewish fanaticism to abate, in the belief that even if a part of the Jewish people were lost, the bulk would survive.

This belief that Nazi persecution could be survived played into the hands of the mass murderers. The Germans were careful to disguise their goals. As Gerstenfeld observes:

> Over the perspective of time, reflecting upon the behaviour of the Germans from the very first day of their entry to Lvov it can be seen that all the separate actions, requisitions, confiscations, and abuse come together into one deceitful plan, worked out with typically German cunning. It was obviously figured out in detail. They did not allow one moment of respite to the Jewish population. Mass slaughter called *Aktions* were interlaced with periods of relative calm but these were marked by mass abuse. The ultimate objective was to destroy morally, to torment psychologically and spiritually people doomed to death, and to bring people to such a condition that in no one would the thought of defence or resistance arise. This devilish idea, spawned in some pathological imagination, was unfortunately realized to the full (p. 65).

Yet who could believe that mass murder was possible and that it would be carried out in the twentieth century in the heart of Europe by one of the continent's most advanced nations? When in late 1943 he met his brother who had fled in mid-1941 to Romania, Gerstenfeld had great difficulty in convincing him of what had really happened to the Jews under Nazi rule:

> Among other details, I told him that in the so-called "small ghetto" in Lvov there were 45,000 people whose food supplies had been completely cut off. My brother jumped up in protest, the better to express his doubt: "You're exaggerating! That's impossible! Why, that would mean mass murder!" I was struck dumb. I did not tell any more stories. I had only been giving him some facts about the "small ghetto" and not the most cruel ones at that.
>
> At that moment I realized that a normal person, brought up in ordered conditions, could not grasp what the Germans had done. The mind boggles at the thought of deeds which exceed in brutality and cruelty anything we could ever imagine, actions compared with which even the loathsome exploits of Genghis Khan pale into insignificance. The enormity of it by far exceeded normal human understanding. Only a person who had had direct experience could understand what had happened (p. 301).

The failure to comprehend the enormity of Nazi goals explains the collaboration of the Judenräte, and also why the Germans sought this collaboration:

> Organizing the Judenräte in Lvov and other towns, the Germans knew exactly what they intended to use the members of the Judenrat for. They contrived everything very carefully, and actually succeeded in convincing many distinguished social and political leaders to let themselves be used to aid them to achieve their purpose. They went like sheep to the slaughter and led thousands with them, trusting the explanations of the Nazis, who posed as people governed by law and not, as afterwards came out, by brute force alone.
>
> The Germans denied that their goal was the extermination of Jews. They said that indeed the Führer did not intend after winning the war to allow Jews to remain in Europe, but that meant only deportation to various colonies. Yet the best proof that their goal was solely to exterminate the Jews can be found in the wide powers and responsibilities they gave to the Judenräte.
>
> People working in the Judenrat were relatively protected from being caught on the streets for labour. The councillors of the Judenräte got very wide protection; personal immunity, immunity for their family and

> even of their homes. With such privileges, the Germans managed to entice people who at first were very reluctant to collaborate with them. The Jewish militiamen got better conditions of life than the rest of the Jewish population. They obtained protection of their home, the right to be on the streets after curfew hours, greater food rations and of course the uniform which gave them full personal protection. By such trifles, though necessities in those times, the Jews were divided into two groups; one extremely harassed and a second favoured. From this point, it was only one small step to use one group against the other, and not long afterwards this occurred (pp. 65–6).

It was this perception that no good could be achieved through working in the Judenrat, but that, on the contrary, one would only find oneself in an increasingly compromised position, which led Gerstenfeld, after a short period, to abandon his position there:

> I was disturbed by the uselessness of working in the Judenrat. I was working in the inner control department and every day new difficulties were made by the Germans. They alone were blocking the execution of their own decrees and orders. Something peculiar must be going on. On the other hand the oppressive atmosphere of the Judenrat, the misery seen at every step, without any chance to help, became darker and deeper. We felt like animals in a trap, and it produced in me a deep state of anxiety. I felt the atavistic fear of a trapped animal. To try to break at any price from the hands of the Germans, from this trap, before the small crack which still admitted a little light into the abysmal darkness into which the Nazis had pushed the Jews closed, I decided to take the post in Galikol, to be further away from this place of torture that was the Jewish quarter. I made the decision (pp. 69–70).

At the same time, he understands the motivation of those who continued to work in the Judenrat, pointing out that after its collaboration with the first large deportation, its members could no longer be "bluffed into cooperation" (p. 97). Accordingly the role of the Judenrat diminished, and Gerstenfeld reached the conclusion that there was nothing it could have done to resist Nazi genocide. Some of its members distinguished themselves by their courage in the face of Nazi brutality, and Gerstenfeld honours its chairman, Joseph Parnas, murdered for refusing to yield to every Nazi whim, as one of the heroes of the Jewish struggle to survive.

His account of the Jewish police is also fair-minded, bearing in mind how soon it was written after the events it describes and how much hatred the body had by that stage aroused within the Jewish community. Initially, as he points out, the Jewish police did help to create some necessary order:

> In September 1941, the Germans became filled with concern about the efficient functioning of the Judenrat, and insisted upon the need to create a Jewish "Order Service." They even brought the commander of the Jewish militia from Warsaw to instruct. At first the Judenrat assembled 20 men, as the cadre of the future militia. A short time afterwards, the roster of militia was increased and they took responsibility for order in the part of town inhabited by Jews, around the building of the Judenrat, at Jewish groceries, at warehouses, at bringing the recalcitrant to work etc. The idyll was very short-lived. Before long this Jewish "Order Service" would degenerate into an instrument in the hands of the Nazis, to sow destructive disorder in the life of their fellow Jews on their way to ultimate extinction (pp. 74–5).

This process of corruption did not take long to occur:

> The Jewish militia developed enormously, growing more and more into the role of police, more and more separating itself from the mass of Jewry, becoming completely an executive arm of the SS and Gestapo. The police spirit, it may seem, is immanent in objects like a police cap or police uniform, invading living bodies and playing havoc with the souls of people till now normal. The height of infamy, however, was to be found in the *Sonderdienst* (special squad) of the Jewish militia. From the moment it was created in April 1942, this detachment was the executive organ of the Gestapo and constituted a sort of link between the central Gestapo office on Pelczynska Street, the Judenrat and the HQ of the Jewish militia. The commander was a man named Goliger Schapiro. He wrote himself with letters of blood into the martyrology of the Jewry of Lvov, the wounds bleeding perhaps more than those inflicted by Germans, since they were inflicted by a Jew. Goliger's deputy was a man named Krumkolz, a refugee from Krakow. These two very often outdid the Germans in cruelty to Jews. They both took even the most trifling opportunity to extort fantastic bribes, threatening to give the victim to the Gestapo and actually doing this, when the need arose (p. 100).

The incredible character of the Nazis' genocidal plans and the hope for survival also account for the Jewish failure to embark on active resistance; as did the sedulous use of terror by the occupiers.

People have charged Polish Jewry with submissiveness and lack of

> courage. Someone who did not know much about the conditions might say that he would have chosen a quick death, than a slow torture, leading inevitably to death, that he would have preferred to perish in a hopeless fight, to take with him at least one German. People do not realize the sum of two things in this situation. First of all, none of us dreamt that the laws about the status of Jews were a dead letter and that the aim of the Germans was the murder of the whole Jewish population. On the other hand, as I have tried to describe, the Germans, by greater or smaller harassments, annihilated the morale of the Jews, destroyed the feeling of being human, pushed us down to the level of undernourished brute slaves, deceiving us until the last moment by pictures of a life of some kind, even within the framework of Nazi law. Never during all that time, even during the finishing off the remnant of three and a half million mass of Polish Jewry, the tiny handful which in no case could be a danger, did the Germans find enough moral courage, to raise the visor and say openly "our aim is to kill off all the Jews" (pp. 85–6).

Ground down by the constant harassment, the Jews were kept going by the hope of outliving the Nazi regime. Within a few weeks of the Nazi invasion of the Soviet Union, hope, seemingly irrepressible among the Jews, began to blossom. Gerstenfeld comments bitterly on the belief that the Germans had not been able to crush the Soviets in the initial phases of the campaign. Perhaps they were not, after all, invincible.

> Slowly hope began to gleam that perhaps this time the Germans had slipped up. From this side perhaps the rescue for the Jews would come. Hope, stupid hope, tottering, flickering, hardly visible from afar, bore us up. We must hang on somehow. Unfortunately the dawn was far away, and before the sun was to rise, the abysmal darkness of the Nazi night would swallow up millions of human beings. No! Not human – only Jewish (p. 73).

He also described how, after the long hours of compulsory labour, the Jews, in their overcrowded quarters, nourished their hopes of outlasting the Nazis:

> People got together for half an hour's injection of optimism. During the day, the theme was the horror of the day, so in the evening, the radio news was commented upon with perpetual optimism, despite the nightmare awaiting us in the morning; our Jewish optimism dictated our opinions. Although the Russians were hundreds of kilometres away from Lvov, we saw our saviours already at the gates of the town. If someone reminded us that an *Aktion* or some other Nazi harassment

threatened, he would receive from all sides the answer that surely the Germans would wait before acting, as for example, in another town there were riots because of the lack of potatoes ... One man claimed: "Stalin has decided by a certain date to clear Russian soil of every German" ... A quietly expressed doubt that this news originated perhaps from the "A.J.W." (as Jews want) news-agency was drowned in the flood of optimism without anybody paying attention (p. 168).

An important tool of Nazi rule was the constant use of sadistic terror. Gerstenfeld gives many examples of this almost mindless fury and of the devastating effect it had on its victims. He refers to the impossibility of living in "constant fear" and graphically expounds the impact on the Jewish community:

> We lived in terror of torments, insults, violence, robberies, murders, and before everyone's eyes stood the spectres of hunger and torture. We were hurled beyond the orbit of society, even beyond the compass of men. Our thousand-years-old traditions of culture were torn out of us like living flesh. We were systematically degraded to the role of animals, herded, worn out by endless toil, baited by endless harassment. The Germans operated with the help of such perfidiously camouflaged methods that wider and wider circles, even people of the strongest character, descended completely to the state of brutes. Very few during the two years 1941–1943 were tough enough to avoid this – perhaps the worst of the means of crushing the spirit (p. 75).

Terror took various forms. There was the random murderous violence on the streets, sometimes on a small scale, sometimes taking on larger dimensions as in the pogrom which accompanied the "Petlura days", ostensibly Ukrainian revenge for Petlura's assassination by a Jew in the 1920s. Then there was the fear engendered by the round-ups which accompanied deportations:

> On the night of 15–16 November, about midnight, people knew that on the following morning an *Aktion* would begin. The Jewish militia was ordered to be in readiness. Warnings were at once sent to relatives and friends, to be prepared. AKTION! The sound of this word – even now a year later – when I write it, the very thought of it makes my blood run cold. I cannot find the few words to put onto a scrap of paper, to describe the stream of blood and tears, implicit in the word. Before, we never had any real idea of what fear meant. Now, a few hours before an *Aktion*, people in the ghetto understood. Wild primeval animal terror, before an

> elemental calamity that had invaded and paralysed every mind. Human beings felt like dust in the face of the vast power that opposed them. The feeling of fright during such a moment can be compared to that of an animal running from a prairie-fire (p. 158).

Fear of being sent to the concentration camp established by the Janowska road on the outskirts of Lvov increased the terror:

> Several letters were smuggled from the camp. The horrors in them were appalling. I do not feel equal to describing this, only one hell on earth among many created by the Nazis in the world, words fail me. That horror hung over our heads day and night like the sword of Damocles. Over everyone, everywhere, in the workplace, on the street, at home. The fear of the camp deprived us of our will to live, froze the blood in our veins, sent a shiver down our spines (p. 91).

This fear pervaded the souls of the Jews and made escape from the ghetto more difficult:

> The deep-seated sense of bearing a stigma of abasement was the greatest source of danger for those fleeing the ghetto. A Jew crossing to begin a new life on the Aryan side first got rid of the Jewish armband, which served as the external symbol of humiliation. This seemed difficult: how to do it, where, someone might see me, etc. But all these difficulties were trifles. Nobody was aware of the real obstacle: the stigma branded into our souls by the Germans, the stigma of inferiority, of the cattle trains, of hunted game, of fear of one's fellow humans, stigma invisible but branded deep within. It was not noticeable in the ghetto as there it was ever-present and natural (pp. 100–1).

What of the reaction of the bystanders to these horrendous events? Gerstenfeld is very critical of the behaviour of both Poles and Ukrainians. He reserves his deepest scorn for the Ukrainians; it is striking that the famous appeal to his flock by the Greek Catholic Metropolitan Archbishop Sheptytsky in which he affirmed that the two primary commandments were "Thou shalt not kill" and "Thou shalt love thy neighbour as thyself" does not seem to have worked any resonance in the ghetto. In this respect, Gerstenfeld's account should be set against the memoirs of Rabbi David Kahane, who survived the war hidden by the Metropolitan.

He is less harsh on the Poles. He points out that when, in the immediate aftermath of the German occupation, the Jews were required to pay a 20,000,000-ruble fine, many Poles were induced to show solidarity:

> ... the venom of the omnipresent German propaganda had not yet poisoned the souls of the Polish population, nor yet immobilized the conscience of Polish society. It had not yet fallen so low that for a bite of white bread they would renounce their fatherland. Cases occurred, though not too often, of impulses of solidarity. I knew personally some members of the Polish intelligentsia, who paid appreciable sums to help with the contribution. Although the sums made little difference, the gesture of good will showed a spirit that counted and had a strong moral meaning. A handful demonstrated their solidarity, but not for long; they also were to abandon us and throw us upon our own sad resources (p. 63).

Later, cases of Poles denouncing Jews or seeking to improve their position by declaring themselves to be *Volksdeutsche* became more frequent. Yet Gerstenfeld also reveals that it was a Polish peasant and his family who finally persuaded him, when in a labour camp, not to give up hope, and that it was a Polish railwayman who finally gave him the courage to jump off a train bound for the death camp of Belzec.

The personality of the author emerges clearly from the narrative. Appalled by the immensity of what he has seen, Jacob Gerstenfeld after describing the therapeutic effect of attempting to describe his experiences, comments:

> I struggled hard to find words which would help the reader understand the nightmare I was trying to describe. The reader, I knew, had not experienced all those things and would frequently be unable to grasp events which have no equal in human history in the immensity of their cruelty and the degree of brutality employed in the implementation of the cruel design (this inability may be one of the givens of human personality) (p. 305).

He does often allow his savage indignation expression when describing the horrendous character of Nazi atrocities. These passages are among the most moving and powerful of the memoir. Perhaps not surprisingly, he has greater difficulty in finding words to describe his reactions to his own sufferings. His father was the first to die:

> On the second day of this *Aktion* I received information from my mother that my father had been missing for 24 hours. He was called to the commissariat of the Ukrainian militia to get a visa on his passport. We never saw him again (p. 61).

His wife was seized in the *Aktion* of August 1942:

> Only in the afternoon did the news of the purge in the workshops reach me. My colleagues getting the news hid it from me knowing that my wife worked there. After I got the information at last, I began to run to various colleagues and persons of influence to try to extricate my wife from the camp. It was in vain. Twice I myself barely escaped from the claws of the thugs. In the evening without reckoning the risks I went in the direction of the camp, where a German checked my documents and beat me up badly. Finally like a beaten dog stupefied from fatigue, I returned in helpless despair to my empty home. I consoled myself at first that perhaps the women were not taken to death; after all they were healthy, in the full bloom of their strength as workers. I could not conceive that the only aim was the senseless murder of thousands of women. Perhaps they yet lived, maybe there was even the most trifling hope? Maybe ... No! Unfortunately, those who had fallen into the hands of the Gestapo had not the smallest hope. All perished, like pebbles thrown from a cliff, leaving behind only ever widening circles, weaker and weaker, till very soon they also disappeared ... Among them, my wife ... (pp. 133–4).

His mother died before the closing of the ghetto in September 1942:

> On the night of 4 September, she survived the only bombardment of Lvov by the Russians and fell asleep not to awaken again. The whole night I sat at her bedside. In the morning, I learned that she had been granted Heaven's greatest blessing in this vale of tears and had departed this life in her sleep, to a better world where there were no Germans, no Hitler, no *Aktions* and no Ukrainians. Can such a place really exist? Maybe only in the next world. The *Hevra Kadisha* (The Holy Brotherhood) interred her the next day in the old Jewish cemetery on Spitalna Street without a funeral service. I had nobody now. The world was unreal, my eyes reeled. All my bonds were severed. What really held me here? Where should I go? (p. 143).

These were heavy blows:

> I had nobody. Within one year my father, my wife, had been taken away, disappeared and perished, my mother had died, the rest of my family was destroyed. What had I to live for? For whom? I wanted to care for somebody, to do something for somebody.
>
> I had nobody, I hated the now empty corners. Not to look at these surroundings among which – not so long ago – I had been together with

> my wife and mother. To burn everything which had felt the hands of my nearest and which now would serve the Germans. To fight? Against whom? What for? I had nobody. Like a gloomy refrain these words molested me at every step with every movement.
>
> One of my colleagues informed me that there was a chance to enter a farm-camp of the SS near Lvov. Well! Let it be a camp. Only to leave, only not to look at all that had surrounded me up to now, after all ... I had nobody (p. 143).

One episode was so traumatic that he was unable to record it in his testimony. In an *Aktion*, he and several others were seized by the Germans and forced to dig a common grave. Gerstenfeld fainted as the soldiers fired and fell into the grave. He was left for dead and thus survived. It was this episode, according to his son Ron, which led him to change his surname on his arrival in *Eretz Yisrael* to Maltiel – "God saved me".

Under the stress of his ordeal, Maltiel temporarily lost hope. But his determination and inner strength brought back his will to live:

> Yet ... after several days, maybe after several weeks, I am not sure, since we lived without dates, holidays or Sundays, I began to awaken from the spiritual torpor into which the last ordeals had thrust me. Time eased the pain of my wounds. A worry slept on is no more a worry, it became recollection. I made contact with one peasant family. Often in the evenings, I would visit my new acquaintances and I entertained their small daughter. The peasants – unusually – extremely kind-hearted people, saw my apathy. They urged me to flee. They even promised to put me in touch with a smuggler, who would smuggle me over the border. They appealed to my common sense to brace myself and strengthen my resolution, as the Germans, in their opinion, would not long maintain the farm camp and would finally shoot all of us like dogs. The overwhelming instinct for life, the deepest desire of every living creature, awakened and raised the alarm. At last, in a way unknown to me, in a place where I was supposed to end my life, the will to live returned. I came to my senses. Everything around me emerged in another light. Only the strong, physically, spiritually or financially would endure and maybe manage to extricate themselves. *Let me be strong* (pp. 145–6).

As his will to live returned, so too did his desire to deny the Nazis the opportunity of destroying him. He resolved to leave the ghetto, where death was certain. After weighing his options, he decided that it was too risky to attempt to escape to Hungary or Romania across the Carpathians. Hiding on the "Aryan" side would expose him to the perils of blackmail and was at odds with his activist temperament. He thus determined, like a number of Jews from Galicia before him, to masquerade as a *Volksdeutsch* and move to the German-occupied Ukraine as a civilian craftsman ostensibly working for the German Army. As he describes, this enabled him not only to survive, but to assist a number of other Jews to escape from Lvov, including Gina (Hela) Nachman, who was to become his second wife. Most eventually made their way to Romania.

This is the most unusual part of the memoir. There have been a number of accounts of Jews who survived the war on German papers, including that of Solomon Perle, which has been made into a successful film, *Europa, Europa*, and that of Makower, who was a member of the Todt organization, responsible for military engineering works. What Maltiel provides is by far the most detailed account of what it was like to be a Jew living on German papers in German-occupied Ukraine. A vivid picture of the chaotic character of Nazi rule and of the very varied reaction to it of the native population emerges clearly. By mid-1943, the situation had become too hot for Maltiel, who succeeded in crossing with his future wife to Romania where he encountered his brother, the only other close member of his family who survived the war. In August 1944 Romania left the Axis and went over to the Allied side. This created a new situation for the Maltiels, and at the beginning of 1945 Jacob and his wife crossed, after a last nerve-racking confrontation with the Red Army then occupying Bulgaria, to Turkey, and from there to *Eretz Yisrael*, where he spent the rest of his life.

His first years in Israel were difficult. He took on many different jobs, including that of shoemaker, in order to support himself while he learned Hebrew and requalified as a lawyer. This he finally achieved in 1955 and he worked in this profession for the remainder of his life. In 1960 he published a book on tax law, in which he specialized. He was an avid collector of stamps, ancient Israeli coins and Israeli and Jewish art. His stamp collection won a prize in an international competition in Paris in 1964. In the last ten years of his life, he wrote two books about ancient Jewish coins. He had two children, Ron Maltiel and Talma Eshel, and four grandchildren.

He suffered his first heart attack in 1952 and was plagued over the years by various ailments. He died in his sleep on 25 January 1990, and his wife passed away soon afterwards.

I got to know him in the course of editing his manuscript. Like most survivors, he was determined that his voice should be heard and often expressed to me his fear that he would not live to see the publication of his book. Unfortunately his premonitions were justified.* Yet I take some comfort from the fact that this memoir appears in the year in which we commemorate the fiftieth anniversary of the Warsaw ghetto uprising. Jacob Maltiel concludes his account of the mass murder of the Jews by listing what he refers to as the "nameless heroes", those who refused to submit to Nazi brutality, from the individuals who collected information on Nazi crimes to anonymous women who died cursing the Nazis and the chairman of the Lvov Judenrat who refused to be cowed by a Nazi thug. His highest praise is reserved for the heroes of the Warsaw ghetto uprising which occurred barely a few months before he penned his autobiography. His paean to them sums up his whole attitude to life and perhaps more than anything else makes clear why the Nazis could not break his spirit:

> But I close with those who should have been at the head of this chapter of unsung heroes – the heroes of the uprising in the Warsaw ghetto. The Zionist and pioneer organizations which did not bend under the boot of the German soldier, united despite their political differences in the fight against the common enemy. There remained after innumerable *Aktions* only some 55,000 to 60,000 with hardly any arms. With almost bare hands they decided to fight a fully armed enemy, to defend their national dignity with the hundred or two small arms they could purchase. Some 56,000 were burned and buried in the rubble of the bombarded and burned-out ghetto, but the Germans too paid a price; some hundreds of casualties. Should one describe specific episodes of this heroic struggle? Perhaps it would be worth citing the splendid deeds of one or other leader of a fighting group, but most worthy of all was the collective heroism of the anonymous mass, which fought ferociously, attacking not to remain alive, but to perish with hands constricted on the throat of the enemy, instead of being murdered by perfidious and deceitful means; to defend their dignity as human souls and as Jews, heirs to three thousand years of heroism, steadfastness and endurance. They threw out of the ghetto the Germans who came to execute the first of the final *Aktions*. The Nazis returned with tanks and cannon under General Stroop. The ghetto fighters resisted from 18 January 1943 to August 1943. Only 50 of them escaped alive, but they inspired the whole of Europe to resist (pp. 188–9).

ANTONY POLONSKY

*A shortened version of the second section, "Beyond Revenge", was published in Hebrew in 1947.

BOOK I

The Soviets: A Backstairs View

1 · The Assault

The first day of war was a day like all others, but totally different. All that was sure had become unknown, everything that until now was ordered lost coherence. Bombs, grenades, the fight for a mouthful, hunger, misery. Homeless wandering and in the end, crowning it all, death. At the request of one of my colleagues, I went together with him to Otwock, to bring his wife and child back to Warsaw. On our way through the suburbs we had our first sight of war. A small house on fire, domestic effects thrown into the street and people trying to rescue whatever possible from fire. A little further lay three corpses, unmoving, quiet and indifferent to everything around them. For the first time we came into contact with death. Death of a kind unknown to us bourgeois: violent, wild, shocking in its contrast with yesterday's life. Totally pointless, even compared with the slaughter of cattle in a slaughterhouse. None of us could have conceived of death so foreign to our life-style. From now on, the ghostly personification of death, stripped of the sentimental garment in which civilization usually dressed it, haunted me at every step.

The next day, I went as usual to the bank where I was employed, but normal work was out of the question. No one had any inclination to work. During the morning, there were two air-raids. Some people with the instinct of rats sensing the nearing disaster, were already preparing secretly to abandon the town. On Wednesday, the sixth day of war, Warsaw indeed took to flight. Anyone owning any kind of vehicle prepared for departure. Panic grew from hour to hour. Banks and businesses, following in the wake of state offices, paid their workers several months' wages in advance. The news from the front was alarming. Suddenly at about 9 p.m. Radio Warsaw announced that the entire male population was ordered to gather at once for digging anti-tank ditches. Full of enthusiasm, people gathered in response, but they were also seized with fear and horror at the direct danger. I returned home at about 2 a.m. discussing with a neighbour the need – not yet pressing – to leave Warsaw. Nearing my quarters I went by a police station and saw policemen with bicycles ready to leave. Answering my question "What news?", one of them said "Get out, go across the bridge before it's too late".

At home I was told that there was a radio call to all men able to bear arms to leave the town. So it was time to leave Warsaw. I packed some warm clothes and a little food for the way, and we started our wanderings. Not for a moment did I imagine that they would last for years and lead me through many countries and regimes, through adventures that would turn my blood to ice and would lead to my final emigration from Poland.

2 · The Refugee Trail

Nearing the bridge we met more and more people with rucksacks and bundles. By the Vistula a few military sentries stood at the last tollgate. On the road there was a dense crowd of people of all social classes, including people with their own vehicles. The road made a strange impression, full of people carrying something, something which at the moment of leaving home seemed to be the most valuable or necessary. People on the move, not knowing where they were fleeing. I asked some people close by where they were going: the answer was that they would go together with the crowd. Where? Wherever the Lord will!

During the day, the string of cars in the centre of the road increased; a string of cars of such variety that it seemed to me that the human eye had never seen anything like it. Private cars, sports cars, ordinary taxi-cabs, luxurious limousines, trucks, buses and crowning all, a fire engine, heavy with packages, wives, children and heaps of bedding. But you couldn't even dream of a free drive. The line of cars and vehicles came to a stop every few metres. The people on foot chaffed the drivers, who, in turn, cursed the disorderly crowd. The crowd, leaving the cars behind, looked back with real satisfaction. At about midday we reached a crossroads, one road leading to the east to Minsk and the other to Lublin. We decided to go eastwards to Minsk, to create greater distance from the Germans, who supposedly would attack the line along the Vistula River. The road brought people together. Total strangers talked and discussed politics as they went. Of course, there was no lack of gossip and rumours. The central theme was the possibility of revolution in Germany.

For variety, there were the German aeroplanes circling from time to time above the road. During the first day of wandering we lived through three air-raids on the defenceless crowd of refugees. The plane dropped to a height of several metres above the road and machine-gunned the crowd. Of course, there were several victims. They left a horrible impression, but eventually one became accustomed to the sight and grew indifferent to the atrocities. In the evening we got to Minsk Mazowiecki. The town was overcrowded and it was impossible to find an appropriate place to sleep. Before dawn we set out on our way in the direction of Siedlce. Thanks to my foresight, we took some food with us on the way, so that in this matter we were independent, as attaining food was an impossibility.

The war's disregard of human life deposed death from its great height. This was a massive blow to our sense of importance and inviolability. We had absolutely to change our course of thinking as our lives could be counted in minutes only. We lived only for the current moment. No one knew what was awaiting us.

The refugee trail was continually crowded, but the type of refugees changed – so to say – from unofficial to more official. Now the refugees consisted mostly of officials, police, communal officers and prison-guards, but most of all of soldiers. All were in a miserable condition, especially soldiers returning from the front. No one carried arms, this unnecessary burden having been discarded long ago, but they lacked even overcoats and headgear. The stories told by the soldiers were terrifying. Nothing had been prepared for the outbreak of a war. In their opinion, they were the victims of treason, recklessness and incompetence. It could perhaps be clarified by a future historian. They only knew that the staff had let them down totally, the extreme lack of responsibility of the officer corps defied the imagination.

One could not complain about monotony during the day on the refugee trail. The landscape was diversified: hundreds of cars were abandoned at the side of the road as a result of the lack of petrol, giving the pedestrians real satisfaction. The things caused by the war in its first moments were really extraordinary. People attached to their possessions learned contempt for earthly goods. The important thing was to save one's life. The rest was trifling. Nearing the River Bug the crowd grew denser and every trifle caused a gathering of people. At one such gathering we stopped and heard – in my opinion – of a most horrible event. A wounded soldier lay beside the road on a stretcher. The orderly related that about an hour before an officer had stopped the ambulance and ordered him under the threat of a gun to pull out the stretcher with the wounded soldier, after which he, together with a woman and a mass of luggage from a nearby private car, took over the ambulance and drove away.

By the time it was evening we approached the River Bug. Near the river we met some sentries – the first we had met during our wandering. After a very cursory check-up we continued, encouraged a little that not all was lost and some authorities were still working.

On the other side of the Bug was Byelorussia. The peasants, unlike the Masurs (on the western side of the Bug), behaved very badly towards us. Until now finding a place to sleep had not presented any special difficulty; now we could only find such a thing after a great deal of trouble. To get food became even more difficult from day to day. Despite the food that we had taken from Warsaw, the spectre of hunger began to stare us in the face. One peasant treated us with great hostility: he refused to sell food even for exorbitant prices. The following day the situation became still worse. During the whole day, we only managed to get a few old beans. A little pulp from the beans without salt was our only nourishment and we were obliged to walk a minimum of 30 to 35 kilometres daily.

We set out on the road to Kowel – a distance of about 20 to 25 kilometres. But we reached Kowel at about nine p.m. only, as continuous air-raids caused inevitable interruptions. Of course, there was a blackout in the whole town. The streets were almost empty, a rare passer-by slipped through the dense darkness. After many attempts, we found lodging for the night with a well-known lawyer. His comfortable apartment brought to mind the recent pre-war times. We had been no more than a week on the refugee trail, but the quiet comfort we had left in our homes seemed to us very remote. We listened to the radio and heard disturbing news. The situation at the fronts was bad. Our host told us that besides the mass of refugees, almost all the embassies and representatives of foreign states had passed through Kowel. The town was destitute of anything edible. We were advised to go at four a.m. if we wished to get a piece of bread. Of course in the morning we went to the bakery. Despite the early hour there was a huge crowd. We were told that only at 4.30 a.m. would they begin the distribution of bread. There was no order; people were pushing and falling one over another, it was a fight of wild beasts for a bite of food. It really was all about one bite, as no more than half a kilo per person was distributed. After an hour the bakery was out of stock and the majority left with nothing. I remembered World War I. One must accommodate oneself to various shortages.

These paved the way for theft and looting. In the rule of disorder and chaos, nobody hesitated. Fearing to remain in this dangerous state of affairs we decided to leave the town and departed hastily. Considering the exhaustion of the women we decided this time to use the railway.

3 · The Refugee Trail by Train: Meeting the Soviets

At the railway station a huge crowd was awaiting for any train that would take them further from the Germans. I tried to get some information about the time-table or the direction of the trains, but received such empty answers that we decided to do the same as all the others, to wait and eventually to go towards the unknown.

After about two hours of waiting, a train was formed going directly eastwards to Sarny. The train consisted of several freight cars in which some military horses were loaded, and the rest stood at the disposal of the refugees. In a few minutes every inch including steps, was occupied. Soon the train started. It was a beautiful autumn day. People were basking in the sun and on the stubble along the track, cattle were grazing. The quiet and peace of the surrounding fields soothed our nerves, wrecked by the last few days. But the quiet presaged a storm.

Sixteen kilometres after Kowel, we saw three planes from afar. The driver gave a signal of alert and braked the train. Even before the train stopped, the planes were above us. They flew through and machine-gunned us intensively. At last the train stopped and people fled into the fields. In the meantime the planes returned and began to bomb the emptying cars. They dropped about 20 bombs on this civilian train. The planes came back for the third time gunning the fleeing passengers. Our group lay not far from the track. At my wife's insistence, I covered my head with the rucksack. The bullets whistled around us, but fortunately they avoided us.

After the air-raid we returned to the train. The damage was colossal. Dozens of wounded needed immediate help and nobody had first-aid kit. Waiting for a rescue train was like waiting for the Messiah. We gathered some shirts and blankets to help the most severely wounded. Some volunteered to bury the dead. Nearly two hours passed and we had to think about moving. The train was badly damaged. Two cars were totally crushed and another three seriously damaged, one irreparably. A refugee engineer who was with us took charge of the necessary work. With our own strength, without any machinery, the damaged cars were cleared off the embankment. The embankment was repaired in two places and at last, after eight hours of heavy work, we succeeded in moving on.

On the seventeenth of September, in the afternoon of the second day of our stay on the train, the few military officers on it became very nervous. They constantly sent messengers to Kostopol, not far from us. At last, in the evening, two of the officers changed into civilian garb and the others disappeared. From an unknown source came the rumour that, before noon, the Soviet army had crossed the border of Poland. Confirmation of this from Kostopol came very soon.

During the night we remained in the train. The following day we decided to go to Rowne about 20 kilometres off. The peasants of the surrounding villages regarded the entry of the Russian troops as a signal to open robbery. Along the railway track we watched the peasants with horse wagons ride alongside the train and load them with as much as they could carry. No Soviet military units were seen. About two or three kilometres before Rowne, after the railway tracks were cleared, the trains began to move. Of course we mounted the nearest train and met with the Bolsheviks for the first time. A military patrol entered the car and demanded that arms and other military items be handed over to them. The soldiers were kind and after hearing that we had no such things departed, taking us at our word. We arrived in Rowne in the evening.

The following day we went early on to the street, curious to see the Bolsheviks at close quarters. The town I had known before the war as a small, provincial, sleepy hole was now completely changed. We met old acquaintances from Warsaw, Krakow, Lvov, Katowice, Wilno and even Gdynia. The Russian military were not stationed in Rowne and were rarely seen in the streets. Two or three official buildings in the town had been taken over by officials, but all day various formations crossed the town on their way westwards. We were informed that the Russian occupation had taken place with the full agreement of the Germans, whose military units withdrew when the Russian military units neared. The Russian army made a great impression on us. We saw various branches of service which we never dreamt of in Poland. The military did not have that smartness or elegance which we were accustomed to see in Polish soldiers and especially officers. Most units had lorries, a few were marching through the town singing. When a column halted, groups of people instantly gathered around the soldiers, interested in getting first-hand information about another country and another way of life, until now enveloped in a fog of propaganda. Despite some mistrust, the soldiers were very kind and good-natured and gave us all kinds of information, unfortunately interrupted at the most interesting moment as the column moved on.

The first signs of the omnipresent Soviet propaganda machine were the loud-speakers installed on almost every lamppost, which dominated everything with their roar over the noise of a town which was loud enough in any case. Characteristic of the first days of communist authority were the long lines before all sorts of shops, beginning with food shops and coffee houses, through clothing and shoe shops and ending with upholstery and furniture. Everything was characterized by a state of being only temporarily, awaiting something firm which would change all this into a wholly new state.

It seems that the overcrowded condition of the town was also very inconvenient for the authorities, so that on the third day of the occupation an office issuing passes was installed. Everyone who wished to move from the town was obliged to get a pass. This was something wholly new to people accustomed to move about freely. At the eight windows of this office long lines formed. After four days of pushing, we got the necessary passes to move on to Lvov.

In the meantime, we tried to get some information about the possibility of returning to Warsaw. The town commander, a full colonel, informed me personally that it was advisable to wait a little, as the Soviet army had approached Minsk Mazowiecki (about 40 kilometres east of Warsaw) and probably in two or three days Warsaw would be seized. Despite the official information that the movements of the Bolshevik troops were coordinated with the Germans, the conviction that prevailed among the soldiers was that they were off to fight the Germans. A sergeant on duty in the town command, for instance, answering my question about whom they were fighting and where they were going answered: "Of course the Bolshevik troops are fighting the Germans and we are going to Berlin." Unfortunately, as it later transpired, the good intentions of the soldiers did not find expression in the orders of the Soviet government.

Immediately after we got the passes, we boarded a train. The trains were going very irregularly, without an exact timetable. We were told to prepare for a two-day voyage (normally six hours). We purchased an appropriate stock of food, though we did not believe that the journey would take so much time. In reality we made an error as the journey lasted not two but five full days. Five long days passed as in a Gypsy hovel dragging at a snail's pace from one station to another. The long stops, sometimes lasting several hours, we passed baking potatoes or basking in the sun. When we neared Lvov we saw many signs of war. Instead of the imposing liquor factory of Baczewski on the suburbs of Lvov, we saw only a heap of rubble.

4 · Lvov under Soviet Rule

We arrived at Lvov in the last days of September at the railway station Podzamcze. It was a small station in the suburbs, not especially damaged by war, in spite of German fire. Outside the station the evidence of war was more apparent. With my heart in my boots, worried about my parents, I went, or rather, ran in the direction of their apartment, which was not far from the Podzamcze. They were well. Nothing had happened to them during the few days of the German occupation of Lvov. My stories filled the most part of several evenings. But we were worried about my younger brother Poldek. He lived in Zaleszczyki, a town on the border of Romania. He had a drugstore. It was clear that something must be done, first, to get information about him – he had not stayed in Zaleszczyki – and, second, one of us would have to take care of his apartment and the drugstore. I was determined to get some information about what was going on from my acquaintances in town. I had not decided what I should do. To flee further to Romania? What to do about my brother? A horrible dilemma – what to do? I had never been, after all, enthusiastic about the Bolsheviks and life under their system.

Lvov, my beloved native town, where I had spent 25 years of my life, was and always would be beautiful in my eyes, particularly as it was gilded by memories of my youth. There were two natural parks – Kilinski and the High Castle – on a hill dominating the town. Opera, theatres, a concert hall, superb, museums, countless coffee houses, clubs and dancing accounted for the town being called "little Paris".

On the streets of Lvov, received an impression similar to Rowne. Though Lvov was not a small town (350,000 inhabitants before the war) it was treated by the Polish government stingily, and had lost its character of a capital city. Before the war there reigned on the streets a sleepy quiet, rarely disrupted by a car horn. People moved more slowly than before and the town grew slack in the provincial way of life. The town which once had an opera and several theatres had barely two vegetating provincial theatres. Famous from the times of Austrian rule for its entertainment and dancing clubs, it now had only a few – in short there remained only a small trace of a bright past. The literary and bohemian fraternity moved to Warsaw. Places of entertainment that were not frequented closed one after another. Boredom and emptiness dominated the town, once full of life.

Now the streets acquired a more animated character. The sidewalks were full of pedestrians, the majority refugees from the western and central Poland. The roads were full of private and military cars. During the night places of entertainment and night clubs sprang up and were crowded from morning till late at night. Life was boiling, bubbling, preparing itself to take on a new and unknown form.

The 22-month stay of the Bolsheviks in Lvov could be divided into two periods – the first during the winter and spring of 1939–1940 was the period of hatching of the new form, the impetuous remodelling of the economy from individual capitalism into an extreme state economy. The second period from the summer of 1940 until June 1941, the end of the Soviet occupation, was a state of stabilization and higher control. The beginning of the first period was characterized by a certain amount of chaos. The Bolsheviks found themselves in new terrain. On the one hand, the country was unprepared for the drastic changes which would be introduced in the near future; on the other hand, the Soviet state and the Bolshevik party organs lacked experience in remodelling the economy of a newly occupied country from individualistic forms into a state-ruled economy, despite the fact that the means were long ago established in the USSR. It must be emphasized that from the moment of the invasion of the Bolsheviks, the Bolshevik party and the authorities made intense endeavours to win over the population, not by compulsion, but rather by a liberal approach. The authorities avoided repelling the population by severe measures, and often avoided the repressions which were previously applied in Russia. According to the order of the authorities, all shops had to stay open as before the war and to sell everything they used to sell. In fact the majority of merchants opened their shops, though I am sure they put away most of the merchandise, fearing it would be confiscated or nationalized. Despite fears, after several days of the occupation and the entrance of the Russians into Lvov, the majority of shops were open and business went on. The merchandise in them was not nationalized and they remained in the hands of their owners or committees spontaneously created among the working staff. Simultaneously the sources of propaganda were set in motion to prepare the population for change and to provide the psychological foundation for transformation according to the programme of the Bolshevik party.

5 · Zaleszczyki

To get information about my brother was very difficult. The phones were out of order in Lvov and one could not even dream of a long-distance call. Fortunately there was the so-called “slipper” mail. From this, we learnt that the Romanian border was open at Zaleszczyki on the second or third day of the war and everyone could pass to Romania without formality. My brother used this method and on the fifth day of the war, he had passed over the bridge to Romania. Two days after him, his wife followed. Their drugstore and apartment were closed. A friend of my brother’s living in the immediate vicinity was taking care of it.

My informer who returned from the border advised against trying to pass through the Romanian border as he knew the conditions there well. According to his information, strong anti-semitism ruled in Romania, the Iron Guard had the prevailing voice. Going to Romania would mean homeless wandering without aim or shelter. Besides, on top of everything else, in his opinion the Romanians had now closed the border. He considered that it might still be possible to cross over the Carpathian mountains, but it was very difficult, as the border-guards shot without warning. In his opinion staying in Lvov with the Russians would not be so bad; one could live with the Bolsheviks. The Jews were not persecuted and anti-semitism was punished severely. In the USSR there were several million Jews, proof that we would also live. On the other hand, he advised us to go to Zaleszczyki as quickly as possible and open the drugstore, otherwise the authorities would themselves open it, which would be equivalent to confiscation.

After a family council, I decided to remain with my parents in Lvov and not to go further. In the meantime, as it was necessary to take some steps with regard to the drugstore, it was decided that I must go to Zaleszczyki. After a long wandering through various offices, I received permission for this voyage – without it, it was impossible to go – to open my brother’s closed store as he was absent. The journey to Zaleszczyki was normally a long one, and now it took four full days. My brother’s friend received me with undisguised joy, for at last he saw the possibility of escaping the constant explaining to the authorities about why my brother’s store was closed.

In the end I packed up my brother’s personal effects and some trifles from their apartment. All of this would come in very handy, as I was without clothes after my flight from Warsaw. The way back to Lvov with two big suitcases and a huge bundle was not a pleasurable experience. Two revisions and endless explanations were most unpleasant, but I had got an attestation from the Soviet administration of Zaleszczyki that all these things belonged to my absent brother and the affadavit avoided confiscation and an accusation of profiteering. At last I arrived at Lvov. At the railway station I found a wagon, which brought me and my baggage to my parents' flat. Again, a detailed and almost endless report of my voyage was necessary. My parents were pleased to receive the considerable sum of money. We decided that besides the things that I kept for my personal use, the rest should be sold on the black market, which had began to flourish in Lvov. Certainly, huge demand together with the lack of new sources of supply created this trade done in a corner. There was nothing which could not be bought on the black market. Everything in any quantity could be bought, from a length of English fabric, French silk and French silk stockings to diamonds and gold. Centres of illegal trade arose as every day more and more shops, cleared of all merchandise, brought down their shutters.

6 · In Search of a Job

In the first days of October 1939, posters appeared on the streets, published it seemed to me by the town authorities, calling upon anyone who had arrived in Lvov after 30 September 1939 to register in order to get a flat. Naturally I registered as did every normal citizen. To whom, accustomed to the law, would it occur that the registration was a trap, aimed only at providing evidence of refugees who had come to Lvov from other regions of Poland? I do not intend to claim that the authorities in Poland were always honest and that government announcements were a source of truth, but such a decidedly false announcement was for us a total surprise. There was no intention of allotting flats, which in any case did not exist. Anyone who registered himself was a candidate for deportation, which began in January of the next year. This registration stayed with me as a warning, and from this time, I never registered for anything.

Jobs were in surplus. The demand for workers, intellectual and physical, was almost limitless. There was no profession in which specialists were not demanded. To get a job, it was enough to call on any new office or factory where places were waiting for workers. Among white-collar workers the most sought after were book-keepers. I decided to look for a job in this line of business and tried in the Post Office. There were several free places in book-keeping for offices in the province.

I must emphasize that in the USSR there was a permanent lack of book-keepers and it seemed to me that there always would be a shortage of specialists in this line of office work, as in every institution, office, factory, workshop, theatre, clinic or any economic unit there had to be regular book-keeping, according to Soviet principles. The state economy demanded the calculation of figures of any activity of the state, aimed at getting an all-embracing yearly balance of the state economy, almost analogous with a balance of any business or industrial concern in the capitalist system.

In the Post Office, I was directed to the personnel department. The examination was primitive. The examiner, a deputy director, a young Russian, saw himself as an excellent specialist. There was a long discussion on o amortization, and our examiner, instead of examining us, gave us a long lecture, showing the typical loquacity of the Bolsheviks, explaining the Soviet principles on the subject. After getting the qualification I had three provincial towns to choose where to work. I went to Bobrka to acquaint myself with the conditions before I took the job.

The conditions there scared me away. What a difference between the provinces and a big town. The Bolsheviks appointed to the leading position in Bobrka a primitive person lacking any appropriate qualifications apart from his membership of the Communist Party. He governed the town as a gulag. He raged and wreaked his anger upon the bourgeois. He fulfilled his task by giving orders to confiscate furniture or even whole apartments of bourgeois or people suspected of not favouring the Soviets, not forgetting on such occasions to provide himself and his family with goods of all sorts, linen, suits and furs, inaccessible to him in the conditions of the USSR, because of their rarity in Soviet markets and their high prices. Against the lawlessness of this tovarish no redress existed, at least in this first period of organisation and the chaos associated with it.

I returned quickly to Lvov, anxious to forget the unpleasant impression from the province. I decided to learn Russian intensively to increase the possibility of an appropriate job in Lvov. My job-hunting ended shortly in my getting the post of bookkeeping controller with the District Council of Industrial Cooperatives. The institution was in the very first period of organisation of its offices and a whole network of producting cooperatives in almost all branches of industry. The work seemed to be most interesting as I would be active in the organisation of small producing cooperatives and would have the best opportunity to observe the creation of industry in Lvov, one of the least industrial towns in Poland.

I worked in the finance department. The manager was a Russian Jew named Perl. The work, like all work in state offices, was nothing special. Its main feature was meetings. They were arranged in every institution. For us, the locals, it was something new and instructive. One kind were gatherings providing information about various institutions in the USSR which were interesting. The other kind of meetings, which to me personally were a revelation, were for criticism and self-criticism. After the details about the execution of the quarterly production plan were ready, the chairman of the *Oblpromsoviet* called a special gathering of the staff and the heads of the cooperatives and informed us about the results and fulfilment of the plan. A broad and serious discussion took place.

It would have been unthinkable in pre-war Poland for someone to dare to make in public an open criticism of the activities of his director, about even the smallest details which could negatively influence the fulfilment of the year's plan. As we could ascertain later on, criticism under the Soviets seemed to be welcomed and did not seem to cause disagreeable reactions from the chairman, as the worker could always ask for protection from the omnipotent Party. On the other hand he could leave his post and without any difficulty find another job. Even more astonishing was the self-criticism of the director of a concern, which might be compared with the public confessions of the early Christians.

7 • Meetings, Discussions, Self-Criticism

During the winter 1939/40 an event took place of great meaning for the west Ukraine (formerly East Galicia), namely a general vote annexing these parts of Poland to the USSR. The way this important event took place is interesting in terms of the differences from the forms used by us. Without any propaganda, without preparations, huge throngs of workers from various state offices and state institutions gathered on Lagionov Street, from the Grand Theatre to Mariacki Square. The gathering, according to the media the next day, was a spontaneous demonstration of the population in favour of annexing those parts of the Ukrainian nation torn from their roots, again to its mother country.

In my office, as in other offices and factories, all the workers were ordered to gather at 10 a.m. with the aim of going to a meeting. It was underlined that participating in this meeting was obligatory, though the goal of the meeting was of course not even mentioned and nor was the setting of the daily routine of the meeting. Of course we all went, and the meeting was really massive. No one, despite the many recently installed megaphones, knew what it was about nor could one understand the speakers, but hearing the speakers – multiplied by the megaphones – and the shouts of "*Khay zhive*" (long live!) and being in the mass (where most people feel the best), people began to shout "*Da zdrastvuyet Batko Stalin*" (long live Father Stalin), "*Da zdrastvuyet tovarish X* and *tovarish Y*". People were glad to have this unexpected break in everyday monotony. The majority of the crowd for whom there was no room on the square did not even see the tribune or the speakers, but despite this they warmed themselves up shouting. Imagine my astonishment and that of most participants in the meeting when the following day we read in the daily papers that at the mass meeting of the workers, it had been decided to send a resolution to the Supreme Soviet of the USSR, with the request to annex the lands of former Poland to the USSR, as well as to nationalize the factories and private properties. Almost all outside appearances of democratic general voting were supposedly kept up, although the meeting described had nothing in common with democracy. This method seemed to me to be not significantly different from the methods of our German neighbour where, without asking anybody, various new laws were forced upon a whole nation.

MEETINGS, DISCUSSIONS, SELF-CRITICISM

On 19 December 1939, an order was published that within one day everyone was obliged to change his zlotys into rubles. From 20 December the zloty went out of circulation. It was emphasized that only a maximum of 300 zlotys per person could be changed. The order came like a bolt from the blue. No one had taken such a thing into account. At the few places where the change was possible huge crowds gathered. The change was carried out at snail's pace so that only a minimal part of the population was able to change even the permitted 300 zlotys. The intentional result was to deprive people possessing large sums of cash and was doubtless achieved, dragging along victims from among the less guilty, people who had nothing in common with capitalism. The poor were deprived of their last penny, without even the possibility of buying themselves a loaf of bread the following day. This order dealt the strongest blow to the peasants, who lost all the capital gathered during the prior speculations. Now they lost their trust in the new authority and in its currency and refused to sell at any price, wanting only to barter. It was a common sight to see a piano, clothes or drawing-room furniture on a peasant wagon. The severe lack of fuel compelled the townsfolk to give up everything from their homes to barter with the peasants for firewood. On the other hand the peasants were compelled to plunder the forests surrounding Lvov, which of course did not belong to them, and to bring into the town wagons of wet wood to exchange for furniture, dresses, coats, furs and sports suits made of English cloth. From this time dated the devastation of the forests around Lvov.

8 · The Omnipotent Black Market

The whole winter of 1939–1940 stood in the shadow of speculation and black marketeering, supported to a very great extent by the immigrating Russians and new people coming continually from Russia for several days to make purchases. We "locals" felt most keenly the speculation in food-products, which raged all the winter. Rumours were diffused from an unknown source about food shortages which shook faith in the new currency.

This development began relatively modestly; the peasants who brought dairy products and other agricultural products into town began to raise prices. Sometimes they tried to justify this by alluding to the difficulties in obtaining industrial products, sometimes claiming that paper money was without value, demanding silver. Prices jumped daily, for instance the price of milk rose from 15 groshy per litre (about 20 cents a day) within two weeks to the level of five zloty (about $7 today) – 35 times. Every item was affected. The authorities tried to control prices and the supply of products, trying to take over the mediation between village and town, prohibiting entry to peasants with products and opening instead purchasing points for agricultural products in the villages. The result of this order, carried out in a most slapdash manner, was hostility and a refusal to cooperate by the peasants, who were extremely conservative and wedded to old methods.

Open supply – free competition – regulated prices quite well. In this system, the hero who managed to penetrate the town with merchandise dictated prices, which after a very short time reached fantastic heights. The authorities soon abandoned coercion and after a short period, they allowed free delivery of the villagers' products. They hoped this would regularize in some way the conditions of the food market, as almost simultaneously they promulgated their decree on the change of currency from zloty to rubles.

In textiles, shoes and watches, arrests and confiscations did not bring significant results. The Russians who came to Lvov with the intention of buying clothes or watches did not need orders and prohibitions and favoured the black market.

9 · Acronyms and Abbreviations

During this winter, unfavourable to any growth as is every winter, there grew as if by the touch of a magic wand, plaques of various colours on many houses, dominated of course by red flags and the five-arm star. Very few houses, especially in the town centre, remained without a plaque of some office or government department. During the first four months, branches of every government department existing in the USSR and industrial establishment were created from nothing. The local population got lock-jaw, spelling the monstrous acronyms of the names of various government departments and establishments. It was also very difficult to get accustomed to calling hotels or restaurants by numbers. For years I was accustomed to visiting the restaurant Bristol or Hygiena; suddenly it became restaurant number 56 or 73. It sounded to our ears like a mathematical riddle: "Where did you eat yesterday? I lunched at restaurant 56!" "I was at the coffee-house 43, but took my supper in restaurant 58, where in, my opinion, the chef is much better"!

In December 1939, the *Spetsoddiel* (Special Department) announced that everyone had to submit a *curriculum vitae*. Of course I submitted one. Several weeks later, at the end of January 1940, there appeared again a demand to submit a life history. In my naiveté I asked the boss of the *Spetsoddiel* to show me the one which I gave him in December. He answered: "There is no need. I am sure you know the history of your life". One of my colleagues told me not to dare to write anything not conforming to the first declaration in every particular. Luckily bribe-taking in Soviet Russia was omnipresent. For a Waterman fountain pen, the assistant manager of the *Spetsoddiel* gave me a short look at my prior declaration. From this time on, I gave nothing without a copy. Spying on one another in Soviet Russia was such a general thing, that later on I understood a warning from a Russian with whom I was friendly, that one should not talk in the street. One never knew who was behind one who might hear something suspicious.

Once, during the breakfast break, in an unrestrained talk with colleagues whom I knew from before the war about films and theatre, I remarked casually that I could not bear Soviet films, because of the propaganda that pervaded all films so that every scene, even the smallest one, had its propaganda aim. It was only a throw-away opinion in free talk. To my enormous astonishment, after a day or two, the boss of the *Spetsoddiel* called me in for a talk. He asked where I went after working hours, about entertainment in general, what I did to relax after hard work in the office. I answered that I almost never went to cinemas or to theatre at all, as I had no time, because of my study to deepen my knowledge to achieve promotion. His reaction was almost outrageous. "How is it possible! You, a cultured person, have no time to be interested in art? No! It is not normal! Or perhaps you do not think the level of our films is good enough?" At this point I realized which way the wind was blowing and naturally I denied this hotly, praising the great artistic value of Russian films and Russian art generally. I thanked God, when at last I was outside the door in the corridor. Innumerable similar stories could be told.

10 · First of May Preparations

I was promoted in my office. I officially received the nomination to be the deputy manager of the finance department, the deputy of Perl. I had the impression that he had proposed me and gave me backing for this promotion, at any rate an important enough post. Our relations might have developed into friendship, but this support was of greater advantage for him than myself. He could now officially shift a great part of the work on to me and – what was more important – the greatest part of responsibility of the daily work, for instance the approval of the credits from Gosbank. He admitted to me that he was not equal to the level of lies, which we had to fight daily.

On the approach of the first of May, everything was specially decorated and a special monument was built. Monuments were built ad hoc on the occasion of major holidays. The building lasted two to three days. The monument was built of plywood, plaster of Paris and papier maché. Such monuments were gigantic and looked very impressive and magnificent but did not have the durability of monuments made of bronze or marble. After a month, sometimes only days, the tooth of time with the help of rain, snow and wind impaired its base a little and it would be taken down and in appropriate time a new monument for several months would be erected in its place.

Such building for the short term was typical of the system. Buildings were not built in Lvov, but shops were built en masse. The first of May was established as the appointed time for finishing such a work to give the town a sense of holiday and to take into account the propaganda aim. There were plenty of places for this task but the population certainly would be most satisfied if only there were enough merchandise to fill the shelves. This time enough merchandise was provided not only to fill the shops, but even to satiate the town famished by a very meagre winter. Apparently the Soviet authorities intended not only to please the population with the amount of merchandise, but to impress them with the almost luxurious arrangement of shops. The authorities knew perfectly well that a satiated person would see everything rose-coloured.

Five shops of "Gastronom" were created, well provided with all one could desire: white flour, coffee, cocoa, spices, chocolate, sweets, poultry, pork, vodka, wine, liqueurs, butter and sugar, which could normally only be had after queuing for many hours. This even became the theme of a folk song: "In a queue they made acquaintance when sugar was sold ...".

A new product was introduced, unknown before the war, "maslomiod" (butter-honey) similar in taste to butter with honey, but having nothing in common with either. Besides, special shops for fish-products, an industry of dimensions and assortment not known in Poland before the war, were created. Several shops selling ready-made silk and woollen clothes as well as shoes were opened. The infamous Mikolash passage, the centre of black market and speculators, was transformed and shops were opened there. The Russian merchandise and manufactures fell well below the quality level of such products in pre-war Poland and could not really compete with the black market, which flourished as before. Nevertheless, there were metre-long queues before the fabric shop. The Russians saw this all as a matter of course and were astonished about our seeing it as a regrettable affair. They did not want to believe that before the war we had no idea of queues or the black market. They considered this a normal or even necessary sign of life.

Such trifles did not spoil the high spirits of the holiday. Feverish preparations were in full swing in every factory and office, to appear adequately at the parade in which everyone was obliged to participate. All the houses in the centre of the town were plastered with portraits of Stalin and all the other members of the Politburo several metres high. The Communist Party committee published a two-page section of the daily paper, complete with slogans which could be held in the march. Of course a special new symbolic monument was erected. The town, a day before the holiday, was red with thousands of flags and swarming with hundreds of artistically constructed kiosks for selling chocolate, sandwiches, beer or wine to the participants of the march who were active the whole night from 30 April to the first of May.

On 30 April, we were ordered to be present the next day in the office at 7 a.m. at our working places to be ready to go to the rallying point. I was on duty in the office. The whole parade passed by the office, so that I had the opportunity to observe the march of the workers.

The army opened the march, various branches of the service went by, orchestras played untiringly to create an appropriate frame of mind. At last the workers began to pass before the tribune, organized in accordance with the factories they worked in. The larger factories prepared trucks decorated with various symbols as in a carnival. Every column was crowded with posters, with signs and slogans and of course portraits.

The portrait of Stalin was everywhere with the inscription "Our Father", "Liberator", "Thinking for us", besides portraits of other members of the Communist Party and the government. The portraits were made from various materials and by various techniques, as if to unload the artistic fantasy of the creators cramped in their theme. One could see Stalin painted on canvas, made from coral beads, printed on gauze, made from string, normal photographs, a bust from plaster of Paris, a bust made from wood or cut out from some picture or poster and stuck on a rod. One was dazzled by this deluge of portraits of one single, living human, risen from dust and who would return to dust. It reminded us of the worship of Roman Caesars. He was omniscient. He would make everything for us and instead of us. He was our father and we his small brainless children who could only stay at the foot of his heaven-reaching throne, to burn incense, to sing obsequious songs and pray "Care for us and think of us, our beloved father!"

The propaganda endeavoured to do its best to perpetuate the Stalin cult and relied, maybe rightly, on the experience of the Tsars (Batiushka-father-Tsar), giving the primitive intellects of peasants of the east a living image of divinity in place of that which had been removed, who would care about all the thinking for the whole nation. Icons of this type were perhaps well received in the east, but made an unpleasant, even a ridiculous and sometimes depressing impression on us. It was very difficult for us to accept as an axiom every word expressed by Stalin. Anyone daring to think individually of problems in which Stalin announced his opinion was the enemy of the State and a counter-revolutionary. I remembered one of the lectures about the "Stalin" constitution. Answering a question from one of the audience, the lecturer quoted the opinion of Stalin on this problem and added: "Now no doubt there cannot be any further question after the elucidation of Stalin himself."

But returning to the parade, the march stretched on uninterruptedly for several hours. From the tribune fell a new slogan every few minutes, repeated by the crowd of several thousand. At last at about 2 p.m. the forest of red flags, posters and portraits came to an end. People dispersed to assemble in the evening for banquets, parties and dances.

11 · My Promotion

Some days after the examination of future bookkeepers, the secretary of the Communist Party in the *Oblprosoviet*, Tovarish Brodski, called me for a small chat. He asked what I was doing after working hours and what studies I had completed. I saw that he was very pleased with my behaviour and the questions in the examination. After he became aware that I had finished two branches of higher study (the academy of trade and law faculty in the University) he said that he understood the level of my questions at the notorious examination. He spoke so highly of me that it became almost embarrassing. He emphasized that the Party needed such positive elements, especially from among the *miestny* (locals). He said that he was aware that my salary was insufficient and that he would help me if I wanted additional work. He offered me the job of a lecturer in the *Uchkombinat* (a sort of technion) in the subject of trade-accounts and the economic basis of the bookkeeping in the Soviet system. As to my question about what an *uchkombinat* was, I got a whole lecture about the socialist system of teaching workers. The *uchkombinats* were filling the gap between high-school and university studies. They were schools with various courses for specialization for students with very different levels of education. Courses lasted from three months to a year. The difference between them and courses in factories was that the *uchkombinat* had a stable team of professors and its own laboratories with a curriculum for a whole year. The technion type of school and the scope of the syllabus were close to level of universities, the period of learning one to three years. In addition to normal subjects, special emphasis was placed on learning the history of the Bolshevik party, which "developed" the social feeling of the citizens.

I liked the description of the system of schooling and of my eventual duties. A short time afterwards I was offered to lecture on the same themes as in the *Uchkombinat* in the *chlebtrest*. Of course my income was raised considerably. I worked very hard, often until late at night preparing the lectures or setting the exam papers, but I got satisfaction from my work. I received even more satisfaction after the summer holiday when I received an invitation to lecture at the University of Lvov on the theme "The economic basis of the settlement of accounts" (*economicheskiye osnovy gosudarstviennoho raznchota*). Admittedly it had its bad aspects, namely I had to prepare the draft of the lecture some time in advance and submit it for confirmation to the Secretary of the Party and to the NKVD. Only after approval could I begin the lectures. Economic themes were very dangerous in the USSR as I learned later – everyone tried to avoid this theme in any way possible. Even the smallest deviation from the recognized axioms meant departure from the Party line. This was worse than sabotage and hard forced labour in a Siberian camp was guaranteed. My first lecture was given to an almost empty lecture-hall, only three students risking going to hear some wholly unknown lecturer. According to schedule it was a two-hour lecture. At the second lecture there were already a dozen or so students. At the following lectures, the lecture hall filled up with more and more, and at last after a short time I had a full room. The satisfaction from such proof that my lectures were interesting was simply exhilarating. The dark side of it all was that there were always one or even two informers in the lecture hall. I was not afraid of their presence as I kept exactly to the confirmed text of the lectures. The interest of the audience expressed itself in an innumerable flood of questions from the students. Those waiting to drive me to the wall with their difficult questions caused me sometimes to writhe like an eel to extricate myself with honour or at least to extricate myself with my skin intact. However, the satisfaction from the apparent interest of my lectures compensated fully for the unpleasantness.

On the other hand the competition between the lecturers and professors did not impress me. It was the other side of the coin. There was an artificial competition among the professors to give students high marks. This sometimes resulted in ridiculous situation, when a professor forced himself to seek among his students a candidate for honours (the Russian *otlichnik*). I prefer not to recall my problems with the director of the *uchkombinat* about "*otlichniks*" in my class. On my explanation that there were no students deserving the merit of an "*otlichnik*" I got the answer: "How are you teaching? There should always be about 20 per cent of students with top marks, and in your class there were only 12.5 per cent. This is impossible! I am sure you have made an error". No argument could reach him. The result must be as recorded in the statistics. At the end of every half or full year there was a statistical analysis of the results of the work of all students, on the basis of the marks achieved by them. Professors were evaluated according to the marks of their students. Of course in such a system everyone endeavoured to produce the greatest number of top students.

12 · Getting a Russian Passport: Deportations

To get a passport in any capitalistic state was a trifle, an administrative move only, but in the USSR it was a grave event and was necessary to be a 'normal' citizen. The passport was identical on its outside appearance for all, but differed widely in its purposes. There were normal passports without any limitations, valid for five years, entitling a person to a stay in any town and a move from one town to another. The second category of passports were those with a shorter validity than five years. Another sort was a passport with the number 11, authorizing the holder to stay in the province only, with exception of district towns. Other passports were valid for some specific districts and last, there was a passport with the name of the place of stay.

The issuing of passports was conducted by the organs of the N.K.V.D. It was announced two months in advance that everyone had to provide a confirmation from his house-manager at what date he was registered and was a permanent resident of Lvov, and of course a birth certificate.

According to the interpretation of the authorities a permanent resident was anyone registered in Lvov before 1 September 1939. Due to this interpretation there were a colossal number of questions open to doubt in relation to people temporarily not living in Lvov, who had arrived back after the date as well as the problem of a whole mass of refugees from various parts of Poland, living in Lvov. The interpretation of the rule was left – as in most such rules – in the hands of the executive organs, with much freedom to use their own discretion: to give a normal passport or to refuse giving a passport at all.

This was only the beginning. Immediately afterwards, even during the issuing of passports began the deportation of those refused a passport. I learned of this during May 1940, when the first deportation or to use the official term, "removal of part of the population to other districts of the USSR" took place. Despite the fact that I was born in Lvov, and only lately living in Warsaw, I found myself in the same situation as all the other refugees. The problem of the refugees became even more complicated, as the mass of them declared themselves willing to return to the part of Poland occupied by Germany.

The first deportation, whose details I could not observe as I was in hiding for 12 days (the duration of the deportation) led me to make efforts to acquire a passport at any price. The deportations were executed during the night by delegated Party people, who, with the assistance of soldiers, went from house to house. They visited every house according to addresses given at the registration of refugees and took everyone found in the flat, whole families, single people, allowing them in most cases to take along almost any luggage they liked. The people together with their luggage were conveyed to the railway station, where cattle-trucks were awaiting them, which were destined to be their living quarters for for a month or more until their arrival at the place designed to be their place of abode. Conditions of the train ride were horrible, 30 or 40 people crowded together in a cattle truck, without heating or any hygienic facilities, without water, without any possibility to move, as the wagons were closed and guarded. Many of the old and children could not endure this ride into the unknown to the end.

My wife and I were hidden in my acquaintance's place, living in the suburbs, in an attic above a pigsty, as I had obtained advance information that the deportation would take place. In really horrible conditions, on bread and water, unable to move or speak to one another, not to arouse the suspicion of the neighbours, we were locked up for 12 full days.

Hiding was necessary for people without passports. A great number of refugees, officers of the Polish army, who had registered two or three months earlier, prostitutes and some known bourgeois were deported. It was clear to me that all registrations were to be avoided, as no-one could know when and to what purpose the registration would be used.

To live one must have a passport so I had to take energetic steps to acquire one. I used all possible ways and acquaintances, but in spite of a somewhat more liberal attitude on the part of the authorities after the deportations I did not find a way to get a passport. The refugees got in optimal cases an "eleven" passport obliging them to leave Lvov for the province. I would not agree to such a development, despite the fact that many did so and moved into the nearest provincial location, almost the suburbs. At last I decided to visit the "*nachalnik*" (manager) of the passport office. After great difficulties, I got to him, instead of his deputy. He read my application and answered: "You are a refugee."

"*Tovarish-nachalnik*, here you see my certificate of birth in Lvov, here are certificates of schools in Lvov. This should convince you that I am a citizen of Lvov".

The Russian heard with full concentration and answered: "You are a refugee."

"*Tovarish-nachalnik*", I returned, showing him documents. – "Here is my certificate of work in Lvov, the booklet of Social Insurance in Lvov. Here is proof that not long ago I lived in Lvov. My parents were living all the time in Lvov."

The Russian answered unerringly: "You are a refugee."

The official seated before me listened with rapt attention, so I thought that at least I had convinced him of my rightness. But to all my arguments, I got the answer as from an automaton: "You are a refugee".

Convinced of the hopelessness of my efforts to get a normal passport, I returned to the office and told one of the senior officials about it. My friendship with him proved beneficial. Of course, he knew what was going on with the passport action and knew what threatened me and my family, and I must admit that he behaved like a true friend. He advised me to type out the application in Russian and to formulate every point in a separate numbered passage, underlining the name, number and date of the document certifying the facts, and, ignoring today's refusal, to go again tomorrow.

Without any real hope, I went the second time to my automaton sure he would say only "You are a refugee,". To my astonishment I heard a demand to show the documents. After checking every one of their numbers and dates, the *nachalnik* recommended giving me a normal passport. It may appear ridiculous, the same man, according to identical documents, one day refusing to give a passport and the next day accepting the same application, but the second time he had an opportunity to check the documents without the need to read the document in a foreign language which he did not know.

In the second half of June 1940, the issuing of passports was at last finished. A great number of people – merchants, industrialists and senior state officials – received no. 11 passports and were obliged to leave Lvov. A great number did not get passports at all. On 25 June, a sad piece of news leaked out, that on the last night several hundred known merchants and industrialists were arrested. Russians warned people with whom they were friendly about the possibility of deportation. On 28, 29 and 30 June, the great deportation-action took place. The signs of an approaching deportation became obvious to the enlightened when in the early evening before the stations of the NKVD stood a long row of trucks and wagons mobilized for the night. The streets emptied very early. Everyone tried to be at home or in an appropriate hiding place. People were waiting nervously at home listening intently with a quake to the rumble of passing cars, praying inwardly not to hear – God forbid – the stopping of a motor before the house. Nobody in the whole town dared to sleep. The cars circulated according to the addresses listed. I too was visited, but after I showed my passport, they apologized for disturbing me at night in a very polite way and went on to the next delinquent. From the house I lived in, a retired general was taken together with his whole family. People prepared for something of this sort and packed up their goods. The delegate executing the action explained that one could take anything one wanted – apart of course from furniture – if only one had enough strength to carry it. The soldiers helped to pack the bundles and to carry them to the truck.

A slip of official paper, somebody's stroke with a pen, could tear apart whole families from the place they lived in from birth and transfer them to the confines of earth, to foreign countries – people not adapted for pioneer life, not prepared to break new ground in a wilderness of new settlements, which they had to build. The ruthlessness of this action provoked disgust not only among the locals, but also among the Russians, who usually praised every step of the authorities. They, being beyond any suspicion, gave shelter in many cases in their flats to those seeking a hiding place. They cheered up the frustrated, telling them that they knew their authorities, advised them to hide during the hot time, since when tempers cooled it would be possible to settle everything. About the rightness of this opinion, I had the opportunity to be convinced myself.

Despite the hardships of deportation, the majority lived through it to arrive to the assigned place. From the description in letters of the deported we came to know about two centres they were deported to: one was the forests at the northern part of Ural mountains and the second was Khazakhstan, the district around the town Semipalatinsk.

Into the forest or rather primaeval wilderness were sent a mass of people. No buildings to live in or even barracks were awaiting them there. The newcomers got axes to cut down part of the forest for cultivating in the future and for building there houses for living; in a word, they were forced to live the most primitive life of pioneers. Once or twice a month bread and other food products were brought. It is clear from the above description that such conditions were especially hard for people from the intelligentsia, officials or lawyers who were completely unprepared for such a mode of life. In consequence, various illnesses and accidents grew in great numbers, and almost daily we heard news about diseases.

The conditions of life in Kazakhstan were a little different. People were located in various villages and were assigned to very hard physical work. Living standards were below any European level. For instance, a chimneyless cabin 1.5 metres high, with a hole in the roof for smoke, and a dirt floor was regarded as very fine living quarters. Work conditions were extremely hard. The workplace was several kilometres from the living quarters. Payment was so low that it was scarcely sufficient to provide the most modest food. The sort of food was different from that used in Europe; for instance European bread was unknown. The climate was different, the night temperatures in summer were often 8°C below zero, yet during the day they reached 40°C in the shade. It was clear that many could not survive in such conditions.

13 · Trip to Kiev: Paranoid Distrust

The Party delegate in the *Oblpromsoviet*, Brodski, did not forget me, or, perhaps, to be more exact, kept me in mind. At the end of the summer he picked me up again for a friendly chat and declared that it had been decided that I should take more part in social life, namely become a member of the workers' committee of the *Oblpromsoviet*. The function of "*kultrabotnik*" was assigned to me, and I was placed in charge of cultural matters in the committee. He emphasized that he was intensely interested in my work and that I should increase my qualifications, as there were interesting higher levels in book-keeping. The next level was "book-keeper of the collective balance" (*zodnoho balana*) of a whole branch of industry or even of a whole republic. He promised to help me to achieve this position. It was necessary to participate in a seminar at the Secretariat of the Party in Kiev, which would last about a week, but this of course was a formality. What would be my answer? Naturally I could only agree with a smile of satisfaction. In the meantime he proposed that I should give a series of lectures at the Lvov University on economic themes. He then promised me a "*putiovka*" (an order for a railway journey including a ticket) and an official order to go to Kiev to attend the seminar. He also made vague mention of his intention to propose me as a candidate for membership in the Party. This perspective for my future in the USSR gave me the creeps. Every one of us, subconsciously, awaited the return of pre-war times. At present, the war raged throughout the world, at least in Europe, but this could not last forever. Perhaps there would arise the possibility of living in the free world. Yet he wished me to bury myself for all time in the Soviet system. This talk gave me material for thinking things over. How could I protect myself eventually from a career, even if it was the greatest I could achieve in this system? I would not call it a hateful system – but it was, for sure, barely and reluctantly tolerated. I had no one who could advise me.

In the last few days of September, I received the *putiovka*, with an order to start my journey to Kiev in two days' time for the six-day seminar. I took with me only a small bag, with one change of underwear. Provided with a thousand admonitions to be careful, to consider what I said, what I did, and how I behaved, I went to the railway station. At the train there were two cars reserved for Kiev. The majority of passengers, as it later proved, were going on shorter journeys within the Western Ukraine (i.e. occupied Poland). In the Kiev car there was a reserved numbered seat for me and as it turned out later, I was the only one of the few "locals" (inhabitants of "West Ukraine") going to Kiev, to the terrain of the real Soviet Union.

To some extent, I was disappointed by Kiev. A big city, heavy traffic, a few cars and crowds of people. The people were the cause of my disappointment as they were on the whole very badly dressed and full of distrust, especially towards strangers. Of course, I was a stranger and this was noticeable from afar. My suit, overcoat and shoes were too elegant and stood out. My accent was clearly immediately recognized as not Russian. Kiev did not give the impression of a large town. For instance, coming to Warsaw, immediately after leaving the railway station, one felt the atmosphere of a large city. Here there was nothing of this sort, it was little more than a provincial town. I had a reservation at the hotel and got a fine room, but was obliged to leave my passport in order to receive towels.

Immediately after my arrival, I reported to the secretary of the Party Secretariat – as I was ordered – Tovarish Sarkin. He welcomed me heartily. He told me that Brodski had recommended me warmly. He asked me about my duties, about the relations at the universities in Poland, the ways of teaching, lectures and exams. Later he introduced me to the organizer of the seminar, which I had to attend at once, that very afternoon. The lectures were not impressive. Their content was well known to me from the theoretical Russian books which I had been able to buy and study. Naturally inescapable were lectures about the Stalin Constitution and the history of the Bolshevik Party. The lectures took the whole day, morning and afternoon, with a short break for lunch in a mess in the same building of the secretariat of the Party. Often during the six-day course, at least two or three discussions were arranged in the evenings. I was obliged to participate, but as far as possible I tried to avoid talking. The purpose of this course was to prepare staff for positions higher than the chief-bookeeper, for instance managers of finance departments, book-keepers of the collective balance in the ministries of republics or combines of factories. Naturally a colossal amount of time was spent on the political side of work, which was characteristic of the Soviet system. There prevailed an opinion that there was no sphere of life not influenced by politics and without a political tinge. I thanked God when the seminar ended and I could return to Lvov. The continuous bumping against the wall of mistrust and suspicion and having to be extremely careful with every move and every word was really exhausting.

In Lvov my wife and parents received me almost as newborn. My fellow book-keeper, a Russian, Partionov, was so glad that he invited me for dinner with a litre bottle of vodka. I returned to the inspections together with him almost with joy after this short stay in the USSR and a real readiness to give lectures in both *uchkombinats*. I also began the lectures at Lvov University. Owing to the enormous amount of work, I returned home very late every day, often after 10 p.m. and some times later. One of our neighbours told my wife to warn me to be more careful, because the caretaker asked him very eagerly – even over-zealously – what I was doing and who my friends were, since I came home so late every day. It was generally known that every caretaker and house manager were working, willingly or not, for the NKVD.

It is not my intention to describe in great detail the system and methods of surveillance which prevailed at that time. It is enough to say that there did not exist in the USSR an institution, office or factory where there was not installed a "*Spetsoddiel*" (special department). This department was supposed to be the representative of the military with the task of preparing the specific institution for mobilization in case of war, and of holding exactly to the Party line. This gave the *Spetsoddiel* the opportunity to become almost the official representative of the NKVD which did not exclude the additional presence of at least one secret agent of the NKVD on the premises of every undertaking.

The meddling of the Party in the most private affairs of an individual was not isolated or rare. One of my colleagues was in a café together with some of his friends and colleagues. The line of the conversation, as often occurs among older men, tended to frivolous themes and one man present, a Russian, a member of the Party and a person in a position above any suspicion, showed a pornographic photo. The occurrence was so petty that no-one of the company paid attention to it. My colleague told me some days later that he met in private the Russian who was with him in the café, who told him the consequence of this agreeable evening. The following day he was invited by telephone to the NKVD. He did not know the cause of the invitation, which was not to be ignored, and obediently went. The department which invited him had not yet received his file, so he was asked to come the next day. On the next day, an official of the NKVD asked the official to hand him the photo, which had been shown on this and this day at this and this hour in the café, as it was not fitting for such an serious person and a member of the Party to possess such dirty things.

Thousands of such cases from various spheres of private life could be quoted. A call to the offices of the Party to explain "improper" behaviour towards one's wife or children was not a rarity. One could then imagine with what severity all sorts of political behaviour were put under surveillance. In the case of an arrest of a politically suspicious person, all his friends and acquaintances were exposed to long enquiries and thousands of inquisitorial questions, before being relieved of suspicion of participating in disloyal thoughts. The living quarters of the suspected would be spied upon for a long time and anyone nearing the area of the contagion exposed himself to an interrogation and detailed investigation of his past and present (it was unfortunately not possible to check on the future!). The inspection was very detailed and if the suspect mentioned – God forbid – a name like Stanislaw without any other details, the NKVD would investigate all people with that name living in the town: all mothers who had a son named Stanislaw or who intended to give that rare name to their son; all girls with a friend named Stanislaw; of course all inhabitants of the town Stanislavov would be interrogated. I have exaggerated, but I have the impression that not too much.

In the first months in Lvov after I left Warsaw I met one of my colleagues from the bank in Warsaw, Stasek Weiss. He fled at about the same time as myself and came to Lvov. He had no relatives there and only a few acquaintances. I saw him once in a while on the streets or in a café. After I got my job in the *Oblprosoviet*, I met him and he complained that he had to earn a living and could not find a job. I found him a job in one of the co-ops. He was very pleased and thanked me. He told me that he had found a very cheap room together with a Ukrainian. He boasted of having ideal living conditions, as the Ukrainian worked at night, so he almost never saw him, as he slept during the day while he (Weiss) worked and when he returned at evening from his work his Ukrainian partner had gone to work, or, at least, so he told him.

Some months later, perhaps about February or March 1940, Weiss suddenly disappeared from the co-op where he worked. I was questioned several times as to why he did not come to work. His private address was not known to me and I could not give any explanation. I was even angry that he had done such a thing and had not informed me what he was doing or intended to do. I must admit that in the turmoil of my new job and the spate of work I forgot all about the matter.

After my return from Kiev, during October, Weiss suddenly appeared in my office. He was pale-faced, or rather had an almost green complexion, starving, asked for a small loan and an appointment as he had to tell me something. Of course I made an appointment and learned about the unlikely events in which fate made him an involuntary victim.

One night he awoke suddenly in the presence of three soldiers, who entered the room without any ceremony and turned on the light. They ordered him to dress and go with them. Naturally he had no choice, dressed and went with them. They brought him to the prison at Loncki Street or perhaps Pelczynska. The leader of the patrol alone registered him, not allowing him to speak at all.

He was led to a cell with five other prisoners. He wanted to speak, to shout, to ask what was wanted from him, why he was arrested, in short to make a fuss in the middle of the night, hoping it would help him. His fellow prisoners in the cell advised him to be quiet. He would have enough time to do something in the morning, if anything were possible. In the morning, Weiss appealed to one of his fellow prisoners, a Russian. He told him that in prison, especially in Russia, one must be infinitely patient. Not long ago, he told him, there was one man without patience, continually demanding an inquiry. Once he even banged at the door, when not immediately answered, and asked to be led to the "sledovatel" (examining magistrate). After an hour, during which he did not cease to make fuss, two jailers came and took him. After some time they threw back him into the cell, stained with blood and only half-conscious. From then on the delinquent was patient and quiet. Some days later he was taken for an inquiry and did not return.

In the course of time the Russian told his personal story. He was a Captain in the Red Army and a member of the Party. He was arrested because he "left off" on the black market four tankers of gasoline. He was convinced that he would be released at least with his hide whole. He said that "with us in USSR anyone who has achieved something must have a little prison in his past". He asserted that he had made a profit from this black market transaction of about 1,000,000 Rb. In his opinion the "sledovatel" would cost him some 400,000 Rb, about 200,000 Rb would buy the magistrate, so that he would be freed and remain with some 400,000 Rb. Of course his rights would be restored. With such a sum of money – as he said – one could live. Weiss said that hearing this story terrified him. During the visit of a jailer to the cell, which took place once in a while, Weiss asked for some paper to write an application to the "sledovatel" asking for an inquiry – in vain. The jailers only laughed. In this way days, weeks and months passed; nobody was interested in his existence.

After more than six months of such torture, suddenly, unexpectedly the jailer came to the cell and ordered Weiss to go with him to the "sledovatel". Weiss told me that he repeated inwardly various explanations, which he intended to place before the "sledovatel". He was led to an office. Behind a desk sat a man, in all probability the "sledovatel", who ordered him to sit down; but when Weiss tried to open his mouth, he was immediately ordered to keep silent. The "sledovatel" was writing something and said that he knew everything Weiss intended to say, and continued to write. At last he signed the written document and affixed the seal. He gave the document to Weiss.

"It is your release. You can go home. I said that I know all." Weiss thought that it might be a trap, that this release was perhaps a macabre way of tempting him. The "sledovatel" called a jailer and ordered him to escort Weiss to the front door. The jailer conducted him to the gateway and showed the guard the document given to Weiss. Weiss told me that he went out into the street on trembling feet. Later on he learned that his lodging partner, the Ukrainian, had been sought, as he was allegedly active in some Ukrainian subversive group. As in the USSR arrests were carried out only at night, he was arrested just for being at the address at night. To check who he was and what he was doing there at night only took six months!

This incident and other similar incidents, were the result of the belief – impossible to dispel – that the USSR was surrounded by enemies and that every stranger was, at least potentially, a counter-revolutionary with the task of overthrowing the Soviet system. At every step treason was suspected from the new citizens, resulting in fantastic suspicion towards them. Distrust which we could not cope with till the last moment. This mistrust towards the Ukrainians, as was proved later on, was fully justified.

An accident which occurred to my wife in December 1940 was typical of conditions in the USSR. My wife lost her bag with her passport. We went together to the NKVD station to notify them of the loss. When the official heard what was the matter, he attacked us, shouting that we should admit that we had sold the passport. The way he approached the matter was remarkable. He did not say that he suspected that we had sold the passport, for him it was certain, he only wanted to discover what price we had received. Not for a moment did it enter his head that we were telling the truth. We underwent a cross-examination so severe that when we at last left the station, we were drenched in sweat, afraid that, perhaps, despite all, we *had* committed some crime. The following day, a worker in the factory where my wife worked found the bag and returned it to the director of the factory.

Triumphantly – naturally sure that now we would convince the sceptical NKVD official – we went to the NKVD station to inform him that the passport had been found. We were received as repentant criminals, who, seeing the futility of misleading the authories, now pretended that the passport had been found. This was not the end of the incident. Some days later the director of the factory called my wife to tell her that an official of the NKVD in the factory had ordered him to pay special attention to her doings, as she had tried to get rid of her passport and such people were capable of anything.

This attitude was present at every step. Everybody's blood boiled experiencing it, when every opinion was investigated and checked to absurd limits. The slogan put up in offices in Poland just before the war: "Beware of

Traitors" was engraved by the omnipresent propaganda on the brains of every USSR citizen.

14 · Elections – Soviet Style

Whoever has not been in Soviet Russia or did not live through the propaganda machine of Hitler's Germany does not know what propaganda is. Colossal yet elastic, the propaganda machine is overpowering – an inexhaustible number of leaflets, brochures, posters, agitators, pictures, speakers and equipped with films. It starts slowly, gathering pace with time. Citizens of non-totalitarian states cannot imagine the dimensions of the propaganda effort and its huge suggestive power. Twenty-four hours a day people saw, heard and read only what the state wished to delude them into believing. The conceptions were repeated so often in various forms, sometimes so cleverly veiled, that they were hammered into the heads of everyone, even independently thinking people. Untiringly the inexhaustible propaganda machine crammed by a thousand means loyal ideas into our speech. It even happened to me that I suddenly discovered myself using the opinion of some party agitator, or that I thought in categories smuggled into my head by continually meeting at every step, at every move, the same opinions, ideas, slogans or watchwords. An industrialist having at his disposal such an advertising apparatus would conquer the world.

The Communist Party, the promoter of every activity in USSR, overwhelmed society. The Party and its members collectively were the only ones who had the right to think. The Party grew to the dimension of a giant: the rest of society gave the impression of being made up of midgets, or perhaps a better image of the state of things is that the Party was the only one living entity or thinking being which thought for the present and the future; the rest of society was made up of puppets, set in motion by threads invisible to the eye.

Some years ago, about 1925, a play was put on in Poland under the title *Jan Karol Maciej Wscieklica* written by the prominent author, philosopher and painter Stanislav Ignacy Witkiewicz (Witkacy). The hero of the play was a social worker and a politician with a range of thought so vast and an intellect so great that those around him could not afford an independent opinion and only repeated ideas heard from him. Personal life ended when Wscieklica was around. When the hero of the play died it was as if fetters fell from his circle and they returned to life, but during his life no one dared to think how to free himself from his overwhelming influence. The author surely never dreamed that his play would mirror the conditions of life in the USSR – in the relations between the Party and the rest of the population.

Especially so since at the Party's disposal was the formidable propaganda machine, an unscrupulous way to concentrate in the hands of the Party all the threads to put the Party in a position to set the rest of the nation in motion, according to the ideas of the Party. Besides the means of propaganda, which I have mentioned, there was also the daily press and plays. The press, according to the nature of things, was almost entirely the mouthpiece of official opinion, but the overpowering strength of the Soviet press was based on the fact that there existed no opposition and whatever was printed in the papers supported the government.

Everyone met with agitation at every step, everywhere there was smuggled in a didactic idea. Propaganda presented itself as a gigantic machine with 1,000 superstructures, but at the front was a huge wide roller. At the highest superstructure in the leader's room the Party directed the roller to roll over the 180,000,000 USSR citizens, levelling every thought and idea, to sow into the created emptiness suitable new, lawful slogans from prepared reserves.

In this system and this atmosphere were carried out the elections for the central authorities. About four or five weeks before the day set for them, it was announced in all the daily papers at gatherings and institutions and factories that elections to this or that council would take place. The factories, offices, state institutions, schools, universities, trade unions and other associations delegated thousands of their men for propaganda work in connection with the elections. But this was barely the first step.

After a short course of instruction, these thousands of ad hoc delegate-agitators were let loose on the inhabitants of Lvov like a pack of hounds, whose task was to draw the exhausted voter to the poils. Every agitator worked on one or two houses. By arrangement with the caretaker he was allowed to organize meetings in one of the flats. His task was to prepare housewives for the noble duty of voting for the best and most suitable people to proclaim new laws to improve the life of the workers. At the gatherings the constitution was read and interpretated and the agitator was obliged to answer any questions to dispel doubts which might arise in minds of the enlightened. At factories, offices, schools and universities there were similar gatherings. Everyone had to learn about the constitution.

In addition to these gatherings, regional meetings were organized in parts of the town for a greater number of participants, at which agitators of a higher category spoke, extolling to the skies the paradise created for workers in the USSR and burning incense for the ubiquitous NKVD (of course without metaphysical allusions) in form of portraits of "for our Father Tovarish Stalin". It was impossible to ignore such meetings, as several hours beforehand, agitators visited every flat in the vicinity and pressed the inhabitants to "honour" the meeting with their presence, making more or less subtle threats to people reluctant to go.

The Lvov radio station broadcast uninterrupted propaganda speeches, cinemas projected only propaganda films, which showed how full was the Soviet Union of benevolence for the worker and how "Father Stalin cared for all." The daily papers were crowded with articles about the elections and interpretations of the constitution.

At last, two weeks before the election-day, was published an electoral list under the single name, "The List of Bolsheviks and Non-Party Candidates (independent)." Yet the name alone suggested some doubts. It was generally known that "Bolsheviks" would be the members of the Party, but what did "non-party (independent)" mean? Were they people not belonging to the Party, or people not tied to any other party at all? In such a case who would put up their candidacy? So from relatively innocent seconds of reflection, clouds of doubt were gathering. In the first moment, the question arose as to where the other lists of candidates were. The answer was that there were no others, but there could be if 80 citizens would sign such a list. This was not achievable in anyone's dreams, as who could possibly organize such a list – to gather the signatures was impossible as any political association was prohibited. The agitator claimed of course it was possible to vote for other candidates, as the elections were general, equal, secret and direct.

Finally the election day drew near. Shops were filled with colossal amounts of merchandise. Restaurants and cafés prepared especially huge stocks of food and beverages. The electoral committees that had worked or for some time controlling the registers of voters and settling complaints now concentrated on organizing buffets in the polling stations (so that the term "electoral sausage" had a literal meaning), arranged separate booths for voters (the vote was secret) and decorated the walls of the polling station with portraits of the "leader and father" and other politicians.

Election day was in full motion from morning till the late evening. Everyone voted, even the members of the army. The activity ensuring that the greatest number of people voted was enormous. From the morning, on the average once an hour an agitator visited our flat, asking if we had already voted. The electoral committee went with ballot boxes to the hospitals and even to private flats of the bed-ridden. People who were not severely ill were brought by cars to the polling station. At the polling station everyone was received at the entrance like a guest of honour, taken around the premises, led to the buffet, to the register of voters and finally to a great room with booths around the walls and given a printed list with one or two names of candidates who would be elected; here he was directed to a booth, to put the list in an envelope or if he wanted to cross off somebody's name from the list, in 'secrecy' in the booth. At last the citizen, exhausted by all the honours, threw the list with the names of all the delegates of workers for some council (Soviet) or other into the ballot-box.

One might ask what all this was for, since *de facto* the elections of candidates were already decided when the list was prepared. It was partly for the statistics and partly to give the crowd counterfeit instead of real money, something that usually satisfied the wishes of the crowd for political fulfilment. The elections were supposed to be free, secret, proportional and universal – they were only universal. Perhaps secrecy was also achieved – the elections were 100 per cent secret; no one knew when and by what means the election of this or that person was decided upon. Triumphantly the daily papers announced that 99.25 per cent of the population had participated.

The entire elections were blown up to the dimension of a gigantic soap-bubble: it was colossal and it caressed the eye with its rainbow colours and brilliance, but after one touch it burst and vanished into oblivion as do all soap-bubbles.

15 · New Laws

The USSR was awash with new laws. Scarcely a week passed by without a new law, and sometimes one of great significance. In the years 1939 to 1940 many laws were issued with regard to the nearing possibility of war, for instance working hours were extended, latecomers to work were punished, there was a compulsory transfer of workers, a law prohibiting arbitrary leaving of work was introduced, as were laws about sustaining the quality of production.

At this time, not long after the elections, a law was announced about "progul" (unjustified late arrival) drafted by Malenkov. The law was draconian in the full meaning of the word. In the event of coming five minutes late to work two or three times, a punishment was imposed of two months' forced labour in a remote region of the USSR. One day it seemed as if I would be late to the office, due to damage to a tram. I returned home and went to bed. My wife phoned the office to say that I had an attack of lumbago and was in bed. Of course I could not come to work. The office immediately sent a physician, not so much because of my health, rather to ascertain that I had not run away. Because of the severity of the Malenkov law it was ordered that the text should be read aloud. We were ordered to come to a meeting during the breakfast break. Tovarish Pronin explained the text and the meaning of the law. At the end he asked "Who is against the law?" Naturally no one dared to express such an opinion. After we dispersed and went to our work, I asked Weinbaum, an auxiliary clerk, a local, what he thought of this new law. His answer came as a shock. He said that one could say what one wanted about the Soviets, the law was really extremely severe, but the authorities had at least asked him if he was against it. Such a thing could not have occurred in pre-war Poland. The long and short of this was that Soviet propaganda seemed to be succeeding in its ways of treating the simple and primitive parts of the population.

Another abuse was the law persecuting hooligans, with its wide interpretation of rowdiness and the severity of its punishment. I suppose that the lawmaker wanted to eliminate arbitrary administration of justice by anyone and to raise the level of public behaviour. Rowdiness was defined as verbally abusing anyone on a tram, on the street or in a café, knocking somebody intentionally, shouting during the night on the streets, making a fuss in public premises or on the street, not to mention beating somebody up. The punishment was also draconian – one to three years of forced labour. The court hearing was executed at lightning tempo and the sentence enforced at once.

16 · Outbreak of War

In January 1941 I was offered a post in Russia. At the beginning of the month Brodski called me; he was not alone, with him came the director of the *Spetsoddiel.* Seeing him I felt an unpleasant shiver. Maybe I had done something not 100 per cent law-abiding? But no. It appeared that the talk was very important and semi-confidential, so that an experienced party member like Brodski – probably on his own initiative – wanted to have a witness of what he said and possibly of my answers. I was offered the post of director of the finance department and book-keeper of the cumulative balance in a *kombinat* working for the army; the arms production centre of the whole region of the Ural mountains. This centre was in reality a town with a population of 100,000. My salary would be relatively high; additionally I was assured of membership in a consortium for party members and a two-room flat, fully furnished. Brodski refused to tell me the name of the town or state exactly where it was. He said that the fact that he told me it was in the region of the Ural mountains was enough. I had a month to decide. The director of the *Spetsoddiel* emphasized that I should surely appreciate what an honour it was. I should speak with my wife and inform Brodski when I could set out.

Again I had the headache of deciding what to do. To accept the offer meant burying myself forever in Russia and separating completely from Europe, not so much in terms of the geographical position, as in a total break with European standards, and this was not my plan for the future. I certainly had not the slightest intention of agreeing to such a future. Like the majority of the Polish population, I waited subconsciously for the end of the war and the possibility of return, if not to pre-war Poland then to the west. Again, not necessarily in the geographical sense, but to a system where freedom was not an empty propaganda slogan. My family was divided in their opinions and the deliberations took every free minute of my time throughout the whole week. Partly my family was inclined to think that the Urals would provide the best shelter during the war, but partly they were afraid of the possibility of being cut off from the west. A talk with Parfionov decided me. He knew of course from a Party conference or from Brodski about the offer and he entered into conversation with me only about the recognition and the great honour to myself in being offered such an important post. The greatest value of the post

– in his opinion – was that naturally I would be accepted as a Party member since apparently my candidacy was already under debate. This conversation decided me and it convinced me to give a definite "no". With apprehension, I went to Brodski to tell him that due to a definite refusal by my wife, who did not want to leave her old parents, I must unfortunately turn down this magnificent opportunity. Brodski tried to persuade me, offering to wait a little longer and promising an appropriate post for my wife and other incentives. After some days he called me again, but naturally I had no intention of changing my mind.

In the meantime, attitudes about the war situation became more uneasy. I am sure that the Soviet authorities took into account the possibility of a German attack and decided to be suitably prepared. Everything done in the USSR was done under the consideration of opposing the armed fist of any possible enemy and to be so well armed that no one would prove to be more powerful. War preparations used up any profits from work and the state even obliged the citizens to be prepared, accepting in advance the opinion that it was impossible to insure itself 100 per cent. Heavy industry was working exclusively for the army, as was the chemicals industry. Light industry was ignored. Its time would come when the war danger was over.

For us, remembering the crushing defeat of the Polish army, the hope arose that maybe this time the Germans would face a fitting opponent, at least in terms of armaments. Once in a while there were notices in the daily press, which created the impression that relations with Germany were not as harmonious as they should be, though the general tone of the press was pro-German. On this point the propaganda was unconvincing, perhaps because it was not wholehearted. The population, almost without exception, was anti-German, even more, they were all filled with enmity towards the Germans. They were aware that politics demanded at the moment a seeming concord, but they reckoned that war against Germany was inevitable. The general opinion was that the greatest enemy of the Soviets was Germany. It was remarkable that people accustomed to accept slavishly the slogans of propaganda were not prepared to be misled on this issue. This attitude could be seen everywhere. On my journey from Rowne to Lvov in 1939, a soldier whom I asked where they were really going answered without hesitation: "To Berlin!" Once I witnessed a scene in a private shop. An officer wanted to buy a razor. The merchant showed him a razor, praising it as an excellent German product. The officer returned the razor refusing to purchase German merchandise. When the merchant expressed his astonishment at such an attitude toward products of a friendly nation, he heard a short but significant answer: "That is politics". This frame of mind was prevalent and despite the current political line, everyone agreed that Hitlerism was the enemy of the whole world. Hitler would be surely disappointed if he expected an anti-stalinist revolution in Russia. Under the pressure of war, opponents would disappear, everyone would give everything he could, and "Matushka Rossiya" (Mother Russia) would remain free.

The tone of the press remained pro-German, but once in a while some small article surfaced representing the real attitude of the population. Though no one thought of war in the near future, the government, through appropriate laws, prepared the nation for war. At the end of April 1941 the omniscient press-agency OWT (one woman told) spread a rumour, later confirmed by the radio, that Germany had grouped a huge number of armed forces on the border and the engineer. Todt had inspected the fortifications on the border.

An evening with my friends and acquaintances in the café Wells at the end of April 1941 is still fresh in my mind. Naturally the coming war was under discussion. The political situation, clear from the tone of the press and radio, was very tense. There were no Russians in our group. Everyone was in agreement that the Russians were not over-optimistic about their ability to stand up to the formidable military machine of Germany. They were aware of their shortcomings and were nearly overwhelmed by the manifestations of the might of the German army, shown in the German war against France or Belgium. They were saying directly that they were not up to this level. Parfionov, who was very cautious, also expressed himself in a similar way and that meant that it was the opinion of the Party. Naturally our talk passed to the theme of German atrocities against us, the Jews. From private information we knew about the concentration camps, murders, smaller and greater pogroms. I am not ashamed to admit that at that time in my simple naiveté or direct stupidity, I maintained that those full of pessimistic prophecies did not take into account the number of people involved. In Poland there were 3.5 million Jews. For the sake of argument let us assume that the Germans, with all their atrocities would murder 100,000 maybe even 200,000 Jews, or, let us take the worst-case scenario – half a million Jews, which of course was an impossibility, who could imagine such a thing? This would mean that every seventh Jew would be murdered. Why should I be the seventh? I would do everything possible to be among the six that would not be murdered. We considered the eventual possibility of flight or evacuation to Russia. The majority would not even consider such a possibility. It would mean cutting oneself from Europe.

Before long two thing happened, strengthening the population's conviction that relations with Germany were not so rose-coloured and that we stood on the verge of war. The first was an official communiqué, denying rumours that the USSR was preparing for war. The aim of this communiqué was probably to provoke a similar denial from Germany. Yet the Germans passed it over in silence. The second was the colossal number of visits to Lvov during May and June 1942 by the leading personalities of the military and political circles of the USSR.

It was clear to everyone that the USSR avoided even the smallest action which could be regarded as provocation. Characteristic of this was the lack of participation of any army personnel in the May Day parade in 1941 in Lvov. The Russians argued that a great concentration of troops for a parade in a town so near the border as Lvov might be interpreted by the Germans as massing troops on the border, and that this could be used as *casus belli*. But all this did not help. The atmosphere was heavy with a storm. Apparently the decision in Hitlerland had been made long ago.

On 22 June 1941 the inhabitants of Lvov were awakened by the shots of the high angle guns. Without any provocation, the troops of the Third Reich crossed the borders of the USSR. The Soviets had tried again and again to avoid any provocation; the army units on the borders retreated without a shot. Only after the announcement of the attack on German radio did the struggle begin.

Already in the first week of war, Lvov was in the hands of the Russians. The majority of the population did not believe that the Red Army could offer resistance to the Germans. On the second day of war, a panic broke out among the Russians and, in cars and trucks prepared in advance, they fled from Lvov taking their families. Through the south-east toll-gate extended an uninterrupted row of trucks full of evacuating Russians. It turned out that an evacuation and mobilization plan had existed long ago, setting out in the smallest detail their behaviour in case of war but ruling out the evacuation of locals in whom no trust was felt.

The mistrust towards the locals turned out unfortunately to be partly justified. On Wednesday, the fourth day of war, Ukrainians, financed and prepared by German intelligence, began a diversion. They shot from garrets and roofs at the passing military trucks. Machine-guns and even small cannons were stationed in the towers of churches. The Russians took energetic steps to secure their rear. Without pause armoured cars and tanks with patrols made rounds through the town. Simultaneously mobilization started.

On 30 June, the last Russian civilian left Lvov. In the evening in the bloody-red light of afterglow of the public buildings set on fire by the retreating Russians, German patrols reached Lvov. On the following day the German army entered the town simultaneously through three toll-gates. The brutal rule of the fist and the horror began.

Slatina-Olt, Romania, Winter 1943/1944.

BOOK II

Beyond Revenge: The Nazi Occupation of Lvov

1 · The 'Liberation'

The German army entered Lvov on a beautiful summer's day. At the head of the army marched the Tyrolean regiments. On the streets, crowds gathered to greet the new liberators. Of course, the Jews did not participate in this reception, which I can only describe as enthusiastic. The population greeted the marching soldiers with cries and applause and even threw flowers to them. These were not only Ukrainians. Most of the people on the streets were in fact Poles, the Ukrainians, a minority in Lvov, were lost in the crowds. It is strange how men can manage to forget so quickly, or shall we put the blame on the unconscious? National consciousness is very strong in Poles, but opportunism prefers to be on the side of the strong and to forget dreams of being a major power. The majority was opportunistic and listened to its perhaps not honourable, but surely more convenient promptings.

The Jews, summing up the situation, and realizing that hard times were drawing upon them, remained in their homes and kept out of sight. It was clear that this would not protect us from the Germans, that the hard times were not to be evaded. It was realized that many lives would be lost but even the greatest pessimist could not imagine through what hells of torture Polish Jewry would pass before its tragic end. Much of the Polish and Ukrainian population – our neighbours for centuries – assisted Hitler's hangmen in their acts of destruction. Very few withstood this acid test of character.

In the first days of the occupation, the Germans felt it was necessary to give the mob a few toys to play with. The mass murder of Jews began without that proper organization so beloved by them and the Jews lurked in their homes and dared not leave them. They had to be lured from their hiding places. The day after the invasion, placards were posted on all the streets calling everyone to go immediately to their work-places during a three-hour period, under penalty of death. As we discovered later, death was not the harshest punishment in Hitler's regime. There are things a hundred times worse than death, as this self-styled highly cultured nation demonstrated, such as the labour and concentration camps. The greatest experts of the Middle Ages, the torture chambers of the Inquisition, could have learned much from the Nazis in our time.

People accustomed to discipline and obedience hastened to factories and offices. No one believed that it was only a trap. On the streets Ukrainan militiamen, mobilized during the night, sought out the Jews. Now folk could run wild; the victims were there. The mob in the streets soon forgot about work, it was more fun to set about the Jews. Not far from where I was living, on Sapieha Street, there was a bomb crater, a place especially created for fun with Jews. The neighbourhood Jews were brought to fill up the crater. From a window of my flat I could observe in this one place the mirror of a thousand other places – the actions of a brutal mob. Old people, children and women, were forced under a hail of blows, to wrench out the paving stones with their bare hands, and move the dirt of the street from one place to another. One woman was tied to a man working nearby and they were forced by blows to run in opposite directions. A teenage boy fainted under blows and others were called to bury the apparent corpse alive. In this one place I saw four or five persons murdered. About 60 people were involved. Throughout the violence life on the street went on in its usual routine. The passers-by stopped for a moment or two, some to laugh at the "ridiculous" look of the victims and went calmly on. Indignation was not expressed by one single word. If someone disapproved he passed by quickly, playing shortsighted, pretending not to understand what was going on.

In other places the mania took even more glaring forms. Groups of Jews were brought to clean up the jails of their corpses, supposedly left by the Russians. Scenes that took place there stagger the imagination. My colleague Advocate E. had the misfortune to fall into the hands of the mob and was dragged to this work. It was a miracle that he returned home at all, in the early hours of the next morning, brought by a fellow Jew and a Pole, who took pity on his agony. He had 16 bayonet stabs, a broken clavicle from a blow with a crowbar, two ribs broken after he was thrown down stairs and various lacerations from blows on his head. During a two-day eternity the mob raged. My uncle, in his 60s, was dragged from his house and on the way to the Brygidki prison was so horribly beaten that before his arrival at the prison he fell on the street with both legs and arms broken. The murderers, thinking that they had done enough, left him on the cobbles to cool down. As I was told later, for three hours the old man begged for help, for a drop of water, till death eased his pain. People had enough strength only to pass by, to hear or to see. Only the next day the Jewish burial society (*Hevra kadisha*) picked up his corpse, together with about 2000 other corpses of the first Nazi victims. According to the statistics of the Jewish Council, this was the count of victims during the two first days of the German occupation. This appeared horrible to us at the time, but it grows pale in my memory in comparison with what took place later during the *Aktions* carried out by the Germans in their well organized manner.

For the time being the Germans gave the Ukrainians free rein. Later on they demonstrated their real cultural level. The slogan "do whatever you want" evoked in these beasts claiming to belong to European culture their congenital instincts to wreak their rage on the weak and defenceless. Cannibals, the wildest denizens of the jungle are ethically and morally on a higher level. They kill only when hungry or in self-defence. The Ukrainians served the Nazis to the end, carrying out the foulest massacres and murders. Among the Germans there were tens – maybe even hundreds – of thousands engaged in the murder of innocents, for the crime of being Jews, men especially trained for the job with God knows what hereditary taints. But almost all Ukrainians were suited to this task. They found their metier and satisfaction in this noble calling, and fully developed their talents for murder and carnage.

After their first two days of their rule, the Germans brought the merry mob to a halt and began to put things in order. First, after the front receded, they organized the civil administration, to the great disappointment of the Ukrainians, who before the war were promised a free Ukrainian state. All important posts in civil administration were taken over by Germans, excluding the Ukrainians who had seized such posts in the first days of the German occupation. Almost a month before the outbreak of the German-Russian war, there were rumours that a Ukrainian legion would be formed by the Germans. This information later turned out to be true. The Germans promised to create an autonomous Ukrainian state, and so attracted almost all the Ukrainan population, forming a very effective counter to the Russians' military recruitment. After attaining their purpose, the German began slowly to limit the range of their promises, continuing to deceive the ally they needed, by putting off the proclamation of the Ukrainian state until the occupation of Kiev.

Meanwhile they quietly but very thoroughly got rid of the most uncomfortable witness to their undertaking – Bandura the leader of the Ukrainian legion, shooting him for some alleged crime. One of the most honoured personalities of the Government of the "General Government" (this was the name of the part of Poland occupied by the Germans) declared at a press conference that the best thing for the Ukrainians was to wait quietly and everything would be as it should be. Translated into colloquial language this meant "as long as we need you, we must stroke you". The Germans actually treated the Ukrainians with great contempt, but as the need for them disappeared, they would stop all this caressing. The Ukrainians, at least that minority who were of the intelligentsia, realized how things stood now, and had few illusions about the future. I often heard this from my Ukrainan acquaintances. One even told me an anecdote. In a public garden, a Jew sat crying and lamenting "How horrible is our fate, we are tortured, murdered and massacred! What shall we do? Where can we hide? O Lord! help us, have mercy on us!" A passing Ukrainan heard this lamentation and remarked: "Why do you Jews complain so much? That your fate is bad now is a fact, but you have hope, you may anticipate a change in this fate. Our fate is not especially rosy at the moment, but we have no future at all. If the Germans win this war they will not give us a thing and if they lose this war Poland will revive and that means we will not achieve independence. If the Soviets come it also means an end to our hopes." The Germans gave the Ukrainian population one of the attributes of a state by creating the Ukrainian Militia, a subsidiary branch of the police, but of course under German command. Their task was to serve the Germans as assistant Jew-exterminators. This task which the German offered them used the Ukrainians' best talents: murder and massacre of the Jews. After the failure to create a government of Galicia, they saw that a free Ukraine was only a vision. But they seemed quite satisfied by their small dose of power and authority. Doubtless the Jews skimmed the cream of German bestiality, but to the rest of the population the Germans gave the feeling at every step, of their own inferiority. It would be beneath the dignity of a German of the master race to mingle with them. From the first days of the occupation there were street-cars "for Germans only" in the Teutonic version of apartheid.

All this of course did not apply to the Jews, as they were beneath any level; completely beyond the law, except for the special laws for Jews. There were shops "for Germans only" (naturally they were stocked with the best merchandise) cinemas "for Germans only", coffee-shops, patisseries etc. This was carried to such an extreme that there were even public lavatories "for Germans only". The population felt very badly about these discriminations, but seeing somebody even lower on the social ladder, like the Jews, who could be beaten by everyone with impunity, spat upon or robbed, made them feel better and tolerate this contemptible behaviour quietly, without any special indignation.

The problem of telling Jews from Poles was solved by introducing the requirement for Jews and people of Jewish descent down to the third generation to wear on the right arm a white armband with a star of David. After the publication of this order on 15 July 1941, a Jew dared not show himself on the street except from dire necessity, so as not to provoke excesses. The Germans, evidently to avoid frightening away the game, did not begin nor allow any brawls. This order was a brilliant handling of the problem. Many people who had little connection with Jewishness or Jewry (even those whose families had been Christians for two or three generations) were obliged to wear this armband, which was equivalent to the brand of death. Many tried to evade this order which worked as long as no compliant fellow citizen pointed out such a person to the authorities as having an unclean racial pedigree. Woe then, to the wretch. Not only was a disreputable brand awaiting him, but he often got a beating impossible to survive. On the other hand, it was not desirable for the authorities to apply the order exclusively. In the first days ofter the order was published I saw a priest with a Star of David armband. But after some days, this sort of thing disappeared and only the accursed wore the armbands. The Polish population during the first period of this harassment displayed a certain measure of sympathy for the Jews, but it found expression only in idle talk and empty gestures. Later, when we stood in need of concrete help, the Poles showed their real face.

Immediately after the entry of the German army, all stocks of victuals disappeared from the shops, partly hoarded by the civil population and partly bought up by the military. The Germans introduced ration-cards that were extremely differentiated. For Germans, the bread ration was 4.5 kilo weekly and other articles in almost adequate quantity; the Poles and Ukrainians got only 2.3 kilo of bread weekly and small amounts only of other foodstuffs (for instance 20 grams of oil monthly) while for the Jews 1.1 kilo of bread weekly, i.e. only 150 grams daily, which is less than a medium slice of bread. Additionally there were special shopping hours for Jews from 12 noon till 2 p.m, so as not to infect the rest of the population with their poisonous miasma. Often at this time of the day there was nothing more to buy, or the merchandise had not yet arrived, so this microscopic ration of bread was often only theoretical.

On street corners trading became rampant. It was in the hands of Aryans (I must use this designation despite the absurdity of the word). The Jews were wholly dependent upon getting food from the black marketers, and had to pay fantastic prices for every bite of food. The non-Jewish population could make up the deficiency in food products on the black market. There one could get everything, but at very high prices. To raise the money, people had to sell their personal effects, as the Jews were doing, or find some other source to acquire the huge sums of money needed for maintenance.

I have mentioned that the Germans, to avoid frightening the game, did not allow mass brawls, which did not prevent individual assaults and robberies. A Jew leaving his home never knew when or even if he would return. Behind every corner the Aryan in the person of a soldier or a Ukrainian militiaman lay in wait to catch you for "labour".

This labour meant not so much work as being beaten and harassed. For instance, 40 men aged between 50 and 65 years were caught to unload sacks of cement which weighed 100 kilos (220 lbs) each. Nobody thinking seriously of getting the work done would pick old men for such hard work. My father, after being caught for such work when he had gone to a near-by shop, returned in the evening with his back cut to ribbons with a whip, completely broken physically and in spirit. For younger men "suitable" work was, for instance, to shift rails weighing 450 to 600 1bs, but only at a running pace. The torturers didn't lack for fantasies.

Remaining at home was no protection against harassment, for officious neighbours pointed out to the Germans, after a vain hunt on the streets, the Jews hiding in their homes. To escape this, one had to hide during the day for hours in extreme secrecy. I was shut away from the neighbours, and let out after 9 o'clock in the evening, also in secret, as it could mean death by beating if I were found hiding by the Germans. After these two weeks I got a good job – that is, one without beating.

Another kind of individual harassment was robbery of apartments. Some officer, soldier, SS-man or common thief in uniform would burst into the apartment and after an affirmative answer to the question: "Are you a Jew?", open the wardrobes and drawers as if he owned them, pick out the best objects, order the Jew to give him suitcases, pack them to capacity and even demand that they be brought to his quarters. Often the victim of such a robbery did not return so as not to be left as a witness. Killing a Jew led to nothing, except perhaps praise. It may be said that such individual acts of violence always take place in time of war. But here they were of such a general nature and on such a scale that it is impossible to define them as cases of occasional wantonness.

In the first days of the occupation it happened that Jews, believing in order and justice, remembering the old-time Germany, or rather not realizing that all this was officially tolerated, even ordered, complained to the civil or military authorities, often emphasizing that they had been officers in the Austrian army. They were received with contempt, held up to derision, slapped in the face, kicked downstairs and thrown out. This was their reception to teach the others not to file complaints.

This first lesson was to make the Jews realize their inferiority and helplessness. The Germans entered methodically upon the programme to undermine the morale of the Jews, to destroy their feeling of humanity, the will to defend themselves, so as to make people destined to be murdered incapable of any impulse of resistance or struggle in the future, perhaps fearing that these individual acts failed to impress the Jews enough. The Germans began to requisition the furniture in Jewish apartments by means of informal commissions constituted from uniformed individuals, often not leaving the most necessary piece of furniture. Often after such a requistion there remained nothing to sleep on. The most bizarre part of the whole action is the fact that the furniture was not needed at all. Some 80 per cent of the requisitioned furniture was left to rot in storehouses, and the rest was used by petty bosses of various offices of the authorities. The effect of this on people who all of a sudden found themselves in their own apartments between naked walls, needs no exposition from me.

2 · Shades of Petlura

Among those persecutions, small seen today from the perspective of time, the Germans unleashed the first *Aktion* planned on a wider scale. These were the fatal three days, 25, 26 and 27 July 1941 called "Petlura days". They were called after Petlura*, because the violence was carried out exclusively by the Ukrainians and not to commemorate any anniversary of Petlura although it was claimed to be in retaliation for the assassination of Petlura by the Jew. I left my house for work, early in the morning. My attention was drawn to the unusual crowds in the streets, which were full of great numbers of youths in embroidered Ukrainian shirts. On one of the streets, I saw a group of Jews led by Ukrainian militiamen. I at once realized that this was not a normal "catch", but something more serious. Unnoticed, I turned into a side street and felt safe only when I arrived at my work place. I knew what I had escaped during the day when visitors brought in horrible stories about the happenings in the town. The Ukrainians went on the rampage. I talked to witnesses of three murders in the centre of the town, where a great many Jews were also beaten unconscious. Everyone advised me not to risk returning home under these conditions. At last I decided to go home, but without the armband with the Star of David, even though I was risking my life if I were recognized. But this was the only chance to reach my home. Unfortunately my way home was right through the town. On my way I met some Ukrainan patrols, but thanks to my self-confident behaviour I managed to evade the "catchers". To shorten my way I crossed a public garden (from the second day of the German occupation taboo for Jews). In the very last minutes of my journey, not far from my house, I chanced on a Ukrainian who knew me personally. I ran into the house, but instead of going upstairs, I went down to the cellar. My pursuers naturally ascended the stairs. The concierge, returning accidentally from the third floor, told them that he had seen no one. Realizing that the hunt had failed, they left the house. My family of course, knew an *Aktion* was in progress and the next day none of us dared go out on to the streets. The *Aktion* proceeded generally in an organized way. People were taken out from their homes, from the streets, from offices, and places of work, herded into the offices of the

* A leader of White Russians in the Ukraine, whose soldiers killed thousands of Jews in the Civil War of 1918–21.

Ukrainian militia and carried off to prison. On the second day of this *Aktion* I received information from my mother that my father had been missing for 24 hours. He had been called to the commissariat of the Ukrainian militia to get a visa on his passport and did not return. By such deceits and tricks people were trapped. We never saw him again.

A very few people were freed after two days. For instance, physicians and those who had close Ukrainian friends who were willing to help. Some mass beatings on the second day in one of the prison courts stimulated collapse. After the rest of those arrested were carried off, and some shots were fired in the direction of the beaten men, they were left in the belief that they were finished. They fled under cover of night.

One of them told me some details. During the day everyone was mercilessly beaten; whoever wanted could go into any cell and beat up anyone; without limit he could torture or murder. During the night, the prisoners were ordered to face the walls, standing in the cells, and told that they would shortly be shot. The prisoners' fear for their lives amused their tormentors extraordinarily. In the morning all were carried off for the obligatory mass beating.

Nobody can escape his fate, and in fact 18–20,000 Jews did not manage to do so, as subsequent evidence from the Judenrat revealed. These people had disappeared from Lvov. They had gone from sight like a stone thrown down a well. No one knew anything about them; where they were taken, what was done with them – they simply disappeared, leaving no trace. The fact is that during two years nobody received even the smallest news about the first instalment swallowed by the insatiable jaws of the Nazi Moloch: fathers of families and mothers, orphaning small children, and children orphaning their lonely old parents. They have gone and are no more, like ripples that spread across the water, weaker and weaker until they disappeared for ever.

3 · Methods of Crushing the Spirit

The Germans, as everywhere in occupied Poland, chose some Jewish leaders to serve as intermediaries between themselves and the Jewish population. After long negotiations with well-known Jews, they selected a committee of six councilors and a chairman. Before this "Judenrat" managed to take office, before its sphere of activity was defined, before it even moved in or collected chairs and tables, the Germans demanded a "contribution" from the Jewish population totalling 20 million rubles to be paid in ten days. Of course the Germans threatened undefined consequences if the entire sum was not delivered in cash on time.

The Jundenrat published an appeal to the Jewish population and asked for their cooperation. Along with many others, I also received such a call and reported the first day for service. Chaos reigned in the building of the Judenrat. There was no census of the Jewish population. There was no paper, no chair or bench to sit on, no table on which to write. We were obliged to begin our work from the beginning but the time at our disposal was too short to allow it. The only solution was to send individuals from house to house to inform the Jewish population of the state of affairs. Of course these individuals were exposed to the same harassment that threatened every Jew on the street. Of the 320 persons sent the first day, only 206 had returned by the evening. We learned about the remaining hundred only from the complaints of families who came to ask what had happened to their loved ones when they did not return home. It would be very hard to call working in the Judenrat agreeable. Every minute some soldier burst in demanding workers. Arguments that the people were needed to collect contributions for the German government contributions did not help at all. To the accompaniment of abuse and beatings, the soldiers took the requisitioned workers, leaving yet more places to be filled. The results of working in such conditions are very easy to figure out.

Everyone worked with devotion from 7 am till 7 pm as only till 8 pm was it permissible for Jews to be on the street. In the offices of the Judenrat every hour passing was counted, as a condemned man counts the seconds separating him from the moment of execution. Suddenly there was heard a rumour (now it is known that it was spread deliberately by the German authorities) that people taken during the "days of Petlura" were in prison in Lvov and only detained as hostages for punctual payment of the contribution. Two or three days later, word came that in Bialystok 3,000 Jews had been burned alive in one of the synagogues, because the contribution was not paid on time. Not long after, somebody came up who saw the Germans deposit in one of the synagogues 10 barrels of gasoline. Understandably the thought was borne in on everybody with tragic emphasis, that the Germans intended to do the same here. The news turned out to be partly true, as later on it came out that the Germans used a synagogue for a storeroom. The Jewish population hastened to several cash desks working from early morning till late evening. The crowds were immense. People often brought their last penny, prepared to be bled white to save their sons, fathers, brothers, wives, daughters, sisters and mothers. Pennies, single rubles flowed in an endless stream. Heaps of money piled up in the offices of the Judenrat, the officials worked till they dropped from exhaustion. They counted 20 million in change and small banknotes; by itself an enormous job. The 50 clerks remained working all night, to make sure of being ready on time. People heaped up more and more money, pulled out from old socks and knots in hidden garments.

This money stank with sweat. The money had perhaps been intended to secure lonely old age, or maybe to rescue a child from death and hunger; perhaps it had been destined for medicine. It was of not the slightest consequence, it fell into the claws of the Nazis to finance further bestialities.

Better-off people brought gold, which the Judenrat was forbidden to receive, or furs and jewellery, asking us to sell them. Unfortunately this too was prohibited. This was a time of inflation, when prices of valuables fell, owing to the enormous supply of articles from wealthy Jews who badly needed cash. There would be many more such inflations, but by this the Germans first gladdened the hearts of the Aryan population, enabling them to buy for a song, for a third or a quarter of their value silver, furs, and objets d'art.

But to give a true picture of these times, it should be mentioned that the venom of the omnipresent German propaganda had not yet poisoned the souls of the Polish population, nor yet immobilized the conscience of Polish society. It had not yet fallen so low that for a bite of white bread they would renounce their fatherland. Cases occurred, though not too often, of impulses of solidarity. I knew personally some members of the Polish intelligentsia, who paid appreciable sums to help with the contribution. Although the sums made little difference, the gesture of good will showed a spirit that counted and had a strong moral meaning. A handful demonstrated their solidarity, but not for long; they also were to abandon us and throw us upon our own sad resources.

These signs of sympathy from Polish society incited the Jews to even greater generosity than they had shown till then.

All the time the clerks of the Judenrat were asked how much had been collected and how much was yet lacking. On the last day of the collection Araleh, a porter well known on the streets of Lvov, asked one of the clerks the state of the collection, whether the full sum of contribution had been achieved. He got a stereotyped answer that some hundred thousands were still lacking. The simple man took this literally, burst on to the street with a clamour passing into sobs: "Brothers help! Help! They will murder our sisters and brothers. Some money is still lacking! Save the innocents, so that their blood does not fall on your heads!". It took a great deal of trouble to calm him. But this outcry did not fall on deaf ears. His call rang through the poor Jewish streets.

The Jewish poor lived in misery, on crusts, its reserves for survival counted in hours, the streets of pedlars, poor craftsmen and even poorer shopkeepers, overreacted in their generosity by selling their last rags and junk to fulfil their duty to aid brothers in need. The sum demanded was paid and delivered on time. However nobody returned home. The disappointment was bitter. Anyone who fell into the claws of Hitler thugs would see the world no more. But the trick succeeded. The Jews had paid!

During the collecting of the contribution, the Germans took snapshots of Jewish crowding to give their last pennies, laughing at the generosity of Jews – in their opinion normally greedy for money. They considered this idea of the authorities very ingenious and funny. To give us Jews something cheerful, the Germans set fire to two synagogues on Shaynokhy Street and Jadwiga Street. In the first, one of the oldest relics of Lvov, priceless objects of craftsmanship and fine art were burned, but being only Jewish, were worthless; as if the cultural achievements of Jews were not part of the general human achievement. To clinch the receipt of the full sum of contribution the Cathedral Synagogue of Lvov was burned. Let the blood-red glow, they thought, throw blood-red light upon bloody money!

Almost immediately after the payment of the contribution, an SS-man appeared in the office of the chairman of the Judenrat, demanding a set of tableware for 24 persons including pots and pans and all the accessories to furnish a kitchen. The chairman told him that in the present state of things, such items were unobtainable, so it was impossible to execute this demand. The SS-man became furious on hearing this answer, slapped the old man in the face and ordered him to follow him. He did not even allow him to take his overcoat. I must stress that the chairman was a very well-known civic leader, Joseph Parnes, 62 years of age, from a well-known Jewish landowning family.

Parnes' secretary who was present during the incident was informed of the reason for his arrest. At once he tried to acquire the needed items by collecting them from various apartments and to deliver them to the SS-man, to obtain the chairman's release. After receiving them, the German still wanted a pair of luxurious high boots for himself. After three days in prison the chairman actually returned to the office; an exceptional event, even at this early time.

This incident led to the creation of a new office in the Judenrat most essential to the Germans, the "Acquisition Dept". From this day on, more and more new Germans appeared requesting each time wilder and more extraordinary things. They demanded high boots, suits, club furniture, women's shoes, paintings, luxury underwear, chemicals long not available in the market, lengths of silk, silk stockings, lengths of English fabric, sculptures, crystal, women's furs etc. The bigwigs demanded, not officially but no less rigorously, jewellery, diamonds and the like. Failure to fulfil such a request meant death for the clerk, and in many cases the murder of a counsellor of the Judenrat, and the Lord only knew what reprisals against all the Jewish population.

Over the perspective of time, reflecting upon the behaviour of the Germans from the very first day of their entry to Lvov it can be seen that all the separate actions, requisitions, confiscations, and abuse come together into one deceitful plan, worked out with typically German cunning. It was obviously figured out in detail. They did not allow one moment of respite to the Jewish population. The mass slaughters called *Aktions* were interlaced with periods of relative calm but these were marked by mass abuse. The ultimate objective was to destroy morally, to torment psychologically and spiritually people doomed to death, and to bring people to such a condition that in no one would the thought of defence or resistance arise. This devilish idea, spawned in some pathological imagination, was unfortunately realized to the full.

Organizing the Judenrats in Lvov and other towns, the Germans knew exactly what they intended to use the members of the Judenrat for. They contrived everything very carefully, and actually succeeded in convincing many distinguished social and political leaders to let themelves be used to aid them to achieve their purpose. They went like sheep to the slaughter and led thousands with them, trusting the explanations of the Nazis, who posed as people governed by law and not, as afterwards came out, by brute force alone.

The Germans denied that their goal was the extermination of Jews. They said that indeed the Führer did not intend after winning the war to allow Jews to remain in Europe, but that meant only deportation to various colonies. Yet the best proof that their goal was solely to exterminate the Jews can be found in the wide powers and responsibilities they gave to the Judenräte.

People working in the Judenrat were relatively protected from being caught on the streets for labour. The councillors of the Judenräte got very wide protection; personal immunity, immunity for their family and even of their homes. With such privileges, the Germans managed to entice people who at first were very reluctant to collaborate with them. The Jewish militiamen got better conditions of life than the rest of the Jewish population. They obtained protection of their homes, the right to be on the streets after curfew hours, greater food rations and of course the uniform which gave them full personal protection. By such trifles, though necessities in those times, the Jews were divided into two groups; one extremely harassed and a second favoured. From this point, it was only one small step to use one group against the other, and not long afterwards this occurred. Besides the fact that privileges provoked great discord between the general Jewish populace and the workers in the Judenrat because of envy, some workers of the Judenrat being only human, took advantage of their official duties for various malpractices, and some even battened on Jewish misery. Owing to lack of funds, the Judenrat did not pay their workers, and because of the very high cost of living, people of weak resolution took advantage of every occasion to derive additional income. There was no lack of such occasions.

In August 1941, less than five week after the occupation of Lvov rumours began about dividing in Lvov into three districts: a German, a Polish-Ukrainian and a Jewish district. People did not take those rumours seriously. Anything that had not happened to date or which one had not lived through seemed to be not real.

I remember one day in August 1941, sitting in the Judenrat checking the final reports of the "contributions". A number of people coming from the town spread panic by reporting a mass ejection of Jews from their homes around the town. Some inner concern prevented me from continuing calmly at my work. Instead of leaving at 7 p.m. as usual, I went home about 5 o'clock. Around the house where I lived everything seemed calm, so that I wondered how to explain my early return home without causing panic. On the staircase I saw my wife sitting on the stairs with a suitcase surrounded by other tenants with bundles and cases.

My wife told me that about 2 p.m. when eveybody was at lunch, there was a ring at the door. This turned out to be a German in uniform. Without entering or offering words of explanation, he ordered them to leave the apartment within 15 minutes. He allowed them to take only what they could carry. What to take within 15 minutes? Particularly in the state of nerves which the presence of a Nazi causes in your head. My wife had packed my pyjama jacket, her right slipper, two pairs of my trousers without coats, and some of her underwear when the 15 minutes ran out; she was expelled from our apartment. It may seem a trifle, but where could we sleep? After two hours of searching – in other places the expulsions of Jews from their apartments had also occurred – my wife managed to install herself, her girl friend and myself at the flat of an acquaintance. The expulsion from apartments was massive. Within a few days, about 6–8 thousand Jewish people were turned adrift. The Judenrat formed a special accommodation department, but could not control the situation and allocate places to the homeless, for there were thousands without a home. The new department had no chance to organize an exact list of flats at its disposal and from one minute to another the number of people in search of living quarters increased.

On 1 September 1941, posters were put up on the walls of the town imposing compulsory work for Jews, men aged from 12 to 60 and women from the age of 14 to 55. Everyone was obliged to work, except sick people certified by special commissions of physicians as incapable for work. Again a new department had to be created in the Judenrat. Up to now, working in the Judenrat was hellish, but from this moment on the old hell became an other-worldly garden of Eden, in comparison with the moral and physical servitude now involved. From now on, not only was working in the Judenrat horrible but even to approach the Judenrat building. From 7 o'clock in the morning the Germans circled the building like vultures seeking their helpess prey, catching Jews ostensibly for "labour" but in reality to be beaten up.

The Judenrat tried to meet some concrete requests for the number of workers needed, but nothing came of this. The Germans would agree to a number and when they were sent exactly in accordance with the demand, they overturned everything. Again and again new Germans burst into the Department of Labour with new demands, then as a punishment took some Judenrat clerks, and released them after a while. Not a day passed that some German did not beat up the head of this department. The continuous fear, uninterrupted annoyance, with the prospect of being hauled out of work, beaten up and tortured, made all work in the Judenrat impossible. Hence the creation of a governmental office of labour for Jews was greeted with joy. A German called Weber was in charge of this office.

This Herr Weber deserves a special page in the martyrology of Lvov Jewry. A ruffian without education, with no qualifications for a responsible administrative position, he considered that the only proper argument was the fist. He introduced the rule of the fist in the fullest, most complete way. In the building specially allocated to him, he arranged the offices and filled them with about 100 Jewish clerks.

Immediately he began the registration of all liable to work-duty. In Weber's building it was forbidden to speak to one another even in a whisper, forbidden to wear a hat even in the corridors. Herr Direktor Weber in person walked about the building supervising the workers, with the help of smashing noses with his fists or knocking teeth out to explain the rules of order. Weber confirmed Jews in their present work places and directed them to new ones. I will return to the details of his work later on, as he and his Office of Labour constituted another of the methods of crushing the Jews' spirit.

I cannot ignore the harassment on the streets, which was perhaps the most loathsome factor in destroying the spirit of human dignity or any idea of resistance. It affected almost everyone. As in a kaleidoscope I see pictures which have stuck in my brain. On the first day of the occupation, after the deceitful call to work, I went out and came across a man of Jewish appearance in a suit torn to shreds, filthy with dirt, with clotted blood on his face, swollen nose and one eye closed. By his side a man in street clothes with a rifle, dragging a woman by the hair; behind them yet another two armed men. No sound of complaint was heard from the one being dragged. The group was proceding in total silence.

These episodes instilled in me a fear of the street. My wife persuaded me to take a walk in the evenings, to counteract this disastrous feeling, as at this time of day it was relatively quiet. Indeed on some evenings we succeeded in passing an hour or two walking, but after a few such evening strolls we met a German conducting ten or more Jews. We were walking without armbands and the German paid us no attention. The sight of the caravan remained with us and it discouraged us from such extravagance as a stroll in the fresh air. They were walking in couples, men only. In the first couple was a man with a red weal from a whip on his face, the other with marks of a beating. One had clotted blood on his face, another a bruise on his forehead. Of course all were hatless as this was forbidden to Jews in the presence of a German. They were dragging their feet, inhumanly tired, ragged, soiled with faeces and the mud of the street. The German drove them with a long-handled whip. Woe betide the unhappy man upon whom it fell. The pain would jerk the nerves for a while, the traces on the body would disappear after a few days, but the humilating brand on the soul would remain for ever.

4 · On the Margin

At this time the Germans organized an office called the Financial Enterprise Commission to hold stewardship of the private property nationalized by the Russians. Not long after the occupation the Germans declared that they would return all private possessions taken by the Russians to their legal owners. After a short time the Germans concluded that it was better to profit from this property than to return it. The gesture had been made, by promising to return private property, and there would always be time to give it back. Tenement-houses in Lvov provided a respectable income and a whole clique could make a magnificent profit but this was only possible by stealing what was being administered. Managment of factories and cooperatives became a gold mine.

Huge firms were created by combining cooperatives according to their trades: chemicals and food were under a firm called Chemia, later Galikol, The metal co-ops into the firm named V. E. M., wood-treatment as the firm C. H. B. and so on, of course the directors were mostly German, but they employed many Jews who were excellent experts, engineers, technicians, qualified workers. Creating these firms from private concerns nationalized by the Russians was a clear-cut fraud on the original proprietors, who had been grandiloquently promised the return of their property. This should have been a warning signal for the Judenrat of the real value of German promises, even those given in such a solemn form.

I was disturbed by the uselessness of working in the Judenrat. I was working in the inner control department and every day new difficulties were made by the Germans. They alone were blocking the execution of their own decrees and orders. Something peculiar must be going on. On the other hand the oppressive atmosphere of the Judenrat, the misery seen at every step – without any chance to help, became darker and deeper. We felt like animals in a trap, and it produced in me a deep state of anxiety.

All of a sudden I was offered the post which I had had in the time of the Russians as specialist book-keeper in the firm Galikol. I returned home deeply disturbed. What should I do? Go and work for the Germans, or remain in the trap? I pondered the question through a sleepless night. I reflected on the horror I had seen.

Finally the ghastly dreams turned pale. The sky began to lighten with the dawn. Slowly the contours of the furniture began to stand out. I got out of bed; another depressing day like the days before, overcast despite the sun. The phantoms of the night shunning the light of day slowly disappeared. I realized that I must get up and go to my work in the Judenrat. To bear all day the contemptuous behaviour of every boorish pipsqueak dressed in Nazi livery, to hear from morning till night the anxieties of the Jews (unfortunately with no way to help). One related that his wife had been kidnapped by the Germans, another's son had not returned for two days, another's apartment had been robbed by an unknown German, and under the eyes of fathers and husbands women had been raped. On this or that street, there lay the corpse of a man, murdered by Germans some days before. An SS-man proclaimed a pogrom: as he did not manage to get a pair of slippers for his mistress, the Jewish hospital will be without food in a day and so on. This again and again all day, day after day, week after week. Getting worse; tighter and tighter every day. A bewitched or accursed circle, or rather a circle described around us the accursed Jews, made us hold still tighter. I felt the atavistic fear of a trapped animal. To try to break at any price from the hands of the Germans, from this trap, before the small crack which still admitted a little light into the abysmal darkness into which the Nazis had pushed the Jews closed, I decided to take the post in Galikol, to be further away from this place of torture that was the Jewish quarter. I made the decision.

Good? Bad? Who knew?

The Galikol company was one of the 12 or 13 of the trade firms in the framework of the Treuhandstelle craft workshops, created from one-time cooperatives. Galikol united the chemical, cosmetic and food manufacturers, and was at this period in the process of being organized. The director, a German of course, was named Fuchs. He was a very enterprising man, liberal in his relations with Jews, who readily surrounded himself with Jews. Later on it turned out that he himself was part Jew. In the space of two to three weeks 24 cooperatives were united. Ukrainians meanwhile tried to grab these as Ukrainian workshops. The Germans did not enter into long discussions with the Ukrainians and quickly put out of their heads the idea that the profitable business could be Ukrainian. Doubtless it was much better to grab the business themselves and exploit it as war booty. Fuchs had the opportunity, and recruited a great number of Jewish experts. He paid no attention to obstacles, and filled most of the posts in the works and factories, even the leading ones, with Jews. The Poles and the Ukrainians came forward en masse for jobs. In a very short time the offices and factories were fully filled. Almost without special preparation the machine started to roll. Preparations were not needed. All the raw materials remaining from the time of the Russian occupation were used up at quite an American tempo and no one even tried to bring in new raw materials from Germany.

The economy achieved was an absolutely incredibly wasteful exploitation of all resources. The director stole for Germany as a whole, and for himself personally as a German. Every German thought the firms were created for those who were near the high altar – that is closer to the Nazi Party – so that they could grow rich. The enrichment took place at the cost of reducing the revenues of the state and the ruining of alien property but it did not affect the Nazis' tender consciences. Every one of them gorged like an animal as soon as he reached the trough. Their general attitude was: "Guzzle as long as the swill stands before you, before they can take the basin from under your nose". The effect of this principle was complete ruin – after a short period – of all the excellent two year plan achievements of the Russians; the industrial centre which they had created by almost superhuman efforts, the Germans destroyed, dismantling factories, selling off machines and stealing raw materials. They stole them as they were, or remodelled for personal needs. Herr Director Fuchs ordered for his private use 850 kilograms of 60 per cent soap for washing and about 300 kilograms of high-class toilet soap, from which he presented about 100 kilograms to the leading personalities of the government, as good quality soap had been for a long time only a memory from the good old days. In Germany at that time only soap with 10–20 per cent fat was produced.

It is a little difficult to speak about our fellow citizens of the Polish republic – the Poles. A not insignificant number of them now declared themselves to be *Volksdeutsch* (ethnic Germans). A short time after the occupation, the Germans announced that people wishing to demonstrate their belonging to the German nation should register and present appropriate documents attesting to their German descent. This proceeded with great difficulty, as people of German descent were in fact rare enough and almost no applications were registered. Those few who presented themselves got some privileges, first of all, bigger and better allocations of food, the right to travel on a street car "for Germans only", entry into public lavatories "for Germans only" and so on. Owing to the small numbers, the Germans began to look "with a kindly eye" at the documentation on German descent. This news spread quick as lightning among the Poles and immediately thousands of thoroughbred Germans were born. One with a German-sounding name or whose mother had been lucky enough to "forget herself" with a German, one who could claim some family connection with the Germans, and of course everyone speaking German. At last even people who had once purchased a subscription for a German paper applied to the appropriate department of the Government and registered themselves as *Volksdeutsch*. The most ardent patriots found it useful to give an account of their persecution by the Polish authorities because of their Germanness, and gave this as a proof of their belonging to the German nation. Their grail was really "holy", a double ration of white bread.

Relations between Jews and Aryans now seemed to have settled down. The latter dumped all the work on the Jews, and did not find it necessary even to pretend to be working. For work there were Jews, for Aryans there were good salaries, premiums, fringe benefits, additional food rations. These gentlemen got together in some free room, carried on conversations for several hours, discussing all current themes, such as the price of cigarettes on the black market, what one could get now on ration cards, where were the best places to get black market articles. And of course what hard war-times they were living through, where were the best sources to get valuable objects from the Jews for a song, and the lamentable impossibility of getting a loan, as the German director found fault with the Poles and treated them almost sadistically, refusing to give advances even to the value of a mere half-year's salary. The director took great care that "his" Jews worked, realizing that he must, under the present conditions, keep also his Polish workers. Besides, he had himself enough opportunities to fill his purse with money. The expansion of the concern was not his worry, as he understood that the far future was in fact not even a dream, and all that he could wring out now was his. Management in all the firms was similar. Every German was stealing for himself, partly dividing with other Germans working in the government, whatever was unavoidable, so that they would cover him when needed. He allowed the Aryans working with him not to work and to steal a little, while he himself took care that the Jews worked well so there would be enough to leak through the holes, great and small, and in the end enough would remain at the bottom, for the dear German nation and the "beloved" Führer.

All were working or rather bullying others to work for victory. All for the victory of savagery over culture, boorishness over civilization. On every railway-station were signboards with the slogan. "The wheels must roll for victory", but the more intelligent Germans who spoke out loud of certain victory, inwardly stopped believing in victory from this time, as the USSR had not broken at the first blow. The horror of the approaching winter campaign in the terrible Russian snow imbued the Germans with fear, and shattered their belief in victory.

Once, sitting in a coffee-house with my Aryan colleagues from the office, of course without my Jewish armband, as the place was prohibited to Jews, I overheard the talk of three young soldiers. One said that the war against the Russians was difficult, but he was sure that after three or four years they would finish them. The second added that the English would also be conquered, but he thought that the Germans would get even with them also in four years. The worst nut to crack would be the Americans and they would take perhaps six to seven years. The third, listening till now to the talk, burst at this moment into loud laughter and finished this harsh dialogue ironically.

"Oh! Wonderful! This means that after another 15 years, the rest of the cripples will be home. Excellent!". This and similar news spread with lightning speed among the population, and people saw with the eyes of fantasy, the retreat of the Germans. Everybody enjoyed this, as hatred of the Germans was inborn in the Poles, especially as then they would be the only masters of the trough and would be able to steal without restrictions, admitting no one else to the bowl. The Jews – completely understandably – listened to the highly exaggerated communiqués and to news from the front line, trying to find a little hope for a better tomorrow. Very few had faith in the possibility of great resistance by the Russian troops. We were afraid of what the Germans were waiting for, a revolution in Russia and the disintegration of the USSR At first it was reckoned, after the sad experience with Poland and France, that the war would last weeks only.

"See, today it is already over three weeks and they still hold on!"

"What do you say, after five weeks they are still fighting!"

Such were the remarks even then, twelve weeks later. After that, people ceased counting days and slowly hope began to gleam that perhaps this time the Germans had slipped up. From this side perhaps rescue for the Jews would come. Hope, stupid hope, tottering, flickering, hardly visible from afar, bore us up. We must hang on somehow. Unfortunately the dawn was far away, and before the sun was to rise, the abysmal darkness of the Nazi night would swallow up millions of human beings. No! Not human – only Jewish.

5 · The First Camp and the First Ghetto

After installing himself in the office of the Jewish Labour Department, Herr Weber began to register all those liable to work in accordance with the government's order. The penalty for not registering was death. To register was itself death, either way led to death. Weber ran wildly through the building, wreaking his rage upon people for no cause, threw out his clerks for the smallest over-stepping of his regulations, each with his due dose of beating. Whoever was not a bad enough character, whoever could not deal out satisfactory brutality to his brother Jews, was dismissed. Finally there remained an appropriate team around Herr Weber, to serve his purposes and to become the shame of Jewry. The German masters, playing on the lowest instinct of weak characters, selected for themselves everywhere suitable teams from among the people to be annihilated, only at last to eliminate also these assistant hangmen once they had completed their despicable work.

The Judenrat grew enormously at this time. About 2,000 officials were working, hoping to help, after a fashion, the Jewish population. At the disposal of the Judenrat were several bakeries, a few dozen groceries. Kitchens for the poor were organized, hospitals opened and so on. The Department of Social Welfare expanded more and more, as more and more had to accept the fate of being recipients of public welfare. The Germans did whatever they could (and they could do much) to make this apply to the maximum number of people, and to make it difficult for the Judenrat and its clerks to succeed in applying good order and organization.

In September 1941, the Germans became filled with concern about the efficient functioning of the Judenrat, and insisted upon the need to create a Jewish 'Order Service'. They even brought the commander of the Jewish militia from Warsaw to instruct. At first the Judenrat assembled 20 men, as the cadre of the future militia. The Germans provided caps, boots and other pieces of uniform, the heritage from the Polish police. The men were drilled in this police service, so completely alien to Jews. A short time afterwards, the roster of militia was increased and they took responsibility for order in the part of town inhabited by Jews, around the building of the Judenrat, at Jewish groceries, at warehouses, at bringing the recalcitrant to work etc. The idyll was very short-lived. Before long this Jewish 'Order Service' would degenerate into an instrument in the hands of the Nazis, to sow destructive disorder in the life of their fellow-Jews on their way to ultimate extinction.

From the deformed imagination of a psychopath, a horrible plan of murdering millions of people was spawned. Two means were the basis of this plan. The first were the camps, officially described as labour camps. These would prepare and teach the Jews "productive work". The second were *Aktions* serving more directly the aim of fishing out recalcitrant elements, and deporting them to work places. Between these two poles as between Scylla and Charybdis – we dragged out our existance in daily distress, in a grey, red-splashed anger, which was perhaps the third means, most far-reaching in effect, for the extinction of the Jews.

We lived in terror of torments, insults, violence, robberies, murders, and before everyone's eyes stood the spectres of hunger and torture, We were hurled beyond the orbit of society, even beyond the compass of men. Our thousand-years-old traditions of culture were torn out of us like living flesh, We were systematically degraded to the role of animals, herded, worn out by endless toil, baited by endless harassment. The Germans operated with the help of such perfidiously camouflaged methods that wider and wider circles, even people of the strongest character, descended completely to the state of brutes. Very few during the two years 1941–1943 were tough enough to avoid this – perhaps the worst of the means of crushing the spirit.

The first camp for the Jews of Lvov was established in a farm belonging to the town, in the nearby village of Sokolniki. As principal work-place, a small swampy field around a pond was allotted. The commander of the camp was a Ukrainian named Tshubak (Czubak) and his deputy was also a Ukrainian called Jaworski. The Germans did not pay much attention to this camp, knowing that they could trust the Ukrainians in the matter of sadistic treatment of Jews. This camp was liquidated in December 1941, and a new camp near the Janowska toll bar was then organized. It lasted during all the time the Jews were still in Lvov, till the liquidation of the ghetto and even longer.

The Janowski camp was organized completely differently from Sokolniki. A very large area was fenced in, without any special accommodation for workers and with no buildings. The Jews would themselves build the barracks and other buildings. Sokolniki camp was destined for "training": these who withstood two or three weeks of its torment were discharged; if one got sick he was moved to a hospital, but anyone who could not keep on working perished; his bad luck or perhaps his good luck. Anyone who fell into Janowski camp could never get out alive, at least by normal means. As long as he lived he was destined for torture. When anyone fell ill or became incapable of work he was rushed to his death, or as it was called there, went "beyond the wire" or "onto the sands". In December 1941 the organization of this torture centre began, but its real activity started in January 1942.

In the meantime, Herr Weber's Work Department informed all the interested institutions that after the statistics on all working Jews were completed, to avoid them breaking the law which obliged the Jews to work, the credentials of Jewish workers must be extended by him monthly on the first of every month. To check that this demand was satisfactorily fulfilled Weber ordered the Judenrat to set up a Jewish militia post in the Work Department. From this moment the Jewish population began pushing continual bribes and presents onto Herr Weber. His jackals, unfortunately recruited from among the Jews, nourished themselves on the crumbs of the loot. At the same time, there also took place in this period an expansion of the Jewish militia and the evolution of a police mentality and corruption among up to now normal people.

About 80 per cent of the Jewish militia was at this time at the disposal of the Work Department. It may be understandable that they did not want to be left out in the cold – and they also opened their palms, greedy for their share of the loot. The militia increased rapidly. From the several dozen militiamen who at first constituted the Jewish Order Service of the Judenrat; already in December we had about 300 militiamen imbued with the "noble police spirit" and devoted with fervour to their German masters. The principal occupation of the Jewish militia was to aid the Work Department. and to assist the clerks of the Acquisition Department. in taking goods from Jews and seizing people for the labour camp.

On 11 November 1941 an order was published, awaited for some time, creating a Jewish district. It was in the north-east section of the town, or rather a suburb, consisting of shabby huts, without drainage, without water supply, without gas and mostly without electric light. It was separated from the rest of the town by a railway track, traversing the four main streets leading to the toll bar: Kleparowska, Zamarstynowska, Zolkiewska and Peltewna. These four streets passed partly under railway bridges crossing these streets. The position of this district was significant, as there was no other way to this part of town apart from passing under those bridges. The Germans of course took advantage of this convenient situation and assigned this area for the living quarters of the Jews. The whole town was divided into 10 districts. For one month, beginning on 18 November all the Jews of every district had to move at the due time to this ghetto district. The Aryans living there, beyond the bridges, had to leave the district. But to prevent the transfer proceeding in an orderly fashion the latest time for Jews to move was fixed at 18 December 1941 and for the Aryans 25 January 1942. The confusion that such a seeming trifle could bring about is hard to imagine. The number of Jews in Lvov according to the evidence of the Judenrat was about 160,000 people, and from the statistics of the Germans 180,000. This number of people had to accommodate itself in this small sector. In the whole district assigned, about 30,000 people were living.

After enormous doubling up it might be possible to lodge 60–70 thousand people, but what could be done as the Aryans did not want to leave their mostly privately-owned one-family huts, delaying the removal till the last moment. None of the Jews could justify his not having removed by the lack of a place, as this excuse did not interest the Germans. It was arranged so as to cause a lack of places for many Jews. For those not complying with the ordinance, or behind the time for removal, the penalty was death. Immediately after the publication of this order, a wild scramble began among the dozens of alleys and back streets full of mud 20 to 30 inches deep, among grudging Aryans, to find some corner for living. The neighbours touched by the carefulness of the Germans, perhaps not so much for their own good as to make life more difficult for the Jews, thought it their duty to add their share to the godly work of oppressing the Jews. They offered closets, coal bins, stables, sheds, pigsties and hovels as residences, demanding fantastic sums of compensation for giving over the lease. I paid a sewing machine, a bicycle, a man's fur coat, a length of fabric sufficient for a suit, and 3,000 zloty (about $7,000 today) for two very small rooms in a ramshackle hut. In addition to all that, only after several day-long petitions did I succeed in persuading the owner to desert these living quarters in time.

Similar difficulties met all those living in the districts of town with an early time for removal, who had to hasten. On this occasion, the Judenrat was able to intervene effectively. The Judenrat was negotiating with the Germans to widen the district for Jews and to prolong the time for removals. The protracted negotiations continued and in the meantime (this was the most important!) the Judenrat was greasing the palms of Germans with every possible means. Thanks to colossal bribes, the Judenrat succeeded in getting an enlargement of the Jewish district to include a part of the town adjoining the bridges, the district of the town the most densely inhabited by Jews, and also to delay the deadline of the removal for three districts. The rest still had to remove on the previously fixed dates.

The Germans designated exactly the route for Jews to carry out removals to the Jewish district, namely under the bridge on Peltewna Street. All the bridges were lined by German sentries, who would on no account let Jewish pedestrians or a country wagon with Jews pass, directing everyone to Peltewna Street. Under this bridge there was a special guard of SS-men. For them and a crew of Ukrainian militiamen an old bath-hut, which stood near the bridge, was refurbished. By the middle of November 1941, hundreds of country wagons trailed with the rubbish of those obliged to remove through the gate. It was an unbelievable sight; wagon after wagon in an unbroken line, from 6 in the morning till 7 p.m., inching along foot by foot. The Germans checked under the bridges lest – God forbid – somebody tried to transport anything too good. One could not of course see furniture vans at all, between the rare trucks were many small peasant wagons. The contents were almost routine, a bed, a table, several chairs, a primitive chest and one or two suitcases or a bundle with bedclothes. Mainly broken, battered stuff, the remnants of once decent furniture. These humble remnants the Germans inspected to fish out something worth stealing. The more valuable items such as food reserves, a better shirt or suit, were transported before dawn, when it was impossible to ride a wagon and the sentries were not so many. They would be carried in a small bag, hidden in a pocket and so on. Taking this risk to carry valuables, slipping through in the dense darkness before dawn, along the walls of houses, like thieves, taking a careful look around on all sides, went the thieves of their own property, while a severe penalty awaited them if caught. The attachment of people to inanimate things was amazing, many risked their lives to rescue some piece of linen or underwear. Many lost their lives, because the watchful eyes of German sentries only sought an occasion to work off their bad temper.

The street was wide at this place, but was encumbered with a bar, leaving only one sidewalk and a narrow part of the roadway. Through this bottleneck everyone had to pass. In the morning the guards were not numerous and did not pay much attention to those going downtown. But the movement from the town into the Jewish district was thoroughly controlled against the appearance of gold, jewellery, furs or food being smuggled. On both sides of the sidewalk stood SS-men and Ukrainian militiamen armed to the teeth, with whips and cudgels in their hands. From the first day the Germans tried to instil in the Jews a proper respect for the bridges, killing some people on the street and crippling dozens physically and mentally after torturing them in the barrack near the bridge. The corpses were left on the street like used rags, to impress the people. Day in, day out, the cries and howls of the tortured in the nearby barrack were heavenly music in the ears of those SS-men who were unable to participate in the fun.

After I was thrown out of my home on Listopad street, by happy chance I moved to the part of town over the bridges, but the street where I now lived was not included in the Jewish district. I was obliged to move again. Together with my family we moved to the Zniesienie suburb. As I have related, I paid a respectable compensation for the "apartment". The removal, although I did not need to pass under the bridge, was not a simple thing. To find a farm wagon in the mass rush presented a very serious difficulty. At last I found something that the driver called pompously a furniture van. It consisted of a platform of splintered planks and cracked frames, held together perhaps by faith, the earnest prayers of the owner, and a broken-winded nag with barely the strength from hunger and old age to carry its spavined back. Hearing the price, I was staggered, despite having been toughened by the present conditions, by its astronomical impudence. The owner-driver, an Aryan of course, thought it a sin against this new magnificent Aryan God not to take advantage of the situation of the "yids", created by the coming of the saviours of humanity from the west. He demanded 650 zloty (about $1,600 today) for a haul of a mile; 40 minutes of his time. Seeing the bewilderment on my face when I heard this exorbitant price, he knew at once that I could not haggle, as other people were waiting for him. Willy-nilly I must pay the price demanded. But this was not extreme. For transport of a ton of fuel (probably illegal), I paid in addition to a similar price, kitchen furniture and lamps from my apartment. Prices such as this were not unusual. The cost of transport exceeded all imagination. The exploitation did not end with such trifles. Many Aryan neighbours took steps apparently to help the Jews – by receiving their most valuable things for safe-keeping, helping in this way to rescue at least some of the belongings of their "poor dear persecuted Jewish neigbours". Naturally acquiring so cheaply the property of others led to betraying the confidence placed in them, and led the "benefactors" into forgetting the truth and regarding it as their own legitimate property. They began to revel in the cherished furniture, clothes and other things they had acquired.

Eventually I loaded my few remaining sticks of furniture which I could accommodate in the new apartment (or rather hut) and moved after the nag, shuffling at a snail's pace with the wagon threatening to disintegrate at every pothole. This slow vehicle and its pieces of good furniture seemed to the local kids created especially for them. Scarcely had we turned into the Zniesienie neighbourhood than we were beset by a cluster of boys and girls from the suburb. Their provident parents had sent them out to provide their households with a few Jewish belongings. They threw themselves onto the wagon like a cloud of locusts. Repelling them had no effect, and to strike anyone could be provocation for a pogrom for "assaulting an Aryan child". The hungry jaws of empty sacks, which the thrifty mothers had provided, gaped open, and greedy paws grabbed for pillows, often the last remaining one. A desperate impotence from the fear of all Jews being charged with collective responsibility shackled our hands and choked the cry of fury in our throat. But nothing being forever, at last I reached my new home.

The new apartment was two rooms without electricity, with small windows, in a hut caving into the earth, which should be a home for 9 persons. The stale damp smell of the long unaired rooms struck one on entering. The flat included what was gradiloquently defined as a toilet. At best it merited the name of open sewer, and there was a bin in a plank shed. There was no cellar, only a pit for potatoes. Water had to be brought from a well 60 yards away. Because man is the most adaptable animal, we began to arrange things and to settle down in these primitive conditions. We arranged our things partly in the living room and partly in the bin. We finished in the middle of the night so tired, that even our desperate thoughts did not move us and we lay down to sleep. Long before dawn I must rise and go to work if I did not want to fall into some trap and be carried off to a labour camp or some other pleasant place. The following day I rose early. The way to my work-place was long, and as I could not use the tram, it took more than an hour. Before I went, I had to bring water, chop wood and so on. On entering the porch I noticed that during the night we had been burgled and the chest with our provisions had been emptied. At the sight of the broken furniture and the scattered remnants of the supplies I was horror-struck. The burglars had left us without an ounce of food, and there was no chance of more as there was no place where victuals could be had. The loss was irreplacable. We collected from the floor the precious remnants to break our fast.

Unfortunately the sight of the traces of burglary, once rare enough in the disappearing memories of pre-war times, became almost an everyday occurrence. During our three-month stay in Zniesienie, our hut was broken into nearly 30 times. Every two or three days, some nocturnal guest paid us a visit. Foodstuffs, wood, coal, furniture from the bins, empty suitcases, even the wicket gate were worth stealing, not to mention the fence with its excellent value as fuel. Affairs came to such a state that on rising in the morning I was astonished when a night passed without a break in. To be sure that something would not disappear, one had to sleep on it, literally. People slept on suitcases containing their most valuable possessions, and a sack with food served as a pillow. Listening to the noises every night gnawed away one's nerves. There was the continual fear that the thieves might steal the remaining necessities of life. The tide of thefts, robberies, murders, robbery with murders, the helplessness engendered by the impossibility of any active defence, and finally the thieves' total impunity, incited the insolence of our brave fellow-citizens, and forced us to secure the house as best we could. We abandoned anything that could not be placed in our rooms. The windows in the attic were walled up. Near the outer door of the attic we heaped together a pile of stones and bricks, so that if someone tried to open the door, it would fall on the robber and hurl him from the ladder. The professional thieves did not fatigue themselves for such a trifle as robbing a flat. At 8 o'clock in the evening, the curfew hour for Jews, our hut transformed itself into a fortress. The entry door was secured with bars and supported by a baulk. The windows were closed with heavy shutters from the inside. Nobody could go out or come in till 4 a.m. when we allowed ourselves to look out upon the world. This precaution turned out to be completely justified. Every night shrill cries reached us; the only possible means of defence of the robbed and murdered; not a rare occurrence. The Jewish militia was totally helpless; they could not arrest an Aryan. The Jewish militia were only permitted to whistle to call in a Schupo (*schutzpolizei*), so every night one heard whistles, and for a change horrible cries for help. On Sloneczna Street nearer the centre of the town people made an arrangement among themselves for a collective defence by mass outcry. When one cry for help sounded, everyone opened their windows and began a terrible outcry for help in the form of beating on pots and stewpans, honking on children's trumpets, whistling, crying and so on. This method proved to be very efficient, succeeding in most cases in repelling the robbers. Cowardice is inseparable from the nature of a thief, accustomed as he is to working furtively in the shadows, the row alarmed him. Who dared to defend himself would perish, killed by the thief and no one cared a fig for it. No one troubled the authorities about such a trifle as the murder of one or two Jewish families, better to avoid a bad time for himself on this account.

I have mentioned that our Aryan collegues did not condescend to stain their hands with any systematic work. Every now and then, one of them would write something and was sure that he had caught up with his arrears of work, for his – in his opinion – insufficient salary. For work there were after all the Jews. Really we were the only ones to deserve worker credentials, although we got nothing more for our work. We racked our brains for a way of getting some food, to ensure a tiny shelter for our families and ourselves, and most important, to hold on at work so as not to lose the credentials, as this meant death. Around these poles our lives revolved. The officious Aryans, understanding the impossibility of our moving in the town, brought various foods to work. At factories, workshops and offices, all day various Aryan dealers or rather peddlers appeared, bringing with them bread, dairy products, meat, sugar, cigarettes and altogether everything to anyone's heart's content. They did indeed everything they could to alleviate the heavy fate of the Jews. This, however, was only one side of the coin. For this favour and service one must pay very well. For instance 1 kg. bread cost about $15, 1 kg. meat $20, 100 cigarettes about $10–15 and so on. On such occasions they offered the sacrifice of their mediation in selling various things for Jews needing money. In numerous cases they themselves bought the offered goods. If one was compelled to trust some goods to the middlemen for sale, if they didn't embezzle the things entrusted, they would pay such a low price that it would not be worth selling anything. Yet better to sell and to be relatively satiated, than to be robbed by Germans on an empty stomach.

But God forbid, if we let such a trifle distract us from work. The work in the office, which forced us to concentrate, had no depressing effect on us and the work conditions were bearable. Only a few individuals managed to find such work. The majority were working at the hardest physical labour in factories, on construction, clearing away the rubble, on railway stations and military warehouses; ten hours daily of harassing labour for a little pot of dishwater laughably called soup, without a crumb of bread. The only quality of this soup was that it was hot. The ruinous tempo, the overburdening of the worker, the horrible working conditions, hunger and cold, and worst of all, the whip over one's head, not only hanging there, but more often slashing till it drew blood, ruined completely those unpaid workers. Salary was quite out of the question. A soup, labour credentials and sometimes a few pennies – not enough to purchase a slice of bread – meant that after some months the ranks of those learning fruitful (that is, physically ruining) labour had become much depleted, and the workers were more like skeletons or shadows than men. Everything in this world comes to an end, so the work hours dragging at snail's pace came to their end. It was deep evening. The blessed dusk, generously lending its wonderful protection, cloaked the streets of the town. At last one could go home. Perhaps I would yet see my family alive, maybe I would even get a bite of food and maybe even – if the Germans and the local robbers would allow us Jews a breathing spell – I would succeed in having a little rest. But nothing was without payment. For everything, one must pay and pay well. The nightmare of the route through town was enough payment for the short moments of rest and relaxation after the strain of the day. It would seem likely that the crossing under the bridge was enough for variety's sake on the way home, but no! It appeared that it was not all. The majority of those working had to go almost all the way through town. The Aryans in their Christian abnegation wanted to free the Jews of the trouble of this world's goods, such as overcoats, fine suits and so on. They therefore robbed the defenceless Jews in broad daylight. They tore overcoats off shoulders, ordered one to remove one's shoes, with full tolerance for such acts from the German police. The poor man whose overcoat was torn off his shoulders often had trouble to avoid being beaten up by the robber and had to flee; in most cases with teeth clenched from fury to avoid being murdered if one tried to defend oneself. The laughing crowd advised the robber what needed to be repaired or changed so that the newly acquired coat would fit 100 per cent. Often a Polish policeman was in the crowd of the actors in such a scene. At first he stood at the side and observed the scene with authoritative interest. After some complacent citizen informed him that the object of the robbery was a Jew, he lost his stiffness and observed it with a smirk of sincere joy. In such a short time, the seed of Nazi propaganda had flowered in this new soil. Hundreds of such scenes could be seen at this time. I myself lost my coat in this manner on 4 January 1942 at 5 o'clock on Krakowski square.

The robberies on the streets were a speciality of our fellow-citizens. The attacks on the streets and beating without robberies the Germans reserved for themselves. Very few could escape being attacked and hurt in a more or less grievous manner on their way home from work. A passing German, often for the sake of fun and to demonstrate his good humour, now and then to show off before his girlfriend or simply from boredom, found it desirable to beat a passing Jew on his head or face, to hurl the hat from his head or do something similar.

In November/December 1941 the Germans reported that the Russian army had ceased to exist, that the front wedged deeply into Russia. On the Russian side, supposedly there remained only small groups of soldiers, completely disorganized with no communication between them and without command. The articles in the papers were expressing astonishment. What could be supporting these detached bands, and what kept them from final capitulation? Everything, according to the German press, pointed to the ultimate disintegration – after all the German army was on the outskirts of Moscow. The BBC broadcast did not announce any such thing about the Russian army; on the contrary the tenor of the news was full of optimism, but it was impossible to deny that the Germans had approached Moscow.

After the daily portion of hypnotizing radio-propaganda, one began to see the future in a little rosier light. Some things were incredible, but we were eager with our whole souls to give credence to this pleasant news, so in line with our dreams. We listened to the radio in the cellar of a ruined house. After every session everything had to be taken to pieces. One by one we would go to the apartment of one of our acquaintances, who lived close by, to discuss and critically examine the communiqués, to find among the countless lies meant to beguile the masses the smallest grain of truth.

Quietly though, in the deepest recesses of our hearts, we cherished the pleasant delusion of a better tomorrow. To ourselves we would deny that we trusted some of the fantastic delusions in the face of the tragic reality. But this belief, the hope for a better future, supported our consciousness of self so near to collapse. Optimism, self-delusion, muddleheadedness based on radio propaganda – whatever you call it is not important. It was important that this existed. Indestructible, uncrushable, our Jewish optimism, perhaps our reward for our one-time deep faith in God, was our mainstay. The belief, blind, stupid, baseless, contradicting reality, that perhaps someone would, in spite of all, do something for us. Perhaps England or the USA would threaten reprisals against Germans living there, perhaps our outcry would induce the conscience of the world and would influence at the last second the ravaging madness of the Huns. These hopes were all that was stopping us from committing mass-suicide. They held us back from total brutishness and total collapse. Today 19 months after extricating myself from the hell of the ghetto, I myself cannot comprehend what then restrained me from ending this long-lasting suffering. What gave us the strength to endure the torment of a normal day and the hell of dozens of *Aktions*? Hope? Trust? In what? Expectation, of whom? Only irrational Jewish optimism. Nobody could take it from us as, unlike our worldly goods, perhaps nobody envied it. However, I have the feeling that we should all thank God for this priceless gift.

6 · The First *Aktion*

Anxious that everyday monotony should not upset the Jews, the Germans unleashed at the beginning of December 1941 the first of their *Aktions*. An *Aktion* was an activity on a large scale, undertaken with the aim of eliminating the Jewish population at a faster and more brutal rate than was possible by everyday harassments. During a normal day the number of victims in the ghetto and Janowski camp was about 100 people per day, in one day of *Aktion* the number of murdered was increased to 1,000 or even 5,000 men, women and children. The *Aktionen* followed one after another every 2–3 months, sometimes more often, without apparent cause. To distinguish among them they were christened as follows:

“Aktion” on old men under the bridges from	1–10.XII, 1941 – 2,000 victims
-″- before the Holidays	14.XII, 1941 – 1,000 -″-
-″- for deportation	20.III–10.IV.41–22,000 -″-
-″- of catching for labour camps in the whole year 1942	40,000 -″-
-″- in June (two hours only!)	14^{h}–16^{h}9.VI.42 – 6,000 -″-
-″- August	11.VIII–22.VIII.42 – 62,000 -″-
-″- on “W” and “R”	18–20 XI. 1942 – 8,000 -″-
in January 1943	6–8.1.1943 – 10,000 -″-
-″- of retaliation	17.III.1943 – 1,100 -″-
-″- “every third”	22.V.1943 – 3,000 -″-
-″- for liquidation	1.VI.1943–16.VI. 1943 – 16,000 -″-

The character of these *Aktionen* was similar. Rapes, murders, robberies, fulfilment of the wildest bestiality the Germans and their Ukrainian helpers could dream up, wreaking their rage upon the helpless to complete the total annihilation of the Jewish population.

People have charged Polish Jewry with submissiveness and lack of courage. Someone who did not know much about the conditions might say that he would have chosen a quick death, than a slow torture, leading inevitably to death, that he would have preferred to perish in a hopeless fight, to take with him at least one German. People do not realise the sum of two things in this situation. First of all, none of us dreamt, that the laws about the status of Jews were a dead letter and that the aim of the Germans was the murder of the whole Jewish population. On the other hand as I have tried to describe, the Germans by greater or smaller harassments, annihilated the morale of the

Jews, destroyed the feeling of being human, pushed us down to the level of undernourished brute slaves, deceiving us until the last moment by pictures of a life of some kind, even within the framework of Nazi law. Never during all that time, even during the finishing off the remnant of the three and a half million mass of Polish Jewry, the tiny handful which in no case could be a danger, did the Germans find enough moral courage to raise the visor and say openly "our aim is to kill off all the Jews". All the time with cowardly perfidy, they insisted that their only purpose was to eliminate the Jews from the life of the Aryans, to keep the healthy minds of the Aryans apart from the destructive influence of Jewish mentality. It was not their aim, they claimed, to touch one hair of our heads. This really was the truth. Verily they would bend no hair on the heads of the Jews, but they would torment us with tortures. The German experts worked miracles compared with the torturers of the Spanish Inquisition, who seem now to be small children in their ridiculous effort to subject their fellow-creatures to hell. We Jews fell for the deception, but what healthy, normal human being could believe that *à propos* of nothing in particular, with no reason, in the twentieth century, a national government would decide to murder four million people? Helpless people, not dangerous, not in a fight, not in the heat of emotion even artificially generated, but in cold blood, systematically, by specially created state-organs, with government offices, statistics, full office apparatus, directors, clerks, references etc. Their aim, to fulfil a degenerate plan. To annihilate a population consisting of two-thirds of women, children and old people. Was it so?! NO! Nobody could believe such a possibility. To carry into effect such a macabre plan, hatched in the heads of the Nazi leaders, they began in December 1941 the realization of the plan of murder on a wider scale than just to kill old men under the bridge.

I returned from work not anticipating anything special. About halfway to the bridge I noticed some unusual excitement. We were accustomed in our new set of conditions, to react quickly to any general sign of nervousness. My questions were answered, that there were rumours that today they were taking people in masses and retaining them in the barracks near the bridge. I went on with greater caution. The crossing under the bridge was empty. In a small side street I saw some people and accosted them asking for information. They told me that today they had taken all the old men or rather all men with grey hair. From the barracks sounded horrible groans and moans. What to do? It was evident that they had taken our old people, but if a German suddenly got the idea of taking also young men or women we could do nothing. There was no chance to appeal, as there was no regulation or offence. All of a sudden the few people on the square before the bridge disappeared as if blown away. Some trucks drove up. The street glared with deadly emptiness, except that from time to time from beyond a corner, from the cavity of a house-gate, a head looked out with a pair of deathly afraid yet curious eyes.

The trucks stopped in a row before the barracks. From beyond the fatal boarding a mass of old men was being driven out like a herd of sheep. But I have expressed it incorrectly. One could hardly know that these were once people, now they were almost rags. One day only in the hands of the German thugs had made them so. Ragged, soiled, filthy, bedraggled, clothes in shreds, vacant stupefied expressions on their faces, shoulders bent, oppressed by boundless apathy and resignation. On tired feet already heavy with the inertia of death they dragged on the few steps from the place of torture to the truck, which would drive them in comfort to the place of death. The loading was accompanied by beating, the moaning of the victims, the shouts of the SS-men, the crying of the families watching from afar the torture of their fathers and grandfathers, the laughter of the Ukrainians, when one of them fell, took an endless half hour. At last the death-load left. Respect for grey hair – what could have happened to that German virtue? Reverence for parents, the ten commandments – ethical rules – all this was folly, banal platitudes imposed by Jews on the whole world.

Only after an hour did people had gather the courage to pass pale-faced, with eyes widened with fear between the thin ranks of guards under the bridge. After fruitful work the workers in the Lord's vineyard were being allowed rest.

Some days later from the shreds of information collected from Ukrainians, from freed Jews and even from Germans, one could essay a more or less detailed picture of this *Aktion.* On the first day about 400 old men were gathered in the barracks. A mental defective was found (handicapped or mentally insane Jews from the asylums were killed or thrown out) and after being beaten into a state of fury he was set on people, attacked them, bit, clawed, gnawed, threw down old men and danced a crazy dance. His wild jumps, howling, laughter changing to insane moans, and gurgling took from the victims what little remained of their senses. They dispersed in all directions, only to be driven back by the whips of the Ukrainians amid the laughter of the delighted Germans. Whom could I properly call "poor"? Whom would one describe as "poor", the mental defective, unconscious of having done anything, or the grey-haired victims, now the object of "amusement"? Finally the madman, exhausted by the attack, fell in convulsions, and a German, having had enough of this entertainment, finished this first act with a shot from his pistol.

After a short rest a new game began. The victims were divided into two groups and ordered to beat one another. One group was armed with sticks. If someone did not put all his energy into the fight, he was drawn out of the crowd and – to induce respect for orders – beaten to teach him how a beating should be administered. Such an example was of no further use for continuing the game, but the rest of the victims would show the necessary enthusiasm, so that the fight would be interesting. The victims forced to beat one another – with tears in their eyes – made an excellent theme for the thugs to scoff and sneer at Jews. But this also palled after some time and considering that it was late in the afternoon, the Germans ordered a prayer out of doors, to change the custom – in the nude. Everyone was forced to undress, even hats were removed – a disgrace for the Orthodox. The victims remained in their tzitzes or Talit Katan (a ritual garment worn under the shirt) and were ordered to pray. The victims were turned out into the courtyard. It was a frosty December day. It would be a day of miracles as the Ukrainians boasted later – that God would warm up the bodies of the praying sons of Israel. Many refused to be forced to pray with bare heads, a great offence against ritual. Those were forced to kneel, an even greater offence, and with the help of whips "persuaded" to pray. With some people faith is stronger than the fear of lashes. It gave them the strength and resistance, which the unbelieving cannot understand. Several of those deeply faithful accustomed all their life not to depart from their holy rules refused to bend and perished under the lashes. The rest, the weaker in spirit, covering their heads with their hands prayed and profaned ... NO! It was not they who profaned the words of the Lord, it was their executioners.

Beseechingly, old men said their prayers. They prayed for a quick death. Let us hope these prayers reached the throne of God. Very soon the trucks took those living ghosts to give them back to mother earth in perpetual rest. Let the hellish torments before their death expiate their sins. Rest in peace!

People after slipping through under the bridge tried not to tell their wives and mothers that their nearest were erased from the circle of the living. Perhaps they did not yet know; leave them their illusions, let them have hope.

Another of our axioms was destroyed. Respect for the aged, for hair turned grey in the daily struggle for bread. The Jewish districts were horror-stricken. The anguish spread its tentacles, intruded into every home or hide-out. It choked voices to a whisper, hobbled unsure steps, bent the shoulders to earth, congested throats and lips, flushed the eyes with fever, changed the course of our thoughts and feelings. Horror at greater or lesser intensity dominated the Jewish districts continuously from then on. Horror, our omnipotent master, henceforth dictated our desperate steps, closed our lips with dumb complaint.

The hunt for old men continued under the bridge several times between 1 and 14 December 1941, till eventually on Balonowa, Piastow, Panienska and

Wybranowska streets the Germans carried out an *Aktion* in the houses. Several lorries prowled about these streets. The Germans burst into apartments, took the old men and women, threw them, often from second and third floors through the windows into the waiting lorries, beating, harassing and murdering them in horrible ways before the eyes of their helpless children.

Following this day of blood wallowing, after injecting a sufficient dose of horror to last for a good while, the Germans calmed down. They withdrew the Ukrainians from the sentry posts under the bridge, and began travelling home to Germany for the holidays, while those remaining prepared themselves for Christmas. All was done, after all, to ready their hearts to celebrate the Birth of Jesus, who laid down the basic commandment of Christianity: "Love your neighbour as yourself".

7 · Intermezzo

The usually sharp winter began in 1941 exceptionally early and attacked us severely. The majority of people did not worry much about this, as they rejoiced that this severe frost would be felt by the Germans unaccustomed to such a sharp climate. More important, they were unprepared for winter combat. In fact in this period occurred the first collapse of a German front; the retreat of the German army nearing Moscow. Everywhere discussions continued, that if the Germans did not finish off the war against Russia in the first assault, they would lose this war, as the Russian winter would finish the Germans. There were already rumours that there were hunger riots in Germany and that revolution was about to break out. An the turn of December 1941, there were also rumours about a military *coup d'état* which had been foiled at the last moment. The more serious did not trust these rumours, but to our great astonishment, we heard after several days on the BBC, that something of the kind had taken place. In connection with this there followed a whole series of "heart attacks" among German generals. Everyone knew what this meant. Radio London published the names of about 20 generals. Enthusiastic hopes grew from one minute to another, people already saw the Germans in flight, disarmed them, dividing among themselves various functions. Delightful were these moments of rosy hope.

The Germans strengthened us in our convictions by ordering an immediate requisition of furs, fur-collars, mittens and shoes, ski attire and ski equipment. This was officially announced, with the warning that any Jew found with any of these items after 10 January 1942 would be liable to the death penalty. They took 10 hostages from the Judenrat to ensure that the handover would be scrupulously carried out. The barometer of our hopes jumped so rapidly that the optimists leapt for joy. Could the Germans really be in such a bad shape, that they need to protect their army with the help of some Jewish furs? Some hundred sets of skis and boots were apparently needed for the front line. Who could believe that those who had to grasp at such measures were not *in extremis*?

A new unofficial news agency expanded its activity and the "famous" A.W.T. (a woman told me) was outdistanced. This was the A.J.W. (as Jews want). What could be more characteristic of our indestructible Jewish optimism than attributing this flood of rumours, gossip, pseudo-radio news coming from a most "reliable source", to the source "Jews want"! It would have been much closer to reality to describe the source as what "Jews want it to be" since the gossips expressed only what we wanted to be the truth. The reality was very sad. I didn't believe in all these tales invented by the A.J.W. but told myself that a total fantasy would not be repeated without some reason. Maybe at the bottom there was some small percentage of truth.

The fur-*Aktion* surprised a sufficiently great number of people, so that despite resistance, enough was collected to satisfy the Germany. As a result, for the first and *only* time the hostages were freed. This was so unusual that it was never repeated. Anyone who fell into the hands of Nazis, no matter for what reasons, never returned. The rumours whispered among the Jews probably reached the Germans, who had special informers for this task and were presumably not specially palatable to them. When women appeared in overcoats with the uncovered inside of their collars stripped of fur staring everyone in the face, the German policemen called their attention to this, ordering the women to cover the tears in their collars. To rob was permitted, but it was unacceptable to see the traces of the robbery shown so openly.

In the meantime, the winter did not subside. It began with sharp frost, but of snow which normally relieved the frost not a trace could be seen. We, the Jews, awaited the snow with trepidation, as we feared this would be an additional occasion for German harassment. Finally in January 1942 the first snow fell but as everything in this year was abnormal so it was with the snow. It snowed and snowed without end. Immediately the hunt for Jews to clear the streets of snow began. The whole Janowski camp was mobilized to work on the snow. The cadres of the camp were increased. Several letters were smuggled from the camp. The horrors in them were appalling. I do not feel equal to describing this, only one hell on earth among many created by the Nazis in the world, words fail me. That horror hung over our heads day and night like the sword of Damocles. Over everyone, everywhere, in the work-place, on the street, at home. The fear of the camp deprived us of our will to live, froze the blood in our veins, sent a shiver down our spines.

The 2–3 square km of the camp site were surrounded by two rows of barbed wire. The camp bordered almost directly upon the Janowska highway, hence its name. Between the camp and the highway remained several private one-storey houses, where some families of Poles lived. The first information of what was taking place in this camp came from the inhabitants of these houses. Of course the Germans intended that when the camp was developed, this populace would be removed and their houses occupied by camp officials, often with their families. On the site of the camp there were no buildings. The inhabitants of the camp would have to build barracks.

The camp began to function from December 1941. The commander was Gebauer. He was a very handsome man, with an almost dollish build, a dandyish face and suave blue eyes. On anyone unprejudiced he made a pleasant impression. He had several helpers and, of course, for guards he had a number of Ukrainians.

In various round-ups and raids, 400 to 500 Jews were gathered, and this embryo of the camp was used to build the barracks. They lived on food parcels smuggled in for enormous bribes by the Ukrainian guards. After several days Gebauer allowed one to receive food parcels through the Judenrat twice a week. Discipline in the camp was severe. For any forbidden move or even breaking the rule of silence, extreme penalties were fixed. An 18-year-old boy caught eating a raw potato which Gebauer thought had been stolen from the kitchen of the camp was ordered to be boiled alive in a huge pot of hot water: camp hangmen scrupulously carried this out.

The main occupation of the camp's inhabitants at this time was crushing the tombstones in the Jewish cemetery and transporting the rubble for paving the streets and paths. The Jewish cemetery was totally desecrated and devastated, not a stone was left standing. The camp was destined for hard labour. The essential aim was by all possible cruel means to murder the greatest number of Jews – so that beating, shooting and hanging constituted the everyday essence of life in the camp. The labour was only accompaniment. Untersturmführer Gebauer personally finished off some of the victims. He did not shoot, possibly in his opinion a waste of cartridges. Maybe the sight of spilled blood offended him, or perhaps another way of killing suited his character more. He strangled two or three people daily, the victims gave up the ghost in his hands.

The Germans seized the opportunity of the especially sharp winter. With the help of the frost they finished off a greater number of people. In January and February 1942 the first German defeats on the Russian front occurred. Reports came in that a great number of German soldiers had perished because of the cold. What was easier than to take revenge on the Jews? During the sharpest frosts, they ordered people almost without clothing to stand – very often without shoes – in an open field "as our brave soldiers must". This entertainment they arranged usually at night, when there were not many witnesses, and when the frost bit sharpest. From the guard tower the lines of prisoners were illuminated by searchlights. Anyone who tried to support himself, to kneel or to sit was shot on the spot. To stay motionless in over twenty degrees below zero of sharp frost for three or four hours caused pneumonia and almost generally frostbite of the second and third degree. I was present once in the Jewish hospital when such a victim was brought in: a young man not more than 20 years of age, both his feet totally blackened, gangrenous, dead as clogs. It was already too late for an amputation and in any case what sense to amputate feet or legs on a person destined for death? This and similar stories leaked to the town caused a wild fear of the camp in all our people. Everyone trembled just on hearing the name of the place. The authorities were satisfied with the results of the working of the camp, because in March/April 1942 they enlarged it and nominated a new commander Wildhaus. The German crew of the camp was increased by a specially trained overseer, new barracks were built and of course a greater number of victims was demanded, as the maw of Moloch must be increasingly filled with Jews.

In the Jewish district, we became accustomed to robberies day and night. Anyone not robbed felt happy, while those robbed despaired at first but very soon put up with fate. Slowly everyone grew accustomed to life in primitive conditions. The food supply provided by the peasants reached more or less normal levels. The Jews were allowed to buy in the market places from 10 a.m. to noon. Of course, none of the peasants sold at the fixed maximum prices, and, therefore avoided "Aryan" customers, who could go to the authorities, preferring to supply the Jews, who paid fantastic prices for this favour.

The prices were certainly insane. But thank God for this. Jews were selling everything they had from their homes, personal things – everything, only to fill their stomachs. Trade disappeared completely from shops, and did not stay on the street but descended deeper to cellars and basements. Almost every janitor was running a brisk business in his room, selling food products from bread and flour to spices or preserves. Every janitor was buying or an agent in selling everything: suits, shoes, pianos, sewing machines, looking-glasses, underwear, sets of table china, rugs, old overcoats, stockings, everything that was offered. We learned to chop wood, to draw water from a well, to eat once a day, to feed mainly on soups, to bake bread if someone managed to get flour, to end the day at 6 p.m. and to begin at 5 a.m. To everything a human being could get accustomed. Despite the nightmare of the Janowski camp hanging over our heads, despite the fact that almost every day someone in our closest circle disappeared, despite the robberies, assaults, somehow or other, life went on.

8 · The March *Aktion* – Deportation

During the middle of February 1942, rumours began to circulate that the Germans intended to deport thousands of Jews from Lvov. Allegedly similar deportations had taken place in Krakow. Jews were deported to the provinces to avoid too great a concentration of Jews in the cities. The councillors and the more important workers of the Judenrat denied these rumours so as not to cause panic, but achieved only very limited results. Some Jews were warned directly by friendly Germans who knew the intentions and plans of the Gestapo. Some not especially discreet councillors in the Judenrat spread new rumours, repeatedly new pieces of information appeared. All these rumours contained the same information, that the first group subject to deportation would be anti-social elements, "such as people on police registers, prostitutes and beggars". The last mentioned category would include social welfare cases. Fear increased daily. Early every morning people would come to the Department of Social Welfare in the Judenrat asking for their names to be struck off the lists, some even borrowed money to return the allowances they had received; nothing helped.

At the end of February 1942, the German firms employing Jews collected detailed information about their workers. At last, on 10 March 1942, they began issuing certificates signed by the Economic Department of the General Government (i.e. German-occupied Poland), with the following statement: "The Jew X.Y. is employed as such and such an expert and is indispensably needed. This certificate is issued on the basis of an agreement signed February 1942". The certificate was sealed by a round stamp with the Nazi eagle and a signature. Such certificates were issued for the worker and one member of his family, who were defined as Jews who were "economically worthwhile" (*wirtschaftlich wertbar* – WW). Some Jews made green armbands for themselves, but there was no official announcement requiring this action.

Presently the scare reached the level of a panic. Everyone endeavoured to be recognized as "economically worthwhile" which was not simple and sometimes impossible. A period of large-scale bribery began in German factories and offices. My director, seeing that the employed Jews were not only working for nothing but also willing to meet an extra charge for proper credentials, tried to get all he could, demanding of course considerable payment for the trouble. Despite bribes, many people could not get certificates. Some firms obtained certificates for only half their employees, some firms like insurance offices were totally rejected. Afterwards it appeared that the German authorities thought this work to be too light for Jews. I got a certificate for myself and my wife, as she had recently lost her job, but for my mother I could not obtain one by any means. I approached my boss for advice. He advised me to hide my mother, as "a good hiding place is the best certificate"; his words.

I went to the Judenrat to get more reliable information. I had many friends and colleagues in the Judenrat. Under oath to keep the information in strictest secrecy, I was told what was in preparation. The SS police superintendent of Lvov, Katzman, had demanded that the Judenrat carry out, using the Jewish militia, a deportation *Aktion* against "anti-social elements" such as thieves, prostitutes, speculators and other law-breakers. The next group for deportation were those who did not come to work despite registration and those on social welfare. Katzman pledged his word of honour that nobody would lose a hair of his head, that all would be directed to labour in the province. Simultaneously he guaranteed, again with his word, that nothing similar would be repeated. The Judenrat had to made lists for the deportation and submit them to the Gestapo.

Admittedly it was not yet known what "deportation" meant and there was no concrete reason for doubting a General's word of honour. The Judenrat would not take on its shoulders the responsibility for deporting people even from town to the countryside, and called upon known social personalities for cooperation. The secrecy did not last long. The Germans were pressing to bring forward the date of the deportation. As I learned later, after long discussions in which the argument was stressed, that if the Judenrat would not prepare the list, the Germans would carry out the *Aktion* in their own way, at last it was decided to prepare the lists. From specific district commissariats and from the verifying commission, lists were drawn up. The rest was done in the Judenrat. Additionally it was announced officially that since a section of the Jewish population had to be deported to the provincial countryside, the Judenrat called for volunteers to leave. One was allowed to take along some items, for instance one blanket, one spare suit, a pot, a spoon, knife and a fork, and up to 200 zl. ($ 300 of 1988) in cash. It was forbidden to take pillows, gold and jewellery. There ended the role of the Judenrat, as the lists had no meaning whatever during this *Aktion*. The naiveté of people at this time was without limit. But our naiveté was not only at fault, for we had grown up in law-abiding circumstances and lived with the conviction that obligations and even "promises" of the authorities were sacred. As a result about 2,000 volunteers answered the call of the Judenrat.

On the night of 18–19 March 1942, the Jewish militia began the *Aktion*. Patrols of 3 to 5 men went to addresses of people on the lists of the Judenrat. But this lasted only a very short time. People expecting this visit were hidden. Afterwards the patrols began going from house to house. According to the instruction of the authorities they had to take everyone not having a certificate as "economically worthwhile", but during this first *Aktion* the Jewish militiamen behaved in exemplary fashion. The police spirit had not yet soaked through them, and had not yet suppressed their communal feeling, had not yet choked the voice of conscience. The patrols almost all remained in the home of an acquaintance chatting and drinking, as the nights were cold. After dawn they returned to headquarters to report that all those they visited had the correct certificates. Of course there were exceptions. Some, from the moment they donned police uniform, found in it a second skin. The people taken were brought to Sobieski School on Zamarstynowska Steet. Here a sort of transit camp was arranged, and here was staged a mockery of a tribunal, which had to decide if a specific person qualified for deportation. All this was to show that they Germans were working strictly in accord with the promise and word of honour of Katzman, that only anti-social elements were to be deported. The tribunal consisted of Ulrich, President of the Police, Weber, the boss of the Work Department, a representative of Wirtschaft Abteilung, an SS-man representing the Gestapo, and a representative of the Judenrat, who of course had no say at all. All those captured were brought before this tribunal. After a brief comedy of interrogation, those who were found to be qualified as engineers, artisans and so on were allowed to remain in the town. The rest were to be deported. Before World War II police had been impervious to bribery. Now it was possible to buy oneself out from the Germans. For a ring with a diamond, SS-men would remove people and even accompany them to their homes in the middle of the night. The Jewish militiamen took their example from the Germans, demanding their portion in addition to German bribes, for which they often did nothing. Others went further and gave their assistance for appropriately smaller bribes. The comedy of the tribunal did not last long. After one night everything was settled, and in the morning the school building was empty. But everyone was stricken with dismay when the prophecies of the pessimists proved right. The deportation proved to be a term on paper for taking people to an unknown destination for an unknown purpose. All the luggage which people had brought, according to the instructions of the Judenrat, remained abandoned in a chaotic heap in the courtyard of the Sobieski School; people had left everything behind.

THE MARCH *AKTION* – DEPORTATION

In the following *Aktions* the Judenrat was no longer bluffed into co-operation. The Judenrat could neither help nor harm. Participation in the first *Aktion*, despite the fact that the Judenrat was also deceived, left everyone with a bad taste in the mouth. The Jewish militia cut not too bad a figure during this *Aktion*. They risked the dissatisfaction of the German authorities, which was very soon expressed.

Seeing greatly insufficient results after the first three days – only a few hundred people, not even one full train-load – the Germans took the further execution of the *Aktion* into their own hands. After one day of intermission the Ukrainian militia under the leadership of SS-men systematically surrounded whole areas of the town, and checked street by street, house by house in the Jewish district, taking whole flocks of people to the Sobieski School every night.

My mother, after sitting two days in a hide-out, returned to the apartment, just in time for an unexpected raid. Luckily the SS-men who burst in our apartment "flung their cap over the windmill" regarding bribes. On my wife's imploring mercy and taking 150 zl, they left my mother at our home. Others failed to save their skins so cheaply, unless they had vodka handy. A bottle of vodka was the best bribe. Apparently the riff-raff were compelled to inebriate themselves in order to execute their villainies.

The ever-present feeling on leaving home for work, that one never knew if one was seeing one's family for the last time, now increased and overwhelmed everything. Could you expect efficient work in such conditions? All day one was awaiting information from the town; where was today's raid? The Aryans were sent to get information, which they did willingly for presents in cash or in kind. Being far from home in continual uncertainty unnerves one more than being home within range of a round-up. On the eighth day of this *Aktion* I returned home at about 5 p.m. Already in the centre of the town there were rumours that today the raid was on the Zniesienie Quarter. I could barely wait till the end of working hours to run home. In record time I made the 5 or 6 km. separating us from Zniesienie. Before entering the Zniesienie district I saw from afar a cordon of Ukrainian militia. Of course I had to stop at one of the nearby factories of Galikol. I hoped at the HQ of the Jewish militia, to find out from an acquaintance who commanded this post whether everything at my home was all right. He was not in the office, and I was told to wait. These several minutes of waiting I count as the worst in all my life. At last I was told that the raid had ended. Almost simultaneously somebody entered from the street with the news that the cordon was gone. I ran home.

On my way I met crowds of old men and women with children being driven by Ukrainian militia to the Sobieski School. Nervously I looked at them to see whether there was anyone I knew. I remember that a German with a sadistic smile on his face, enjoyed my nervous look, seeking faces in this crowd driven like a herd. On the threshold, my wife told me that my mother was hidden, but could not yet go out as some Ukrainian militiamen were still in the vicinity. At last at 7 p.m. after nightfall we pulled out my mother from a potato pit where she was hidden. We pulled her out literally, as there was not enough room to stand or lie, the only possiblity was to sit curled up. My mother was 60 years old. She begged us to give her poison, so that she would not have to endure such torments. Instead of being able to do something to ease her pain and troubles, I had to condemn her to additional pain. This helplessness ate away our already shattered nerves. During the night that followed, I weighed long in my thoughts whether it would not be better to end it all. Some small obstinate hope that perhaps my father was yet living, and we might get some news of him, prevented me from taking such a decision.

The raid on Zniesienie was the final event of the *Aktion* in the Jewish district. After a thorough combing out of the district, the Germans began nearly a fortnight of raids in the Aryan districts of the town where a few Jews were still living. Every day, people caught in the town were brought to the Sobieski School, and every two or three days a train load was made up.

More than 22,000 people passed through the Sobieski School during those three weeks and were removed. In the last days corruption grew to colossal proportions. The Germans and Ukrainians directly solicited bribes. A considerable number of people were rescued in this way.

A characteristic feature of this *Aktion* was the preservation of the appearance of legality. The interrogation before the tribunal, and the carrying out of the *Aktion* essentially during the night hours, although they increased the horror, at the same time created the impression that the Germans still attached some importance to public opinion. This, naturally, suggested that perhaps the situation was not catastrophic since there was still some restraint. Very soon came bitter disillusionment, but at the time Ulrich's mild behaviour, the mild behaviour of other Germans, avoiding murder and brutal scenes on the street fooled us. It is worth mentioning the loyal conduct of the Jewish militia and the possibility of buying oneself out relatively for pennies. All these impressions deceived us, seeing the future in rose instead of blood-red. Unfortunately bad news travels fast. After some days' several escapees returned bringing horrible news. All the supposedly deported were brought to a forest between Rawa Ruska and Żółkiew, ordered to strip, and afterwards massacred by machine guns. Some days later loads of men's and women's clothing, torn and bloody, were brought to the raw materials store. The horrible news was confirmed.

9 · The Register of the Damned

Very soon after the end of the March *Aktion*, a new decree appeared on the walls widening the age groups of Jews liable for the general obligation of labour. The announcement referred to "*männliche und weibliche Juden*" (male and female Jews) as if describing animals of masculine and feminine gender. The timing of this announcement was characteristic. The department set out at full steam to prepare a new registration. A whole phalanx of register cards, inquiries, questions, ground out ominously. We knew now from experience to avoid the light under dangerous conditions. A form merely made it easier to discover addresses and increased the possibility of seizure. It seemed especially dangerous to register, in view of the almost limitless powers of the Work Department and a total absence of written law. To go to work, accepting work, changing a work-place, even changing the kind of work, was possible only with the agreement of Weber. Everyone received a number (mine was 3966) and an armband with a star of David in the middle of which was a great letter "A" for Arbeiter (worker). Under the star the number was distinctly stamped. In the meantime – according to rumours – it was claimed that there was only a limited number of armbands with a number, so that Jews who did not receive an armband would be liquidated in the next *Aktion*. It was already known that the aim of every new measure was sifting and thinning out the Jewish population. The Work Department as a result of these rumours was overcrowded. People stood on their heads to get a number and a *Meldekarte* (proof of registration) as quickly as possible. This was a special certificate with a photo and detailed description and personal data. For one additional member of the family (wife, mother, sister) it was possible to get another *Meldekarte*, but without an armband with an "A" and a number. These were called *haushaltführende Frauen* (housekeeping women, housekeepers for short). If up to now the Work Department was a goose laying golden eggs for persons knowing how to steal them, it was now laying golden eggs. A thousand and one problems resulted from the new registration of the families' housekeeper, with the fiction of an agreement from Weber, who theoretically reserved for himself even the transfer from one kind of work to another, the sequence of numbers (people feared the high numbers), the chance to buy the official armband from the Work Department. All these problems could be solved by stuffing the greedy jaws of the insatiable Work Deptartment officials. No more corrupt institution could exist in all the world. From the doorman, who would not answer the simplest question without his baksheesh in accordance with the tariff fixed by him, right up to Weber himself, almost nobody, settled anything unless he got his tribute in cash or in kind.

The Jewish militia developed enormously, growing more and more into the role of police, more and more separating itself from the mass of Jewry, becoming completely an executive arm of the SS and Gestapo. The police spirit, it may seem, is immanent in objects like a police cap or police uniform, invading living bodies and playing havoc with the souls of people previously normal. The height of infamy, however, was to be found in the *Sonderdienst* (special squad) of the Jewish militia. This was a squad under the direct command of the Gestapo. From the moment it was created in April 1942, this detachment was the executive organ of the Gestapo and constituted a sort of a link between the central Gestapo office on Pelczynska Street, the Judenrat and the HQ of the Jewish militia. The commander of this squad was a man named Goliger Schapiro, descendant of a well-known Lvov family of grain merchants. He wrote himself with letters of blood into the martyrology of the Jewry of Lvov, the wounds bleeding perhaps more than those inflicted by Germans, since they were inflicted by a Jew. There was no lack of renegades, and it is well known that they are the worst. Goliger's deputy was a man named Krumkolz, a refugee from Krakow. These two very often outdid the Germans in cruelty to Jews. They both took even the most trifling opportunity to extort fantastic bribes, threatening to give the victim to the Gestapo and actually doing this, when the need arose.

My wife lost her *Meldekarte*, a document without which one could not take a step. The duplicate in the Work Department was not expensive and cost only 10zl, but one had to pay 10 or 20 times this sum in bribes. Of course, this presupposed no complications or objections from Weber (in this case the bribe would reach the level of thousands). But before we decided what to do, there appeared at my wife's work-place a Pole trying a small extortion. He demanded 1,000zl. for the return of the document, threatening to hand it to the Gestapo on Pelczynska Street, with an appropriate story. My wife naturally came running to me for money. I tried to haggle a little with the blackmailer, pointing out our situation, that not so long ago we were fellow-citizens of Poland, we were fighting the Germans together, that the Germans were our common enemy, etc. All in vain. Our dignified fellow-citizen did not care a damn; on the contrary he even raised the ransom, demanding 1500zl. This sum he must have within an hour, or else ...

I managed to raise the cash in time but our noble helper, tired of waiting, went away. Full of disquiet we awaited developments. My wife naturally did not sleep at home, I did not undress, to be prepared for any development. The night passed quietly. The following day a Jewish militiaman came with a summons to the *Sonderdienst* office, to Mr Goliger, who had received the *Meldekarte* from the Gestapo – it was handed over as worthless to them. Goliger wanted 1 kg. coffee (i.e. about 700zl. = $100) for returning the document. What could I do? …

10 · *Z.A.L* (Zwangsarbeitlager – compulsory labour camp)

The Janowski Camp now appeared impressive compared with its modest beginnings. There were now four barracks completed or under construction, bath house, toilets, kitchen and office buildings. The staff consisted of 25 SS-men and about 30 askars (Ukrainian guards). The commander of the camp was SS-Untersturmführer Gustav Wilhaus, distinguished with the *Blutabzeichen* (blood award, an important Nazi Party award for participation in an assault on a town). By profession a printer, he was about 28 years of age, and tall. He had a leather overcoat, which he wore constantly. He gave the impression of a slender man, presenting himself beautifully from afar, despite his knock-knees. His steel-grey eyes, with their piercing glance, remain in my memory. Those cold eyes, as if already seeing a corpse, affected everyone like the hypnotizing glance of a snake. People preferred anything to being brought before Wilhaus. A handgun, which he used often, completed his attire.

His deputy, SS-Untersturmführer Richard Rokita, was a Pole from Silesia, well-known there in artistic circles as a violinist and conductor of a jazz-band. In appearance he contrasted strongly with his boss. He was about 40 years of age, of middle height, sturdy, bald, with the wide good-natured pudding face of a corpulent man. The narrow tight lips did not harmonize with the general impression of his face. For people not believing in the geniality of tubby men, Rokita made an excellent argument, since in cruelty and bestiality he not only equalled his German mentors, but surpassed them in meanness and perfidy and in maltreating his former fellow-citizens.

The second deputy SS-Scharführer Adolf Kolonko, also a Pole from Silesia, was about 30 years old; by profession a mason's journeyman, blond and of middle height. Due to his broad shoulders he was reputed to be clumsy. But this stocky and clumsily shaped man knew how with lightning speed to make a leap on his crooked legs, in order to beat up or liquidate a victim.

From among the other SS staff I must describe SS-man Fox: tall, slender, an oblong face with a tapering nose, wide thin lips and a cross-eye. This murderer's appearance was wholly justified by his deeds. He was 24 years of age and described himself as a professional poacher. Later came SS-Scharführer Schonbach, SS-man Grusshaber, SS-Scharführer Bittner and lastly a type worthy of special attention among this group of Hitler myrmidons. This was a Hungarian called Peter Blum. Very young, only 17 years old, a shoemaker's apprentice, he found here his proper metier. He was short with a youthful freckled face, snub-nosed and with red hair like hog's bristles. He made at first an impression of a candidate for cinema stardom, the type of the ugly but good boy. He was one of the cruellest beasts ever born on the face of mother earth. His constant weapon, apart from a pistol of course, was a whip with a short handle and a very long lash like those used in the big top. Accompanied by wild shouts, like those used to frighten wild animals in circuses, he would place himself near the kitchen and woe betide the poor man who from hunger gave the impression of hastening to the kettle. With an ear-piercing shout – "Juuuaaacha!" – he would bring down the horrible whip. It lashed the poor man wherever it fell, to coil around the neck of the victim. Only the smallest jerk and the victim was lying on the earth. Now, depending on his humour, he released the victim after kicking him properly, or finished him off with a shot from his pistol. This creature was engraved in everyone's memory. The others vanished in the blood fumes which veiled our recollections of the camp; he remained.

Similarly almost no one remembers the askars in detail. They were partly Ukrainians and partly Russian P.O.W.s who agreed voluntarily to go over to German service. After a short training in Majdanek or Trawniki, in a special police-school, they were directed to auxiliary service in various camps. By the cruelty of their conduct they endeavoured to equal the noble example set them.

The barracks of the camp need special description. They consisted of long sheds with an endless row of board bunks. These were constructed in four levels, one above the other. Apart from these the barrack-shed was empty, not a table or a chair, a bucket or any personal object. The cleanliness shone from empty corners. The wash room was also a shed, not so big with two rows of gutters and water-pipe. The kitchen shed had six windows, through which what pleased the camp commander to call food was dealt out to the prisoners.

Every day, at 5 a.m., the SS-men burst into every barrack with wild shouts and shots, announcing the morning reveille. This was the unchangeable start of the camp day. The prisoners rose in fear. Not long ago they had lain down to sleep with fear, to rack through the night on the hard bunk. The stomach, filled with some suspicious gruel, could not be deceived and demanded its rights, particularly because the continual movement and working beyond everyone's strength increased the appetite. Everyone tried to deceive his stomach by pouring in as much of the only food one could obtain, the so-called soup. This soup was the principal and almost the only food the prisoners got. Consumption of so much liquid, without food of some consistency, had evil consequences on one's quantity of urine. During the day it was only a half-misery, but what could one do during the night? To descend from the fourth floor of the bunk in the darkness would be difficult for a fully fit man, for people half-starved and weakened by excessive work, it was almost impossible. We did everything possible to save the effort. People urinated under themselves and continued to sleep on a wet bunk, others fearing the neighbours on the lower floors used their mess-tins as chamber pots. In the morning they would pour out the urine and take coffee in the mess-tin. Life in the camp was hard and brought people to such a condition of brutishness that they lost their sensibility to such trifles. One fugitive from Janowski Camp told me that he saw someone pour out urine from a bottle and having a rare opportunity to get water, took it in the bottle without rinsing it.

I wrote about descending from bunks to fulfil the needs of nature, so that one might think that there was a latrine, and only the negligence of the dirty Jews expressed itself in that they used their mess-tins for convenience. I must underline that after 10 p.m. and until till 5 a.m. it was strictly forbidden to leave the barrack. For overstepping this rule or any other regulation, the penalty was torture, for death had totally lost its importance. Discipline in the camp was brutal. One cannot speak about discipline or the maintenance of order in a place where the only aim was to harass people to death; in cases where the endurance of the victims appeared to be greater than the inventiveness of the thugs, murder in cold blood was resorted to.

Their sense of good order did not allow some people to wet the bunk or piss onto the heads of people below, or to use a mess-tin, and the pressure of an overfull bladder caused a feeling of not caring for anything, so they walked at night to the latrine. The camp authorities took pleasure in the opportunity to show what they were capable of. Three men were caught going at night to the toilet. At the morning roll-call, Kolonko, after a lengthy oration in which he pointed out to everybody the need to maintain proper standards of human behaviour, sentenced the three "criminals" for their scandalous offence to be flogged: 50 lashes each. On the spot the first victim was stripped, tied to a bench and two askars started the execution. They lashed simultaneously so that the victim actually got 100 lashes. The heart-rending howls of the victim tore the ears of the 3,000 prisoners forced to look silently on the spectacle. Pretty soon the skin on the victim's back burst apart under the hail of lashes. The cries of the victim became weaker and weaker, they subsided more and more into silence, he scarcely moaned. The last lashes were laid on an unconscious man, to the disappointment of the SS-men, at this waste of the beating and pain. Something had to be done so that the entertainment would be more complete. The second victim was not totally stripped; the shirt was left on his back and continually wetted with water. Now the shouting, howling, imploring to be killed struck the deaf ears of executioners inaccessible to human feelings. The prisoners felt every lash, which fell not only on the bodies of the victims, but struck into all and lashed their souls. All of a sudden Rokita appeared. After being informed about the matter, he cynically expressed his indignation. For such a horrible offence, a few lashes would not be enough. Kill! Without another word he walked to the half-corpse, who had already been punished once for his crime and shot him along with the third victim waiting for punishment.

Understandably, people so inculcated to discipline started immediately from their bunks and after receiving a fairly small beating at the barrack door from the SS-man ensuring that all got up, went outside. Anyone who could not get up was shot on the spot in his bunk. Unwashed, dirty, unshaven, they went to get coffee in their mess-tin/chamber-pots and a slice of bread issued through the kitchen windows by foremen. From here they could go to the wash room. The wash room was intended for 20 to 30 people, and there were about 3,000 who wanted to wash themselves as fast as possible; every moment counted. The result was an impossible crowding, pushing and real fighting at the water pipe for every drop of water. Once again a good opportunity for the Germans to carry out a massacre. The SS-men burst in to restore order and kill a little. Almost every day several prisoners were killed. These criminals wanted to wash themselves! What cheek!

One especially nightmarish incident remained in the memory of my informant and its horror is still before his eyes. In the washroom press, an SS-man burst in and reached a naked man standing below the water-pipe to wash his whole body. The poor man bent in the process of washing himself was unable to straighten, as muscles paralysed from fear could not raise his body. The SS-man shot him down. The man fell on his knees, his head in the washing gutter, his body bent in an unnatural posture, from his rectum protruded a piece of faeces, released in the moment's tension of maddening fear. The German seeing this, burst out laughing and called in his SS pals quickly to admire such a rare phenomenon.

Many prisoners did not even try to wash. Some tried to wash with coffee. The majority was degraded to such a level of brutishness that they ceased to feel the need to wash at all. Yet mostly there was not time enough, as exactly at 6 a.m. everyone had to be at roll-call. At the roll-call all inmates of the camp stood in their work gangs. These gangs were variable groups, according to the number of foremen nominated by the camp commander from among the Jews or the local Aryans. The number of prisoners in a gang was variable at first owing to the fact that from one roll-call to the next some inmates were shot, hanged or tortured to death, and secondly the gangs were organized according to the demands for workers. The German firms which demanded workers paid 45 groszy for a day's work. Of course the Jews never saw a penny of this microscopic payment. The power of the foremen was not especially wide, but like foremen in factories, each could become an additional hindrance to life. Before the appearance of the commandant, Kolonko led the roll-call. Till the arrival of Wilhaus or Rokita he filled in the time with drill. For instance "caps on! caps off". Sometimes, this continued for one or two hours. His helpers prowled between the rows seeking an opportunity to harass the less resistant people. Again an overloaded bladder could cause trouble; to leave the line was unthinkable. But if someone could not endure the strain and urinated under himself it was a very short wait for death. For one of the thugs going between the rows would see it and shoot the poor man on the spot ... It was the daily entertainment – a pleasant start to the work day.

Finally the commander of the camp or his deputy came. The foremen reported the number of people in every gang, the number of sick, and at last how many had died in the night. Normally no-one had the courage to admit being ill, as despite the existence of the camp hospital, all the sick were put beyond the wires, i.e. between the rows of barbed wire surrounding the camp to be finished off. After the report, the gangs working in town went to work and the foremen reported at the gate-guard the number of prisoners that went to work. Usually about 40 per cent remained for work inside the camp. It was the routine of any work-day. But once a week or perhaps every 10 days the camp commandant, apparently wanting to increase the number of murdered, arranged a special selection of the ill and weak. From gate 2 a run was ordered, called by the prisoners "the death run". The SS-men stood in lines and the prisoners passed running through the lines. Anyone who stumbled or did not please one of the SS-men was put "beyond the wires" for liquidation. Trembling, the prisoners awaited the order "Lauf! Los!" (run) which could mean immediate death, or prolongation of life for some time. The sight was horrible; to look at the harrassed people trying to assume an appearance of health and strength. Hastily they rubbed their cheeks to bring out a blush of health, bit lips so they would seem red, with an ultimate effort they straightened hunched backs to present themselves as fit, to be prepared as well as they could for the struggle against death.

In summertime the run was not too bad. The earth was dry and the prisoners mostly without shoes. But in winter, when the snow stuck to the clogs and one must run through ice, polished by thousands of clogs to an excellent skating rink, it needed a real miracle not to stumble, especially as the SS-men in line took every chance of beating and kicking the men running in their effort for life. On average about 10 per cent of the prisoners were victims of any "death run". In bad weather this number jumped to 20 or even 25 per cent. The result was that everyone in the camp or town shuddered on hearing or remembering the words "Lauf! Los!" which were the watch words of the run for life. It seems that the endurance of human beings is limitless. There were people who endured this hell for several months. As if by a miracle they evaded every day, every hour, every minute, the many wolf traps. There were few such heroes, but even they despite their incredible fortitude could not escape.

At last the gangs left the camp for work in the town under the guard of askars. Feet were barely able to carry the weak body, and the tortured gaunt bodies barely able to carry their clothes. The clothes of a camp prisoner were wholly special and original with nothing to equal them in the world. The fact was that the camp prisoners had been forced down as much as it was possible to degrade a human being, and their attire reflected this. The outer garment was a blanket wound around the body, the waist girded with a cord or belt. One corner of the blanket remained free to cover the head when it was raining. Below the blanket, some wore only a clout which once was a jacket or a shirt. In reality it was difficult to recognize it as a shirt, as the colour had long ago disappeared, destroyed by dirt and mud, mixed with sweat and blood. Washing was naturally impossible. Trousers were in shreds, nobody thought even for a moment of patching and there was nothing to patch with. Holes and tears in indiscreet places showed once hidden parts of the body, yellow or blue from cold, grey from dirt, covered with skin rashes due to lack of washing and bad nourishment. The fringes of shredded trousers fell onto feet black with mud in clogs usually unlaced, as almost everyone was afflicted with swollen feet from hunger. Some had the remnants of socks, with holes on the heels of fantastic shapes and dimensions. An inseparable part of a camp prisoner's outfit was a bag slung over his shoulder containing all his personal property; spoon, knife or pocketknife and a slice of bread. Apart from these, camp inmates did not possess a thing, because it would be taken away from him or stolen by his fellow prisoners to exchange for something edible. Next to this bag hung on a string a jug that served as mess-tin, chamber-pot or water goblet.

Everything a camp inmate possessed he had to carry with him, and to guard like his own eyes, because as the result of a moment's inattention a thing would vanish like smoke. Completing this attire was a stick, a most useful tool for instance to fish out some fat morsel from an occasional garbage-can, or to support the overtired body from falling. On the whole, the prisoners gave a nightmarish impression of scarecrows, stumbling torpidly with uncoordinated convulsive movements.

The worst impression of all was the sallow complexion, the wild glaring eyes of a hungry dog, the sunken cheeks of a starveling, unshaved bristly growth on the face, dry parched lips, all this framed in a children's cap made from a daily paper, like a summer head-cover against the sweltering sun. This march of nightmares straggling through the streets of town had on the order of the camp commander to sing a merry tune. A song was composed by a nameless composer. A song to send a shiver down everyone's spine, but its grim humour, overwhelming with the truth hidden in the gay verses, was shocking with its hopeless cry for vengeance; the tune was the popular Polish folksong, Krakowiak:

THE SONG OF THE INMATES OF JANOWSKI CAMP

We are the riff-raff From Janowski labour camp. When will the world learn about us? Up their damned mothers', snotty whores.	Albo my to jacy tacy Z Janowskiego lagru pracy Kiedy świat nas będzie znać Kurwa ich zasrana mać
When they pull you from the column You won't even get a coffin, You'll sleep on the sands. Up their damned mothers', snotty whores	Gdy wyciągnaą cię z kolumny Nie dotkniesz nawet trumny I na piaski pojdziesz spać Kurwa ich zasrana mać
You have a barracks all beautiful within You can sleep on your fifth level bunk And piss on anybody's head. Up their damned mothers', snotty whores.	Masz baraki, piękne wnętrze Mozesz spać na piątym piętrze I drugiemu na leb szczać Kurwa ich zasrana mać
To two pints of water add four grains of barley That's soup fit for an arse hole The camp fraternity cursed a blue streak. Up their damned mothers', snotty whores.	Liter wody cztery krupy Taka zupa jest do dupy, Klnie więc obozowa brać Kurwa ich zasrana mać
There is a hospital and there are doctors, But for fakers not for the sick Who in their fever could not get up. Up their damned mothers', snotty whores.	Jest szpitalik, są doktory Lecz dla pucu nie dla chorych Gdy w gorączce trudno wstać Kurwa ich zasrana mać
Our Wilus is a brick. When he flies into a passion He'd flog us with his machine gun.	A nasz Wiluś chlop morowy Jak mu strzeli szok do glowy To z maszynki zacznie prać

Up their damned mothers', snotty whores.	Kurwa ich zasrana mać
An *aktion* in August, an *aktion* in February,	Akcja w sierpniu, akcja w lutym
Your wife and your child beyond the wire,	Zonę z dzieckiem masz za drutem
Your heart could break.	Może serce ci się rwać
Up their damned mothers', snotty whores.	Kurwa ich zasrana mać
Shots all day, shots all night,	Strzaly w nocy, strzaly we dnie
Until the boldest face would fall	Aż najśmielsza mina zrzednie
How long will it yet last?	ILEZ TO MA JESZCZE TRWAĆ?
Up their damned mothers', snotty whores.	Kurwa ich zasrana mać

HOW LONG WOULD IT YET LAST? Seconds – years, hours – centuries, days and nights – endless, till the tragic end.

The greatest value of working in town was the chance to get something by begging offal, scraps of food; potato peel was a most precious asset for overcoming hunger. All inmates of the camp were equal, a physician begged together with a simple worker, an engineer or lawyer would willingly hold out his begging hand together with a professional beggar. To get something to eat, to silence the cry of an empty stomach, all were equal, the poor and the rich, the intelligentsia and the simple. All were united by the destitution of their existence, which levelled and obliterated differences. All were equal before God and Hitler.

Another advantage of working in town was that the few who had money, could, for a small sum, bribe the guard to be permitted to drop into their homes, to see their family and to wash themselves, shave, change, underwear and, most important, to appease their hunger. Those working in the camp were deprived of these advantages and had a surfeit of torment with aimless stress and beatings. The most frequent work in the camp was to push a wheelbarrow full of soil at the double. The inmates had to endure the vagaries of humour of the SS-men overseeing the work. One of the SS-men noticed that a father and son worked in one of the barracks. He called them and arranged the following game. First he ordered the father to strike his son. He struck lightly. Now he ordered the son to return the blow. The son barely touched his father. The SS-man burst into a hail of abuse, ordering them to strike harder and threatened them with his gun. At last he forced the father to a full blow. Now was the turn of the son. The SS-man cursed him until the son also struck harder. Now the SS-man increased the pace, ordering faster and faster: "Hit! Return"! and so on. In deadly fear they forgot whom they were striking and in fear of the gun waving before their eyes hit one another till blood was drawn, to the mad joy and loudly expressed satisfaction of the SS-man, this most noble quintessence of Nazi culture.

At last the day neared its end, the gangs returned to camp. Chow time! The camp-kitchen, the most sacred place in the camp; shrine-temple of the uncrowned ruler of the camp – the Master – the cook himself. His gracious bow decided if you received water from the surface of the kettle or a wonderful collection of small musty beans from the bottom. The kitchen was distinguished only by an enormous quantity of flies coming from a nearby latrine and refuse-heap, which drowned recklessly in this doubtful beverage. The hardened inmates of the camp not only paid no attention to such trifles, but on the contrary valued such thick soup seasoned with flies, for its greater nourishing value.

Like all holy places, here also access was made difficult. Here stood no angel with a fiery-sword, nor did harpies or other creatures of fantasy guard the entrance, only an SS-man trying to ruin this moment of getting some hot food, by vexations and torments evergrowing with their invention of the most fantastic ideas. Anyone demonstrating his hunger in too striking a manner was killed after a briefer or longer harassment, depending upon his mood. The SS-man Fox constantly arranged an entertainment by shooting at a small coin of one groszy (about 7–9 mm in diameter). He fished out a victim from the queue, ordered him to hold the coin between his forefinger and thumb and shot at it with his machinegun. Sometimes he hit the coin with the first shot, now and then he shot away a finger, sometimes the whole hand. Afterwards he released the victim with the shot away finger, and fished out a new victim. At the next morning roll-call the victim was found to be sick and unfit for work and sent “beyond the wires”.

The other SS-men had even better ideas. The inmates of the camp tried to behave so as to get the thickest soup to fill the stomach. Very soon afterwards, the evening roll-call took place, almost always brief, with rare exceptions. Complications occurred when the flight of a prisoner were reported. All gangs trembled. If Wilhaus was in a good humour, he would order only two from the gang killed for every fugitive, if he was in a bad mood ten would go. Maybe he would do nothing? One could not know. But at last this also passed. Now black “coffee” without extras and into the barracks.

In every barrack there were 800 to 1,000 people; strangers one to another, torn from various circles, sometimes antagonistic, who had become savages from hunger and destitution, crowded by force into impossible living conditions. The most primitive and rough adapted most easily to these conditions. It would be possible to write books on the psychical changes in yesterday’s human beings.

One must be struck with horror when the darkest recesses of the human soul exposed their gloomy insides. All the barriers of civilization, the superstructures of culture, collapsed from the human being like a needless rag. *Homo homini lupus* (Men one to another were wolves). We repeat this immemorial truth without understanding its content. For us it sounds a trite platitude. Here in the raw life-conditions of the K.Z. (concentration camp) this gloomy sentence achieved its full meaning. People illustrated it by every deed, every move. The barter unmasked various types and queer fish in all their shabbiest nakedness. One could wonder what could be the object of the commerce as people possessed nothing. But, for instance, for a mess tin full of thick soup, one could get a quarter of a loaf of black bread soggy as if made of mud, for thin soup, an eighth of a loaf only. The inmates whose families still remembered them used their soup to get hold of some precious bread. Inmates from outgoing gangs bartered treasures they had obtained by begging or had fished out from garbage heaps, like a raw or baked potato, corn-cobs, saccharine, sugar, cigarettes. For five cigarettes one could get a mess-tin of thick soup. There were also some new-comers. They sometimes had well-concealed diamonds, dollars, watches or gold. Old stagers of the camp would very soon find means to swindle them away from the greenhorns and get these treasures, under the guise of being a go-between in selling them. At the most they would afterwards throw a mere pittance to the owner, who put away this treasure against a rainy day.

At 9 o'clock, the lights were put out. People ran to their bunks so that – God forbid – a check would not catch them out of their bunks. In haste they crawled on heads to the accompaniment of beating, kicking and biting. All this in extreme silence, so that not a sound would penetrate to the outside. Finally all lay on their bunks amid incredible dirt, coexisting with vermin and bugs, for which every bunk was a refuge. Bedbugs were such an inseparable company for an inmate of the camp, that you had the impression that if anything was changed, not one of them would sleep. The fugitives from the camp could not sleep on a mattress and bedding for several nights. After all who would dare to allow himself to sleep well and deeply in the camp; this would mean awakening without shoes or some other piece of your wardrobe. Everyone slept in all he possessed, laying his most needed things under his head. If one did not want to sleep in his shoes, he had to sleep with them as his pillow. Robberies and theft were everyday occurrences in the camp. Only the strongest and most brutal could survive.

Shoes were the most precious part of one's belongings. It was worthwhile to risk even one's life for such valuable loot. I was told of an incident in which when three prisoners were hanged in the evening, during the night, in spite of the fact that it was strictly forbidden to leave the barracks, the shoes of the hanged men were stolen. My informant saw one of the prisoners take off the shoes from a shot fellow-prisoner still warm, as soon as the SS-man turned and looked away. No one dared to allow himself a deep sleep. Very often about 10 or 11 p.m. the SS-men burst in for a check with fantastic ideas, for instance whether people had clean feet. Of course after checking several bunks with most unsatisfactory results they carried away a group of prisoners ostensibly for a wash, in reality to a place from they would not return. This also passed. Silence fell; a relative silence. The barrack was full of snoring, moaning, grunting, wheezing and various sounds typical of restless sleep. At last the camp day ended. Another day had passed. How long would it yet last?

I have tried to present the camp in its full horror, to reflect certain trends, to picture in full the SS-men human-beasts, the background, the conditions, tortures, invariably leading to martyrs' death. I hope I have succeeded but to complete the picture, I must report some incidents, unquestionably authentic, characteristic of the behaviour of the Germans, the inmates of the camp and the background.

Between the latrine and the wire was the garbage heap. Here on the garbage heap were brought prisoners who had expired and were found in the barracks hospital, or who had been shot, but had not yet died. The "certains" were not worth an additional bullet. Constantly there were 15 to 20 people here. They could suffer for some time. People lay in agony, an hour or two, sometimes a day or two, wheezing, kicking the inhospitable mother-earth in their death agonies till they died. This was one of the refined means to influence the psyche, to show the victim his place.

One of the orderlies cleaning the barrack was caught giving his overcoat to his wife working in the laundry. He was tied to handrails (similar to parallel bars) head down, and beaten on the testicles till he died. Naturally such an entertainment took place in the sight of all the inmates of the camp at roll-call, as otherwise the aim would not be achieved, and the pleasure of morally torturing 3,000–4,000 people would be lost.

In July 1942 Rokita solemnly celebrated his birthday and invited all SS-men. A mad drinking-bout began in the evening. About 11 p.m. Rokita called all the foremen and delivered a fantastically optimistic speech. Apparently confidentially, he disclosed that better times were approaching. He was already an old man so they should trust him, that soon all their troubles would reach their end. People did not want to trust, but every soul was eager for some glimmer of hope. After he finished his oration, he ordered them to show him through the barracks. On entering the first barrack he burst out into drunken laughter at the success of the joke and began wildly shooting at the crowd lying in their bunks. In his tracks followed his buddies the SS-men, rushing into various barracks and entertaining themselves in a similar way with blind shooting. In the morning several dozen bodies were carried out and more than 10 people were left in agony on the garbage heap.

Engineer Keil, a well-known architect in Lvov, was caught and delivered to the camp. He was in a gang working on buildings of the firm Hans Schladt. The construction manager was a Viennese named Birk; hearing whom he had got among his workers, he gave an appropriate job to Engineer Keil and accommodated him so far that after a short period, Keil was unofficially directing all the construction work. Incidentally in the camp, engineers were needed and Keil was fished out to supervise some construction on the site of the camp. Fate decreed that after several days Engineer Keil fell ill with typhus. To confess to being ill with typhus meant death. He had to go about his work with a fever of 104[ssdeg]F and conduct himself as if well. Unfortunately the human being is not made of iron. In a moment of weakness he sat and closed his eyes. Exactly at this moment Wilhaus saw him. He ordered him to be tied to a pole and to be given 50 lashes. By a miracle, his friends managed to smuggle him out, though he was sentenced to death, to the camp-hospital. After his recovery, Engineer Keil was allocated to a gang working at the railway station. Again he had bad luck. Several days afterwards on the "death run", Wilhaus recognized him, took him from the row and despatched him "beyond the wires". To avoid another "miracle" he personally watched to see him shot, and commented cynically at the end of this episode, that intellectuals were the most dangerous demoralizers of the environment. After all, they were the greatest leeches and sluggards.

At the evening roll-call, it was discovered that in one of the gangs a man had escaped. Rokita ordered five men of this gang to be shot for not preventing the escape. Among those destined to be killed was a well-known merchant in Lvov, Korikis by name, once the possessor of a large umbrella-store, an elderly gentleman. Hearing of his inevitable death, this quiet man was seized by a sort of madness. He grabbed a brick and lifted his hand to throw it at Rokita. O wonder! This hero of the gun, exercising his cruelty upon thousands of defenceless people, this brave murderer of hundreds of people daily, began to run away, running in panic despite his weapons before one harassed old man with brick in hand. Very soon the brick was taken away from the old man and then Rokita returned. He could take revenge as the enemy was now "disarmed". The victim would die 100 times! The poor soul was tied to a post and Rokita started the execution. On his head was placed a small mug, which Rokita knocked off from his head after several shots. Now he shot at last to kill, but missed. Again he took aim and at the last moment he tore out the magazine so that the trigger fell on an empty chamber. Several times under various pretexts he tormented the victim, amusing himself like a cat with a mouse. He shot all around his head, in the shoulder, in the arm and other places. Finally he left him with several shot wounds until the next day. Next day, as the old man was in an agony of emaciation and loss of blood, he ordered him to be thrown on the garbage heap.

Rokita was sentimental, and in memory of old times organized a band of the camp inmates for his private use. A well-known fiddler called Striks played there. Schilhorn and many others sang, changing very often, as one false note was punished by death. Sometimes in an especially sentimental frame of mind Rokita played himself, sometimes playing Kol Nidrei, watching to see if this wounded the religious feelings of the hearers enough.

A truck arrived at the gate. In the cab an SS-man was sitting on the corpse of a woman. There were also two children, a boy and a girl. He ordered the girl to get off. The child asked if he was going to shoot her. The German answered smiling "Go! I will go with you to a cinema". After several steps, he shot the child. Now it was the turn of the boy. He ordered him to get down. The boy didn't make a sound and went down silently. After several steps he turned around, asking the German why he was not shooting. On the shout "Lauf" (Run), as the boy turned round he was felled by the shot.

In the houses near the camp, with a wonderful view of all that occurred there, lived the wife of Wilhaus and her seven-year-old child, the wife of Kolonko with two small children, and the families of other SS-men. They were privileged to obtain a beautiful picture of the new Nazi order of the world under the power of the *Herrenvolk*.

11 · Vegetation Normalized

It was not the hand of the militiaman that weighed on your shoulder, it was the hand of no living creature. It was the merciless claw of death, which tightened on your shoulder, to prevent the escape of an easy prey. The militiaman was only a chance tool in the affair. He trembled for himself. He himself feared the camp and his fears soon proved to be fully justified.

At the end of April 1942 the Germans ordered a roll-call of the Jewish militia. During the *Aktion* of March, the Jewish militia force reached its maximum of about 700. When they received the order for the roll-call they did not suspect anything special. The general opinion among the Jewish commanders of the militia was that this roll-call was a sort of parade, to show it in its entire splendour. The militiamen did their best with spit and polish, to show themselves as smart as possible. Boots were shined, whoever did not have a short jacket borrowed one from a friend. All were cleanshaven and marched in squads to the square for the roll-call. What a bitter disappointment awaited them. Machine-guns on all four sides of the square bared their ominous muzzles. It turned out that the purpose of the roll-call was to select 100 to 200 militiamen for the camps, the majority for the Janowski camp, and some for smaller newly set-up camps in the area. It began quietly. People went for a parade, but did not return to their families. Militiamen who had renounced their brothers, who thought themselves secure and immune fell into the same category as yesterday's victims. Again we should have learned that the Germans did not care about their helpers and should have drawn appropriate conclusions – to quote from Schiller – "The moor has done his work, the moor may go". They would not go where they wished, but would be liquidated like their former victims in the service of the hangman, once their job was done. There was another purpose in the purge. The Germans of course had informers among the Jewish militia. On the basis of denunciations, they picked out on this occasion all the decent and reliable men who had not succumbed to the destructive influence of the uniform. Only the proven remained in the militia. On the other hand these militiamen would be of use in the camps under the direct control of the Germans for performing various helpful functions. such as guard duties, to act as foremen and so on. The Germans would pressure them appropriately and force them to perform their duties in the desired manner.

Taking one third of the militia was the end of one period. This was the last part of the March *Aktion*; the tool needed to execute the *Aktion* had been used, now it was unwanted and superfluous, therefore it was scrapped. A new registration was under way, a new *Aktion* was in preparation. In the meantime, to preserve the stupid Jews in their idiotic hope, so that they would not get wise and try to defend themselves, a new dose of the narcotic of legality under the name of *Städtische Werkstätte* (Municipal Workshops) was required.

A year earlier, the problem of giving work to the masses of the Jewish population had been under discussion. The problem of employment was especially difficult in Lvov. An almost total lack of raw materials, and to a large degree of machines and tools, created an almost insurmountable difficulty. To sit still with folded arms could never give any result. On the other hand the indefatigable and irrepressible Jewish mind, with its limitless resources of initiative, did not sleep. At one of the sessions of the Handcraft and Industry Department of the Judenrat it was decided to establish a textile cooperative. The director of this department, Dr Mehrer, had to get the approval of the Town Governor for this institution. The settlement dragged on and on endlessly; on the one hand because the officials of the Judenrat were looking no further than their personal gain, and on the other because of the indecision of the Stadthaupman.

In the last days of January 1942 a half-Polonized German came to Lvov. His name was Dorman and he proposed to one of his acquaintances, a Jew, to start a repair-workshop for tailoring and hosiery for the Luftwaffe located on the border of the future Jewish district. The location of the place would present a great opportunity for the supply of raw materials from the town, and also would furnish comfortable possibilities to smuggle things most needed from the town into the ghetto. The beginning of this work met new obstacles every day and dragged on so that rumours of a March *Aktion* took the organizers aback. They installed the shop in rooms supplied by the Judenrat. However, several dozen female workers employed as members of the cooperative were without any documents when the *Aktion* began. Dorman, who had made great efforts to establish the work-shop, got about 500 Ausweis passes from the Luftwaffe, so that people would be shielded during the *Aktion*, despite the Judenrat's refusal to issue any credentials.

After the March *Aktion*, all of a sudden a Jew appeared from Bochnia, a certain Greiwer, on an inspection tour of the embryo-workshop already operating. It later became evident that he was a confidential agent of Dorfman, a director and organizer of similar Jewish workshops in Bochnia. He was called to Lvov on the initiative of Leib Landau, the director of J.S.H. to start at last the organization of work-shops in Lvov. The problem of giving work to the masses of Jews became crucial under the current conditions. The March *Aktion* demonstrated that without a work-pass it was impossible to live, even with the apparent settling of conditions in the Jewish district. To find work was not an easy problem, particularly the regrouping of a large number of Jewish working intelligentsia, the almost complete lack of office work, a mass of women unsuitable for employment in military institutions and with no professional qualifications. Finally the Judenrat had to be relieved of the large number of surplus workers, given the demands from the SS to reduce the number of clerks, under the threat of appropriate action. In the end, it was decided to establish the work-shops together with Greiwer, and the agreement of the *Stadthauptmann* (Town Governor) Dr. Raisp, a Viennese lawyer and theatre critic, was obtained.

The principal mistake was establishing the work-shop under the sponsorship of the *Stadthauptmann* (the civil authority) instead of under the military. I must admit that he was a man of positive character, and very favourably inclined toward Jews. The work-shops were intended to work for civilian needs, instead of a purpose that could provide some protection, for example working for the Air Force; this last basic principle became the cause of controversy between the general government and the SS, which lasted long after the liquidation of the *Städtische Werkstätte*. The formal battle was under way between the civil authority and the SS; the victims were the Jews. The number of workers anticipated was between 5,000 and 6,000. Our leaders were blind. The unanticipated demonstration of fair play by the Stadthauptmann, which the Judenrat accepted without giving any thought to the possible consequences, was really unfortunate. The machines and tools which people brought with them were accepted as borrowed, that is, the property rights remained with the present Jewish owners. This appeared to be one of the greatest disasters which the Germans – Dr Raisp and Dorman – should have foreseen. No workshop without its own machines and tools could exist. Afterwards when it was announced that all Jewish property was the property of the SS, the raison d'être of the municipal workshops and the 3,500 people employed there was doomed. This and some smaller causes such as a real struggle between Greiwer and the Judenrat, a minor quarrel with the Work Department and the refusal to pay a bribe, were bad omens for the supposedly well augured institution. By a phone order of Herr Greiwer the registration of people and machines. especially sewing machines, began at 20/22 Kazimierzowska Street. The chaos from the first moment to the last was characteristic of the municipal workshops. One single person had to register and accept the sewing machines, check their condition and degree of wear, draw up and issue an appropriate certificate. The crowds, the arguments and shouting were beyond all imagination. The number of people applying was enormous. All who had hidden themselves after the March *Aktion*, now sought – as the opportunity occurred – to obtain the pass of a worker.

Apart from a pass, no one was even thinking about any other wages. The work of Jews for the Germans was almost everywhere unpaid, though here it was even worse; one had to provide a sewing machine. Only people who brought in something were employed. People who could bring in any sort of working machines were accepted. To the offices were brought typewriters, desks, chairs, bookcases and safes. People brought everything, that could possibly be needed, and all that merely to get a a pass. They were eager to attain the secure feeling of possessing a pass. It would perhaps be too easy and too quick, if there were order, therefore a little confusion more or less did no harm. The registration, despite the fact that it proceeded at a very slow pace, was going on, and after some days was completed. Yet in three days, the gathered data of the registration would be worked out and it would be possible to work out a detailed scheme, based on the human material and machines tools available. But what could be done when we met Herr Greiwer again as a peremptory tyrant? Despite all this, the organizing of the *Städtische Werkstätte* made progress. The human material was immense, but there were fewer workers in relation to the number of foremen, managers, directors, etc., not only those pretending to this distinction but real experts in organization and leaders of mass-production. About three to four thousand people and some hundreds of sewing-machines were gathered. After lengthy internal haggling, a fledgling in the form of a haberdashery department was born. Not long afterward a shirt-making department was opened. Slowly people got the longed-for passes in the form of a *Meldekarte*.

To the eyes of bystanders not going deeply into the matter, the institution developed magnificently. By creating new departments a greater number of people were employed. After a month or two, the institution grew greater and greater so that the few clear-headed people, knowing organization and experienced in the management of large undertakings, were afraid of this colossus. The Stadthauptmann Dr Raisp, a person as serious in character as he was without any knowledge of industry, gave his full backing, introducing even such an innovation as payment for work, at the time in the form of one loaf of bread weekly, to the municipal workshops, but paying no attention to such trifles as inefficiency. On closer examination, the reasons for the catastrophic state of this production unit are clear. Lack of the right machines, lack of adequately qualified workers, total lack of capital, and most importantly the lack of raw materials. The directors of the municipal workshops Turski,

Reisler and Sokolski realized that in this state of affairs the colossus would tumble down at the first slip.

At the foundation of this seemingly healthy creation gnawed a worm – the Town Workshops worked for civilian needs only. This itself was an irritant for the omnipotent SS, who thought of the Jews as their monopoly. When the case of the Municipal Workshops came up before the Town Governor Dr Raisp, a formal struggle flared up between him and the civil authority on the one side and Dr Wagner, but in reality the SS in the person of Katzman stood behind him. Regrettably, the unsatisfied ambitions of the directors hindered co-operation with the Judenrat, preventing them from obtaining money for indispensable bribes. The whole Department made difficulties in issuing the workers cards and demanded a bribe of 40,000 DM for Weber, and for Bindel and Schapiro 10,000 marks. Of course the greater sum needed for the SS or the Gestapo was out of the question. The end effect of this quarrel was that the Gestapo got a ripe fruit. I am convinced that at the very beginning of the Municipal Workshops the SS acquired an appetite for this tasty plum, but with all the perversity and perfidy of a cannibal-gourmet reined in their lust till the fruit was completely ripe for picking, waiting to pluck it at the right time, so as to get the maximum amount of pleasure for their blasé nerves, with countless murders and the chance to delight themselves with the fear of the victims surprised by the unexpected attack. On the other hand Dr Raisp and the civil authorities dealt with the subject seriously, not even taking into account consequences from the all-powerful SS. In the last days of June 1942 it was decided by the general government that the Jewish question in German private enterprises must be controlled by the SS. The fate of the municipal workshops was sealed. There were rumours about some new shops, new management under the control of the SS, but of course, this was not the problem. The fruit was ripe for picking!

Life continued on in its normal course, under our horrible conditions of manhunts, beatings, camps, murders and robberies. People became accustomed to being pushed down to the level of draft animals. Even when all Jews employed in the insurance offices were arrested about the end of May 1942, this did not interrupt the relative psychological quiet of the Jewish district.

In practice, this was the first sign of the dangers of the exact data which the Work Dept. had accumulated and which had greatly worried us. Some clerk with an aversion to insurance-men enacted a regulation dismissing all Jews from the insurance companies. The SS of course also gobbled this windfall. The Jewish *Sonderdienst* received the exact addresses of all the people who had some connection with insurance either present or past from the Work Department with an order to arrest them for delivery to the central offices of the Gestapo and SS at Pelczynska Street. Altogether there were 54 "guilty" persons. All were brought and Goliger had a magnificent idea. If the person sought was not found, he ordered the whole family to be taken. Naturally there was not one who would accept such an exchange, knowing that it was not a mere formality of taking hostages. As a result of this brainwave of Herr Goliger, people who perhaps might have escaped death were obliged to report in person. The small group was brought to Pelczynska Street, before the director of the department for dealing with Jews, a Major Engels. After a short interrogation he gave the order to "liquidate these parasites".

This episode however sank in the flood of other events. Till now there was not a ghetto in the full meaning of the word in Lvov. There was only a district designated for Jews to live in. Jews still lived in front of the bridge which was settled by colossal bribes of diamonds – a diamond had became a unit of measuring bribes. About the middle of May 1942 rumours of a Jewish district in specific streets for experts and craftsmen began to circulate. Beyond the bridge would be a closed ghetto for the rabble of labourers.

The existing Dwellings Department grew, presently occupying a whole building, and was growing still further. Every apartment, or rather every room in the Jewish district was available and could be occupied only by the permission of the Dwellings Department. The offices of the Dwellings Department presented a picture similar to the Judenrat. The two-storied building was full of offices, departments, officials in charge of departments, managers, who instead of facilitating, put all sorts of difficulties in the way of the petitioners seeking to obtain a roof over their heads.

The manager was admittedly a Jew, but his position was very difficult, since often, as the result of the demands of the Germans (managers of firms employing Jews), in fear of his own skin, maybe even against his will, he was obliged to declare himself against people not having such a German director as a sponsor. Clerks subservient to him did nothing without an appropriate bribe.

The hard conditions of life, tore away the veneer of civilization grafted on to us by our bourgeouis upbringing and showed us naked, undisguised human nature in its savage and ruthless egotism.

The directors of the German firms from self-interest took great care of "their" Jews, and they approached the Dwelling Department with fantastic demands far beyond its capabilities. These demands had to be satisfied to some degree. The director of one firm, an SS-man in the civil service, demanded 12 two-room apartments including bathrooms, for three- and four-person families, because as he maintained, "people must live in human conditions." The cynicism of such a pretence aroused everyone's indignation, but had to be dealt with in some way, as it was impossible to oppose him, despite the total lack of free apartments. This and similar demands destroyed every plan for the future. It was fixed, on the basis of the living space available, that 3 to 5 square metres could be allowed per person (including kitchen, etc.). The demand described above – and it was not an isolated one – upset every calculation and forced the Dwelling Department to evict from quarters, Jews who had no chance to hide behind a German. Ejections and removals from quarters were one of the main and continual nightmares of the Jewish district, and afterwards of the ghetto.

To enforce the orders of the Dwellings Department, a special unit of Jewish militia was placed there, enlarging the number of leeches seeking blood from the weak and powerless. The man in the street, coming to the Dwelling Department without the backing of a German, simply made a wasted journey. You wandered about and made no impression whatever on hundreds of officials. Some times a month passed before living quarters were secured. Nobody cared that someone had no place to sleep, or to leave his wife or children. There were people who for months on end put up with acquaintances, having no place of their own. Nobody thought about storing of furniture, as in most cases this had become stuck in the Acquisition Department or had been sold. Our life, if one may call this existence life, we passed slinking about, continually afraid, among grim monsters with whimsical names, with hundreds of new, unknown dangers:

A UNIFORM met on the street was itself a potential threat, to be avoided by all possible means. Seeing a uniform, everyone tried to retreat as far as possible, to walk on the other side of the street or to walk around – if possible – through side streets or alleys. A call of "Komm mal hier"! (come here) which no one could disobey concealed many unpleasant possibilities: to be beaten up, robbed, shot down and sometimes a proposal of some dirty business. Similarly a JEWISH MILITIA man was to be avoided; perhaps today he had to catch a few for some "extra-pleasant" work – loading coal for instance – at a murderous tempo under a hail of blows, or to punch through clogged sewer channels or, the most frightful, to supply a number of Jews to the camp.

The DIRECTOR or MANAGER must see you at your work-place always smiling, sad, serious or joyful in conformity with his mood. Woe betide you if you could not respond to the mood of your work-card provider and switch on a suitable countenance. To fall into his bad books meant to lose your employment, and another monster was then waiting for its victims, the LABOUR DEPARTMENT for Jews. Everyone who lost his occupation had to apply to Herr Weber for a new allocation to work. This meant being swallowed (especially in May–June 1942) by the growing Janowski camp whose maw was ever hungry for Jews. Even in your home, you could be surprised by a degenerate renegade. The JUDENRAT with greedily outstretched palms – the Jewish Order service, with the help of its smaller offshoots such as: the *Taxes and Finance Department* for your last pennies in taxation, poll-tax, contribution for an unknown use; the *Acquisition Department* for your couch, furniture, rugs, shoes, fine suits, clothes, lengths of suiting, crystal, sets of china, bedclothes, pictures, mirrors. Everything was needed for the never satisfied Germans; the *Dwellings Department* supposed to see to your living quarters, would leave you without a roof over your head, not caring what you would do with yourself and your family. These monsters caused great suffering.

The *Jewish Militia* carried out arrests on direct orders from the Gestapo. To wriggle out or to hide from them was impossible. About once a month it carried out a purge: it got together all people recorded in the police registers or who even got in touch with the police, for instance, as witness, and would march away this "merchandise" to the Gestapo. From here they would be sent "on to the sands". This special service executed commendable functions and the recollection of its famous deeds is especially unpleasant. Especially disagreeable was a visit and search executed by DEVISENEUEBER-WACHUNG STELLE in search of foreign currency, gold and gold coins. Of course the opportunity was taken to get in some beating. If they actually found something, the provident financier would disappear like a stone into water.

The CRIMINAL POLICE must be mentioned in this worthy company. One night in the last days of November 1942, the right side of Sloneczna Street was surrounded. About 9 p.m. every building was blocked, by soldiers and police. People thinking for sure that it was the start of a new *aktion* prepared themselves for death. In the morning the police only started a search. They searched house after house, apartment after apartment. Several hundred people were beaten up until they were unconsciouness, robbed of everything of any value and the raid finished. What the aim of the round-up was no one knew. The omniscient news agency "O.W.S" (One woman said) claimed that it was a search for spies, weapons, deserters or whatever. This event seems to be only a trifle but the fear it provoked in the Jewish district is indescribable. Such lesser events included arresting someone because he irritated a police detective. The event could end with sending the victim to the prison at Lacki Street or at least with a severe beating, but it is hardly worth mentioning so as not so spoil a picture in this beautiful gallery. The king-monster the GESTAPO, the most menacing part of this line-up, was never satisfied by just a beating or a killing. This was an insatiable Moloch. Its jaws engulfed thousands, its appetite was measured in millions. What was concealed behind its facade at Pelczynska Street one never knew. What new *aktion* it would think of, who or what it would strike with lightning speed when it would fall again and again onto our heads – we could not know. The everlasting threat ceaselessly suspended over us the greatest danger. The Gestapo, the ruler of our world, grown from the hellish depths of the degenerate brain of the "genius" they called the Führer.

We all had to steer our daily course to avoid these many-headed and multi-handed monsters. To sneak through like a shadow, to grow small until one became invisible. No endurance, no struggle or courage would help. Even the cunning of a snake would not help. Perhaps though, a bit of luck would gain you an easy death.

In the first days of June 1942, the excellent machine of the Work Department finished handing out work cards. Altogether 60,000 workers numbers and 20,000 "housekeepers" numbers were issued. Everyone had his number like jail-birds or dogs. In the meantime everyone who possessed a number could move freely about all the town.

A very interesting sign was to be observed, a sign never observed in other circumstances and times As I have described, the Work Department issued armbands with the letter "A". These "holy" armbands must be guarded against dirt, rain or staining. Somebody had the idea of making protective casing from cellophane. Others found other ways to protect the armband against staining. This started from utilitarian reasons, but later to the great astonishment of the sober thinking, the casing of armbands became a matter of fashion and even of luxury; armbands were invented of leather with a window of celluloid, from white oilcloth with a window, from impregnated silk, entirely from cellophane and so on. Those who say that the stupidity of men is limitless are correct. This sign of shame, or worse this seal of death, this symbol of our misery, this jail-number, the fools chose to demonstrate their vanity and chase after cheap glamour. The depths of this stupidity did not offend, it rather caused laughter. The condemned were proud of the beautiful frame in which they had mounted their death sentence. Women who could not express their coquetry by fashionable clothes, would want the armbands in various colours, if possible with ribbons, knots, laces, tucks, and other devices. "Unfortunately" Weber would not allow this. Armbands must be white, 10 cm. wide, etc.

About the middle of June 1942 an acquaintance warned me – naturally in deepest secrecy – that I should obtain a housekeeper's stamp of the firm I was employed by. Of course I did it immediately, and learned that I was not the first asking for such a stamp. It was interesting that despite the secrecy in which the Germans wrapped the hammering into shape of their plans against the Jews and fixed the date of *Aktions*, almost every time it was known in advance that an action was in preparation. This may demonstrate that an office without a leak does not exist. Despite the abyss dividing the Germans and the Jews, despite the total lack of connection, despite the fact that plans were made in the closed circle of the Gestapo elite, something always leaked out; by what ways only God knew.

Disquieting rumours circulated from time to time in the town. The Germans tried desperately to suppress this talk of an *Aktion* and met the charges with a flat denial at every opportunity.

On 9 July 1942, I was by chance in the Judenrat about noon and learned from one of the more important officials that a short time before Inquart (aide de camp of the Police Führer Katzman) and Wepke (one of the leading officers of the Gestapo) had been in the Judenrat, answering questions about a coming *Aktion*, declared that nothing was proposed at that point that all these rumours were baseless and that they vouched for total quiet for at least two or three months. The declaration of Inquart had to be taken seriously, as he was the Director of the department of the General Government, District of Galicia for Judeneinsatz. This made plans for *Aktions*, set the date and fixed the "contingent" of victims. Those responsible for executing these orders of the Gestapo were SS-Hauptsturmführer Engels and Untersturmführer Wepke.

Pleased by this information I returned about 2 p.m. to my office. Just as I passed on the good news to my colleagues, a German together with a Ukrainian militiaman entered the office, asking if all of us had work-cards and if there were living quarters in the ground of the factory. After we had been checked, they left the offices. Full of disquiet, we phoned other offices to warn them of the visit and heard that precisely at 2 p.m. simultaneously from all the toll-gates of the town a round-up began making its way concentrically towards the centre of the town and from the centre a star-shaped group spread out to meet the other half of the round-up. To divert the attention of the population from these movements, the normal police, the *Schupo* together with the Ukrainian militia were charged with the task. The increased movement of Gestapo and SS-men would surely have called the attention of people to them. The *Aktion* was carried out coolly by the normal organs of order, which at any rate meant that there was some degree of law, without violence; this was a characteristic of this *Aktion*. Excitement, even when provoked artificially, with the help of liquor, helped create a sort of madness, in which massacres could be executed, something which did not happen on this occasion. Yet during this *Aktion*, a plan was made and coolly executed without "unnecessary" murders, something which shook even the strongest nerves and disabused us of our last illusions. The *Aktion*, in spite of Inquart's guarantee of the two-month quiet, started not two hours after his official promise.

Hauptsturmführer Engels led the *Aktion.* It lasted 12 hours, from 2 p.m. until 2 a.m. The Schupo and the Ukrainian militia went from house to house, from apartment to apartment, checking work-cards. People without a card or firm-stamp (especially housekeepers) and crippled persons (hump-backed, lame, blind) were taken and gathered in the police stations. Afterwards they were transported to a special part of the Janowski camp called the *Durchgangslager* (transit). Altogether about 8,000 people were taken. The largest part were women, and old people of both sexes. People returning from work found that their wives, mothers, daughters, sisters or parents had been seized. People began desperately turning to police stations. All was in vain. People had to wait until the next day, when their German director might intervene and extricate some people. During that sleepless night, thousands counted the slow seconds to dawn, wandering through suddenly empty apartments. Other thousands lay on the earth in a bare field awaiting help and wondering if their husbands, brothers or sons would manage to extricate them from the claws of death. Finally dawn. The faster one could find the dircctor, the quicker he could intervene. Everyone readied the sweetener needed to induce him to quicken his steps. Yet before 8 a.m. no German would appear in an office or factory. At last, when at 8 o'clock, the petitioner arrived before Engels, the German cynically declared with make-believe sorrow: "Unfortunately, my dear, you have come too late. At 6 o'clock, everything was finished, now I can do nothing".

The wheel of life of many people had completed its full turn. And mine – meanwhile is turning on. …

The lack of brutal scenes made the impression on the multitude that the Germans' attitude had improved. Those personally afflicted remembered the blow, but after some days, the rest recalled only the fear they had passed through. It was amazing how quickly everything returned to normal. Of course, to what was normal before the *Aktion*. However, something was added to the norm: hunger. The reserves which people had possessed lasted long. But finally they came to an end. Personal possessions sold or bartered for food were also not inexhaustible, particularly as the Germans spared no pains to help the Jews to get rid of their movables faster. Hunger and misery spread over the Jewish population every day in widening circles. There were many more begging than those able to give alms. To make matter worse, the currency that the Germans imposed upon the conquered territories devalued more and more from day to day. On the street at almost every corner you could hear the shout: "Fried cakes!" "Fresh! For one zloty only!". These cakes were the most striking sign of our misery. Their outer appearance was not especially tempting. Round, heavy, the colour of clay spotted with grey mud, they were made from bran and by some mysterious art adhered together. For many they were – despite it all – a dream only. They could not afford them. On the streets many lay unconscious from hunger and emaciation. It was almost impossible to go through the streets of the Jewish district without coming across people who had collapsed from hunger. All were so accustomed to this, that no one paid any attention to the people lying on the streets.

Once when I passed by such a man, a German accosted me. The recumbent figure presented a picture of extreme misery. Bones covered with bluish skin, some days of unshaven growth. The feet and legs overlaid with mud and dirt, more like a child than the legs of a grown man. Finger-claws impotently dug into pavement as if to tear at the inhospitable mother-earth. Clothes in shreds completed the picture. The German asked me why the man was lying here. After I informed him that the man had fainted from hunger, the German – an old person – stared at me. Astonishment full of indignation appeared on his flushed cheeks, and in a controlled toneless voice he threw at me a question – a grievance, as futilely incredible as our Jewish ones – "This is what the nation which gave birth to Goethe has done?!" He gave me a salute and, as though ashamed, he left with bowed shoulders.

Those who had collapsed usually remained lying so until they regained consciousness. Sometimes, though, they might get something by begging, if not – they must perish.

One of my colleagues, who worked in the Judenrat, took great pains to record the statistics of the death rate from hunger and suicides. He showed that taking into account that the number of births was close to zero, within five years, even without the help of the Germans all the Jews of Lvov would die out. At the time when the Germans came to Lvov there were about 180,000 Jews and including converts more than 200,000.

The Aryan district displayed a flagrant contrast to the Jewish districts. The black-marketeers took the lead and constituted almost 50 per cent of the population. They lived particularly from the Jews, wallowing in luxury. The black market brought enormous profits and it was hard to spend these ill-gotten gains. Illegal pastry-shops or cafés and restaurants helped the black-marketeers and those Germans who were in contact with them to spend this unclean money. Even though in the town a great dearth was felt and it was very difficult to obtain bread, meat or fats, yet in these places one could get everything as before the war, various sorts of meat, eggs, vodka, liqueurs, brandy, rolls, sandwiches – all that one's heart could desire. The prices were even more fabulous than the choice of dishes. A modest breakfast for two persons, cost 200–250 zl. ($15–20). In these dives the profits of the speculators and the black-marketeers were soaked up. But of course these were only for a small part of the population. Some shops full of merchandise glittered, but with a protective card "Nur für Deutsche" (only for Germans). It is interesting that clothes and textiles were mostly of Russian provenance. Apart from these, there were very few shops for the rest of the population. From afar they glittered with bright crowded windows. But when one came nearer the gilt was off. In the show-windows bright with fabulous colours, the fancy wrappings hid only ersatz; ersatz tea, ersatz soup, ersatz pepper, ersatz eggs, pudding made of a combination of surrogates. A living illustration of the proverb "all that glitters is not gold", the beautiful wrappings hid missing constituents in a fine garment. Apart from all this ersatz, the shops were actually empty. The non-profiteers had no other choice, but had to try to make a living from this. Their attempts to manage strange results. My colleague in the office tried to make an illusion of scrambled eggs, from ersatz egg powder. He mixed several powders with water, salted with real salt, added ersatz pepper, in a small pan – because of lack of fat – smeared it with stearine (as such ersatz was recommended by some as kitchen grade), finally from lack of fuel he heated this mixture on a candle flame. What the result of all this was we do not know, yet I do know that he did not eat it, not trusting the colour. His dog was also hungry but turned away from this delicacy, perhaps astonished that despite the hard times a man could play such cruel and foolish tricks.

In the Aryan district, only the Germans – beside the black-marketeers – sparkled with full, fat faces. Life there, apart from the various shortages, was not strewn with roses. Of course, it could not be compared with the misery of the Jews, but sometimes it was really bad. The Germans, ever brutal, ruled everwhere by fists and not by law. I witnessed a traffic policeman grab a delinquent and shower blows on him with a truncheon. The coachman tried to explain, but the policeman paid no attention, called some passing soldiers to help him, and beat the carter to death. People bit lips in anger, fearing to utter a word. The pessimists said that once the Germans had finished off the Jews, they would do the same with all the others. The harsh attitude of the Germans against the Jews was the only consolation of my fellow-citizens. They did not feel so bad, seeing that there were people suffering a much worse fate, one that not even the most fertile fantasy could imagine. And the Jews ... they became accustomed to the beatings, to the murders, to hunger and misery, to being exploited, to lawlessness, and lived somehow or other; that is those who up to now had managed to wriggle from a thousand traps, whose guileful jaws lay open for new victims.

12 · "62,000" (August 1942)

In the first days of July 1942, one of my colleagues in the office greeted me with some unpleasant information. He believed that something new was being prepared by the Germans, as in the Town Workshops new stamps were being issued to all the workers. From experience we knew that every new regulation dragged behind it further reductions in manpower. I was astonished because my boss (the managing engineer of Galikol) had some days before discussed the transfer of Jews working in the food factories to the chemical branch, because this was demanded by General Government as condition for allocating to Galikol supplies for the army. He was making plans for the distant future. Usually he was well informed. He promised to ask his acquaintances, what was the matter. I later got the details of what occurred in the Town Workshops. On 6 or 7 July, it was announced that there would be an inspection by some top brass. Actually on the 9th a committee appeared consisting of SS Untersturmführer Inquart, Stadthauptmann Dr Raisp, a delegate of the Zentrale für Gewehrbelieferungen, Mr Kaufman and some other men from the SS and the Gestapo. The commission visited all shops. Immediately the Jews who managed the Municipal Workshops came to guide the party through the production halls. Inquart, before starting the inspection pulled out a stamp and demanded a stamp-pad. Walking through the halls, he stamped on the cards of the workers with the SS-polizeiführer stamp for the old, infirm or crippled; the colour of the pad was violet. I must stress this detail because it became important later on. At the end of the tour of inspection and stamping – which took all day – Inquart thanked Dr Raisp in the following words: "I am obliged to thank you, for you have created something magnificant. You should get a medal for the fact that from parasites and idlers you have created such a beautiful work of labour, which can bring benefit to our fatherland. I beg you to prepare an album of photos for the SS-polizeiführer for the Government and for me."

The cynicism concealed in this speech was only later revealed. Inquart knew then what fate he was preparing for this "praiseworthy" foundation. The management of the Municipal Workshops was, of course, in the seventh heaven. Finally, they thought, an appropriate protector had been found. Now the Workshops and its 4,000 workers would have the right backing. Reassured by this revelation, I returned to my office and my boss informed me that all workers would get stamps from the SS-polizeiführer, but that he had received instructions not to pay attention to this and to proceed with his normal plans. The information sounded to him not very pleasant, and, of course, worse to me. I realized that some new *Aktion* was in preparation. In the meantime in the whole town – extremely sensitized by present conditions – the distress signals began to sound. In various firms stamps were given to workers, but some did not get them and their work cards were not returned. The German directors pointed out to their trusted Jews that the SS was pressing for a reduction in staff. An even more depressing impression was made by the second purge of the Jewish militia. The same day that they affixed new stamps at the Municipal Workshops (9 July 1942), in all the town, the "12 hours *Aktion*" of July was executed and a roll-call of the Jewish militia was ordered. The roll-call was led by Engels and Stawiski. About 250 militiamen were chosen for the camps. Now the militiamen were directed as assistant guards to camps and especially to the Janowski labour camp. This fact gave everyone food for thought. Rumours surfaced that the camp would be enlarged and of course a new hunt for victims was on the way. But nothing concrete was yet known.

Suddenly in the second half of July 1942 came the news of the dissolution of the Arbeitsamt-Judeneinsatz and the farewell speech of Weber to his workers. Beside clap-trap thanking them for their fruitful work, Weber advised them where would be the best place to work. He advised against working in offices; in his opinion it would be better to be a rag-collector than a book-keeper. In the building where all the activity of the Jewish workers was centred, where life seethed in the diligent extraction of bribes from numerous clients, out of about 140 men and women working, there remained only five or six. Weber was so trusted that he was placed in enterprises working for the Army, *Rohstofverfassung* and so on. His advice diffused in a broad wave throughout Lvov and provoked fear among those not working in the institutions he mentioned.

At the end of July or beginning of August, Dr Raisp was informed that, by a decision of the general government, the Municipal Workshops were to be liquidated. Only a few departments approved as efficient and productive would be transferred to the direct management of the SS. The refusal to give stamps to all workers in the Judenrat caused the greatest consternation and horror. Four thousand people together with the 15,000 members of their families spread panic through all the town. Negotiations were going on, though probably without much chance.

The news spread from mouth to mouth and gathered to an ominous cloud swollen with the storm that would soon rage over our heads. Everyone spoke only of this, as there was no more important theme. When would the *Aktion* take place, against whom would it be aimed, how many Jews would be left in

Lvov? From morning to evening in all work-places, at home, wherever two or three people got together, at once talk began about the horror awaiting us. *AKTION*! This became so depressing, the atmosphere so stressful that everyone wished "that the abscess would burst more quickly" to relieve themselves of the torment. Every passing day, new information increased the panic. They took work-cards from the workers of the Judenrat, allegedly to be stamped, but did not stamp them, and refused to return them. In one firm, of 18 cards, 14 were withheld, and only four got stamps. Allegedly the Luftwaffe had been ordered by the SS to reduce the girls employed in its workshops. The number of workers at the airfield in Sknilow was reduced by half. About 40 men were summoned to Sknilow for work, but on the way they were taken off to the Janowski camp. There was no end of bad and worse news indicating that the *Aktion* was close.

On Saturday 9 August, an announcement appeared on the General Government bulletin board that interested German firms should, before 11 a.m on the following day, Sunday the 10th, seek stamps for the Jews working in their firms. If they did not do so, they would forfeit the right to get them. This was the final sound of the alarm bell. In the office where I worked, nothing had been done up to now. The director was away. He was returning that day, Saturday, in the afternoon. In Galikol, there still worked about 450 Jews. Almost all came together in the office to await the return of the director. At last he came; all the cards were gathered and the director went with them to the district agency of the general government. In my room were several colleagues. We sat quietly under the terrible stress through the thickening dusk. The darkling hour normally disposed people to be sentimental, but threw us off balance with the long hours of waiting. The impossibility of living in constant fear, was worse, incomparably worse than being at war; in the trenches one was doing something by risking one's life and had to be fatalistic. One would perish if one had bad luck, but with good future one might escape. Our situation was unprecedented, we could not do a thing; we were not so exposed to sudden death as in the front-line, but we know that inescapable death was awaiting us. Finally we interrupted these joyless reflections and without the director having returned we went to our homes.

That night I had a horrible dream. I dreamed that I saw a row of sieves, one above another. Around the sieves stood SS-men who all the time reached with their paws into the sieves to catch some objects which were in the sieves. I myself with a crowd of people was in one of the sieves, which shook continually. The sieve let some people pass into the next finer sieve. Each time seven people passed into the following sieves. The SS-men guarding the sieves caught up those who did not pass through with their bare hands. With horror – bathed in cold sweat – I awoke. How long will I continue to pass through the sieves? On which will I remain and be caught? Better not to consider such an eventuality and prepare for myself an appropriate shelter. Above one of the offices was a small pigeon loft. I checked the plan of the house and found that a small part of the attic was separated – God only knows for what purpose – and a separate entrance had been arranged direct from the office by a ladder. This seemed to me to me an ideal shelter, as in the building there were no living quarters. I hid there two loaves of bread and a bottle of water for emergency.

In the office, I learned that the director had received only 200 cards, i.e. about 250 had been held up. Mine was O.K. Perhaps I would pass through another sieve; I gave a selfish sigh of relief. One forgot in such moments the tragedy of thousands who remained without this scrap of paper that decided life. These altered at times the tone of everyone's life. One thought only of oneself and one's nearest and dearest. As there was no need to use the shelter at present perhaps I would give it to someone else. In the evening of Sunday, 11 August at 3 a.m. the *Aktion* would begin. My information was right. In the morning going to work, I saw it in full swing. Under the bridge at Sloneczna Street thc *Aktion* had not yet begun. But beyond the bridge it had already started. Here in the "district of experts" it was advisable to hold one's card in one's hand and show it from afar to every *Schupo* and SS-man. People feared to walk alone. A small group got together. Everyone held his card in his hand. Perhaps some SS-man would not have patience to wait until he could pull out his documents and would put him on a truck or even shoot him down on the spot.

Beyond the bridges, the *Aktion* was in full swing. SS-men, Schupos with specially trained units of Ukrainians in black uniforms and black helmets marked "S" for *Sonderdienst* – (special service), were the worst among the thugs and put themselves in the right mood by intoxicating themselves with fumes of victims' blood. People were murdered in their houses and apartments. They gathered all the people they found in their apartments, and took them away leaving whole houses empty. For entertainment they threw corpses from windows on to the street. People tried to sneak through the bridges, but this had been foreseen by the painstaking German strategists and under the bridges were guards checking everyone's documents. When they caught a Jew without the proper stamp on his card, they beat him to death with the butts of their rifles. Others undiscouraged kept trying this million-to-one chance to evade certain death. The carnage went on uninterruptedly.

The sidewalks under the bridge were drenched in blood. The gutter under the bridge on Zamarstynowska Street was running a sluggish red. People whose cards had the right stamp were allowed to pass. With pale faces and horror-dilated eyes they arrived at their factories and offices, unable to describe the horror of the *Aktion*. Everyone prepared shelters against the moment the tidal wave would reach him.

Those caught in the *Aktion* were brought by tram-lorries through the town to a transit camp at Kleparow. The lorries were overcrowded, the majority of those on them women. The trucks were drawn by a street-car in which were the guards. The women cried, shouted, imploring the passers-by to inform their relatives, husbands, brothers, children. Passing the Aryan districts the scene was the same. The view of this caravan, full of victims destined for butchery made a frightful impression. Everyone was seized with dismay. The horror and terror hung over the town like a cloud and sent cold shivers down everone's spine. Desperate shouts, not for help, but only begging people to inform relatives of their tragic fate, sounded day and night. The first two days the *Aktion* was performed uninterruptedly day and night. The tram-lorries with human victims rolled and rolled and rolled ...

On the third night of the *Aktion*, there was a temporary rest for the thugs. At last one quiet night. It seemed unreal after the anguish of the two preceding it. People in the grip of fear did not dare to believe it. The majority of working people were held in their factories. It appeared as if all was petrified. However, something moved in this motionless darkness. Hyenas prowled for loot. The houses were empty – the apartments of the enemies of all humanity! Why not take advantage of such a wonderful opportunity. Let's go to rifle human bodies and to strip dead-houses. In the pre-dawn darkness, whole phalanxes of these hyenas laden with booty returned to the Aryan districts, but each went alone, they did not unite into groups. They sneaked furtively along the walls of houses, bent over. Was this because the excessive load weighed down their shoulders? Or could it have been shame? Yes, shame! And rightly so! Hide your face, you despoilers of corpses. Your face is unimportant, your attitudes symbolize your behaviour towards us – the accursed. You feared to be recognized; that much humanity remained in you.

On 13 August, the number of people in the Janowski camp including those brought in as a result of the *Aktion* was, at morning roll-call, 13,500 people. On the same day the evening roll-call produced only 2,000 persons. Where were the missing thousands? – "On the sands".

At the Municipal Workshops there was despair. Their stamps were not respected because of their violet colour. All other working people had received stamps in red ink. Inquart's joke with the stamps had succeeded excellently. They alone suffered from the mistake. Why was he given a violet pad? Perhaps if they had given him a red one, the authorities would have given all the other working people a green stamp. As a result of the intervention of Dr Raisp with the general government, the workers of the Municipal Workshops were kept at their work-places. There were about 3,500 workers and about 2,000 of their families. The halls, offices, corridors, toilets, stairs were full of people. The hubbub and clatter were deafening. News from town about who had been caught was repeated with despair. The crying and shouting set everyone's nerves on edge. Madness hung in the air. Thursday morning, the atmosphere of fear reached its cumulative intensity. People walked up and down, circling like animals in a cage. About 9 o'clock, some trucks pulled up at the front of the building. Gestapo-men burst in like wild beasts hungry for their long-sought quarry. People on the staircases were immediately hurried onto the trucks accompanied by wild shouting and beating. Afterwards Wepke began the real inspection of the workshops. Presently he would show what it meant to really exercise control.

– "You wear glasses? Los! Off with you!"

– "Blond? Los!"

– "Book-keeper? Los! Off with you!"

The department of hosiery and haberdashery took his fancy. He took all the workers. After two hours of inspection, in the building that had been full of noise, dead silence reigned. Of more than 4,000 people, only 1,000 remained. Fear checked tears and dried throats incapable even of shouting in despair. The bloom of the young people of Lvov was gone. A work place created with great pain for the Jewish intelligentsia became its coffin. At last the Gestapo satisfied its appetite with the meal for which they had waited so long. People were taught the lesson by the murder of 2,500 workers that the Gestapo had the monopoly of Jews.

Only in the afternoon did the news of the purge in the workshops reach me. My colleagues getting the news hid it from me knowing that my wife worked there. After I got the information at last, I began to run to various colleagues and persons of influence to try to extricate my wife from the camp. It was in vain. Twice I myself barely escaped from the claws of the thugs. In the evening without reckoning the risks I went in the direction of the camp, where a German checked my documents and beat me up badly. Finally, like a beaten dog stupefied from fatigue, I returned in helpless despair to my empty home. I consoled myself at first that perhaps the women were not taken to death; after all they were healthy, in the full bloom of their strength as workers. I could not conceive that the only aim was the senseless murder of thousands of women. Perhaps they yet lived, maybe there was even the most trifling hope? Maybe ... No! Unfortunately, those who had fallen into the hands of the Gestapo had not the smallest hope. All perished, like pebbles thrown from a cliff, leaving behind only ever-widening circles, weaker and weaker, till very soon they disappeared … Among them, my wife …

After the liquidation of the Municipal Workshops, the *Aktion* raged with increased strength. Gestapo-men and the black-uniformed Ukrainians burst into homes, smashed the doors with hatchets seeking further victims. One could delay them a little by offering vodka. In some apartments whole tables laden with liquor were prepared. By such means some succeeded in saving their lives. The beasts drowned their madness in vodka, shooting at the walls, through windows, till drunk almost to unconsciousness, they left to quench the heat of their blood in other wild and beastly deeds. At No. 6 Gazowa Street in a secret bar, a mad drunken spree went on day and night with continually changing clients. Alcohol flowed in streams. Street whores brought in, danced amid blood, murders, liquor and rage. Tirelessly, the Germans murdered people on the streets, and a few moments later, they participated in the wild dance and the mad celebration. The revelling mob roared with joy and, for no reason, burst into wild, raucous laughter. Were they human? Which of them was still able to laugh? Caesar described the *furor Teutonicus*, and in 1980 years this maniacal frenzy of the Germans had not abated.

At No. 5 Gazowa Street, Ukrainians were searching the house. By a fatal mischance they found a shelter in the attic. Together with a German they climbed onto the roof and shooting blind into the windows – as they feared to enter the attic itself – forced the people to leave the shelter. The only entrance was through a window. They stood at the sides of the window with axes and hacked those coming out on their heads, on shoulders, or wherever they could reach. Two others threw the victims from the roof into the courtyard. There another SS-man awaited them, entertaining himself by shooting them from about five yards with his pistol. He was so drunk that he had to fire two or even three times until he hit, and if the shot was not lethal, to try again.

Two Ukrainians burst into the apartment of my friend K. In the apartment were an old mother and her son. The Ukrainians ran up to the old lady – prepared for death – and slapped her in the face. The son, usually a quiet person, seeing this, went mad. He attacked one Ukrainian and with one stroke felled him. He caught the second one before he could reach for his gun and threw him with such force against the closed window that the window frame broke and the murderer fell out onto the street from the second floor. At the sound of a brawl, an SS-man entered the apartment and saw what was happening. With a burst from his machine-gun he almost cut the culprit in half, for daring to defend himself. The old lady seeing this lost consciousness. After the *Aktion* I met her in the Jewish hospital. She had only a light gunshot wound, but had lost her mind.

Some of the thugs, knowing that according to Jewish belief touching a corpse defiled a Cohen, arranged a special joke. I personally witnessed a scene on the opposite side of the street in which several Germans burst into an apartment and shot down a woman. After a moment they brought in two bearded old Jews, ordered them to take the corpse and throw it into the street. Later the Germans went together with the two Jews. On the street they called a cab, ordered the Jews to place the corpse into the cab and sit on it. In this way, they took the Jews to the Janowski camp. All the way the Germans were choking with convulsive laughter.

The laughter and shouts from the bar on Gazowa Street re-echoed through the empty Jewish street. At night, the sound of a harmonica joined the drunken hubbub and there was loud raucous singing. The murderers could enjoy themselves to the full! Nobody would object. The houses were dead. The corpses lying on the street were devoid of feeling. Their debauchery offended perhaps only the night, which covered all with a dark shroud, the bestiality of the Germans, the helpless despair of the bereaved, the stains of blood and the robbed houses. Yet even the night could not hide the revels of the beasts at the shambles. They went all beyond all bounds.

The *Aktion* went on and on. Every day, a new wave of thugs rolled through the houses of the Jewish district. Every day the searches and examinations became more exacting. The Ukrainians were going around with axes to force entry into closed apartments. Often the Germans brought dogs to uncover every possible hideout. At last when there remained nobody without a card, they confiscated valid cards and seized people who, in fact, should have been exempt. Sometimes they amused themselves in another way. To my good friends went a whole gang of SS-men. After checking their cards, it seemed that everything was in order. The Germans took away the cards and drove the people into the courtyard to be shot. They ordered them to face the wall and fiddled ostentatiously with their machine guns. It was astonishing how quietly, without hysterics, people awaited their fate. People stood and waited. Behind them only silence. At last one of them turned around and saw that the Germans had crept away. The Germans had gone and left all the cards on the ground. This was one of their more successful jokes!

The overcrowded tram-lorries arrived at the camp. Here SS Polizeiführer Katzman spent most of his time watching personally that the *Aktion* was carried out in the most rigorous way, without exceptions or appeals. The majority of the victims of this *Aktion* were women and it was chiefly aimed against women. All appeals to Katzman met with ruthless refusal. To some especially insistent German, he answered: "What is the matter? Is this woman especially necessary to this Jew? Let him take another female!

In the camp square or rather on the loading ramp square, every transport was greeted by Rokita with the demand to hand over jewellery, gold, foreign currency, watches that people had with them. Those guilty of concealing anything would be severely punished. Most gave up all the valuables they had, perhaps not so much from fear of being punished, as all knew they were going to be murdered, but rather from utter apathy. I was told that on one of the days of the *Aktion*, buckets of valuables, watches and jewellery, were taken. I should not say taken but rather re-allocated since all Jewish possessions were the declared property of the SS. After giving away their valuables – the last tickets to life – everyone was free to move around, but of course only within the area fenced with barbed wire. The majority, seized by apathy, lay down on the first empty piece of ground, but others gathered in groups. They talked and considered the situation. Very soon they too would be seized by apathy. The Ukrainian guards were very numerous. Several searchlights illuminated the square during the night. Everyone who approached the wire-fence was immediately shot at. A group of old Orthodox Jews provided a characteristic picture. They gathered together and prayed fervently "Shema Israel Adonai Eloyehenu, Adonai Ehad" (Hear o Israel, the Lord is one, our only Master!) O God! What is man? The life of men is nothing. Days pass as shadows. KI AFAR ATA, VE EL AFAR TASHUV! (You are dust and to dust you return). Everything you do O LORD is just". The holy words of the psalms gave them consolation. All the torment was without meaning. It had all occurred before. Others cried and wept, or broken by fate, did not react at all. For the believers, their sufferings were a test. They were a fate sent by God. With humility, they bowed their heads before His holy sentence.

Reveille. The train arrived on a specially built spur. They began to load people, arranging them in fours and drove them into the cars. At the sides stood SS-men and counted to check whether the crop had reached the anticipated number. People were loaded up for a journey into the next world. Somebody shouted through the window of the cattle-truck a word of farewell or a curse. Then everything subsided into silence. The square was empty, awaiting new tenants.

After nine days of intensive *Aktion* came a break. The streets were dead. People did not yet believe and did not want to lose their shelters and fall victim to another piece of deceit. Business and barter was totally dead. It was impossible to get bread or anything else. Selling anything was out of the question, due to lack of buyers and lack of wholesalers. The Aryan districts were well provided with merchandise but at present there was no demand at all. After a day or two, a little by little, people came out into the light of day, with pale faces and the fear which had remained in their eyes, a fear which died only with life. With dilated eyes, with ears cocked, they looked around, to see and hear whence danger might come. The first steps were to get information on what had happened to family, relatives, and friends. They received distressing news. No house, no family, was without victims. In normal times when somebody was murdered or some unfortunate accident had claimed several victims, it would be said "the family was plunged into mourning". But what could be said now when tens of thousands had disappeared together during a few days. There was almost no person, who had not lost a wife, a sister, mother or daughter. All would have to wear mourning, but that would be inadequate. To deck oneself in black crepe? For whom first? For wife or mother? For brother or father? Who was nearer? No! Better not to wear mourning at all. Mourning had reigned in every home for a long time now. From the moment the whip of the Huns cracked over our heads, from the moment they profaned our houses of prayer, when they desecrated our Holy Books, when thousands began to fall victims, children, women, old people and nobody reacted as they should have, save a very few mouthing empty phrases. The mourning in our hearts was the only light in our solitude. "How long would it yet last?" Who knew? But surely long enough. Hard and deaf is the conscience of the world; an unchanging constant in a changed world.

The far-sighted rightly feared. After a two-day interval, perhaps because the desired quantity of fodder had not been reaped, or perhaps it was just a deceitful plan to draw people from good shelters – the *Aktion* raged anew. As the last squalls of a storm are the worst, the two last days of the *Aktion* were marked by the most bloody deeds. Blood flowed – literally – in the streets. My colleague, whose wife was taken after they tore up her card, went after a column of seized women to a police station. The whole way, from where they had caught the victims in a house-to-house search and were hurrying them to the police station, was marked by the blood of the beaten and maimed, and littered with the murdered corpses left on the street.

A shelter uncovered in Sloneczna Street was so peppered with shots that the cellar afterwards presented a monstrous view of heaps of corpses of the 60 persons who had hidden there.

At the end of the *Aktion* on Saturday, 22 August all those in Jewish hospitals were taken. The sick who could not walk were shot in their beds. Every human being in the place; the whole staff including the nurses were taken.

On that night, 22 August 1942, the *Aktion* ended.

On Monday, as usual, several colleagues, gathered in my room in the breakfast-break. Some were missing and conversation faltered. What could we talk about? We were unable even to despair, hardened by the recent past.

My boss told me that he had heard from a most reliable source, that the *Aktion* had really ended. The number caught and murdered had been 62,500 people; of this number about 40,000 were women. Ciphers. Statistics. Some dead strokes of the pen, but who can perceive that under them were concealed hearts formerly vibrant with activity, plans, intentions, dreams, unsatisfied longings. Stupidity! Ciphers. Statistics. A macabre plan to exterminate the childbearers; it had been accomplished to the letter – a nightmare!

13 · Alone

After three days a postcard came from one of the women taken away from the workshops, from a small place called Zaszkow. She wrote that almost all of those deported were together and that they had thrown the postcard from the train going north-east from Lvov. After studying a map, it was found that Zaszkow was a small station on the railway line between Lvov and Rawa Ruska, the last important junction. But before this junction was Belzec, a destination which evoked horror. For a long time there were rumours that a special camp was located there. After the March *Aktion* the rumours claimed that in the forests around Belzec people were "deported" to a better world. Perhaps this was relevant to the matter at hand, but nobody knew anything for sure or anything concrete. Afterwards, mostly from some railway-men, it became clear that none of the trains had reached Rawa-Ruska. People made enquiries in the most fantastic ways. I myself participated in such efforts by sending "Aryans" with ample remuneration to get some concrete information. Unfortunately beyond the facts given above nothing was uncovered, but what we now knew was enough – to our deep sorrow. Gathering together for the mutual exchange of news, became very difficult. The streets were uncannily deserted. During the day the only movement seen was that of militiamen clearing deserted apartments on the orders of the SS. Everything was taken away: furniture, bedding, personal effects, loaded on cars and brought to the storehouses of the SS. There was nobody to walk on the streets and there was no purpose in going anywhere. Of more than 100,000 Jews there remained about 40,000. In the evening, the lifelenessness diminished a little. Those returning from work to their homes did their best to leave the street as quickly as possible, to hide themselves in the twilight of home, not to stand out or to show themselves. Despite the fact that movement on the streets was allowed until 8 p.m., by 7 o'clock you could see nobody there. A gruesome, oppressive atmosphere. We were too few in relation to the space occupied. Yet soon a remedy for that, too, would be found.

In September 1942 an announcement of the general government appeared on the walls of the town establishing a closed ghetto in Lvov. It would be exclusively beyond the bridges. Every Jew, living in the districts not slated for the ghetto, had to move before September, as on this date the ghetto would be closed. Naftali Landau, one of the councilors of the Judenrat, got the job of building a fence around the ghetto at the expense of the Judenrat. Simultaneously there appeared placards announcing that all Jewish possessions were the property of the SS and every appropriation of such property either by Jews or by Aryans was punishable by death. A third order announced that anyone guilty of hiding Jews in the Aryan districts or helping a Jew to hide himself, would also be liable to the death penalty.

Now everyone realized that all was lost. The trap would be closed any day. Between the lines the placards shouted S.O.S. Many did not want to be pushed into a ghetto in any circumstances. Thus began the 'flights'. For a flight, documents were needed. At once there appeared dark but very useful types dealing in documents. The trade in documents existed, of course, before that boom, but now, during and after the *Aktion*, when a stamp determined one's life or death, the real production of false stamps began. This made it necessary for German directors to add a second stamp confirming that the first had been given in the signer's presence. You could obtain almost any document: identity cards, birth certificates, certificates of baptism or marriage, the documents of an Aryan worker, and so on. Principally there were two types of documents. There were genuine documents given up in rare cases by Aryans to their friends, usually for a large payment. The second type were documents falsified from A to Z. Forms were printed, rubber stamps made. The documents were prepared according to the wishes of the customers, with ficticious names, false personal data, signatures, and all necessary etceteras. To possess Aryan documents became highly fashionable, but this time the fashion was justified and reasonable. Many bought such documents, even when they did not intend to use them immediately, saving them for a rainy day. In prewar times, conscience would not have allowed them to make use of a false name or document. Conscience now had to stand aside. People with children rightly feared to wait, and gave their children to Aryans who demanded huge payments for hiding them. The payments varied between 1,500 zl. to 2,000 zl. for accommodation plus 500 to 1,000 zl. monthly for board, payable for several months in advance. The Aryans readily accepted children into their homes. Such sweet tiny tots, and in addition so well "gold-plated". Suits, furniture, and other things they had got enough of, even too many, now some cash would be of use.

Jesuitical outpourings of sympathy and fellow-feeling found place in almost all transactions and negotiations involved in hiding a child. Imagine the feeling of a parent, compelled by conditions to take leave of a child. People gave up all they possessed only to assure their children's survival. They might perish, but their child would be rescued. Everyone refused to admit the slightest shadow of mistrust in the honesty of the Aryan who had agreed to hide their child.

After all he had been given enough money, it would be an utterly cold-blooded individual who would let you down in such a situation, especially when there was the life of a child to take into account. "It is such a sweet creature. God will surely watch over it".

Others left alone without wife, mother or children, were resigned, apathetic and only awaiting death. But to have the chance to end it all when the time arrived, they provided themselves with poison. The blow was too strong, they could not bear it spiritually. To supply them, a new kind of business developed, the macabre trade in poison. People constantly discussed which were the best, most potent poisons, those taking effect like lightning. Various kinds of death were considered. It was an often-discussed theme, and soon nobody was astonished at its appalling character. The most sought-after posion was, of course, cyanide, but it was very difficult to obtain, considering that the price of one dose was about 1500 zl. The crooks had a free run, knowing that it was not possible to test the quality of the merchandise. Other poisons, such as strychnine, arsenic, luminal, morphine were also popular. Escape or death, were two poles between which our life plans revolved. A long torment and then ... either freedom or a short agony and then a different sort of freedom; you could take your choise!

During the August *Aktion* the Judenrat was ordered to remove its offices beyond the bridges. A corner building on J. Hermann and Lokietek Streets was chosen. After the August *Aktion*, no more than 10 per cent of the officials in the Judenrat remained. The most important department became the Housing Department. On this department rested the task of allocating 40,000 to 45,000 people among 87,000 square metres of living space. A proper re-organization of the Judenrat was simply impossible, due to the results of the August *Aktion*. But nevertheless the Housing department worked day and night, seeking some solution. No one had any illusions that life would become somehow stable. Any such illusions were laid to rest on 1 September.

We feared that the anniversary of the beginning of the war would bring unpleasant surprises. But what occured exceeded in its grimness our worst misgivings. On the night of 31 August – 1 September, a *Volksdeutsch*, an agent of the Kripo, in a brawl with a Jewish criminal as depraved himself, was stabbed several times and hospitalized. About 9 a.m. some Germans came bursting into the offices of the Judenrat to seek revenge. Almost all the known leaders of *Aktions* and mass-murder appeared: Wepke, Engels, Hildebrand, Petryk, Streicher, Fischner, Staviski, escorted by a mass of black-clad Ukrainian "S" men. First they sought Jewish militiamen. Everyone they met was slaughtered by blows from their pistol butts. Engels called for the counsellors of the Judenrat. Nobody knew what was the matter. When two of the Judenrat Landau and Hochs appeared, he demanded that they provide him with ropes and scarves. There were no ropes in the store, so some were sent for in the town. In the meantime, people who were present on the ground and first floor, both officials and petitioners, were hurried out to the street. There was a wild fusillade, several hand-grenades were thrown and the matter was settled. Bodies and wounded were scattered on the street in front of the building of the Judenrat. At last the ropes were brought from town. Engels ordered a roll-call of the Jewish militiamen and choose 11 volunteers, among others Adv. Tunis and Dr Tafet, and ordered them to be hanged from the windows of the first floor of the house at Lokietek Street. All the people there and especially the victims were so terrified and stupefied, that no one fully realized the dire nature of this nightmare. One of the militiamen requested – as a former officer – to be shot and got only a sneer for answer. The 12th to be hanged was the chairman of the Judenrat, specially brought from Lecki Prison, where he had been held for several weeks. In recognition of his function as chairman, he was hanged from a second-floor window. The corpses were to remain hanging for 24 hours. Now Wepke ordered chairs to be brought to seat the the wounded, who had lain till now on the street. There were about 40 of them. He reassured them that he had sent for a physician, who would dress their wounds. Afterwards when the chairs were brought he called several Ukrainian thugs and ordered them to kill the wounded one by one by a shot in the head from behind. Sated with infamy and cloyed with pleasure, the thugs went, after a job well done. So ended this incident.

No! Not yet. The hanged men had to remain hanging for a whole day and night. The Germans and the population of the Aryan districts apparently thought that they should not miss such an opportunity to feast their eyes on such an edifying view. All day long, huge crowds walked to the Jewish district to enjoy the wonderful sight and take photos. In the evening they installed special floodlights to illuminate this part of the street for people whose work had not allowed them to participate in the holiday, so they should not lose the opportunity to fill their delighted eyes with the edifying culture of the Third Reich. This incident cost about 170 victims. It demonstrated with finality that there was no place for illusion, even the smallest, that final extermination was inevitable.

Immediately afterwards the escapes into the Aryan districts increased to great proportions. Almost every day people disappeared and we learned that someone was missing. People kept their plans in the deepest secrecy, till the last moment. Perhaps some might succeed in escaping in this way. Surely the Germans would sooner or later learn about the flights and by the aid of innumerable traps would also decimate those who had half-escaped.

As the ominous date of 7 September 1942 neared, the removals were in full swing. In contrast to the earlier removals, no wagons or vans were seen. There was nothing left to be driven. Removals took place mostly by handcarts. A bundle with bedding, several pots, a chest, suitcase, rarely a trunk and a box-bed. The rest were carried by hand.

My mother had suffered for a long time from Parkinson's disease. The continual running to shelters and sitting with no chance to move, the continuous nervous stress ruined an organism weakened by illness. She would not even hear of removing to the ghetto. She slept for very long periods and prepared herself for death. She longed for this deliverance. All the time she worried what I would do, where I should hide myself. Her sober and clear-thinking mind worked endlessly on this matter until her last moments. On the night of 4 September, she survived the only bombardament of Lvov by the Russians and fell asleep not to awaken again. The whole night I sat at her bedside. In the morning, I learned that she had been granted Heaven's greatest blessing in this vale of tears and had departed this life in her sleep, to a better world where there were no Germans, no Hitler, no *Aktions* and no Ukrainians. Can such a place really exist? Maybe only in the next world. The *Hevra Kadisha* (The Holy Brotherhood) interred her the next day in the old Jewish cemetery on Spitalna Street without a funeral service. I had nobody now. The world was unreal, my eyes reeled. All my bonds were severed. What really held me here? Where should I go?

I had nobody, I loafed in my empty apartment. Supposed to be packing, getting things together, but dead, empty, deaf to everything.

I had nobody. Within one year my father, my wife, had been taken away, disappeared and perished, my mother had died, the rest of my family was destroyed. What had I to live for? For whom? I wanted to care for somebody, to do something for somebody.

I had nobody, I hated the now empty corners. Not to look at these surroundings among which – not so long ago – I had been together with my wife and mother. To burn everything which had felt the hands of my nearest and which now would serve the Germans. To fight? Against whom? What for? I had nobody. Like a gloomy refrain these words molested me at every step with every movement.

One of my colleagues informed me that there was a chance to enter a farm-camp of the SS near Lvov. Well! Let it be a camp. Only to leave, only not to look at all that had surrounded me up to now, after all ... I had nobody.

14 · The Farm Labour Camp of the SS

After several days in the camp, I recovered enough to pay attention to my new surroundings. The camp was in a village called Winniki and thank God, not at all similar to the Janowski camp. It was a farming camp on a former noble estate, the property of a Jew, at present in the hands of the SS. Jews – men and women – altogether about 160 people, were the unpaid workers. The majority were Jews living in the surrounding villages, we, members of the Lvov intelligentsia, were only a small handful, just 14 wrecks. We lived, as in all camps, in a small shack with two-storey bunks. I got the upper bunk. Beneath was an engineer-architect. He had lost his wife and a six-year-old daughter. He himself, after many experiences which would provide the material for a separate book, got stuck in this camp. Spiritually, he had been completely destroyed as a result of his tribulations. He could not concentrate on anything, spoke about himelf only by his title "Engineer", without a name or his surname. The next bunk was occupied by a veterinary surgeon, the only survivor of a once numerous family, now working as a herdsman. The following bunk was occupied by an 18-year old youngster, both of whose parents had been taken in the June *Aktion*. Further on was the proprietor of a large grocery in Zakopane, with a mass of memories from a past when he was still a human being. Others were so lacking in individuality, apathetic, spiritual cripples, that there is nothing to say about them. Memory was our only spiritual comfort. It was the only thing that could cheer us up, awaken those hurled into an abyss of melancholy, sadness and boundless despair. Like automatons we got up in the morning, before dawn, and after hog-swill coffee, we went to work in the fields. The work was the usual work on the soil, with the addition of four slave-drivers from among the local peasants, who kept watch over us slaves. It gave the peasants great satisfaction to see physicians, advocates, engineers, students working at this sort of task. People who yesterday had stood above them on the social ladder. The commander of the camp was an SS-man called Rose, a disabled war-veteran. He ran all day from one end of the camp to another, making sure that everyone was working at maximum tempo. He took care of the farm as if it were his own, and took great pains to ensure that most of it really became his own, stealing whatever he could.

At 12 noon we had a lunch-break. We got soup made from the waste of vegetables boiled in water without any fat or even salt. There was, indeed, a supply of natural products (a small amount of fat, bread, salt, etc.) sent for Jews working at the farm, but Rose sold everything on the black-market. Fortunately our farm camp was not closed, and we had the chance to buy provisions from peasants. From two p.m. till dusk again constant work. We were not accustomed to physical work and returned in the evening to our hovel so tired that most of us had not enough strength to cook or even to wash. At sunset our day ended, as the hut had no electricity. Anyone who could allow himself the luxury of a candle, endeavoured as quickly as possible to settle things that needed light, since to obtain a new candle was not simple. Exhausted, we lay on our pallets in thick darkness, and there appeared the ghosts of our past. Wives, mothers, children, circled around us. Recollections, Memories. All of a sudden someone – with no provocation – began to spin out the long-drawn-out, often extremely tragic thread of his memories. The darkness swallowed his words, empty, pale, weak sounds, which were inadequate to describe the tragic nature of wasted youth, ruined happiness, broken life. We listened, not interrupting, although fate had not treated us much better – a wife was shot down – a child killed – parents "deported" – before the eyes of a father, a dear one was raped and murdered. The stories, full of the incredible crimes of the Nazis, almost knocked one senseless, but it was good, as one was distracted from one's own ghosts. Sleepless nights of spiritual torture were our rest after the hard workday.

A new day – the same again.

Yet ... after several days, maybe after several weeks, I am not sure, since we lived without dates, holidays or Sundays, I began to awaken from the spiritual torpor into which the last ordeals had thrust me. Time eased the pain of my wounds. A worry slept on is no more a worry, it became recollection. I made contact with one peasant family. Often in the evenings, I would visit my new acquaintances and I entertained their small daughter. The peasants – unusually – extremely kind-hearted people, saw my apathy. They urged me to flee. They even promised to put me in touch with a smuggler, who would smuggle me over the border. They appealed to my common sense to brace myself and strengthen my resolution, as the Germans, in their opinion, would not long maintain the farm camp and would finally shoot all of us like dogs. The overwhelming instinct for life, the deepest desire of every living creature, awakened and raised the alarm. At last, in a way unknown to me, in a place where I was supposed to end my life, the will to live returned. I came to my senses. Everything around me emerged in another light. Only the strong, physically, spiritually or financially would endure and maybe manage to extricate themselves. *Let me be strong.*

The visit of Engels from Lvov had a decisive influence on me. One day Engels came with some friends to our farm-camp for hunting. In various amusements they spent the whole day, together with our commander Rose. After all they had to live, to amuse themselves, to play, after millions of murders and massacres, while we had to perish unavenged. This could not be! To control ourselves, to collect all my strength, to pull out and avenge? Maybe I would succeed in rescuing myself and in making public what had occurred. There were no impossibilities!

Our Herr Rose stole the vegetables of the farm *en masse*, and sent them to the black market, mostly to the ghetto in Lvov, as there he could obtain the highest prices. I made an effort to go on such a transport, of course for an appropriate bribe, in order to prepare in Lvov a way of escape for myself in the near future.

The fence around the ghetto was not finished yet, and despite the fact that from 7 September the ghetto was supposed to be closed, almost unrestricted contact with the town was still maintained. Engineer Naftali Landau, who was organizing the construction of the fence dragged out by every means the completion of the work, laying the blame on lack of building materials. A German police post was established in the ghetto, whose function was to preserve order and hunt for Aryans coming into the ghetto on their business affairs. The Aryans visited the ghetto because they could obtain everything dirt cheap, almost for a song. Every day the Germans made raids with a plentiful catch. Conditions on the streets were worse from day to day. A lonely Jew in the streets in the Aryan districts was a rarity. The risks of such a stroll, both from the Germans and from our Aryan fellow-citizens, were so great that only on extremely rare and important occasions would one allow oneself such an escapade. I went about my business while the driver – a confidant of Herr Rose – disposed of his merchandise, I succeeded in contacting a dealer in documents and ordered an appropriate set of papers. I could collect them in several days' time. I came to an understanding about my journey to the formerly Soviet, Eastern Ukraine. In a few days I was to get more details. While in Lvov, among a mass of complaints against the Germans, I learned two interesting things.

On October 1942 an *Aktion* had been arranged – similar to those against Jews – against the Aryans, especially physicians. In one night about 400 physicians were seized and deported. Nobody knew where or why. No one knew why these 400 were taken and not others, whether they had been killed, or employed in hospitals. Their fate was unknown. The second fact was the disappearance of young women and girls. In two or three cases it was ascertained that they had been placed in brothels for soldiers.

That night we returned to the camp. I brought as a present for Herr Rose a table-cloth and 12 napkins. In exchange, I received the job of repairing the bunks and maintaining the hut, which was in reality a sinecure allowing me to remain half a day in the barrack. From this time on, I did not have to work so hard. We learned from messengers from other camps that the conditions in our camp were almost excellent, comparatively of course. Thanks to the endeavours of our bunch of intellectuals we were free of the plague of lice, but fleas tormented us greatly. We could wash ourselves, we received some, though bad, provisions. In a similar camp in Borki, for instance, there was no water on the site of the camp. The SS-commander kept people longer than necessary at work, so as not to give them the chance to drink water. Simultaneously he tried to make this a source of additional profit. With the help of a rascally Jew as a go-between, he sold water by the mouthful. Scarcely before dawn broke, one could hear in the camp the shout: "A zloty for a sip of water!" Lice and dirt vexed them beyond endurance; not a day passed without beating or murder. So one had to thank God for being in a "good" camp.

Through the driver I sent news to Lvov, and at last got the information that my presence was very advisable to finish the negotiations about my escape. For a dressing gown, Herr Rose again allowed me to go to Lvov. There, I received the Aryan documents ordered for me, and fixed with a smuggler that for a payment of 1,500 zl. he would guide me through the border zone. I had to appear in his apartment on 14 November. I took half a pound of tea, and a pound of coffee as ransom for Herr Rose. After my return to the camp I counted the days. Perhaps they would pass quietly.

Two days after my visit to Lvov, we received information that another brutal *Aktion* had been carried out on Jews working as qualified craftsmen in the buildings of the Gestapo. The *Aktion* was simple to execute, as the Jews lived there together with their families. The harness-maker from our camp managed to arrange an illegal visit to see his wife and five-month-old son. Hearing an unsual hubbub, he hid himself in a niche, which his wife covered with a cupboard. A moment later in burst an SS-man with the usual wild shouts. The woman stood like a pillar of salt from fear, unable to move or say a word. But the child began to cry. This drove the German into a rage. He sprang up to the woman paralysed by fear, and slashed her on the face with a riding whip, but the child did not stop crying and the mother could not manage to quiet his sobs. The SS-man struck the child with such force that the whip cut almost through the child's neck. The boy gave an inhuman cry, like the yowling of cats at night, to use the words of his father, a helpless witness of this scene, and then became silent. The savagery of the German was not yet satisfied. He caught the mother who was holding the corpse of the child, by the neck and threw her down the stairs. The whole scene took only a few seconds. The father seeing the danger, succeeded in creeping out from his hide-out but there was nobody there. The room was empty. The terrible cry of the child would not subside in the father's ear. It drowned out all other sounds. He told me his story with dry eyes. He spoke like an automaton, straining his ears all the time. The terrible cry of the baby echoed still in his ears.

I was stunned by this new piece of news; 300 new victims, each of whom had suffered like the harness-maker's wife and child? Perhaps the Germans had begun to liquidate the camps? At our camp, summer work was practically finished, autumn work was nearing its end. I decided to speak to Herr Rose the next day and come to an agreement. The tea and coffee would surely help to convince him.

I did not like to postpone things which had to be done tomorrow. How correct this principle was I found out – once more – in a most painful way. The next day the harness-maker did not appear at roll-call. Rose sent me and the vet-physician to bring him. We found him unconscious on a bunk in his workshop in a pool of excrement and vomit. He had poisoned himself. He could no longer bear the cry resounding without cease in his brain. We reported the incident to Herr Rose. He was enraged, but did not forget to order that the shoes, watch and money which the undisciplined Jew had on be brought to him. Three days the poor man suffered before he died. It was so hard to get good poison. Nobody tried to help or rescue him; there was nothing with which to help and nobody could do anything. He lay alone in an empty shed and tormented himself to death. At last after three long days and nights, death the liberator freed him and extinguished the barely glowing glimmer of his life. We buried him in a field.

Herr Rose moved like a dark hailcloud, seeking only a chance to vent his anger. One of the older men was beaten with a whip in his bed, so that we had to work to resuscitate the victim for over an hour. With Rose in such a mood I could not speak with him. A week later, sensing something bad approaching I summoned my courage and went to his quarters. As I rightly supposed, the tea and coffee were argument enough. I got permission to go to Lvov on 12 November for three days. In no circumstances would he allow me to go to Lvov earlier. I very much feared this delay. The atmosphere was charged as before a storm. The three remaining days before my departure went very slowly, as I suspected a trick. Unfortunately I was right; one day before my departure, it became apparent that the farm labour camp was to be liquidated. We were rounded up by the SS with the greatest brutality. A crowd of obliging peasants set off in pursuit of a woman who tried to run away. The thugs soon brought her back and beat her unconscious. They kicked her, drenched in blood and unable to move, to encourage her to get up until, seeing that their efforts were hopeless, one of them took his gun and finished her off. A moment later, after a few paces, he phlegmatically lit a cigarette with his worthy colleagues. Where did they grow such people? Could Hitler actually create in a few short years such thugs totally lacking of any human feeling? This could not have been exclusively his achievement. Enough that he could claim the merit of bringing into the daylight the beast which slept in the soul of the Huns.

A column of those left alive was lined up. We were to go to Lvov. In spite of the deterrent lesson, several looked around for an opportunity to run away. Unfortunately we were so completely surrounded by Ukrainians guards that there was not room for a try. After an hour and a half of marching, we arrived at Lvov. We were marching through the streets of the Aryan district. No one deigned to pay any attention to us. Yet more Yids being led to their death – a minor incident! We were brought to the prison on Lecki Street, one of the German hells on earth.

15 · Beyond the Imagination of Dante

The Germans enlarged the building of the former-police-jail to fit their new needs. But it appeared insufficient as 120 people were crammed into a couple of connected cells with a total area no more than 28 sq.feet. There was hardly enough room to stand. It was impossible to sit or to lie down. Though the cells were unheated, the heat was indescribable. In the afternoon a jailer demanded that four people go with him. People in fear of the whip draw aside, fearing to go. At last he took four at random. After several moments he returned and did the same. As not one of those taken returned all were sure that these had been executed. Some old people began to intone the prayers for the dead, someone got hysterical. The jailer repeated the same procedure at short intervals for an hour or two, or perhaps it was a few minutes only. The scoundrel burst each time into the cell, took four people and departed. At last seeing that he had achieved the proper effect, that people were in extreme despair and had become apathetic, he announced that we were going to be searched. The result was as he had hoped. People rallied themselves from their apathy to torment themselves with something new. During a search, one was always beaten, and besides, almost everyone had something hidden in case opportunity presented itself to buy oneself out; a watch, a ring, or money. Where to hide it? I had my Aryan documents. There was no place to hide anything, so I crumpled the certificate of birth and baptism, and threw them into a corner. A document with my photo I tore into small pieces. When my turn came I went, but immediately outside the door the jailer released a dog on us. Running in a breakneck rush on the stairs, breathing heavily we burst into a room through a half-open door, immediately to receive a slap in the face. The search was extremely thorough and they took everything. They did not leave in our pockets even a grain of dust; of course even tobacco dust they took out of mischievousness, throwing it all into a garbage can. During the search, for any answer one was beaten or for the fact that one had dared to possess something. If you had nothing, you would be beaten more as there was no profit from you. Then the return to the cell, again pursued by the dog. Finally, despite small injuries (no one was without a bite or two but alive) and almost whole, we found ourselves in the same cell at about 11 p.m. the search completed. My birth certificate was awaiting me in the corner where I had thrown it. I took it and hid it; perhaps it would still be of use.

It was night. The light was not turned off. We stood crowded like swine in a pigsty. People did not think about eating, but how to relieve nature. No-one dared to knock on the door. The two buckets that stood in a corner had been full for a long time. People were unable to restrain themselves and were relieving themselves where they stood. Very soon we stood deep in urine and excrement. Slowly we were obliged to strip ourselves, because the heat was unbearable. We sweated, breathing heavily, hawked and spat. Nobody even dreamed of sleeping. So passed the first night. In the morning, during inspection, the jailer ordered us to clean the cells of the excrement and urine and as a "favour" allowed us to carry out the buckets.

During the six days of our stay in the jail, we did not receive a bite of food or a drop of water. The stinking air and the unparalleled stifling heat caused an incredible degree of thirst. We sat so crowded, that we simply crawled one over another. We tried to organize groups and place them somewhere to create a chance for a rest at least, taking turns to sit. The dirt and lice increased. If my prior experiences had not hardened me, I believe I would have gone mad from the sights which – as in a nightmare – passed before my eyes. Someone standing near a wall played with a bedbug, wandering on the wall drowsy from freshly drunk blood in a "cat-and-mouse" game. Another one near me, deloused himself and crushed the caught lice on his finger-nail with sadistic satisfaction. Another sight brought me almost to retching. A young boy unwound the dirty rags from a wound on his thigh. The dirty bloodsoaked cloth finally exposed an open, inflamed wound. Around the wound were sitting a swam of lice sucking blood directly from the open wound. The boy with a rotary movement of his finger removed the lice and shook them down onto the floor. Afterwards he bandaged the wound in the putrid rags.

The torment of the overcrowding lasted uninterruptedly for six endless days and six nights. I am sure Hell had not invented such torment, but for the Herrenvolk nothing was too extreme. Four people in the group died, no one even knew when. It was hardly possible to persuade people – stupefied into apathy – to stack the corpses one on top or another in a corner as compactly as possible so as to leave more space for the living. The hunger which tore our guts subsided into silence after two or three days, the more so as thirst consumed us. People fainted, licked the sweat from their faces, to moisten their parched lips a little. At first my lips were so dry that they cracked when I spoke. Afterwards my mouth began to dry out, my tongue was as rough as a rasp and did not want to move; I could not utter a sound. I began to understand the descriptions of thirst in a desert. The day before the last, I was in a state of stupor. I got hallucinations, and believed I saw things. The general theme was water. Before my eyes danced a glass of wonderful cold water appetizing with all the colours of the rainbow. half-conscious I reached for it – only to waken from the wonderful daydream to terrible reality. The thirst brought me to such a state of mind that I devised wild plans, to attack the jailer, to break off the iron bars and jump out to the street and so on.

At last on the seventh day of our stay in the prison, we were marched out of the cell. Our only worry was to quench our thirst. In the court yard at a roll-call, Engels and Wepke honoured us by their presence. During the roll-call, one man fell from exhaustion. Wepke with the utmost composure removed a glove and in cold blood shot him, without interrupting the inspection. Afterwards we were arranged in fours and led to the train lorries that were waiting for us. I must describe one typical incident. A Ukrainian militiaman was not exactly at the designated place, perhaps a yard away. Major Engels attacked him and begun to pummel him, threw him to the ground and kicked him like a dog; a commissioned officer attacking his subordinate with his fists. Wildness, brutality and savagery were the principal forms of relations among the Germans. We, though oppressed, saw with pleasure that someone else besides the Jews got to feel the sympathy of the Nazis. Finally the four tram-lorries were full up and moved off. We went by Janowska Street in the direction of Janowski Camp. Were we returning to the camp? Deadly fear could be seen on all faces. To pass another hell before our death? No! We were going further on to Kleparow railway station for B E L Z E C!

At the last tram-stop, a police squad was awaiting us as further escort. They surrounded us. I heard them say among themselves: "political criminals". They crowded us into waiting freight-wagons. My first move was to the window opening. I found a little snow and moistened my lips. I regained composure and surveyed the situation. The window-opening was barred but only partly, the remainder was closed by barbed wire. It seemed possible to break this out and I might be able to jump. With the assistance of companions who lifted me up, using the confusion on the railway station during the loading of the rest of the people into other freight wagon – I managed to kick out the wire that secured the window opening before the guard was posted by our wagon.

In our wagon were about 80 people. All knew we were going to Belzec, which meant extermination. In spite of this, everyone tried to find the most comfortable space for himself, as if we were going to live and not to die. We were awaiting the movement of the train at each moment. But nothing warned us it would occur so fast. All the time, we observed through the window the traffic at the station. New people were continually brought and loaded into the wagons. Around noon the train of wagons was ready to start. The wagons were surrounded by guards. It would start only after dark so nobody would see the passing death train. I noted that the Germans deliberately misinformed even their own people – trying to hide the truth and not leaving any traces or witnesses. For instance, the escort on the train thought we were "political criminals", the guard by the wagon on the railway-station, who had not seen us being loaded, was told that typhus victims were lying in the cars, others surely heard yet another tale. No one apart from the officers knew for sure that thousands of people in the bloom of strength, young, able to work and thousands of women, children and oldsters were being driven to death.

Most astonishing was that the frame of mind in the car did not agree with the descriptions of various writers about the mood of people being conducted to death. People behaved with the utmost composure, there were no scenes of despair; no crying or complaining. The talk was about the actual state of affairs, about the war, the situation at the fronts. Business affairs were not neglected. Of course, also prophecies about the future that threatened. Even the theme of Belzec was discussed. How long would the ride last? It was not apathy, but some uncanny determination or acceptance of fate. Everyone was lying on the floor of the car, delighted with the chance to rest after six days of standing. In the evening the guards, perhaps fearing rioting or an attempt to break out from the wagons, began a wild fusillade through the boards of the cars to intimidate the victims. Some even pressed their guns to the boards and shot. A shot point-blank above my head deafened me. The swine shot into our car through the planks. My friend Mgr. S.L. from Krakow, on whose knees I laid my head – twitched convulsively. My questions remained unanswered. The bullet had gone through the board and had penetrated his head. He died in a moment – a happy death. We removed the corpse and the living proceeded further on their way as the train rolled along in the direction of Belzec.

16 • A Leap into Life

Immediately after the train left the station, we began jumping from the window-opening. The Germans had stationed machine guns on three wagon-roofs; next to the locomotive, in the middle of the train and on the last car. They were shooting almost without pause. They killed or wounded many of the jumpers which did not intimidate other daredevils, as all knew that by leaping they did not risk more, rather less, having at least a chance. At last after about 20 kilometres my turn came. I extricated myself from the opening and remained hanging on a tiny fragment of the grille by the collar of my overcoat. All my endeavours to free myself were of no avail. I did not want to tear my coat, as it would be clear evidence that I had jumped from the train and was running away. Seeing that I could not jump, I hauled myself back into the car. Exhausted by the enormous physical and nervous strain I laid myself down to sleep in a corner of the car. It is hard to believe but I slept deeply for nearly two hours. The silence wakened me. The train was standing at a small station. I recognized it as Zolkiew. Not yet Belzec. I asked some passing railwayman how far to Belzec. He almost leaped on me, abusing me for being an absolute ass, a coward, and using abusive invective about my family, which would have made every street urchin of Lvov proud. He shouted – "Jump you idiot! Why do you let yourself be taken to death? ! TRY!" This tore me from my sleep. I decided to try another jump and succeeded. Immediately after the train left the station, I prepared myself by stripping off my overcoat and wound it around my neck. Again I extricated myself carefully through the window-opening. The train was going now with much greater speed, to make jumping impossible. The wagons were not made for such a speed, and almost leaped from the rails. I timed my jump so as not to crash into a telegraph pole and leapt. At the moment of my leap I heard the rattle of the machine gun. I fell down and rolled some yards to a telegraph-pole and stopped. A whole magazine from the machine-gun whistled over my head, I heard the plap-plap, a sound like smacking dough, as the bullets hit the pole. I did not even have time to feel fear, as the train had already run away and the wonderful rear light of the last car glittered red. I had ESCAPED!

Still lying down, I began to eat snow. After temporarily quenching my thirst, I raised myself, seeking my cap and the way to Lvov. It was 70 to 80 kilometres through forests. I went back along the rails, till I saw the lights of Zolkiew.

Here I turned through fields to the forest. It was really a strange thing, this leap from the literal embrace of death back into life. I remember nothing of the first hours of my wandering through the snow-covered forest. I did not feel hungry in spite of the seven-day fast, the snow had quenched my thirst. There was nothing but to go straight on to Lvov. In the forest I met another "jumper". We went along together. After some hours of marching, the exhausted organism began to demand its rights. We decided that one of us would go to the nearest village to see about provisions. The lot fell on my comrade. Soon we were near a village. Hiding in the forest we sought a hut as near as possible to the forest. He went. I gave him a sweater for barter. After several minutes he came back with half a loaf of bread, telling me that he had been chased away. They threw him the half loaf of bread, as to a dog, after taking the sweater from him. We devoured the bread in a second, like ravenous wolves while walking constantly looking over our shoulders to check that nobody was following us. At noon I decided to try my luck. In fact fate smiled on me. In the village of Raty in a hut at the edge of the forest I got a helping hand. Not from the calculated reaction of an intelligent man, nor from a humanitarian, but from spontaneous impulse. A man who understood what it means to be in the position of hunted game helped me. He helped me, a jail-bird, a simple everyday offender, perhaps a thief, maybe only a brawler. Never will I forget it. He helped me also because he did not suspect me to be a Jew. My comrade, whom he immediately recognized as a Jew, he would not receive even for a moment. After very long persuasion, he gave in and allowed him to sleep in the barn, on condition that he would leave at first light to contact the Jews in Zolkiew.

I succeded in deceiving with some fantastic story, explaining the reason for my wandering through the forest, unshaven, hungry, not well clothed. A little gambling on his hatred of the Germans, a light twang on the patriotic string and I was promoted to an old friend. I remembered from the short stories of Jack London about hobos, that the reward of a good story was a good place to sleep and a full stomach. Often one's life depended on a good story. My host entertained me like a king. I washed myself and shaved. Afterwards I was seated at a table before a whole bowl of soup. I tried to restrain my wolfish hunger, but in a moment the bowl was completely empty. Some rounds of home-brewed hooch and friendship bloomed like a springtime flower. In the evening, I became acquainted with some colleague of his. He introduced me as a companion from Brygydki (a well-known jail in Lvov for short-term prisoners). I smoked his tobacco, lost money to him in a card game; in a word I got the best possible heart-warming entertainment and all this as a result of telling a fine story and since I hadn't been "identified" as a Jew. My companion from the forest would have to freeze in the barn, because of his reprehensible non-Aryan physiognomy.

The whole of the next day I rested. The following morning, I think it was Monday, my new friend advised me to go further on, because in such a small village I would stand out. He advised me to travel on the main highway, as no one would even imagine that a suspicious type would dare do such a thing. I remembered a Chinese proverb that clever mice hide in the cat's ear and took his wise advice. I circled around Zolkiew and joined the highway to Lvov. A full day's march passed uneventfully.

From a peasant returning from Zolkiew I learned that just that day an *Aktion* against the Jews of Zolkiew had been carried out. Of course I didn't want to leap into fire and decided to seek a sleeping place in a nearby village. My "good" appearance and a new story, induced the at first, very suspicious peasants to give me a night's lodging. Before going to sleep I murmured some prayers, with which I set at rest the sensitive conscience of the peasant, who feared – God forbid – to give a shelter to a Jew. At first light I was on my way to Lvov.

A few kilometres after Zolkiew a Ukrainian policeman on a bicycle accosted me. He tried to trap me, talking to me as to a Jew. After my indignant reaction, he demanded that I show him my documents. With the self-confidence indispensable in such a situation I showed him my birth certificate rescued from the search in the jail. The boor of course didn't understand even a word of the document written in Latin and demanded something else. I answered brazenly that I had nothing else and tore from his hand the worthless paper, proposing to go to the Gestapo, where for sure they would find out if I was an Aryan. The policeman was flabbergasted. Though he was reluctant to let a sure quarry slip from his hands. He demanded 500 zloty as a ransom. I burst out laughing and of course refused. It was very easy for me as my pockets were totally empty. Finally he tried to threaten me as a Pole (he was a *Volksdeutsch*), since I had no documents in order and would find myself in great difficulties with the police. I remained as unyielding as a rock.

It was the one time that lack of money made me better off. The informer seeing at last that he couldn't squeeze out anything of me, even for a glass of vodka, was completely convinced that I was an Aryan. A Jew would have been much weaker. He then enquired where I was going. Again I told him a story. The "kind-hearted" policeman directed me on my way to Lvov and went away seeking a better victim. Following his advice, I passed Zaszkow and found myself again on the Lvov highway. The advice of my host in Raty was correct. Nobody paid any attention to me. Nobody dreamt that a Jew would dare to wander quietly on a main highway. In Kulikov, a Ukrainian militiaman accosted me and took me to the police-station. My heart was in my mouth. At the station he charged me as a Pole suspected of being a black marketeer. I gave an inner sigh of relief. Again after a fantastic story about my brother who had disappeared taken by Soviets, his wife crying her heart out, two children perishing from hunger, told with vivid expressions and gestures and after disarming any suspicion with appropriate nerve and impudence, I walked out of the station with a steady step, but with knees trembling from anxiety and fear. The remainder of my journey to Lvov was uneventful.

17 · Stations of the Cross

From an acquaintance working in a factory in the Aryan district I obtained the obligatory armband for Jews and went into the ghetto. The streets were dead. It was two days after the latest *Aktion.* At the end of October 1942 the authorities began to give to various German firms badges for working Jews, marked "W" for *Wehrmacht* (Army), that is working for the Army, and "R" for *Rüstungswerk* (the war industry). The badges were given to all working Jews. People's experiences made them fear all labels, but some irrepressible characters immediately laughed at this new one. Many realized that a new massacre was in the offing and that the new badges were nothing but a finer sieve. People did not take the new badges seriously because one of the largest and most important of the German enterprises, Cremin's Rohstoffverfassung, which collected on raw materials included in the four-year plan, did not receive badges. On the night of 15–16 November, about midnight, people knew that on the following morning an *Aktion* would begin. The Jewish militia was ordered to be in readiness. Warnings were at once sent to relatives and friends, to be prepared. AKTION! The sound of this word – even now a year later – when I write it, the very thought of it makes my blood run cold. I cannot find the few words to put onto a scrap of paper, to describe the stream of blood and tears, implicit in the word. Before, we never had any real idea of what fear meant. Now, a few hours before an *Aktion*, people in the ghetto understood. Wild primeval animal terror, before an elemental calamity that had invaded and paralysed every mind. Human beings felt like dust in the face of the vast power that opposed them. The feeling of fright during such a moment can be compared to that of an animal running from a prairie-fire.

At 5 a.m., dozens of Gestapomen appeared at the ghetto. Their torches glimmered in the darkness of the night like the eyes of wild animals in the jungle. They drew people in the direction of the gate where Katzman had with foresight ordered electric light to be installed some days before. There others were awaiting, led by Wepke, Engeld, Inquart and Lenard. They beat, shot and tormented old men, women, children and cripples, taking them all on trucks and tram-lorries. The destination was BELZEC. The remainder were directed to go to work. To work?? … More appropriate to say … till the next *Aktion*, when the ring would narrow still more, when the sieve would be finer. Why should I multiply descriptions, once more describing the bloody scenes, once more some freak of beastliness rising above the usual level; it should be enough for everyone to know that about eight thousand helpless people perished, and a few or a few dozen people were authorized to select men for death or life.

I have mentioned several times Belzec camp, without giving more details about the functioning of this and other extermination camps. Several such camps, better termed "finishing off plants", were located on the territory of former Poland–Oswiecim (Auschwitz), Majdanek, Treblinka, Belzec, Malkinia and others. Belzec was – as now we may say with the possibility of comparison – one of the more primitive and less developed establishments of this sort. Surely the commander lacked the creative initiative in the field of extermination of people, or perhaps he was not spiritually mature enough to rise to the level of the creators of Auschwitz or Majdanek.

I met a former inmate of the Belzec camp, who had succeeded in escaping. I heard from him authentic details of the occurrences beyond the barbed wire, at the reception of transports of victims. The train went to a special siding in the camp. Immediately the unloading began, accompanied of course by beating. Forty young and strong men were separated from the rest – my informer among them. The staff of Belzec was composed of Ukrainians, with a small number of SS men in command. An SS-man gave a speech to the people, denying the evil rumours which alleged that in Belzec people were murdered. Germany needed today every working hand, nobody would be killed as everyone was indispensable; here people were sorted for appropriated work not excluding even the oldest, who would be assigned, for example, to weaving mats and similar light jobs. The principal problem of the camp was thorough disinfection. Because of this, all were asked to remove their clothes and go for a bath. He pointed at two buildings, one for women and the second for men. People did not believe him. The scene ran silently as there was no choice. They stripped. Afterwards came a call to hand over gold, valuables and money, and they were marched into the buildings – the gas chambers.

The last ones found it hard to find room to enter the "bath building", it was so overcrowded. At last they were pushed into the gas-chambers with the help of truncheons and whips. The gates were closed with a clang. An old internal combustion engine was started. After about an hour, the 40 men who had been separated were forced to carry the corpses out to the 50 metres-long ditches dug with a bulldozer. My informant carried corpses to a ditch near the fence of the camp. A Ukrainian followed him all the time. After several hours, tired with constantly having to drive, watch and administer blows, he was almost incapable of keeping his attention on the prisoner. My informant then succeeded in getting himself to the fence, beneath the barbed-wire and away. I believe that he was the only man, apart from the Germans, who saw the inside of the camp and lived to tell about it. Martin Gilbert in *The Holocaust* (London, 1986) p. 287, claims that 'from Belzec there were to be no more than two survivors.'

18 · The Ukrainians

The Ukrainians burned with a wild and unbridled anti-semitism. One would think those who had so often been allies of the Jews in political clashes in pre-war Poland would understand the situation of other oppressed people and so would not behave as enemies to the Jews. Unfortunately things turned out differently.

For the anti-semitism of the Polish population, there could perhaps in some measure be the excuse of economic competition, as in pre-war Poland, the Poles were continually outdistanced by Jews. More important their hostility was stimulated by the propaganda of the clergy who inculcated feelings of hatred towards the Jews. All this does not apply to the Ukrainians. In economic matters, the Ukrainians strove during the years before the war for autonomy, and seemingly achieved this aim. Whole streets in the Ukrainian part of Poland were full of Ukrainian shops. Almost all branches were represented. The Ukrainian population avoided Polish shops, buying only from Ukrainians, sometimes even preferring to visit a Jewish firm than a Polish one. The propaganda during the years 1935 to 1939 announcing in large shop-signs "Christian firm" attracted no Ukrainian customers. At this time, the Ukrainians tried to achieve independence in all possible ways in the area of production by the help of their strongly developed cooperative movement. It should be stressed that they were met by friendly neutrality from the Jews and sometimes even by joint action.

Despite all this, at the first opportunity during the German occupation of Lvov, the Ukrainian population threw off their mask. Modern science claims every phobia – including anti-semitism – must have its grounds. The reason for the Ukrainians' phobia may have been the desire to ape the Poles, who were socially at the top, above them, even though every Ukrainian would probably bridle on hearing such an explanation. If such examplars of western culture as the Germans were eliminating and ousting Jews, why should the Ukrainians fall behind? For a nation with a very thin veneer of civilization, rough, without a tradition of culture, in their primitive way of thinking, the times offered an opportunity to find themselves on the same level with the Poles with their imposing traditions, culture and historic past and perhaps even to raise themselves to the heights of the Germans. The fact that this equalizing found its level on the standard of the foulest deeds, on the level of the lowest plane, which would become the blackest page of the history of the German nation for many centuries, was for the Ukrainians without meaning.

The Germans lured the Ukrainians to their side, dangling before them the mirage of a free Ukraine. Very soon after the occupation of almost the whole Ukraine, these hopes were shattered. They were obliged to abandon this dream, and the whole of the not very numerous Ukrainian intelligentsia, abandoned any political activity and separated themselves completely from the Germans. The rabble remained, without any exaggeration, a wild, primitive mob, which the Germans, with their typical perfidy, used as a tool to realize their foul purposes, first and foremost in murdering the Jews.

From the boorish multitude, which included a majority of the Ukrainian population of Lvov, the Germans immediately after entering Lvov, formed a militia. Immediately, the militia was set to its task, which was to help the Germans in the extermination of the Jews. The first days of the Germans in Lvov (1–3 July 1941), were a period of wild cruelty by the Ukrainians against the Jews, ostensibly in revenge for the murdered Ukrainians they claimed they had found in the jails of Lvov. I do not need to repeat the descriptions of savage beastliness of the Ukrainians, which reached such a pitch that the Germans were obliged to take away the rifles they had given to the militia to stop the bloodthirsty attempts of the mob. Among the 15,000 people who perished during those three days was one of the editors of the daily paper *Chwila*, Emil Janusz Igel, murdered together with several hundred lawyers, physicians and engineers.

By this achievement the Ukrainians – especially the militia – won a "glorious" name, which they maintained later when they were degraded from the rank of hangmen to the level of hangman's flunkeys. Even the Germans now had enough of this bloody orgy. The Ukrainians had to be satisfied with scraps, and were only allowed to execute the orders of their great German guides. The latter replaced primitive, wild, murder by the systematic order so beloved by the German character. They formed from the Ukrainians whole units, known under various names: militia, Ukrainian SS group, "S" (*Sonderdienst*), Black Ukrainians (menials for special functions), guards at all sorts of camps (especially extermination camps). But no matter what the name of an actual unit, there was only one purpose; to murder, torment the helpless, torture, to get drunk whenever possible and arrange wild revels among the suffering victims. What a fine aim – the fulfilment of the yearning of thousands of adolescent boys and girls – to murder Jews without getting one's deserts.

The rest of the population having failed to elbow their way into the magnificent uniform of a hangman's servant, managed to find another way of tormenting Jews. This, they achieved by participating in robbing them in different ways. The Ukrainians were for a long time favoured by the Germans and received many privileges compared with the rest of the population. By sheer force they occupied the apartments of Jews together with furniture and all that was in them, turning the owners into the streets. They blackmailed their Jewish neighbours with threats of denunciation. They denounced anyone who possessed what they wanted. Afterwards, when conditions were a little normalized, they began to work in a different way. Under the pretence of friendship they undertook to store valuable things (furniture, furs, jewellery, etc.). The Jews, driven into a corner, were thankful for these signs of friendship and gave up for storage most of their valuables, thus leaving themselves at the mercy of every scoundrel. The Ukrainians, having the goods of the Jews for a relatively long time in their possession, became so accustomed to the fact, that if the owner wanted to get some things back, he would be met at best with refusal and at worst by denunciation to the Gestapo. So by default they became the legal owners of the goods with which they had been entrusted. This should not be regarded as a normal business loss. The only source of livelihood was income from personal possessions sold at the moment of need. Whoever had nothing to sell must perish, and whoever made a bad deal in selling only accelerated his end. The scoundrels perceived all this very well, but being without conscience, took no account of it at all.

The Germans decided to annihilate Jews and did everything in their power to achieve this aim. The Ukrainians, without necessarily supporting this goal, added one more heavy thorn to the crown of thorns which the Germans placed on our heads. It would be difficult today to say whether the Germans would have been able to carry out the murder of European Jews, had they not had such complete and devoted helpers in the Ukrainians. But I am certain that the Germans would not have achieved such an almost complete result, if not for the behaviour of the Ukrainians. The Germans enticed their lackeys by giving them victims to torment since they had nothing else that they wanted to offer them; this was enough. The Germans let them feel their contempt at every step. This did not dishearten their helpers. They found their outlet in harassing the Jews, who were placed far beneath them in the hierarchy of peoples by the Germans. The primitive savagery of the intelligent Germans needs no discussion. They knew perfectly well what they were doing, while the Ukrainians without thought allowed themselves to be used for the dirtiest portions of the infamous task, achieving no gain for themselves by doing so.

19 · Behind the Walls of the Ghetto

The "ghetto" was new to me because during the period that it was being organized and closed off, I was in the Farm Labour Camp. After several days, I became fully conversant with this new German tool for tormenting people. The ghetto was situated in one of the worst districts of Lvov. The whole area was surrounded by a fence 8 feet high, with a closely guarded gate on Peltewna Street. This part of the town was almost completely without sewers, without electricity or gas, without any conveniences, even the most primitive. Apartment houses were few, the majority of dwellings were tumbledown structures and half-ruined huts that long before the war had been condemned to be pulled down on account of their bad conditions. These houses were one storey high, sometimes two-storeys, they had small windows mostly without glass, but fantastically patched up with cartons, rugs, boards or plywood. The colour of the outer walls was a dirty grey, full of mud spots, splattered by every passing vehicle from the ubiquitous deep puddles. In addition, the lower walls of almost all houses were a rotten-greenish colour from the damp. The north wall was invariably saturated with moisture to the top and discoloured. The roofs were mostly shingles with frayed tracery, eaten away by mouldy holes. After closing the front door, one was obliged to stop in fear of the unknown interior, because it was pitch dark. This fear was quite justified as the entrance hall, its floorboards long since rotten, swarmed with treacherous holes awaiting an incautious foot. After passing through this trap, one found onself in a yard. Here there were puddles with stagnant water, the surface sometimes green with a crust, innumerable heaps of garbage accumulated over a long time, broken articles of furniture and, overwhelming with its dirt and stench, a repulsive toilet knocked together from some boards. If the house was "comfortable", on one of the walls in the yard would be a water-tap with an inevitably broken sink, emitting a hellish stink. The living rooms matched this magnificent whole, the walls unpainted or whitewashed from time immemorial. In a corner a small clay stove with a broken and rusted oven.

Into such a district and in such "homes" about 50,000 people were crammed together. The space per person was 1–1.5 square metres; just enough to lie down and store a suitcase. It is easy to imagine the conditions in which people had to live. In a smallish room eight to ten persons were living: men, women, children, healthy and sick, quiet and nervous, familiar and strange, rich and poor, with only one common feature – they were Jews.

How did a "normal" grey day pass within these grey walls of the ghetto? Early in the morning long before dawn, everyone got up. A thorough wash was out of the question, so people could only wash hands and face. Breakfast was also much simplified. Yesterday's soup was warmed upon a kerosene stove or primus-stove. It would be a shame to use the kerosene-stove with hard-fought-for kerosene, acquired by the use of great influence and at a fantastic price (about 20 zloty for a litre) to heat the ersatz coffee. In addition to coffee, saccharine and bread, two expensive and scarce commodities, were required. The little piece of bread, which was available, everyone saved for himself to have something to eat during the working day. About 5.30 in the morning one had to leave home because the workers of each factory assembled so as to leave the ghetto together. Before the exit in every home was a large sheet of paper on the inner side of the door with the inscription: "Attention armband!" It was very necessary to remember the "holy armband" since to forget could mean death. With a last glance at the right arm and chest to check that the band was in place, they left home. Would they return? Who knew?

The columns gathered at a point not far away from the gate. Naturally, there were no street lamps in the ghetto, so in the darkness one heard monotonous shouts, similar to peddlers' cries, but much quieter so as not to awaken the sleeping dragon. "V.H.B.! V.H.B. here." "Where is Lepege?" "Has Rohstoff already gone?" "Galikol, we are leaving." The calling and seeking reached their peak with the approach of 6 a.m. The columns began to leave, the foremen of each group counted the number present; it had to be reported at the gate. The counting needed to be very accurate; a mistake could mean the death of the one not counted or of the foreman himself. These moments of waiting at the exit were the worst when the pitiless frost attacked us, inadequately clothed, undernourished and without bodily resistance, and fear devoured the nerves before every passage through the gate. At last we set off. We marched in threes. The foreman stood at the gate and reported to the SS-man. A nervous tremble went through all the column. Who was at the gate? Mansfeld or Siler? What mood he was in today? It may sound paradoxical, but upon the mood of such an individual one's life depended. Nothing prevented him from killing anyone whom he did not fancy. We marched, trying to appear resilient and in a good frame of mind. The cold glance of the SS-man was gliding over us. No one could know where danger was lurking. The armband might attract his eyes. Such an event meant being taken out of the column and … death. At last we had passed through the gate. Some steps in the glaring light of gate's lamps, and we plunged into the benevolent darkness beyond. People were so browbeaten and intimidated that they felt safer in the protective shadows of the night. Admittedly one could not see even one step before, but one could also not be seen. In the blessed darkness the formation became a little more relaxed. People began to talk, to exchange news, to straighten their clothes, to check their haversacks made from gas-mask holders, an obligatory part of everyone's attire. The march from the gate to the work-place, was, in reality, the only unconstrained period. Nobody was guarding us, nobody driving us. It was a rare moment during the day- without a whip which, at any moment, could fall on one's head.

After the columns of people had gone to work, the streets of the ghetto were dead, with occasional patrols of Jewish militia. Apart from the janitors and the *Putzfrauen* (cleaning women), nobody officially remained in the ghetto. Of course if someone hid, he naturally did not dare to show himself on the street, as this would earn death from the SS-men Mansfeld or Siler, continually hunting for "shirkers" and "marauders". The hollow silence of unnaturally empty streets gave the impression of a dead city, a town of living corpses.

At the work-places, stress did not leave us till evening. The work was not that hard, but every moment was poisoned with fear of the German or Ukrainian overseer. There was no day without new rumours about reductions of workers, of threatened sackings, of selections. Whatever they were called, there was only one meaning – elimination from work simply meant death. The reductions were ordered by the Gestapo, only to exclude a number of people from the circle of the living.

During breakfast break there were discussions of the latest radio news, whispered of course into one's ear by Aryan peddlers of cigarettes, bread, meat, etc. who daily visited every factory or office where Jews were working. It may seem that we incurred an unrepayable debt of gratitude towards our Aryan fellow-citizens supplying us – deprived of freedom – with food. Let this not press heavily on the naive. The provident Aryans included in the bargain a very fair margin of about 300 to 400 per cent profit for their "risky and magnanimous" deeds. The working day ended at 6 p.m. Again, the column went back to the ghetto. Behind every column in the morning and evening, went a militiaman, as from 15 December 1942, it was prohibited for Jews to go alone in the town, not in a group or without an overseer. Sometimes one was lucky and succeeded in making some purchases at a friendly kiosk. At a news-stand, it was sometimes possible to buy milk; at a tobacco kiosk, sometimes there was bread or meat; a soda-water kiosk sometimes sold flour or cereals. Of course all this at exorbitant prices, as these goods were sold surreptitiously. The prices were so high because trade in such products was prohibited, and secondly they were selling to Jews. The full haversack (capacity 2½ to 5 lb) which everyone carried coming back from work, was almost the only way of smuggling food into the ghetto. Officially not one gram of food was supplied to the ghetto. At the time of the return from work the gate was not dangerous. Very rarely did the "masters" Mansfeld or Siler await the columns returning from work. The procession of the returning workers, resembling spectres, trudged through the streets of the town, where once they had lived as humans. Now in rags, dirty, worn out by work beyond their strength, morally oppressed by the Nazi bringers of culture, they did not even see the street nor their former living places. Now they wanted only to return as fast as possible to their homes only to be beyond the dangers of the street, only to rest a little, to wash, to eat something nourishing and go to sleep. To sleep without dreams, as even dreams in these atrocious times carried you to a better world.

After the return of the columns the streets became animated for a short time. At the intersection between Peltewna, Kresowa and Lokietek Streets, within the ghetto, was a square through which everyone had to pass. There bustled Jewish pedlars, bringing goods and selling them at the risk of their lives. On the surface no merchandise could be seen, but something was muttered to the passer-by in an undertone, which to the uninitiated would sound like a password: "Hard only – three a zloty" meant the highest luxury of the ghetto, a sweetmeat concocted from fried poppy seed and potato syrup; "A quarter for a half" meant bread in pieces; "Egyptian Gold, Symphonia, one and a half", various brands of cigarettes, which because of the high prices paid were only within the means of the very rich.

At last home. This grandiloquent title meant a room occupied together with 8 or 10 others. The first thing after entering was to strip naked to check every piece of clothing for lice. Men and women were mutually unembarrassed and during this inspection, exchanged impressions of the day and talked over the results of the search. Afterwards a thorough washing. The finding of lice, nothing extraordinary, aroused the fear of spotted typhus, the calamity of the ghetto. Not all washed themselves, only those who held on compulsively to civilization. Meanwhile, all the primus stoves rumbled, working at full power, preparing supper, as this was the only warm and nourishing meal of the day. It was a plate of soup, but it was not pre-war soup, it was a special gruel, rightly called "ghetto-soup". This soup was cooked from millet, beans, potatoes, hulled barley without any vegetables. In a luxury version it came with noodles. The consistency of the soup was such that a spoon would stand in it. In pre-war soup nobody was interested. After soup, a luxury cup of black coffee made of beetroot syrup with saccharine and sometimes a hunk of bread, or at least what we in the ghetto called bread. The outer appearance of the loaf was normal, but inside it was an agglomeration of unknown and mysterious ingredients. Perhaps it contained some proportion of flour, although its colour, grey-brownish-black reminded one rather of mud. It was sticky, moist and viscous, never drying out and despite its not especially stimulating appearance and even less stimulating taste, was the most sought after titbit. One should not assume that such bread was supplied in a normal way to the ghetto, it was also a smuggled item and was purchased for a great deal of money (about 30 zl. for 1 kilo).

After this Lucullan feast, a break followed for social purposes, but only on the premises. After 8 p.m., there was a curfew and everyone was so tired that there was never enough strength for visiting. There were enough people on the premises, as the house had five or six rooms, so at least 50 to 60 people were quartered there.

People got together for half an hour's injection of optimism. During the day, the theme was the horror of the day, so in the evening, the radio news was commented upon with perpetual optimism, despite the nightmare awaiting us in the morning; our Jewish optimism dictated our opinions. Although the Russians were hundreds of kilometres away from Lvov, we saw our saviours already at the gates of the town. If someone reminded us that an *Aktion* or some other Nazi harassment threatened, he would, receive from all sides the answer that surely the Germans would wait before acting, as for example, in another town there were riots because of the lack of potatoes ... One man claimed: "Stalin had decided by a certain date to clear Russian soil of every German" ... A quietly expressed doubt that this news originated perhaps from the "A.J.W." (as Jews want) news-agency was drowned in the flood of optimism without anybody paying attention. Finally the situation on the home front was discussed, the Judenrat, the extravagances of the Jewish militia, food prices, the chances of purchasing food and so on. Best friends advised one another on the fine points of giving bribes – an everyday necessity in the ghetto.

Nine in the evening approached, and one had to go to the room where one was sleeping and help to arrange the setting out of the pallets for the night. This was not a trifle. A strategic plan was not enough; what was needed was the experience of many many nights in finding the best way to utilize the space available. After arranging the pallets, there could be no further movement, there was no room. Normal beds, camp-beds, trundle-beds, placed in various directions occupied every inch of space. Not everyone had the opportunity of going to bed. Some people slept in pairs in one bed in opposite directions, one person's head alongside the feet of the other. Some, illegally sheltered in a flat of working people, waited on chairs till the people got up to work in the morning to be able to go to bed.

Finally everyone was placed, after a few quarrels, disputes and the outflowing of gall accumulated from helplessness. After one or two buckets for natural needs were taken out, the day ended. At last everybody lay down, tired by the daily grind, stretched their limbs on their pallets and went to sleep.

Slowly the snoring, rumbling, coughing, grunting and wheezing began to disturb the silence of the night. You could not hear a sound from the street, no late passer-by broke the stillness. There was no policeman, guardian of order. Sometimes there reverberated a series of shots – the sound of a vagary of good humour on the part of a German or a Ukrainian and then again dead silence. During the night, almost everyone came to use the bucket several times. Nobody was ashamed in front of others. Someone thinking in pre-war terms would surely call it shamelessness, but this was all right in the right place and at the right time. Living room, kitchen, bedroom and toilet, all were one and the same. The Germans had solved the housing problem. Our former quarters were mostly unoccupied. Perhaps our ghosts crying during the lonely nights in corners where not long ago we had lived, were glad and happy. How fragile had been the basis of happiness. Now no-one thought about it. Everyone thought only how to live through the next day. Everyone held compulsively to every delusory gleam of hope that maybe he would survive this hell.

Unfortunately the night had to come to an end. This was the best time. One could live without the need to think, one could breathe without paying for it, one did not need to eat, or to hide – what more could one desire? Very soon it would be time to get up and recommence the daily carousel. The column, gate, work, again the column, gate, meal, idle talk about delusory hopes, sleep and again …

Getting typhus was very dangerous and, for the majority, fatal. Perhaps a physician would indignantly deny it, quoting pre-war statistics proving that only a small percentage of cases of spotted typhus died. Yet he would not know what complications existed during the war with people ill from typhus. Apart from the dangers connected with the illness itself, when a German discovered anyone sick with typhus he killed the sufferer on the spot; in the street, at home or during work, or on an inspection in the Jewish hospital. An effective way to liquidate an epidemic, but totally futile. People were afraid to lie in bed, and fearing even to betray being sick, walked about with typhus. I knew personally quite a number of cases who "walked through" typhus. Physicians were astonished how a sick, undernourished famished man, with a fever of 39–40°C was able to walk in winter to work, stay long hours at work, often working in rain and frost, be on short rations and yet remain alive. If someone was wealthy enough and had the right acquaintances, he could acquire the necessary injections. The sick man would administer them himself or with the help of an acquaintance during working hours, often in the toilet. To acquire medicine was not at all simple. In the ghetto, there were no pharmacies. Medicines were only available in the Aryan districts which Jews were legally prohibited to enter and for high prices. The epidemic spread more and more from day to day. My colleague, a physician, living together with me, had 20 to 25 new cases every day. He was one of about 80 other physicians in the ghetto. People cared for themselves in any way possible, inspecting their clothes, tried to wash themselves thoroughly, which considering the lack of space was extremely difficult. There was no bath in the ghetto. There was a bath for the militia, but beyond the ghetto walls.

Death rescued many from the claws of the Nazi thugs. The burial department could not cope with burying the dead. Boards were not available, coffins had become a relic of the past. The corpses, wrapped in rugs or even without, were collected in a barrack used as mortuary, and buried in a common grave. Often the corpses lay several days at home as there was no one to take them away, or people did not know where to take them. One of my friends, after some days of waiting, was obliged to carry the corpse of his mother along to the mortuary.

You can imagine my feelings when I found that I had a high fever, the first symptom of typhus. For three days I tried to acquire all that might be needed during my illness, medicines, food and, most important, money. In the end, my friends forced me to lie down in bed. I lived then in a room relatively big, 16–18 square metres, together with seven other men and five women. All – except for one woman – went to work at 6 a.m. I remained for whole days alone in the house, as the remaining woman had to purchase food for us, which occupied her whole day and involved considerable risk.

A horrible headache, sick thoughts and fever-hallucinations filled my daylight hours completely. On the fourth day of my lying ill with typhus, at dawn even before people had gone to work I was warned that an abnormal concentration of Ukrainian militia near the gate of the ghetto had been ordered. Panic spread like wildfire. Again an *Aktion*? Feverishly shelter was sought and people jumped through the fence, became crazy like mice in a trap. I was left alone in the flat. The fever had me in its power. I heard not the smallest sound. After some time a very weak noise reached me and then again silence. I fell into a feverish sleep full of hallucinations. By my bed stood a woman who lived in the same room, and she soothed me. There was no *Aktion*, the scare had been created by a gathering of 50–60 Ukrainian militiamen to liquidate the Galikol firm! At the roll-call, 174 of the 200 Jews working there appeared, including about 25 women. The women were shot on the spot and the men taken to the camp. The affair was minor indeed and was over within an hour. Again death had strolled near me, without touching me. My two companions, physicians, visited me daily trying everything in their power to help me. But there was no way to take away the horrible nightmares which were continually aroused by the fever in my brain, exhausting me nervously more than the typhus weakened my body.

The rumble of our three primuses usually awakened me when they were used at full strength when the people living with me returned from work. The terrible headache which never left me for three long weeks, got worse from this noise. Yet it was better to lie at home in such conditions, than in the hospital, where one had scarcely one chance in a thousand not to be killed during the epidemic.

Man is stronger than steel. Despite the exhaustion from hunger in the jail, the weakening of my body from being in the camp, I passed the crisis and recovered. Fortune smiled upon me, as I succeeded even in slipping through two militia night searches for jobless. At the end of December, I began to walk again and at last went into the street. My principal task was now to acquire food to regain my normal strength. I ate all I could find, I even visited some underworld restaurants. The food they gave me in such places was as unknown and indescribable as everything in a fairy-tale. The prices were, of course, totally fantastic. But there I heard priceless information about the ghetto, life outside the ghetto in the Aryan districts, news of escapes and of general conditions.

The Germans lorded it over the Aryans, almost as they had behaved in the beginning towards Jews. Without a job or a good pass, no Aryan could walk the streets of the town. Continually, roundups were carried out in the streets, in churches; people caught were taken for work in Germany. Strange that the same Aryans who ridiculed us that we allowed ourselves to do all the German wanted like sheep, instead of defending ourselves, now showed themselves no greater heroes when fate caught them in its wheels. Hundreds and thousands of Aryans from Lvov and its province were taken to Germany for work.

Whole villages became deserted. Meanwhile I did not cease to plan my flight from the ghetto. To adopt the attire of a goy and to get to Warsaw or Krakow I did not fancy at all. From the information I received it was clear that life as an Aryan was neither certain nor safe. There were the problems of documents and of hiding in an Aryan flat, which involved many dangers. Many of my friends disappeared from the ghetto into the Aryan districts of Warsaw, Czestochowa, Krakow and so on, but I hesitated. Observed as a whole, living as an Aryan did not present a very attractive picture.

During my sojourns through various secret restaurants, I heard about a Jew named Salek Meisner, nicknamed the great Matyan, who had succeeded in obtaining documents which enabled people to pass as *Volksdeutsche* and hide in German-occupied Ukraine. Naturally, he very soon had several imitators. Friends recommended one of them to me as reliable. I considered which of the two means of flight would be better, but could not decide. I was fully aware that things would not remain as they were for long, and that if I wanted to live, I would have to decide quickly, as the Germans were preparing something new in the very near future. At last I decided to flee from the ghetto in the more dangerous way, but, in my opinion, with a much better chance of success.

There remained two or three weeks to prepare all the things needed for the flight and for settling other matters. No one, neither my guides nor myself, supposed that this relatively short delay in my flight, would get me into trouble and oblige me to live through another cycle of the ghetto hell, the *Aktion* of January 1943.

20 · Beasts – Not Humans

In December 1942, an official order regulating the labour of Jews was announced. By this regulation, the Germans put in order the chaotic terms of employment of Jews. The order laid down in great detail the labour of Jews for 10 hours a day, and what means of subsistence working Jews should receive. Suppressed also were all the minor remunerations or rewards that obtained till then. It was also laid down that for every Jewish worker, the employing firm had to pay 5 zl. daily to the Gestapo. To make possible an exact count, all Jews were to be confined in separate living blocks provided us each firm. A special department was created, which had to supply the appropriate amount of accomodation, according to the number of "W" and "R" badges that any particular firm had. All Jewish matters were from now on to be exclusively submitted to the SS-police commander. He would nominate the undertakings important for defence and the number of men and women to be employed there. There were 35 such undertakings in Lvov. The manager was informed of the amount of workers, after checking that it corresponded to the "W" and "R" badges allocated to the firm, and was granted appropriate accommodation. The workers had to go to work together in columns, informing the authorities at the gate of the ghetto that they were going to work, to enable the execution of the order to be checked. All had to go to work. For "sanitary" reasons, 5 per cent of the number of workers were allowed to work as *Putzfrauen* and remained in the lodgings. The confinement in block-barracks had to be completed by 31 December 1942.

Naturally the confinement caused a new wave of removals. People were crowded together where they had installed themselves, and now had to transfer to even more restricted space. Once, on removal, there were a bed, a wardrobe and a trunk. Now, one rarely took pains to transport a bed, one just took a mattress on one's back and went. The removals were not a sporadic occurrence, they lasted uninterruptedly all December. All the time new blocks were designed, changed, transferred, narrowed without taking people into account. During the day, the ghetto was deadly silent and empty. In the evening when people came back from work inhumanly tired, instead of resting in what they called their homes, they had to organize the move to other barrack blocks. The poor "labour prisoners" dragged their luggage to new homes, the depths of misery. The lack of room in the new barrack blocks was so acute that there was scarcely enough space to sleep in two shifts. As a result, sleeping in two and three-storey bunks became necessary. The rooms were very low and hygienic conditions at the lowest level so that it was no wonder epidemics raged. Nobody could be rescued in such conditions, the Germans only speeded up the natural death rate.

Someone spread a rumour that according to a resolution of the Nazi Party, from 1 January 1943 no Jew should remain on the soil of the Reich. Everyone believed the report of this resolution to be true and waited for the blow to fall. Germans very well informed about the frame of mind among Jews tried to prevent escapes and possible plans of defence. Just before the New Year a thug from the Gestapo centre by the name of Figaszewski, during an inspection in the ghetto said allegedly: "Happy are those still living. According to the last orders received from Berlin the number of Jews on January 1943 must remain static as every worker is needed for the ultimate effort to achieve victory." Of course the news of this pronouncement spread throughout the ghetto with lighting speed. People, as always over-trustful, were almost dancing with joy. When 1 January passed quietly, even the sceptics began to believe.

I kept my plan of flight. I prepared everything, documents, personal items, a little money and waited for my transport, which was to take place after 15 January. I decided rather to go with Jews despite the greater risk in passing the border. The preparations necessitated continual visits to the Aryan district. I strolled in the town without the armband. The risk? Never mind! They would take me again to Belzec? Torture? In the ghetto, one was being slowly tormented to death!

I was not spared an additional painful experience with my follow-citizens. I had sold all my posssessions through the mediation of Mania Bilinska, a neighbour and friend of my parents of long standing. Up to now she had shown full understanding of our situation, and despite the fact that she skinned me in every transaction, I had full trust in her. Besides, I was sure that her devotion and my confidence were very well remunerated, as I presented to her all my parents' furniture and a very fair amount of bedding and clothes. But it seemed to me that all this was hardly enough. When I fell ill with typhus and sent a friend to her to get 1,500 zl. which I had left with her, she told him she did not know what he wanted, she did not know me and so on. I thought that this was only caution, but when I recovered and went to her myself, she greeted me in the same way, threatening even to call the Ukrainian militia and Gestapo if I continued to intrude upon her. If good acquaintances and friendly neighbours behaved in this way, how would others behave? This missing sum made a serious hole in my savings but somehow I had to help myself to be beyond the walls of the ghetto. Wandering about the Aryan district was at the time not safe, as the seizing of Aryan labourers for work in Germany was in full swing. This reassured us a little, As the Germans were very occupied with Aryans, perhaps they would leave us alone. Again we miscalculated.

On the night of 5 January 1943, a friend came suddenly after midnight and told us that the Jewish militia was gathered at the gate of the ghetto where there already stood a large detachment of Ukrainian militia. An *Aktion*! A wild fear overcame people. I already heard the sound of traffic in the street. People wandered dementedly about the streets of the ghetto. At first I considered jumping over the fence, but the women in our home totally lost their self-control, so I decided first to put them into our shelters. In the next apartment, a false wall had been made which created a shelter, very small but very well hidden as the entrance to it was by an icebox. In the space of about 2 square metres six people must be hidden. Ten women were crammed lying almost one on top of another. The second shelter in the house was in the attic. There about 30 people crowded. This hiding of people, with the disputes unavoidable on such an occasion, took so much time that before I realized it, it was too late to risk a leap over the fence. A neighbour from the next house rescued me, offering a place in an artificially built shelter in the cellar. The entrance was very complicated. It was arranged through a wardrobe. You had to pull out a drawer, thus enabling you to remove 2 boards from the floor, under which was the hole leading to the shelter, which in reality was attached to the ceiling like a swallow's nest. Cramming 14 people into the space of 3–3½ square metres again took an hour, so that when my turn came it was already after 6 a.m. and the *Aktion* was in full swing. Our house was a corner house. The moment I went through the hole under the drawer on my way into the shelter, I heard the Germans and Ukrainians burst into the house. I had no time to go into a real shelter. I was glad to have enough time to reach and push the drawer and the boards above my head as the thugs burst into the flat. I lay totally motionless directly under the boards of the floor, fearing almost to breathe. The German who burst first into the flat heard some sound and was certain that someone was hidden in the room which appeared to be empty. He shouted that he was sure that someone was here as he had heard a movement.

He circled like an enraged beast in the narrow room. The floorboards bent under his weight, pressing down on my unnaturally convoluted body. My heartbeat was naturally loud, I felt that it was almost impossible not to hear this thunder. The German shot several times at the walls, but, seeing the uselessness of his endeavours, he went away. I was petrified with fear, yet now all my body grew totally numb from cold and bad circulation. I lay motionless and lost all feeling in my body. Unfortunately the head does not grow numb and my hearing functioned normally, perhaps even better than usual.

I heard continuous shooting in the street and banging from the deserted house. On the first storey, directly above me, a German succeeded in uncovering a shelter made in a kitchen stove. Four women were hidden there. I heard the cry of fear in the moment of exposure half fade away, muffled by the triumphant descant of the German. I heard as they pulled out the women, one by one, from their shelter. Afterwards some movement which at first I could not explain and, then, with a painful almost physical feeling of shame the awareness that above me they had raped a woman. Abomination. The voice of the woman could not be heard. This soundless cry of the victim was sharp and painful. After several minutes I heard the voice of one of the thugs: "Hold her feet" and after a moment the sound of broken glass and the hollow sound of the thud of a body falling on the ground. They had thrown her through the window into the courtyard. I heard similar scenes three times with minor differences. After the animals had laughingly satisfied themselves, they went to execute further work. At first, I heard moaning from the court yard. Then it quietened down. From other parts of the house could be heard the cries of the victims and the sound of shooting, the yelling and profanities of the thugs, interrupted by bursts of laughter provoked by some extraordinary bestiality. The wild orgy in the house seemed to last for centuries. At last the noise subsided and it seemed that the tempest had passed over our house. In the distance continous shooting and shouts could be heard. Our house became deadly silent. Not a sound. Every one was petrified.

People beneath me in the shelter were afraid to budge. Only an hour or perhaps two, and they dared to move, as the continual silence aroused their suspicions of a trap. I pulled myself into the inner part of my shelter. I was not in a position to make the smallest independent move, I was totally cramped. I was seated on the bucket that served in place of a toilet. There was nowhere else to sit. The man standing next to me gave me a sip of vodka and I massaged myself as well as I could. Of course the shelter was without light and though it was unheated, because it was so crowded it was quite agreeably warm. Slowly I recovered. Every minute I had to stand up to allow people to use the bucket. The easing of tension was stimulating everyone's bladder.

In the afternoon, another wave rolled over our house, but nothing happened to us. The first occurrence had been quite enough for us. In the evening about 6 p.m. the sounds on the streets subsided a little. A strong wind arose, its storming and wailing muffling the sound of faraway shots. We decided to come out of the shelter like moles emerging from their den to look for relatives and friends. The need for food leaped into my mind as we left the shelter. We decided that three of us would go out. I was first, being the nearest to the exit. Slowly, weighing every move, I raised myself. Before moving the floorboards securing the exit, I waited a long moment listening for suspicious sounds. At last I came out, and after me another.

The third person decided at the last moment to remain in the shelter. First we carried the bucket out to the courtyard. A snow-storm raged, a real blizzard, as if nature itself wanted to cover up the traces of the bestiality of her hideous offspring. We moved cautiously with sparing use of flashlight in our courtyard. Directly under the window we almost fell over the corpse of a raped woman, thrown into the courtyard. Nearby, another corpse; around it a great bloodstain on the fresh snow. It seemed to me that she was still alive. I bent over and saw in a convulsed hand a piece of glass. The origin of the bloodstain was now clear. The poor thing could not bear her shame and had cut her veins. We went out into the street. The snow-laden wind made us stagger. The street was deserted. The blizzard carried swirling clouds of snow. Taking great care and bent forward, we tried to reach Kleparow Square. When we turned a corner, a scene of horror hit us. The town was in flames. All the Kleparow area, which covered 60 per cent of the ghetto, was burning. The most vivid descriptions of fires pale in the face of the vast horror of this sight seen with one's own eyes. It is difficult to find words to describe the madness of the flames fed by the raging blizzard. Hypnotized, we staggered in the direction of the fire. Where were our dear ones? What had happened to them? We went, blinded both by snow and flames, stumbling at every step over corpses lying in the street half-buried in snow. We fell over bodies, got up and dragged ourselves further. In Kleparow Square, we met others whom anxiety had driven out of safe shelters. The mortuary was full of corpses. A mass of bodies stacked up like pieces of wood: Hitler's harvest. In this macabre labyrinth a small light gleamed from afar. With involuntary shudders we approached it, sure that it must be a madman. He approached one heap of corpses after another and illuminated each with a small candle. The scanty flame shone weakly, making bloody icicles of snow on the bodies sparkle. As he came nearer I saw with astonishment that it was my friend Rysiek Reich. I approached him thinking that he had gone mad, but he was fully conscious and seeking the body of his mother. Conscious? Rather demented, mumbling incomprehensibly and suddenly he fell unconscious. Was it any wonder? Who could understand this macabre situation. On a dreadful night, to the howling of a blizzard, by the light of a tiny flame, to search among heaps of corpses for the body of one's own mother. Happily we had vodka. The blessed spirit brought him back to reality.

The distorted imagination of the creators of Grand Guignol scenes had never invented such wild fantasies as those actually created by life; at least life as it was under the aegis of Nazi thugs.

We took the poor man with us and entered the nearest house – deserted like all other houses in the ghetto during that night. The broken doors did not hinder our entering. Worse guests than we had been here before us. The interior of the house was one great heap of debris, broken furniture, torn pillows and quilts. Rysiek, restored by the vodka, told us what had occurred in Kleparow. The Germans had decided to destroy this part of the ghetto completely. They entered houses, poured kerosene on the stairs and set them alight. They threw hand-grenades into cellars and attics. They did not bother to seek the shelters, they destroyed whole buildings. People they caught they tortured in especially ingenious ways before murdering them. Remembering this he trembled. Sobbing in disjointed sentences, he outlined a story, impossible to repeat, of martyred victims. He tried to stop us from going into this hell. We left him though, and went further. But we did not go very far.

In one of the first houses on Warsaw Street burning fiercely with towering flames, a picture met us which totally deterred us from any further investigation. In a window in the second floor, the corpse of a woman hung by her feet nailed to the window frame. The hungry flames licked her body. Suddenly her hair caught fire and burst into living flame. We ran away. The picture – even for us – hardened as we were, was too horrible to bear.

Dumbfounded by the ghastly scene, we returned to Rysiek and went back. The horrible glow brightly illuminated our way. We met no one alive, though sometimes a sob or the sound of crying reached our ears. We also came across many corpses. ... These kept silent, sprawling motionless in the snow.

In our shelter they were nervously awaiting our return. Unfortunately the news we brought did nothing to elevate the mood. The apartments in our house also stood wide open; empty, deserted, plundered. We visited other shelters in our house. We pulled out buckets, and brought water. Among scattered, broken furniture in the flats of unknown owners, we found some pieces of bread and an onion. This food would have to suffice for the whole day. We did not allow anyone to go out, as it was not known when the *Aktion* would end. The night we spent in gloomy reflection. At 4 a.m. we went back to our shelter.

The *Aktion* went on. On the second day, three waves of thugs rolled over our house, but they did not discover any more shelters. They found a baby in one of the flats, and smashed its head against a wall. The abominable feeling of having to remain motionless, helpless and sit concealed in a shelter, hearing the nearby voice of an SS-man and waiting to be discovered, was unbearable. You held your breath, would hush the beating of your heart. We could not see one another, it was impossible, but everyone felt the trembling of his neighbour. Even the smallest children, perhaps instinctively felt the danger and stood stock still as petrified and motionless as the adults.

At evening, the son of one of the women came. He was with the Jewish militia and brought news that the *Aktion* was ended. The principal victim was the Judenrat, despite the guarantee of Inquart that the remaining 300 working in the Judenrat, who had been given special personal documents, would remain immune. Perhaps it is assuming too much to believe that it was on the inspiration of the commander of the *Sonderdienst* of the Jewish militia Schapiro-Goliger, that the Judenrat was liquidated, but it can certainly be recorded that he was a zealous executioner. This viper, which the Judenrat nurtured in its own bosom, contributed in great measure to its ruin. The Jewish militia, in the beginning an organ of order of the Judenrat, grew from the middle of 1942 and escaped the control of the Judenrat. Officially the management of Jewish matters was in the hands of the Judenrat but in reality the Jewish militia governed tyrannically by terror, extortion, groundless arrests and blackmail, all controlled personally by Goliger, the centre and soul of all the evil tricks.

On the second day of the *Aktion*, on the advice of Goliger, all those working in the Judenrat took cover in the Judenrat building together with their families. Goliger along with Wepke and Untersturmführer Mayer, after surrounding the building, then burst in. Apparently it was not enough for him to enjoy full power in the ghetto, he probably did not want to allow any enemy to exist – undoubtedly he considered the Judenrat his enemy – and he needed to get rid of inconvenient witnesses of his deeds. Wepke was managing things. Most of the workers were shot down on the spot and the rest were thrown "on the sands". There remained only the twelve councillors of the Judenrat.

21 · Scratches in Blood

Now a permanent action began against the jobless and those possessing false "W" or "R" badges. Mansfeld and Siler, the SS-men, governors of the ghetto, commenced their real work. Their official task was the management of the ghetto and the inspection of the barracks, but their real aim was to liquidate the non-working. One of them stood by the gate of the ghetto inspecting the columns going to work, the other with several militiamen inspected the barracks and the other houses, hunting for the non-working. Those caught were taken to prison, from there they would go "on the sands".

The prison in the Aryan district did not fit the German's needs, as from time to time they had to detain Jews in one cell together with Aryans, because the jails were always overcrowded. They ordered a prison to be opened in the ghetto in October 1942, anticipating a numerous attendance. At their disposal was an excellent commander in Goliger, and they knew that they could be sure that under his management the prison would meet its task. In December 1942 Goliger was given complete control of the prison. He chose suitable helpers and adapted for this task a small house on Winiarska Street. To this prison, all Jews up to now detained in Lecki Prison were transferred. I will not describe this additional sore of the ghetto, except that it was an additional place of torture and execution, because it was the only handy place for gathering people destined for death. After reducing the ghetto and the liquidation of the part of the ghetto in Kleparov, the prison was transferred to Waisenfof St.

During the day Mansfeld strolled on an inspection of the ghetto discovering shelters, hunting for people and sending those he caught to prison. No day passed without several dozen victims. Sometimes it was possible to buy oneself out from going to prison. The price Mansfeld fixed arbitrarily at 10,000 zloty. Sometimes in a fit of wild humour, he demanded only a bottle of vodka, saying that this was also too much for a Jew.

In the roundups, mainly children fell into their hands, often homeless, orphaned several *Aktions* ago. Several hundred such orphans were in the ghetto. They dragged themselves from house to house; there was no one to attend to them, the other ghetto inmates were fighting too hard for their own survival. The children hungered, had nowhere to sleep and lived on handouts. During my illness I remember, hardly an hour passed without a knock on the door – a child asking for alms. Not actually asking for alms, but for a piece of something to eat. The child did not even dare to beg for a piece of bread. He knew in response he would be answered: "What? Bread? There is no bread. Here, take 5 zl."

To our flat, regularly as clockwork, used to come a small girl, four or five years old. She said her name was Lucia, she did not know her surname. Her parents had been taken in the August *Aktion*. She found them gone in the morning and they never returned. I asked her how she had been saved from so many *Aktions*. She answered that they – the children – hid together. Where? She could not describe it in detail. How much room did such a mite need? Instinctively she felt the approach of danger and burrowed herself in some hole or a heap of garbage, of which there were plenty on every street. The child was so forlorn that one feared to look at her. Her clothes, gifts, or rags found in dumps, more or less covered a body incredibly overlaid with dirt, swarming with hundreds of lice. Over her face, certainly never washed since the death of her parents, uncombed hair hung loose. Peering from under her fringe gleamed a watchful look, ever sniffing out danger. Even eating the soup offered to her, her whole tiny body seemed to be tensed for a leap and flight if sudden danger should appear. The poor mite came, ate and went. Where was she living? She did not knew herself. There were several hundred such children in the ghetto. Some of them grew savage and avoided men at all costs. Their world was cellars and garbage cans. Is there a punishment for all this? Certainly not. What did it mean for the world, the mass-murder of several millions of people, especially if they. Who cared? Their families alone would cry for a while and that would be all.

The SS-man Siler, who stood at the gate of the ghetto, made sure that the prison did not remain empty. He stood there from 6 a.m. accepting reports of the number of people going to work and checking whether people had real "W" and "R" badges. Usually he stood near the gate, a medium-sized, plain individual with a cold glance, looking piercingly at the passing people, to pick up at random anyone he fancied, and with satisfied sadism handing the victim over to the militia to carry him off to prison. Requests, pleas, proving documents had no effect on this cold-blooded villain, they could equally well provoke him to shoot down the nuisance on the spot.

There were many jobless, who had hidden until now, but this time they fell in masses into the hands of the Germans. The usual means of catching had been unsuccessful, so the Germans now thought up a new trick, providing the chance to use these destined to death as manpower. They formed labour columns. They announced that applications for work at the narrow fence around the new ghetto would be accepted. Poor people still had illusions about the possibility of a legal rescue. Despite the large number of perfidious lies, people continued to be caught in the deceitful traps. The result of the work on the fence was the labour column, partly liquidated by sending the excess workers to Janowski Camp. Finally there remained several dozen people who after finishing work were taken "on the sands". On this occasion Inquart came personally. The idea was not bad – it provided the chance of liquidating some hundreds of people without trouble. Unfortunately in the festive mood of this pleasurable moment the appearance of a Jew made a dissonant interruption and partly spoiled the pleasure. One of the workers, the lawyer, L. Feder decided to tell the Germans a few home truths before his death. The aide-de-camp of the SS commander of the police Herr Inquart had to hear words of bitter truth, that they, the Nazi-dogs, were courageous only if they outnumbered others. They dared to murder and to adopt a manly pose, since they were well-armed with machine-guns, rifles and grenades against people who were completely helpless. These heroes would run if in the hand of the cowardly Jew there were even the smallest revolver. Inquart ordered him to turn round, so that he could shoot him down. The victim with an undaunted look eyed him with contempt and, with the words "Have the courage to shoot an enemy looking at you", awaited his death. A burst from a machine-pistol ended this incident. Here was one who perished not in a crowd, who fought for his honour and human dignity. He defied the Germans: not to rescue himself, but to perish standing on his own two feet with fighting words of truth.

Despite the continual *Aktions*, a relatively large number of people was in hiding in the ghetto in specially built shelters. I have mentioned the shelters built in the house where I was living; such shelters were built in almost every house and even in ruins. People constructed them in deepest secrecy during the night. There was no idea for a hide or a camouflaged entrance that was not used in the ghetto. Some people invested great sums of money in building hides and in supplying them with a stock of food and water, enough for a long period if they needed to stay in the hide. I knew of one shelter built deep beneath a cellar, with an excellent masked entrance. The shelter was covered with a three-foot-thick layer of concrete. Water and sewer pipes were brought in and out. The ventilation was a real masterpiece. In the shelter was a stock of food for five months. Everyone took into account that any day they might be startled by an *Aktion* or the liquidation of the ghetto.

I made an effort to obtain false documents and went daily from the ghetto with the columns to work. Immediately beyond the gate I took off my armband and strolled in the Aryan districts awaiting news from my guides of the exact date of the departure to the formerly Soviet part of Ukraine. I became totally indifferent to the risks; what would be – would be. Night in the ghetto, where I returned every evening, where one was completely helpless, cost me in nervous strain much more than bustling around the Aryan districts. The daily exit through the ghetto gate was the worst. On 10 January I went as usual in a column of chance "work-comrades". Siler stood at the gate. When the column was ready to march, one of the men in the first row did not find approval in Siler's eyes. He was four rows in front of me. Siler ordered him to step out of the column. The poor man, perhaps certain that all was in order, instead of stepping out at once, began to mumble something and reached into his pocket. Siler did not wait and shot him dead with his pistol. Siler continued to rave and did not allow anyone to remove the corpse. All must understand the consequences of not acting immediately on any order of a German.

A friend standing next to me advised me to withdraw, knowing that everything about me was false, documents, name, badge, etc. But for me all had become one – I went along. Like the others I was obliged to step over the fresh corpse. In a moment I was beyond the gate. I decided at this moment, that for nothing and in no circumstances would I go back into the ghetto gate of my own free will. In the town I contacted my middleman for any news and date of departure. Luckily there was news. We were going on the 14th of the month, in the evening. I sent the information through an acquaintance to comrades in the ghetto – the exact date of the escape and the place to meet in town on the 14th. I did not return to the ghetto. One night I spent on the stairs in a house which seemed me to be sympathetic. The next in a similar way in another house. Later I was lucky to have the opportunity to hide in a storeroom of a German firm with the agreement of the Jewish storekeeper. I was locked in for the night, my last in Lvov. The following day, in the evening, I met my comrades according to plan, and was on my way, as I describe in book III of this memoir.

22 · The Purge Goes On

During January 1943 the hunt for the jobless or rather those not working continued. In addition an order was promulgated prohibiting the possession of a sum of money larger then zl. 2,000. This order caused more inspections from Custom control and of course, new vexations and murders. The councillors of the Judenrat held their meetings and had their office in the deserted building. They counted their existence in hours. Rightly so, as on 4 February the Gestapo ordered a roll-call of the councillors. There were 12 and they knew what now awaited them, since they were no longer needed. To the summons responded the president E., Adv. B.K., Eng. N.L., Mr H. and Mr M. They were taken to the jail on Wajzenhof Street and afterwards driven "on the sands". Dr H., Mr M., Dr J., Mr Sch. and Dr J. had escaped (the last committed suicide) and Dr L.L. who was later caught in Lvov and liquidated in the usual way. From now on, over the ghetto gate a sign-board was hung with the inscription "Judenlager RW" (for short Julag RW).

An exact census of inmates of the ghetto was made on 15 February 1943. There were 15,300 legal people, that is, working in German firms or for the Army, militia and their immediate families. In addition there were in the ghetto probably about 3,500 illegals, living in dens and tunnels, not daring to appear in the light of day.

Mansfeld began to clear up the Kleparow, the cut-off part of the ghetto, to ready it for giving to the Aryan population as living quarters. There was no more need for an *Aktion* on a large scale, hunting after those not working was enough, particularly the illegal militia (people who had obtained caps from militiamen), and workers sacked from work in the German firms. In this way, people working for Wohnbezirk Czwartkov, V.H.B., Schwarz and others were liquidated. The circle of people alive narrowed. The following descriptions of the events in the ghetto I heard from several survivors, people who remained till almost the last moments of the liquidation of the Lvov ghetto. I have checked the stories very thoroughly. After my flight from the ghetto I was twice in Lvov in the uniform of a German soldier and able to learn from personal experience what was going on.

The new commander of the Julag was a certain Grzymek of Silesian descent. A slim man with grizzled hair, sharp features, and a piercing, cold look, he was preceded by his brutal reputation. During his activities in

Jaktorow Camp he had been given a Soviet sub-machine gun. He wanted to try out his new toy and used it on the inmates of the camp, killing 165 people in a burst of activity. In Lvov, Grzymek soon showed both his sides, as a maniac about cleanliness and as a bloodthirsty sadist, with an admixture of Grand Guignol black humour.

His first task he considered to be to clear out Kleparow and the ghetto. He started work with fierce energy. He tore down old barracks and fences because the Germans feared to enter such corners. He gave an order that Kleparow should be cleared during a 24-hour period. All the inmates of the ghetto together with the militia worked day and night in fear of death clearing away the traces of the last *Aktion*. People dropped in their tracks from exhaustion and got up to work so that the Aryans could move into tidy apartments so long as the sight of ruins did not disturb them. After a day Grzymek, in the company of Inquart and Wepke, carried out an inspection. The tidiness must really have been impressive, when Inquart is alleged to have said "This can be an example for all Lvov". After he carried out this first assignment, Grzymek made the ghetto his next target.

The streets were blocked by mounds of unremoved garbage from the past month, and heaps of broken furniture. The houses, due to their being overcrowded by an enormous number of inmates, were in a horrible state of repair, especially as they had not originally been an example of tidiness and order. Grzymek did not recognize impossibilities. He ordered 24 signs in the form of a half-moon with a slogan "There must be order" and a number of signs with the inscription "Keep your home tidy – you will be healthier".

He began with the *Putzfrauen*, inspecting their work almost daily and beating them if he found the smallest speck of dirt. He ordered the sign-boards to be hung on specific barrack blocks. Next for inspection were the janitors in the barrack blocks. In white gloves he would check if the stairs or corners in the yard were dirty, harassing the poor men, who had neither the chance nor the ability to succeed in these horrible conditions with a broken sink or blocked sewerpipe. The victims received 25 lashes with a whip administered personally by Grzymek himself and as a decoration, the half moon, with an order to stand the whole day on the streets of the ghetto and shout aloud "I am the greatest swine in the ghetto: there must be order".

Despite these orders to maintain cleanliness, the plague of typhus raged in the ghetto during February and March 1943 taking about 60 victims a day. In the ghetto there were no medicines at all and it was forbidden to supply any. On the other hand there were no sick at home, as it was forbidden to keep typhus patients at home, and in the hospitals Grzymek – on his daily visits – personally killed every typhus patient. The doctors had a hellish life, as they frequently got a punch in the face if Grzymek considered something not clean enough. In fear of being killed, tens and hundreds of people walked about with typhus fever as long as they could stand on their feet. To lie down meant to perish.

Grzymek's idea was to found an orchestra, playing every day at the ghetto gate for those going to work, so that they would march vigorously. When I imagine to myself this march of the harassed slaves of the SS, starving, sick, with shaven heads (also an idea of Grzymek) dragging swollen feet to the lively tune of the Radetzky March, I find myself shuddering. Sometimes he demanded that they sang lively Polish songs, well known to him from the times when he was still a Pole. I was told about an event when after beating, punching, and kicking one of the women because she had put on lipstick, he ordered the others to move her while singing a gay song usually reserved for pleasure trips. The women were forced to sing. They went, singing between sobs, with tears in their eyes, and Grzymek marched along observing with satisfaction the results of his happy idea, beating time to the song with his blood-stained whip.

Life went on with no reaction to the continual liquidation of people in various work places. Several dozen women, seamstresses working in a military unit were killed, allegedly because they sewed something for Katzman's wife. On the occasion of one such liquidation a Jewish driver shot down Kail an SS-man. It took place on 17 March 1943 and became the cause of a new *Aktion*, a revenge *Aktion*. On this particular day in the ghetto area, again in Lokietek Street, eleven militia-men were hanged and remained on show for 24 hours. The twelfth to be hanged was a member of the Judenrat.

The next morning, the orchestra played as usual at the ghetto gate. The columns went to work not suspecting a thing. Before the gate stood several doctors giving injections against typhus. Beyond the gate stood Engels, Staviski and Wepke managing the *Aktion*. They selected people from the columns. For instance, from one column, fair-haired were taken, from another, people with glasses. Those taken were immediately loaded onto trucks and driven "on the sands", The columns inside the ghetto were marching in the direction of the gate, unsuspectingly as inspections were made and the orchestra was playing. People marched, not knowing that beyond the gate, death with its greedy jaws would catch 1,100 of them. The orchestra played on.

Not funeral marches; the Germans did not want this to reveal the execution of the *Aktion*. Obersturmbannführer Staviski stood till the end, until the last column went and until the last consignment for death was loaded. The orchestra played all the time, gay tune after joyful melody, as ordered.

23 · Nameless Heroes

Life in the ghetto dragged on. Only in such extreme conditions is it possible to realize how strong is the survival instinct. Conditions were appalling: 70–80 per cent of the ghetto inmates were afflicted with dropsy because of starvation; 90 per cent of all women had ceased to menstruate; the doctors made the acquaintance of scurvy, known to them only from medical text books; the births in the ghetto, among Jews, fell to zero.

Despite this, all the survivors were eager to live. They fought for the chance to continue life, even in this wretched way. They had not lost the feeling of humanity, of self dignity and ambition. To the large number of national heroes in our history were added new ones. Their deeds were greater and more worthy of praise when we take into account in what conditions they performed these heroic deeds. These deeds of self-abnegation and sacrifice for the honour of our nation and our past are worthy of the highest approbation.

Against the humble background of the Nazi attempt to dehumanize us in order to murder us more easily, among these conditions there remained those who, despite torments, managed to retain their dignity and human pride. They carried high the banner of humanity. They did not wage war romantically in defence of ideas, but were able in the grey of everyday life to maintain the posture of a human being, a person worthy of this designation. From many such in the nameless mass I would mention only a few, not by their names, but through their deeds, heroic amid the desolation of helpless cattle driven to the slaughter. I want to dedicate a few words of remembrance so that their posture, so full of dignity, their remarkable civil and physical courage against a savage enemy unrestrained and taking no notice of anything, should not fall into oblivion; especially as so few witnesses of their deeds remain alive.

I have already described in detail in chapter 3 the stature of the president of the Judenrat, full of dignity, an old man, towards an SS-lout (pp. 64–5). In chapter 10, I gave an account of another old man, a well-known merchant, who, indignant at a baseless sentence of death, tried to assault with a stone a heavily armed SS-man (p. 113).

In a small town of Eastern Galicia, standing on the brink of an open grave one of the women – wife of a physician – had the courage to deliver a passionate speech to the other women to give them courage. Threatening the Germans with a fist, she shouted: "We perish, it's true, but our death will not help you to win the war!" A volley from a machine-gun tried to drown the fiery yell, "You have lost!" and the shout continued to reverberate. Another hero was the President of the Judenrat of a small town in Eastern Galicia, who when ordered to prepare a list of unproductive elements, answered "God gave me my life, so I can dispose of it, but He gave me no power to be prodigal with other people's lives". This noble attitude brought him a martyr's death.

I could tell such stories indefinitely. Worthy of mention is a mother who jumped from the third floor with her baby tied to her chest on to the pavement in the Aryan district, to force by her death a merciful reaction for her child. A boy, when it became evident that his appeal to an SS-man for his mother was futile, tore to pieces his *Ausweis* – "card of life" – and threw the pieces in the face of the SS-man, demanding to be taken also to death, as he did not wish to live among such beasts.

We must also mention those minor officials in some departments in the ghettos, who in secret gathered documentary evidence of Nazi crimes. They assembled the evidence cautiously hiding away documents. They forged a weapon with their modest work against the Nazi beast. Anyone caught was executed, though immediately his place was taken by others, who continued the work. Silent and modest work, but so important, and demanding so much self-sacrifice. Nobody knew them, nobody knows them, and the few who do know about them, are those who with the weapons they forged raised them to strike a blow at the criminals.

But I close with those who should have been at the head of this chapter of unsung heroes – the heroes of the uprising in the Warsaw ghetto. The Zionist and pioneer organizations which did not bend under the boot of the German soldier, united despite their political differences in the fight against the common enemy. There remained after innumerable *Aktions* only some 55,000 to 60,000 with hardly any arms. With almost bare hands they decided to fight a fully armed enemy, to defend their national dignity with the hundred or two small arms they could purchase. Some 56,000 were burned and buried in the rubble of the bombarded and burned-out ghetto, but the Germans too paid a price; some hundreds of casualties. Should one describe specific episodes of this heroic struggle? Perhaps it would be worth citing the splendid deeds of one or other leader of a fighting group, but most worthy of all was the collective heroism of the anonymous mass, which fought ferociously, attacking not to remain alive, but to perish with hands constricted on the throat of the enemy, instead of being murdered by perfidious and deceitful means; to defend their dignity as human souls and as Jews, heirs to three thousand years of heroism, steadfastness and endurance. They threw out of the ghetto the Germans who came to execute the first of the final *Aktions*. The Nazis returned with tanks and cannon under General Stroop. The ghetto fighters resisted from 18 January to August 1943. Only 50 of them escaped alive, but they inspired the whole of Europe to resist.

24 · The Final Liquidation

The echoes of the fight in the Warsaw ghetto aroused everyone. Unfortunately in Lvov the number of people that remained was too small and it was too late to do anything. Lvov after the Russian occupation and the smashing of all Jewish organizations was totally defenceless. The impoverishment of the Jewish population left no chance of buying arms and from the old times none remained, as possession of arms in the USSR was a capital crime. Despite all this the ferment began.

When on 22 May 1943, the German tried to arrange an *Aktion* in their usual perfidious way, demanding that people volunteer for labour on the land (of course a lie) nobody applied. The Germans had to use force. They took every third row from the columns going to work. Under cover of dozens of machine-guns (as experience had taught them) they selected people. The brute force was too great. The *Aktion* again claimed several thousands of victims. But the ferment grew. When the "camping" was announced, that is, the transfer of all those working to the camps, people decided to be killed on the spot rather than to go for additional tortures.

At the end of May at the obligatory inspection at the gate, arms and ammunition were found on several persons. The Germans did not want to risk another Warsaw revolt and even without the appropriate preparations they unleashed on 1 June an *Aktion* with the purpose of liquidating the ghetto. Until now the task of all *Aktions* was bullying, and at the last mass murder. In this *Aktion*, it was clear from the first moment that the only aim was the wish wholly to destroy the ghetto. This did not mean that an opportunity to torment should be wasted; they would still enjoy torturing the victims. The first shots were fired at night. A huge number of SS-men and Ukrainian militia was concentrated; the aim was final destruction. They were searching for shelters, dragged people from flats and gathered them on a square at the intersection of Kresowa Street, Jakub Herman St. and Peltewna, where at a table were seated the Gestapo chiefs; Inquart, Engels and Wepke were attending the feast. At several places they met with resistance, unfortunately not organized; for fighting, the Germans sent in the Ukrainians. The unprepared resistance lasted only a short time against brute force. The Ukrainians avenged several dozen casualties from their force in an extremely wild way, murdering, throwing people from high floors onto the street. Those who fell on the street and were still alive, they strangled, stepping on the neck of the victim and pressing hard with all their weight till the victim died. At the table sat sprawled the Gestapo mandarins managing the *Aktion*. Blood bespattered the streets. The dog of one of the Gestapo-men licked the warm blood and one joker said, laughing, "The dog is committing *Rassenschande*" and got a hurricane of laughter from his comrades. Nearby stood a buffet loaded with snacks and vodka to reinvigorate the workers exhausted by their self-sacrificing labour.

In the first day of the *Aktion*, they sent by tram-lorries transports of 200–300 persons, mostly women and children, "on the sands". On the sands the inmates of the Janowski camp dug a ditch about 6 feet wide and 4½ feet deep. In these ditches the Germans ordered the people to lie down after they had stripped themselves of their clothes. Afterwards on both edges of the ditch went SS-men and shot the Jews with their sub-machine guns. When one layer was dealt with, they forced other people to lie down on the still warm corpses and again the machine-guns fulfilled their part, until the ditch was full almost to the brim like a sardine can. I saw a great deal personally, I passed through not a little, I heard more and I am well able to understand the various appalling situations which occurred, but such wild, fantastic, inhuman beastliness is far beyond the limits of my comprehension. It surpassed anything the brutal savagery of a human beast could invent. The *Aktion* went on. All the time, new transports were loaded on to the trucks. A crowd of Aryans stood near the ghetto-gate and without compassion or pity watched this mass being sent for carnage. Not even indifferently, as one could, for instance, hear: "Nuu, where is your Stalin?"

On the fifth day of the *Aktion*, because the camp prisoners could not cope with digging enough ditches, the means of mass-murdering was simplified. After stripping, people were ordered to go in single file on the edge of a natural ravine which was behind the Janowski camp, and the SS-man shot at the Jews like animals. The victims rolled down to the bottom of the ravine and gathered in a huge heap which afterwards the camp prisoners would clear up. From time to time a grenade was thrown, to reassure the executioners that no one remained alive.

Afterwards the transports were reduced to 100 persons per transport, later to 50 and in the end 10–20 persons only. Now there was no need to seek a special place for the killing. The last victims were murdered on the garbage heap near the camp kitchen. To be sure that nobody remained alive hidden in the ghetto, it was set on fire and the cellars were flooded with water.

Despite this, several dozen people hid themselves in the Janowski camp and several hundreds in the sewers.

The last *Aktion* was finished.

The charred, smoke-blackened houses, stretched out helpless, handless limbs, as if calling to Heaven for revenge. Tens of thousands perished, sunk into the oblivion of a common grave, but even there they would not be left alone. Their tracks must be covered up. Two thousand camp inmates were kept busy covering up the tracks. Brigades of 100 people were assembled to dig up the corpses, and every day after they had finished the work, they themselves were liquidated. All this seemed not to be enough, the corpses must be burned. All over town the foul stink of burned corpses hung like a miasma, the last remembrance of former citizens hovered over their beloved town.

The Janowski camp remained. There were only 800 people. They were driven in the surroundings of Lvov to various jobs. What work? Covering up the traces. This meant digging out graveyards and burning the remains of the fantastic crime. Even the corpses of Jews the Germans did not leave alone. All traces of Belzec, Jaktorov, Winniki, Borki and other camps were covered up. In November 1943 the work was ended. November 1943 also saw the end of the Janowski camp with the murder of all its inmates. A desperate attack by the prisoners with their bare hands was, of course, futile. The hopeless struggle lasted 24 hours. Some SS-men and Ukrainians, and some hundreds of inmates, whom some indefatigable strength had kept alive till now, were killed. Of all of Lvov's 180,000 Jews only corpses and ashes remained. Ashes and corpses.

Slatina/Olt. Winter 1943/1944.

BOOK III

My Private War Against the Nazis

1 · Surviving

A Jew who left the ghetto could survive in a number of ways. He could hide with a sympathetic "Aryan" or try to pass as an "Aryan" on false papers. Both these methods exposed one to the large army of extortioners and blackmailers who flourished in German-occupied Poland.

There was also a third course for these who desired to escape – flight abroad to Romania or Hungary which bordered on Poland. Very few had the means to try this and scarcely a handful managed to escape from the clutches of Hitler by using this method.

Then a real fighter appeared who discovered a different method of survival, a fourth way of escape from the ghetto. It was certainly the riskiest of all, but in spite of its overwhelming dangers it offered an active challenge and was, in a sense, very like combat. The man was Salek Meisner. He was well known among sportsmen because of his many appearances on basketball and volleyball teams. Nobody knows how he got the idea – perhaps he thought it up himself, perhaps a German suggested it – but that is unimportant.

Meisner went beyond posing as a Pole with the help of forged papers. He did not agree to hide. On the contrary, he breached the imprisoning wall itself, he fought back. Meisner decided to take the bull by its horns and put on the uniform of a German soldier. He was the first to tread all the paths of the unknown jungle that was wartime in Europe. He was in Romania as early as 1942 and 1943, wandered across the face of the German-occupied continent and tried various strategies in his attempt to break out of the accursed circle of Nazi rule. He was the first to utilize military and pseudo-military documents and he used them with incredible confidence.

Meisner was probably the inventor of the term "*Wehrmachtsgefolge*" (an auxiliary military unit of the German Army – there was of course no such unit). He and his deeds gave rise to a legend. Unfortunately he did not survive. But it was his method I decided to follow.

2 · The Contact

"Hi there".

"Hi".

I was guided to a nearby dark storage room. Two men stood amidst the jumble of odds and ends. They did not wear the obligatory armbands although they were Jewish. Their rather odd clothing did not astonish me for my eyes were used to the outlandish dress of the ghetto inhabitants. They both wore boots – a sure sign of good financial standing. The taller had a coat of a strange cut and colour which seemed taken from some uniform, his belt was of army issue and on his head he wore a leather automobile helmet which had come into fashion when the Russians arrived in Lvov. I learned later that his name was Marjan Nacht; he later assumed the name Rogovsky. He was a daredevil, without studies, work or profession, from Lvov. The other, who was shorter and stouter, did not wear such eye-catching clothes. He wore a threequarter-length belted jacket, and a common workers' cloth cap. In contrast to my guide and to me, these two were somehow abnormally placid, displayed a self-confidence bordering on cockiness and seemed to make light of danger in a manner which appeared to me downright astonishing.

The contrast between their behaviour and our state of fear gave me food for thought... Our quick nervous movements and darting frightened eyes were so at odds with their strange and incredible calm, that I could not help but look at them as at supernatural beings. They had broken out of the accursed circle of the doomed residents of the ghetto. We, stupefied by fear, only dreamed about doing such things.

The tall one, a handsome black-haired man with large luminous eyes, was the first to strike up a conversation:

"This is the passenger who wants to go? All right."

"Just a moment. I would like to know how we'll do it."

"What is it to you, mister? Do you want to go? Yes or no?"

"Marjan, don't lean on him", interrupted the other one. He winked at me placatingly with his small, rather unfocused eyes and started a normal conversation with enviable indifference.

"We can take you to Dniepropetrovsk with a group of ten people, all of them Jews. Everybody gets faked documents and we all travel very peacefully until we get to the Dniepr river" –

"This means I don't have to arrange anything on my own, right? Good. But what about safety measures? Which firm is supposed to employ us?" –

"That's none of your business, mister. We guarantee that we'll get you through the railway station, put you on the train, cross the border and escort you to Dniepropetrovsk. You'll find lodgings and employment when we are there. Got it?"

"He's shitting in his pants. I'm telling you, Jurek, we shouldn't take this greenhorn with us. Though he looks all right."

While speaking, Marjan took a quick step in my direction and without adding another word he snatched the cap off my head, jumped backwards, took a good look at me and burst out in a peal of shrill giggles. I didn't know what to make of all this. He came close to me again on my other side, laughed, and threw the cap at me.

"He can go like this. But he'll have to make a few changes in his appearance. He looks like a damn intellectual. Jurek will make everything clear. Bye." He left.

Jurek's real name was Icik Mandelkern. He was from Lodz and an actor in a Jewish theatre. He laughed good-naturedly and carried on the interrupted conversation:

"He's a madman. You'll be much safer with us than joining a bunch of Goyim to work for some German enterprise. A few days ago I heard of someone who was identified as a Jew by his Polish fellow-workers. They robbed him blind and handed him over to the police near Zdolbunow. Another one, I forgot which firm he was working for, was thrown out of the window of a speeding train. Why be so choosy, mister? We'll use the same papers as those who really work for a firm. Nobody will know that our papers are faked while theirs are genuine. You won't be handed over by your mates because they are also all 'Chestnuts'" (the colloquial term for Jews).

"How much?"

"Three slices [3,000 zloty]. Half now and the rest in Zdolbunow."

"O.K. I will think it over and tell you tomorrow. Here?"

"Yes, so long."

"So long."

After leaving the storeroom I returned to the ghetto with my friend, moving with extreme care and taking due precautions. We would not speak while on this dangerous route which left more time for thought. Should I go? The devil knew what was best. Well, maybe there wouldn't be any need for leaving the ghetto. That would be wonderful ... But I shouldn't cherish any illusions – something must be done. In any event, it wouldn't hurt me to pay half the money in advance; even then it wouldn't mean I had to leave. Circumstances would decide whether I went or not.

The following day I handed over the money. I was to wait two weeks for news of the arrangements which would enable our group to travel to the East.

3 · Escape

The incident by the gate of the ghetto decided me.* I would never go back to the ghetto. Luckily, my birds of passage have arrived and are going back two days from now. Excellent! After all I'll only be risking my own life. I pass on the news to the others and pack my things.

Only two days ...

One day ...

We're going today!

Marjan and Jurek have naturally designated a meeting-point on the Aryan side. We'll gather there near a small hotel in one of the quiet streets in the centre of the town at seven thirty in the evening, half an hour after the curfew for Jews comes into force, even if they are on a work detail.

I have had my suitcase ready on the Aryan side for several days now. It is quite dark on the streets after seven because of the blackout. Blessed darkness. In these last moments, before it is too late, I consider again whether I have chosen the right path towards my appointment with the Unknown. I weigh the risks, the arguments for and against. An inner voice tells me that the risk of staying surely is much greater. The way I chose at least allows me a chance to survive. In the end I cease my fruitless worrying.

The street is almost empty. I have my small suitcase with me. A backpack would be better, but I don't have anything of that sort. The one I had was left in the concentration camp, there is nowhere to buy a new one.

The moon rises at nine o'clock. Very good. I'll be in a train carriage by then. My steps echo like thunder on the empty street. There is nobody around. Thank you, God. What should I answer if somebody accost me? Where am I going? On a job? Perhaps it's better to pretend I am a black marketeer? No, I'd better run away. The dark of a grave. You can't see your own hand. That's all for the best. What are these steps? Is somebody following me? No, there isn't anything there. Again! I must see who it is. I hide in the niche of a wall. A moment later a shadow passes by, somebody who very clearly is not interested in his surroundings. I breathe easier, as if I have escaped some great danger.

I'm nearing the agreed meeting place. Beware! A trap may be awaiting me here. Careful! My nerves are strained to the utmost. My senses, abnormally acute, almost enable me to see and hear through the walls. Silence and

*see above, p. 183.

emptiness. Too bad, but there is movement now. I leave my suitcase in a gateway. The last few steps I advance slowly like a stalking cat, ready to bolt instantly if the need arises. Somebody looms in front of me. I recognize one of my companions in this escapade. I come closer.

"Hallo!" Although my voice was low, he started in fear as if an electric current had shocked him. I managed to calm him down. He told me that another escapee was waiting at the hotel. I retrieved my suitcase and occupied the gateway opposite his.

The memory of the minutes that passed until I reached the agreed meeting-place and while waiting for the guides are among the blackest recollections of the entire period which I spent in evading the German dragnet on the trip east.

It's seven thirty. Where are the others? Soon a group of six people arrived, our people. We placed ourselves in two gateways and one waited on the street. Staszek and another man stood close to me and described their departure from the ghetto.

"Yesterday an acquaintance in the Jewish police lent me his cap and armband. I led my workers' detail through the gate of the ghetto around six in the evening. Luckily nobody examined my pass to closely. I just yelled 'night shift' and no one took much notice. Siler and Mansfeld were not on guard duty, thank God, well, you've taken a look at these schlemazels – two women and three idiots – worse luck, we had to walk the streets for an hour or so because I didn't want to arrive too early. Then we slunk into a gateway. I took my policman's cap, told them to remove their star of David armbands, threw the stuff into a garden and here we are. But what about Marjan and Jurek?"

What was that? ... Jurek! Praise the Lord! Jurek spun us an unlikely story about a police spy who had recognized them and started to blackmail them. They had had to pay a huge sum to buy him off and Marjan was still drinking with him, making toasts to forgiveness and consolation. Wonders, real wonders. Well, the main thing is that here he was. The hellish period of waiting was over and we could start off for the railway station. Jurek formed us in a column of two and positioned himself at the lead. We moved off. Our little band numbered ten people, including Jurek. We stride through one of the main streets, Jagiellonska, which is completely deserted. The moon is up fortunately and sheds its pale light on the empty streets. Our way leads past the police station on Smolka Square. Each of us endeavours to smother unpleasant thoughts. Nobody dares to open his mouth as if the entire *Schutzpolizei* is waiting to pounce on us.

Our behaviour is symptomatic. The deep-seated sense of bearing a stigma of abasement was the greatest source of danger for those fleeing the ghetto. A

Jew crossing to begin a new life on the Aryan side first got rid of the Jewish armband, which served as the external symbol of humiliation. This seemed difficult: how to do it, where, someone might see me, etc. But all these difficulties were trifles. Nobody was aware of the real obstacle: the stigma branded into our souls by the Germans, the stigma of inferiority, of the cattle trains, of hunted game, of fear of one's fellow humans, stigma invisible but branded deep within. It was not noticeable in the ghetto as there it was ever-present and natural.

Our mood lightened considerably after the police building was left behind. We left surer of ourselves. This feeling was just as unfounded as the lack of confidence which previously had us in its grip.

We are approaching Foch Boulevard which leads directly to the station. Again we feel the strain. The station represents a well-known and often described danger. Here is a concentration of hundreds of spies, agents, provocateurs, and stool-pigeons, all of them ready to discover and turn in any Jew who tries to escape from the trap. If we pass this gate of hell we'll enter paradise and be safe – at least for a few moments. If you survive the railway station in Lvov it means that you have evaded 90 per cent of the traps awaiting the Jew who is in the process of transforming himself into an Aryan.

We're on our way. Our steps echo like a tolling bell. Here we go, to the funeral. The light glares so. What is that? The special entrance for army personnel?! Why, this is marvellous. Clever guys, these two! A tunnel. The tunnel platform. Hundreds of soldiers, backpacks everywhere. Officers, police, railway guards. No trace of civilians.

I feel like a fat piece of meat floating all along on the surface of a plate of soup, but nobody pays attention to our group. Movements, chaos, yells and bustling about. No more places on the trains! What now, do we have to turn back? No way. Here's a station official. A matter-of-fact request made to him masks our agonizing need to move on, to plead for the opportunity to go to the front would arouse instant suspicion.

"Everything's full up! The train is overcrowded. Our brave soldiers can't travel packed in like a swine!!"

Despair. What should we do? Try again.

"Look, we don't have luggage and our boss will punish us if we are late …"

"I've already told you. Wait for the next train. That's it!".

No, we can't wait here, and to return to the station waiting-room is tantamount to suicide as it crawls with agents. This is the end. No, I won't go. But we are forbidden even to stand and wait here. And my papers aren't even with me. They are to blame, Marjan and Jurek, because they were late twice. That wasted an hour which would have given us time to board the train. Damn it to hell! Bad luck has dogged me right from the start. Then a soldier let the women of our group into his compartment so as to while away the dull hours of the journey. His act decided our case as we had a group travel-pass. Hurry up! One of us is still outside the carriage. Where? Why? "Let in one more bold 'Frontarbeiter'". The train official himself intervenes on his behalf. The laggard is seated at last. A minute goes by and our train shudders, bangs and starts moving. I feel perspiration running down my back. These few minutes of tension have left me drained. I've made it. Now just let me find a place in the carriage. And I must not forget that German is a foreign language to me. Only Germans here. No other civilians. Excellent.

The train started off. The chattering wheels picked out a heavenly melody: "You've made-it-made-it-made-it". I chant a song of triumph deep inside. The ghetto, the camp, Belzec. I recall it all and told myself happily that I had escaped a thousand deadly snares and was headed towards the distant goal of freedom which surely existed.

Our guides do not rest on their laurels. They have occupied the toilet, claiming lack of other space, an acceptable form of conduct on crowded trains and they use it cynically as office space, under the very eyes of the Germans, so as to fill in our individual travel documents. They inquire, over the heads of members of the "*Herrenvolk*", which aliases we prefer as our new official names. At first, this risky and unnecessary provocation frightens me immensely, but then I go along with the game and snigger inwardly.

"The wheels must roll on for victory!", say the huge signs erected by the Germans at most train stations. The wheels roll on towards my victory. They roll on and on. They roll me over to the general government border. No problem. Here we are, in the Ukraine and we approach the first station there, with stately speed. The air seems different, fresher, of better quality. This is the breeze of freedom that opens up for me now. This is freedom under false colours, filled with risks, chances of exposure, smaller and larger dangers to be overcome, full of snares and ambushes. But it is freedom which enables me to fight, to show initiative, to overcome fate using my own strength, brains and spirit.

4 · Our Journey to Dniepropetrovsk

Two a.m. A small station, with a waiting room lit by an oil lamp. We go in. A few unwelcoming benches line the walls. The place also boasts an empty newspaper stand and a post of the German gendarmerie. Besides our group, a few others are waiting too, Ukrainian peasants and traders. We eye our neighbours with suspicion but their sleepy faces set our minds at rest. Marjan and Jurek begin to distribute the documents and we start haggling over the sum we owe them. Haggling is unavoidable, of course. Our comrade, Victor, emboldened by vodka, goes out to look for more.

Marjan has just handed me my credentials.

I look it over, quite puzzled.

"This is enough? Why, it's a lot of nothing."

"If you don't like it, go right back to Lvov."

"This is a racket. Who would dare to board a train with such a scrap of paper?" Jurek intervenes when he sees that the discussion is heating up dangerously.

"Look, mister, everything will be O.K. When the train comes, you'll get aboard ..."

"What d'you mean?! You're not coming with us?"

"Nobody promised that we'll hold your hand all the way", Marjan replies. "Jurek and I will get on a goods train and you all will take the 9.30 passenger train to Fastor. There you have trains going directly to Dniepropetrovsk. Jurek, shut up! I'm still talking!"

Jurek, who had thought to smooth over the unpleasant scene, turned about and left. Marjan said goodbye to one of the women and left, too.

We were so stunned that we watched their departure as if paralysed. Nobody tried to stop them, to remonstrate or try to prod their consciences. We all knew that they would not stay, and that if we succeeded in stopping them by means of threats or physical force, they would only slip off at the first opportunity. We were as helpless as babies. I cursed the day when I had bound my fate to these irresponsible brutes. But there was nothing to be done but try to bear up. I had to adapt myself to the new circumstances – otherwise I would perish even before I felt completely free.

Still seething from the clash, I moved over to sit near the women. When I inquired about their papers it became apparent that they were no better than mine.

In the meanwhile, a grey winter day dawned slowly. It seemed that a train was approaching, for a gendarme emerged and began to urge the waiting passengers to leave the waiting room: "*Ukrainer raus! Nur für Deutsche!*" (Ukrainians out. Only for Germans). We were afraid to trust ourselves to the open space outside – another sign of the ghetto complex. I approached the gendarme and started a dialogue in broken German.

"I front-worker, all right here?" – pointing at myself.

"*Ausweis!*" (credentials) – this in a low growl. I showed him my miserable scrap of paper. The German read it carefully from A to Z. Then he looked it over again. My guts felt like lead. Was my cover blown? No, the gendarme handed back the document and I read a positive decision in his good-humoured face.

"Everything in order, Kamerad. You may wait here with your companions." He turned away with a salute, adding that we were permitted to board the train which would remain at the station for an hour.

I went out to the train platform in an incomparably better mood than an hour before. The train, the Berlin–Kiev express, was in sight. I hurried to tell the others but they were already on their way. Soon enough we were squeezing our way into one of the carriages with our meagre luggage. The conductor told us that the seats were reserved for Germans but we could stand in the corridor. Never mind, the important thing was to be on our way.

Four authentic worker types were our neighbours. They observed us for a second or two and I was certain that they saw through our disguise. Sure enough, they started whispering among themselves. Another minute passed and then we heard a sentence – uttered, it seemed, by the leader – which rose above their muttered conversation: "Damn it, let them live, too!" We were sure that he meant us. This time, it seemed, we were lucky.

The train was full of soldiers returning to the front from home leave. Some of them had received a special call-up notice terminating their leave prematurely. Those were openly cursing their fate of having to return to the hell of combat.

A Russian railway policeman in the service of the Germans approached me and started asking all kinds of silly questions. It seemed clear that he was doing it out of pure boredom but at first, because of the ghetto mentality branding in my soul, I thought that his intention was to interrogate me cunningly and that it was all over.

"Where are you going?"

"To Dniepropetrovsk."

"So near to the front?! It's too damn dangerous there. You're not soldiers, eh?"

"No, I'm a furniture painter. We got a job with the Kunz company."

Then I tried to turn the conversation away from a subject of no interest, which is to say, my own insignificant person. When I inquired about his own work it became clear that he had no designs on my life and liberty, suspected nothing and in general just wanted a friendly chat.

In the meanwhile the train stopped at Shepetovka. The soldiers and my policeman friend hurriedly left the train. We didn't know what the rush was all about, but none of us dared to take a step away from the train. They shortly returned loaded with bread, canned food, parcels and canteens brimming with steaming soup. I hadn't eaten since the previous day and furtively had to swallow my gushing saliva. There was no question of leaving the train and getting something to eat. My Aryan skin did not fit me yet, I still felt Jewish. The policeman wondered aloud why I hadn't gone to get my *Verpflegung*. I really wanted to ask him what the word meant (it was the official term for the food rations issued to army personnel in transit) because it sounded rather useful, but I was afraid to reveal my ignorance. So I assumed an expression which could be interpreted variously as forgetfulness, dreaminess, shyness, hesitation and, above all, stupidity – congenital, limitless, hopeless stupidity.

My acquaintance obviously thought to himself: "What a dim Pole." He explained in detail what I was entitled to and where, when and how to get it. His directions were explicit and very clear – everybody so enjoys feeling wiser than the other guy. So I learned what Hitler owed me, as a worker of our fictitious company if only I could summon up enough courage. The courteous policeman then informed me that he was leaving the train and was prepared to be my guide. A monstrous fear of being caught like a rat in a trap almost overwhelmed me, but I could find no excuse and had to go, no matter what could happen. Hell! Let's go!

The operation was painless. Everything went perfectly. I collected my rations (the mysterious *Verpflegung*): I ate a plate of glorious soup and even took some back to my companions. What's more, I was issued bread, butter, sausage and cheese – more than a man could wish for.

The endless snowy Ukrainian steppe rolled on beyond the trains windows. On the endless snow-white waste there was nothing to rest the eye – no tree, not even a hillock. Every hour or so there was a cluster of huts and a railway stop, and then the flat plain once again. I would have sunk into a sentimental melancholia if not all the while the wheels had been clanking out the refrain

"You-are-free, you-are-free" ... I began to spin fantastic plans for the future. The vistas revealed to me were promising: I would go here and there, make such and such arrangements. For the first time I dared to think about the future. This was progress indeed and my brain was so dizzied that I hardly felt the passage of the eight hours it took us to reach Fastov, a railroad junction where we had to change to a train for Dniepropetrovsk, 800 kilometres distant.

The next passenger train was due in four hours but a goods train was leaving in half an hour if we could manage to get on it. The man in charge of that train, a functionary in the Nazi Labour Organization (the Todt Organization), wanted to have nothing to do with us, but when he saw there were two women with us, he let us into the mail carriage. There we were, the seven of us (including the two women) and the Germans: the functionary, two soldiers and a noncom. The train began to move as soon as we were settled in.

The ride was extremely fatiguing, especially when night fell. The German official tried to get off with our women and it took a lot of diplomacy and effort to dissuade him. We also had to overcome a natural inclination to punch him on the nose. He finally realized that all his efforts were in vain and he gave up, surely cursing himself for having let us in.

We fugitives lay down to sleep and soon the cramped space resounded with snores and wheezes. I was too excited to drop off – frantic thoughts kept racing through my head. The soldiers – chewing the fat in the corner – were sounding off again on the eternal subject of war's intolerable burden. Some sentences were daring enough to terrify me: that Rudolf Hess alone was concerned with the welfare of Germany and he knew what he was about when he tried to arrange peace with England; that the Führer was leading the German nation to destruction; that the blood of hundreds of thousands was on his head, and so on.

Nevertheless, their words were of no account, just like all the German complaints I heard. It was all said rather in the spirit of an old toothless grandpa propping up the wall of a church and complaining that the government was no good and that the Kaiser, His Majesty Franz-Joseph, had been much better. Sleep finally overcame me in the middle of a sentence.

We took advantage of the trading on the train to arrange for a night's lodging with a resident of Dniepropetrovsk. The good-natured Russian didn't even wait for the negotiations to open in earnest – he gave his address and promised to help us in any way he could as soon as we began to explain what we needed. We reached the city at about five p.m.

The gigantic station and the street in front of it impressed us – we seemed to have come to a real city. We went to get our rations but left immediately because we were the only civilians there and didn't feel too confident.

Gendarmes swarmed everywhere, as was customary near the front. There was nothing for it but to walk into town through the winter drizzle.

Because of the thaw, we had to cross deep puddles in between the snowdrifts. The women went to seek shelter with the husband of one of them, accompanied by a man from our group, while the rest of us set out in search of our hospitable Russian.

The streets were completely deserted and there was nobody who could direct us in this city of half a million souls. It was pitch-dark. We blundered around blindly. After half an hour, a chance passer-by gave us some directions. We had to retrace our steps and had to run again the familiar gauntlet of puddles, snow drifts and unlit street lamps rearing suddenly in the dark night in front of our noses. It was a miracle we did not encounter a patrol which would surely have arrested us. We were very fatigued after a 48-hours' train ride and dispirited too, because of the inhospitable reception seemingly meted out to us by the dark city. We kept going through black, canyon-like streets, turned a hundred times, retraced our steps again and again …

Finally luck got us – how not to believe in destiny – to the right street. After a short bout of questioning through the closed door we were admitted. It was just a cabin, really, but we could undress and lie down at last. Did we sleep peacefully? Yes, it seems, at last, yes!

5 · We Find Lodgings

Although all four of us slept on the floor, I awoke in the morning completely rested. The first I had to do was find lodgings. During the trip from Lvov I had become friendly with one of my companions, whose assumed name was Michael Baczyński. He was about thirty years old, tall, slim, had Aryan features and, most important, moved and behaved like a common person – the result of constant association with the peasants among whom he earned his living as a veterinary doctor. His clothes were luckily in the height of the prevailing fashion: high boots, breeches made of some ill-defined cloth, a torn jacket, and on top of it a genuine threequarter-length labourer's coat. The two of us had agreed to room together. True, the chances of being discovered increased in direct proportion to the number of people with false papers who lived together, yet a man would feel much better if he had a room-mate. So I gave Michael my address where I slept when he accompanied the women to their hiding-place, in spite of the custom of people in hiding, who usually kept the secret of their location to themselves.

Michael appeared soon after I awoke and we went out to look for a room. It was Sunday but that made no difference for our purposes. We tried our luck at a number of houses whose exteriors looked promising, but these were crammed with German or Italian soldiers. As luck had it, a woman who was visiting one of these houses and saw that we were crestfallen after another rejection, offered to take us to her sister-in-law, who had a room to rent. She accompanied us to the outskirts of the city, only to hear that the room was taken. The people there advised us to inquire about lodgings at a cousin of theirs.

We were quite tired of wandering along miles on miles of streets in this vast city, but the Russian lady exhorted us not to lose hope and drew us on. We were turned away at two locations, but in the end found a closet-like room adjoining the kitchen which would be vacant the next day. Nobody said a word about the rent: we would pay anything we liked. After all, we belonged to the class of the masters here, and if we ourselves were not exactly masters we were at least the immediate servants of the master – several rungs above the level to which the Russians had been demoted by the Germans.

Michael could remain one more night with the woman, but I had to move out immediately because we "masters" are surely accustomed to superior sleeping accommodation and if I stayed in our previous crowded room, it would surely arouse much comment. By this time I had familiarized myself to some extent with the local conditions, and felt more confident in my chosen role. Therefore, I stopped at the first reasonable-looking house along the street and demanded – not requested! – a lodging for the night. I was somewhat taken aback when my intended hosts acquiesced courteously. So I collected my suitcase and prepared to spend the night. The people in the apartment were quite polite, the wife prepared supper for me, and even the bed was excellent.

The sudden metamorphosis from a hunted Jew to a domineering "master" – such was the rank of the Germans and the Polish workers for German firms in Russia – was liable to turn my head! I spent part of the night thinking hard. I began to understand the status of the aliens, who had come with the German army to the heart of Russia, and the necessity to adjust myself to the expectations the native populace had from such an exalted being. Alarming thoughts did not let me sleep. I had to plan ahead – how to behave, what to say, how to explain to my landlord why I did not go out to work, and so on.

I began to realize that although Dniepropetrovsk was a large city, it nevertheless would be difficult to lose ourselves in a crowd. Even speaking correct Russian was no help as the foreign accent was a give-away. In addition, we foreign workers were singled out, by the suffering Russian population, because we were accorded significant privileges: superior working conditions, lodgings in Russian apartments, and much better food. Our dress was the most important factor in this respect as the cut and quality of the cloth, and even our boots were noticably western.

I was aware of all this from the very beginning, a fact which proved to be of great help. I had to remember that we lived in the limelight; everybody took an interest in our doings and knew very well what we did, where we went, what we ate and, perhaps, with whom we shared our bed. So I'd better remember this constantly lest something fatal occur which would remind me painfully that information I preferred to keep hidden was probably well-known. I thought the whole matter over and decided that although in the abstract it would have been best to live in the shadows, unseen and unknown, I had no choice in the matter. So I went to sleep feeling calm and quite confident.

The following day I met Michael and we made our way to the house where we were to live. An unpleasant surprise awaited us there: our room had been commandeered for the use of two Russians, who had come to the city to take a month-long course for surveyors. But our landlady didn't have the heart to let us down (perhaps she didn't dare to). She decided to sleep on the floor in the kitchen and let us use her room. We agreed, with the proviso that we would move after a month to our original room.

Our Russian landlady was an elderly woman with great self-possession, but her restraint disintegrated with the requisition of her room. She poured out all her pent-up grudges against the Germans without regard for the need to be on guard in front of strangers. We had not yet fully identified with our role and it took little provocation to reveal where our true sympathies lay. The landlady then relinquished all restraint.

She revealed that she was the widow of an active member of the Communist Party. All the good things in her life and in the country were the work of the Party. She had the opportunity to learn how to read and write at night courses, thanks to which she could fill the long lonely evenings of old age. There were renegades who licked the boots of the "masters" (the ironic Russian term for Germans) but all they got for their trouble was a kick or two. You couldn't hope for anything more from capitalists. Unfortunately, not everybody held these views, because people were blinded by the opportunity to break into Jewish apartments and cart off a few sticks of furniture. The Germans favoured those traitors, but the war was by no means over. The Bolsheviks emerged from the people; the people would realize in the end where their real interests lay, and would threw the hellhounds out. The two Russians about to arrive were not to her liking either; they were about to serve the Germans after finishing the course. But she was powerless to do anything more than wait for victory.

Her despair was sincere, her patriotism genuine, but I was mainly thinking that we would have nothing to fear from her, when she realized that we did not work and had no intention of doing so. Her Bolshevik sympathies and her enmity towards the Germans could only be of benefit to us. I intended to check at the first opportunity what she thought about the Jews. With regard to the two brutes about to share the house, I was curious about them.

They came home from their studies in the afternoon. When they learned that we were to lodge with them they did not show any annoyance but, on the contrary, remarked that the more the merrier. The shorter of the two was a Russian from the vicinity of Moscow. He had been taken prisoner in the third month of the fighting but had escaped from the P.O.W. camp after a month's captivity. A relative living in the Ukraine sheltered him. He was not enthusiastic about the Germans and was afraid to speak openly about his attitude to the Communists. He always shied away from dangerous topics when we conversed, and reacted with a fixed smile and a hearty laugh, which rang false. The other was a Ukrainian. He was open in his antipathy to the Bolsheviks and did not seem to like the Germans either. Generally speaking, the two seemed harmless companions who could even be of use to us.

The first evening in our new lodgings was spent in friendly conversation and in getting acquainted with the neighbours. In a workers' section of the city, like the one where we resided, it was normal for the people on the street to live at close quarters and know everything about their neighbours. A special occasion such as the appearance of two exotic newcomers was utilized thoroughly, which is to say it was discussed from every possible angle and aspect. A series of curious female neighbours traipsed through the house, so as to observe and evaluate us.

The hopes I had held for Michael were proved correct. The fellow passed the first test with flying colours. He told fanciful stories, argued, and flirted with the neighbours, while I devoted my best efforts to amusing the landlady and the other two lodgers.

The next day I went out "to find out about our work". I went downtown with the intention of looking for a familiar face and perhaps finding a job – this was the best way to obtain an *Ausweis*, because it was not really feasible to survive for long with the document I had. But I did not worry too much – it was not worth it.

6 · A Narrow Escape

Szeroka street was the chief thoroughfare of Dniepropetrovsk. It was a glorious metropolitan boulevard, in a state of glorious disrepair. Many houses were in ruins. The sidewalks and the roads were swept clear of snow but towering heaps of snow framed the streets and threatened a huge flood, when the thaw set in. There were no stores, apart from the two or three reserved for German customers. A couple of filthy bars-cum-teahouses huddled in cellars. The tea one could order there was coloured water to which some suspect ingredients had been added.

The glaring contrasts along this boulevard would have astonished a Westerner, but we knew something about Russia and accepted the sights. A block of tall apartment houses stood cheek by jowl with an aged peasant shack, sunk deep in the earth and roofed with thatched straw. A monumental building in the centre of the town shared one of its walls with a one-storey house containing ten or more dirty one-room apartments – a typical nest of the urban poor. Usually houses of this type were found in the suburbs but nobody wondered or cared that it was right in the centre here.

The larger houses and all the public buildings were taken by the Germans and now served as billets, hospitals or offices. Every few yards soldiers were standing guard in front of entrances. At first, this made me nervous, but then I realized that nobody was interested in me and I got used to the presence of the Germans. There were so many soldiers milling around, that I felt camouflaged in the crowd. This was a city closer than others to the front-line, so it served as a rest-and-recreation centre. There weren't many places to visit, no cafes or restaurants, but the opportunity to walk along a genuine city street is also a treat of sorts. Civilians were few and far between, so I paid little attention to them.

Suddenly I was accosted by two workmen who greeted me in Polish. They were very friendly and eager to know how and when I had come to the city. Though my personal rule was not to trust any Pole fully, I thought at first that these were people thirsting for news from their homeland, and I entered into a conversation with them. Then a sudden thought coursed through my brain just when we were exchanging trifling questions and answers: they knew who I was and were toying with me like a cat with a mouse.

Finally one of them demanded to see my travel documents. This was going a bit too far. I refused and asked why he was sticking his nose into my personal business. They explained that they were working for the police and their task was to bring all the newcomers to the police station to check their credentials. I knew the meaning of that. Although I felt a shiver of horror, my gambler's instinct urged me to go for broke; I knew perfectly well that scoundrels of this kind were impervious to pleading and that only cheek, coolness, and luck could help me.

"O.K. Whatever you say. Let's move."

We marched on in complete silence. Their previous gushing friendliness had vanished without a trace. They hemmed me on both sides to forestall a premature farewell on my part. We made our way through side streets and I noticed that the arrows on the signs showed the way to the police station. My nerves were stretched to the limit, but did not break. A large sign, Gendarmerie, seared my eyes from far off. I was lost. This was a really cruel joke of fate to allow me, finally to get here, and then to let me be betrayed at the beginning of my stay by my beloved Polish fellow-countrymen. Though there was a chance in a million – it was best to keep up a show. Crying and begging wouldn't help. When we were about ten paces from the station, one of my companions opened his mouth.

"This son of a bitch is a tough customer! But I know you from Lvov. You're a 'chestnut', nothing doing. Now, you choose – to sink or to trade. Nu, let's go in this gate."

Well, I let myself be persuaded very easily, since the edge of the precipice was just a step away.

"What do you want?"

"Give us ten chicks [a thousand rubles] and you can fly away."

"Are you crazy or something? I don't have anything like that. Take what you like, you should care if I die of hunger. You should be ashamed to squeal on me. Suppose I die, does it help you? It doesn't matter what I am, but I'm a Polish citizen for sure, just like you. The Germans are the enemies of all of us."

"No stories. Fork out the cash, or ..."

"I don't have it. You can kill me, I don't have the thousand."

I really had no more than 800 rubles on me.

"Show us what's in your pockets."

When I moved my arm to unbutton my coat, the sleeve pulled up and revealed my watch. They pulled it off with the speed of professionals, before I knew what they were doing.

"Nu, that's enough for now. No hard feelings. And you should remodel your style. Anyone can see without trying that you're not our kind, and you'll get caught for sure."

They left. I had been lucky. The drama had been short but significant. My fellow-countrymen had shown their true colours again. They were far from Poland and couldn't plead they were forced to do this. Here they were, in exile really, taking on themselves of their own free will the noble duty of hangman's helpers. Their intention for the present was to extract all they could out of me, exhaust me, ruin me. In the end, after extorting all my possessions, they would hand me over to the Gestapo. They knew very well that I couldn't evade them, that they would meet me again. Then they would rob me of any "treasures" I had managed to scrape up. They would jealously guard their national honour – to rob and rob until nothing remained, and then to finish the Jew off.

They would not abandon the illustrious tradition of the brave extortionists of Warsaw, those we called "greasers", "hyenas", "skinners"; professionals, swimming like fish in the dirty water of their specialized trade. The partners in the economic and physical destruction of Jews, enjoyed in the meantime the approving applause of their countrymen, who were also robbing the Jews, albeit not so professionally. To denounce the Jew to the authorities, to cause his fall was almost a service to the nation. Nobody would even mention it in the confessional booth, because it was no sin. If anyone did, the priest would grant him an easy absolution and praise a person whose tender conscience was uneasy over such a trifle.

It wasn't so easy to escape the accursed circle, drawn around us by the Germans. The incident filled me with loathing but also spurred my will to fight back. I decided not to give up easily. I preferred to go down fighting, for a chance to escape. On my way home I constructed a whole system of deluding my landlady and the two other tenants. I would announce that work would begin in another ten days. This would give me time to find another stratagem, or to move. I understood that the streets were too dangerous and I'd better stay home.

I asked the landlady to buy our food-stuffs in the market until we started working and got our official food rations. She was quite pleased by the arrangement which would permit her to skim off some food for her own use.

In this fashion I began to lead a somewhat regular existence in that circle of hell, which is called "living on Aryan papers."

7 · Our Life in Dniepropetrovsk

Michael, my room-mate, did not dare to leave the apartment after I told him about my meeting with the extortionists. His conduct troubled me quite a lot. He was scared of everybody and everything. The sound of feet going up the stairs or a faint rustle, was liable to make him panicky. It is not as if I had no fear and felt calm at all times, but at least I tried to preserve outward appearances.

Our life together once again proved my point about living on Aryan papers: non-Jewish looks or proper documents were not as important as one's deportment when presenting them for scrutiny. One required moral fibre, a strong character and boldness, with an added mixture of cheek, *chutzpah* and combativeness. It was a pity that Michael lacked these qualities completely and, what was worse, his cowardice repelled me once we began rooming together.

We had to get up early, because lying abed would have been the surest way to direct attention to us. Michael used to procrastinate, as if the bed increased his prospects of survival, but there was no chance – we had no desire to cause the other tenants to speculate about us. As for the landlady, I had told her, as planned that we had a two weeks' wait before beginning work. I did not neglect to curse the Germans roundly, for the impertinence of bringing us all the way to the city and then letting us kick our heels. Our landlady liked to hear that other people, too, were not enthusiastic about the Germans. We held these conversations when the Russian tenants were attending their courses.

I had succeeded in persuading the landlady to cook for us, using the foodstuffs she purchased. It should be kept in mind that shopping in Dniepropetrovsk was no simple matter. All the stores were locked or burned-out, and food could be obtained only at the open-air market. A few peasants were seen there from time to time, but the sellers were mainly black-marketeers from the city. The good woman couldn't understand why we chose to refrain from the joys of shopping – the main source of entertainment in town, and the chance to meet people, talk, and be sociable. She was also afraid that we would suspect her of cheating us as regards prices – these gyrated daily in accordance with the fluctuations of supply and demand, compounded by the whims of the food speculators. It took all our powers of persuasion to convince her that we knew nothing about shopping and she would do the job much, much better. Nevertheless, she sometimes demanded that we accompany her. It was I who escorted her, needless to say, because Michael had absolutely no intention of showing his face in such a risky place as a market.

Once home, Michael and I would remain alone, left with the nagging sense of having nothing to do, and prey to forebodings about the risk of a sudden house-searcher or an unexpected caller. The house was made of wood. We lived on the first floor. Our neighbours on that floor were a widow with three children. The son was a nineteen-year-old drifter, who subsisted mainly on what he could steal. A seventeen-year-old daughter was quite good-looking but was being devoured by untreated scabies. She seemed to be awaiting a propitious occasion to sell herself to the highest bidder. A four-year-old child was tormented by the same skin disease.

The rooms on the ground floor and the courtyard held five families, comprising a gallery of types sufficient to fill the pages of more than one novel. Two "straw widows" whose husbands were serving in the Red Army, hugged to their breasts any visiting German soldier desirous of sharing their beds. An unemployed tram driver had escaped a short time before from a German P.O.W. camp and returned home to find that his spouse had earned her keep in his absence by consorting with men of the enemy's army, whom she entertained in the one-room apartment where she lived with her two children. If a client objected to their presence, she would send them out to play in the yard regardless of the weather and the time of day.

Now everything was back to normal. Her husband, it seemed, was ready to let bygones be bygones and married life went on – quarrels, drunken binges, noisy battles, beatings, reconciliations, starvation and abject poverty in all its most loathsome manifestations. There was a sanctimonious female, mother of two daughters, whose main pleasure in life was haunting the Greek Orthodox churches in the city. She used the worst kind of gutter language when she called on heaven to punish her immoral neighbours. This gallery was completed by a drunkard who got drunk regularly in the company of his wife and stayed up late at night brawling and singing.

Our apartment on the first floor could be reached by a staircase attached to the side wall. The stairs creaked and rattled unmercifully and were a menace to anybody who climbed them. We sat upstairs for hours on end, not speaking to each other, prey to a dull fear that somebody might decide to drop in. Then we would have to explain, why we were sitting there doing nothing, what our sources of livelihood were, and why we had come. A thousand and one tough questions. Each one of us has surely dreamed of sitting idly, in peace, but this idleness was driving us insane.

I was afraid of the thoroughfares, so I wandered around the back alleys. Then I discovered a military cemetery, which served as a haven for those hours that I had to leave the house. Thousands of German soldiers lay there under crosses of various shapes. They had surely never imagined that their crosses would shelter a Jew. It was very peaceful; there were no visitors, for the families were far away. I could wander along the paths for hours studying the inscriptions as if searching for a grave. The cemetery grew rapidly, with new rows added continually. God willing, it would hold many more dead soldiers. It was a pity that the cold spoiled the many pleasant hours I spent there – I would pass an hour or two there every few days.

The rest of my time was spent on thoughts for the future. I had no *Ausweis*, and my *Urlaubsschein* (the document I came to Dniepropetrovsk with) was somewhat outdated. I had to do something so as to acquire a new *Ausweis*. I had absolutely no intention of looking for employment: I would have to work as a Pole and risk being blackmailed by my beloved countrymen. Work would enormously increase the chances of discovery if, as is common on a job, people started prying into my affairs and asking where I had come from, why, and so on. I considered the problem from various angles again and again, and came to the conclusion that it was pointless to risk my life trying to get an *Ausweis* – that road to saving my miserable life hid too many uncertainties and ambushes. On the other hand, I would earn something if I worked, though not enough for my needs – and I didn't have a surplus of money.

There was another way to get money – the black market. Trading, though possible, entailed enormous risks, but so what – I couldn't be killed twice! Trade in matches or in vodka was good business but one had to buy those items from the Germans, with whom I tried to have as little contact as possible. The best course would be to smuggle from Poland quantities of salt (much in demand), soda, or dyes for fabrics. But, again, appropriate documents were needed for that. Otherwise, my plans were vain daydreams. I would have to look for the others who had left Poland and hidden here, and see how they had settled in.

Noon was dinner time; this was much better than the emptiness of the morning hours. Michael was ashamed to display his nervousness, and anyway he was busy helping the landlady with the food. Preparing the meal, albeit extremely simple, was a small ceremony. You always had to pound or grind foodstuffs, fetch and carry, be busy at last. Then there was the ritual of setting the table. Unfortunately, eating the food took only a short time. After the meal we washed the dishes and scrubbed the pots. Then we could take a rest with an easy conscience.

The afternoons were a time for visiting. The attraction of our "salon" was quite strong. Two young men coming from afar, from Europe. Our guests were usually of the fair sex. There were sisters-in-law and nieces of the landlady, workers' wives who were friends of hers, a teacher. Almost the whole of conversation was about current matters, but the situation at the front was – strangely – almost never discussed.

The Jews were an endless subject for discussion. The landlady's attitude wasn't so much pro-Jewish, as decidedly not anti-Jewish. The Communist Party had decreed that the Jews were as good as all the others, so for her it was a self-evident truth, which should not be criticized. Others took advantage of the first opportunity to criticize the party's decisions, and had the time of their lives complaining in a hostile manner about the Jews. Their pronounced hostility to the Jews was mainly motivated by envy: these had acquired, by various stratagems, positions which were or seemed to be better, than those held by the non-Jews. The granting of equal rights to Jews was their only cause for complaint against the Soviet authorities. Their youthful years had been spent in the glow of fires from the pogroms of Petlura, and this had stamped their souls for life.

They had a grudge against the Jews, because they were teachers and taught Ukrainian schoolchildren, were employed in government offices, and so on. Then, a moment later, someone would remark that it was the Russians who had the ill-paid jobs of teachers and office workers while the Jews grabbed the juiciest positions in the state grocery shops and restaurants. There was n0t much logic in these grumblings, but they gained force from the fact, that they couldn't have been aired during the years of Soviet rule. If anyone had dared to utter the epithet "Zhid" instead of the official "Yevrey", he would have been condemned by a court forthwith, to five years' hard labour in a forsaken region of th USSR. Now they were at liberty to have their say.

The mass murder of Jews by the occupying Germans was regarded by the majority as a loathsome, provocative and inhuman crime. In Dniepropetrovsk, about 35,000 Jews were machine-gunned to death three weeks after the town fell. They were all thrown into a huge previously dug pit, whether they were dead, half-dead, or merely wounded, and were covered with soil. It seemed that nobody here was happy about this. But as far as the subject of Jews was concerned, there were so many grounds for personal grumbling against them that their murder, though a crime crying out to heaven, did not hold pride of place among the locals.

The German treatment of the Russian population was so abysmal that we, who came from the West, simply could not adjust to it. Here the Germans could really feel like the *Herrenvolk*. The Russians were put on the same level as cattle. It was inconceivable that a German would walk shoulder to shoulder with a Russian. If it happened that a German was obliged to walk with a Russian, he always strode a few paces behind him or in front. Germans sitting down with the locals in a café or a restaurant? The very idea was ridiculous! A German did not stand in line, whatever his rank was. He would commandeer the barber's chair even if ten people were waiting for a haircut. He had a free ride in the trams and always had the right to a seat. The examples could be multiplied by the hundred, and though these were minor irritations, they humiliated the Russian population painfully and unceasingly. They would not forget, and they would endeavour to make the Germans pay dearly for what they did.

The worst disaster was the kidnapping of young people for forced labour in Germany. Dniepropetrovsk was almost completely denuded of its youth. The round-ups continued in the streets, markets and houses. Information about those taken sometimes took months to arrive and the letters – censored postcards – were few and far between. Nevertheless, news about the new life in Germany infiltrated mysteriously, and reported about scandalous exploitation, hunger, inhuman labour conditions, and so on.

Perhaps some people who still could not cut themselves off from their bourgeois background, had before the conquest secretly desired to get to know the Germans on familiar terms. But now that this opportunity had been granted, they like everybody else were finally persuaded that Soviet rule was infinitely preferable. They recalled regretfully, how in times gone by they could walk the streets without fear, could buy things, send the children to school. Yes, the Germans had closed down the schools as unnecessary for slaves. The local population had enjoyed full bellies once upon a time, but nowadays they were issued 2.5 kg of millet bread a week, and only those who worked for the Germans were entitled to this ration.

Michael and I did not participate much in those conversations and preferred to listen. It was difficult to adjust to the mentality of the locals and we found it hard to join in the condemnation of Jews. Other topics were not much safer. These discussions, or rather grumbling sessions which could go on endlessly, were cut short when the twilight outside signalled that the hour of curfew, 7 p.m., was approaching. The guests would disperse to their homes, and we who lived in the apartment would be left alone.

Supper consisted of a slice of bread and *ersatz* black coffee. It did not take long and then there was nothing much to do. We usually sat in the kitchen – because it was the only heated space and provided a little light from the fire of the stove. Electricity was reserved for the Germans. Oil lamps had gone out of use years ago and were unobtainable. The wealthy used carbide lamps. The gas burning in the lamp stank and carbide was hard to obtain. The lamps needed repairs quite often, but the light they gave was quite bright.

The "*koptilka*" was more popular. It was a small bottle filled with kerosene in which a wick soaked. The burning wick provided the light. It was, God knows, the kind of light which beggars description – a grey wispy trembling flame, which barely shed its light two feet around it. The ceiling was left in profound darkness. Even so, the use of "*koptilka*" was a luxury, too – kerosene was extremely expensive – which we allowed ourselves when we played cards. Sometimes we played with the other tenants a Russian game called "*durak*" (blockhead). This primitive game excited our partners so much that they refused to stop until a bombing raid, which took place almost every night would end the session.

The raids usually began about 8 p.m. and continued until two or three in the morning. Although we lived next to the railway station, the bombs did not bother us overmuch. They did not prevent us from going to sleep calmly, thanking God that we could fall asleep without worrying about the Germans, who feared bombs so much that they surely were sitting tight in a shelter.

8 · A False Dawn

In one of the early days of February, Michael, who was stationed as always at the window, signalled that something unusual was happening. An endless line of sleighs loaded with typical refugee property was moving down the street from the direction of the Dniepr river. The sleighs bore piles of bundles filled with underclothes, broken-down furniture and chests. A cow on a tether frequently followed a sleigh. Children and women rested among the piled bundles. The endless snake of sleighs slithered from early morning: soon we learned from our neighbours that these were German colonists from the region of the Don river, who were being evacuated by the retreating German army. The evacuees answered unwillingly the eager inquiries of the Russians. It was a sign that the front line was really moving. More information kept coming in. There were stories about a Russian breakthrough on the Don, the taking of Rostov, a complete defeat of the German armies.

We were overjoyed. Perhaps the Bolsheviks would manage to liberate us. At the present stage in the war, that would be liberation for keeps. The signs multiplied. I recalled that at the end of January someone had been issued a transportation order to Stalino, but was informed at the railway station that he couldn't go there by train because that location was in the battle zone. He talked to soldiers who told him frankly that Stalino was completely surrounded by Bolsheviks. All of these pieces of information were falling into place. After a day or two we saw the retreat of the army. Lines of automobiles moved through the streets westward in the direction of Krivoi Rog. It was clear evidence of evacuation. Even Michael's spirit rose, and he stopped acting in a way guaranteed to get on my nerves. True, he continued to stand by the window, but now he had something real to observe. Each new group of refugees or a retreating unit were cause for jubilation.

In the middle of February the retreat became a panic-stricken rout, and we had enough experience in wars and retreats to appreciate its true dimensions. All the train carriages disappeared from the nearby station, and the rail sidings shone vacantly. The factories were emptied of anything which could be of use. Each afternoon our guests reported increasingly exciting news about the evacuation and retreat of the Germans. The news about the German flight became more vivid when the soldiers did not find enough living space in the barracks and began to quarter themselves in the houses of the Russian inhabitants. Accurate news from the front came straight "from the horse's mouth". The soldiers spoke about the fighting with a shudder. The front-line was a conflagration of fire and iron. They cursed the Russians and told tales about the inhuman crimes of their enemies, just as the Russians surely related the crimes of the Germans. The reports were so encouraging that we felt that it was time to prepare for the coming of the liberators.

Real chaos begin with the appearance of the Italians. Many Italian units fought in the southern sector of the front line. I recalled the time in Lvov when we used to deserve and admire the uniforms and armament of the Italian units riding to the front in a long motorized column. Their appearance put the Germans in the shade. Our memory of the Italians was a pleasant one because they treated the Jews well. Jews were afraid to approach these fascists, so the Italians invariably made the first move, distributing bread and canned food to anybody who looked hungry.

Now nothing remained of all this splendour. One day groups of tatterdemalions started to wander around town. Lacking shoes, their feet were wrapped in rags or in remains of shoes through which swollen and bluish snowbitten toes peeked forlornly. Only picturesque remnants of the uniform were left, the shirts torn and muddy, the trousers full of holes. They usually walked around wrapped in blankets to protect themselves from the very cold weather. They panhandled like civilian beggars, only more aggressively, and differed from them only because some of them still had rifles. Most of them had thrown away or sold their weapons, which they regarded as useless burdens which only sapped the remnant of their strength. They complained that the Germans did not supply them with food, that the whole front line was broken, that they had abandoned everything and run away. Now the Germans were taking revenge by denying them food. Their unkempt appearance aroused such pity that the townspeople shared with them whatever they could, although they themselves did not have much. Secretly, however, everybody felt good at the sight of such poverty afflicting the allies of Germany. The Italians did not hesitate to curse the Germans, Hitler, and even Mussolini. Their deepest wish was that the great leaders would go to the front, if they really felt obliged to go to war, and fight out the issue among themselves. They, the simple soldiers, had finished with the war, and were going home.

More and more Italians gathered in the city, like potatoes falling out of a torn sack. They flooded the town and instituted what was, in effect, the rule of looters. Anarchy spread like wildfire. Luckily, all their actions were directed against their allies and not against the civilians. A hungry person recognizes no limitations, so first of all they started raiding trains at the station and robbing military stores at gunpoint. Some Italians occupied our courtyard. Our landlady, who had pitied them just the previous day, now told us that they seemed to have got their hands on quantities of cigarettes, in which they traded. I approached them to buy some and realized immediately that their cartons had been taken from an army store. They had two boxes filled with cigarettes, canned goods, sausages etc. My suspicion was confirmed later by the woman in whose rooms they lodged temporarily.

The proverbial irresponsibility of the Italians was best exemplified in their attitude to weapons. Rifles, pistols, hand grenades and ammunition were of no interest to them insofar as they were not edible, so they were abandoned. Before long very many civilians, willy-nilly, had arms at their disposal. The morale of the Germans had also plummeted because of the rout, and they too bartered everything they could in exchange for food – uniforms, blankets and other military items which could be utilized in a household. Nevertheless, their behaviour could not be compared with that of the Italians, who got rid of anything connected with war and the army. They had definitely said farewell to war.

The two Russians in our apartment had finished their course of studies. They packed and left hastily, a little puzzled why we too were not fleeing the Bolsheviks. We breathed a little easier after they had vacated their room. Even the landlady was pleased that they had gone. She realized that we would be quite happy to see the Bolsheviks in town.

On 17 February, 1942 we learned that the military governor's staff had fled in a convoy of motor cars loaded with all they could manage to grab for themselves. The large city was left to its own devices. German soldiers were still in evidence, but only when they were marched on their way elsewhere. All the offices were closed. The townspeople who, on the whole, had little contact with German officialdom, did not realize the extent of this sudden liberty, were perhaps confused by the new circumstances and did not yet take advantage of them. The next day there were rumours that unknown persons were running riot in the city, but nobody was worried because the general poverty precluded any anxiety about robbers.

Our landlady returned at an unexpectedly early hour on the third day. She was about fifty years old but was in good physical condition, as was witnessed by the load she bore on her back. She brought three pails of corncobs, and other foodstuffs – five bottles of cooking oil, a fine piece of salted pork fat, and some flour. We received our share, paid the commission and now had enough supplies to last us for almost a week. She told us that a Bolshevik patrol had appeared on the shore of the Dniepr river opposite the city that very morning. She had also encountered Bolsheviks in a village 60 kilometres distant and these soldiers had told her, they would enter Dniepropetrovsk within three days.

After we heard her story the waiting started to get on our nerves. We hardly left our observation post by the window. We could not sleep at night though there were no bombing raids – perhaps because of that fact. Sad to say, there were no Bolsheviks in sight. The next day we heard with astonishment that the Germans had returned to the military governor's headquarters. Around noon a German company marched through the city with a song on their lips. Nobody took this to heart: the Germans were merely putting on a show, while "ours" were already across the river … So we waited another day, and then another, and …

No, we stopped waiting. The Soviet troops, instead of rushing into the empty area in front of them, withdrew for unknown reasons, despite the law of physics which says that a vacuum is always filled. Our disappointment was extremely painful. Liberation had been so palpably close and now the usual feeling of helplessness overcame us. What was left of my imaginings on the train? Freedom? Yes, in theory, but in practice what was the use of freedom? I dared not stir from the house for fear of blackmailers and I barely had enough to eat in my cloistered existence in the house. My great plans for the future – wide-ranging travel – had proved to be pipe-dreams. I was left to face miserable reality which compared well with that of the ghetto, but remained a pale shadow of freedom. I preferred not to think about the unclear future.

In spite of my painful disappointment I tried to put a bold face on things, but Michael collapsed. The crouching beast of madness was extending its paws and Michael was attracted to its greedy claws like a moth to a flame. I tried to calm him and turn his thoughts away from real and imagined fears. I achieved partial success by making our financial situation clear. I stated that if we put together my "capital" and his, we would have enough money for 7 to 10 days at the most. We had to get more money. Michael told me that Alosha, an acquaintance, had hinted several times that trade with the Germans could be a plentiful source of cash. Alosha had said that it might be good business for both of them, if Michael provided the money and he bought goods from the Germans and sold them at a profit. They would settle account every evening. I told Michael that I did not like the idea, but he was stubborn once an idea took hold of him. What's more, he liked to eat well, spoke and thought continuously about food. Trade with the Germans was carried out mainly in foodstuffs, and this would afford him the opportunity to gorge on good food.

So Michael started doing business with Alosha in spite of my objections. At first everything went swimmingly. Each day Alosha brought loaves of bread, canned food, cigarettes. The capital did not diminish; it even grew somewhat.

A few days passed in this manner. Michael became more confident and parted with increasing sums. He started with 600 rubles but soon Alosha held his entire capital – 3,000 rubles or so. Michael dined sumptuously while I had to make to do with the remnants of my hoard. He was less nervous than usual, perhaps because he always had a full belly.

Then, one day, the catastrophe, I had always feared, occurred. Normally Alosha would come around 5 p.m. to settle accounts, but that day he did not appear even after hours had passed. Michael understandably became very nervous. Alosha appeared only after eight, long past the curfew hour. We heard him staggering on the stairs and singing drunkenly. Michael went to see him after waiting in vain for him to come as usual to our room. Alosha said that he had been robbed at the place where he went to have a drink or two. Michael started to yell. Rage and frustration choked him, he itched to get his hands on the scoundrel. I was afraid of a noisy fight and with great difficulty succeeded in restraining my room-mate. Alosha did not react at first to Michael's threats, but then had his say: Michael could go to the police if he wanted to; he himself had nothing to fear because the money he had (Michael's entire capital) was stolen. When the police took down our statements he, Alosha, would know what to say. This threat cooled Michael down at once. I did not like it, either. I didn't know what the rascal had in mind and I didn't want to probe too deeply.

The fact of the matter was that we had practically no cash left. Michael still had a few cans, we had a little corn, and a few hundred rubles. We had to do something. We had to sell something. I had a spare suit of clothes which could be sold, but how? The landlady, naturally! At first she did not want to handle the transaction because she was afraid of the neighbours' suspicions, after the business with Alosha. After two days of debate she agreed to go to the market.

The day on which we began to sell our belongings, though unimportant in itself, still stands out sharply in my memory because it is associated with an event which made a vivid impression on the minds of the townspeople. The Germans, who had returned to Dniepropetrovsk for good, and ruled with redoubled severity, stuck posters on the walls which called on the inhabitants to return all weapons within three days. Those who didn't would incur to death penalty. The threat of death caused no comment because we knew that death was the minimum penalty meted out by Germans. Torture, in which they excelled, was a subject passed over in silence, especially in official announcements.

Nobody treated the matter seriously. True, plenty of people had concealed weapons, but the Germans had lost much of their prestige because of their flight, and people tended to make light of their decrees. They would find it difficult to unearth the well-concealed weapons and could not make a case without evidence. The Germans were well informed about the mood of the populace. They intended to regain the authority they had lost during their retreat. To do that, they had to demonstrate their power.

On Sunday, at 9 o'clock in the morning, the time fixed for the return of weapons lapsed. All knew this but nobody expected any rapid developments. As it happened, I had just gone out on my customary stroll. I made my way through side streets where every house, gateway and crossing were familiar, where I knew – or let's say I had convinced myself – that no danger lurked. I behaved like a person suffering from agoraphobia. This street was "good" because there was little traffic and it had a few gates, which could serve as hiding places, that one was "bad", stretches of fences made it too exposed. Open spaces were the worst, tight little alleys were the stuff of dreams. It would have been wonderful if the entire town consisted of alleyways, but unfortunately it also boasted broad main streets which were crowded, unfriendly, and did not afford many opportunities to disappear.

My route forced me to cross one of these arteries. I noticed some unusual activity when I neared the dangerous spot, but it was too late to retrace my steps. I had to overcome the reluctance of my suddenly leaden feet by sheer willpower. At the corner, on the main street, several people were grouped around a lamp post. They were looking at something which I couldn't see at first. At least there were no Germans about, so it couldn't be too serious. I just had to pass through quickly and dive into the safety of the back alleys. After a few hasty strides, while already in the haven if a narrow lane, I sent a last glance towards the threatening zone of the main street and was shocked into immobility. A corpse hung from the lamp post, swaying rhythmically in the gusts of wind. People were gathered around the hanging body and no one volunteered to take it down. The distorted face and bluish tongue sticking out between the open lips made such a horrible impression on me that I couldn't stir. Then I drew nearer, as if hypnotized by the horrible sight and noticed for the first time the announcement pinned to the breast. The clumsy, hastily-penned Russian letters formed the words: "Punished for disobeying a German decree".

The Hitlerites had succeeded in creating quite an effect. The people stood there with clenched teeth. They could stand the sight for no more than a few minutes. They looked until they had enough and then moved on. I walked away with one of them and heard the details. After 9 o'clock had come and gone, several trucks which had been parked near the military governor's office deployed in the streets. Dozens of men and a few women were taken haphazardly. When the Germans had the desired number of people they started the executions. The truck would stop at a lamp post, the rope was fastened to a lamp and tied in a noose around the neck of the captive nearest at hand and ... the truck would pull away. About sixty street lamps in the busiest places in town were decorated in this fashion, to celebrate the return of the German authorities. During the night the Germans wrapped the heads of the corpses in cloth – it seems the sight was too monstrous even for them. These monuments of the culture of the Third Reich decorated the city for three days. They were like bloody letters announcing: "Take care! The brown beast is watching you!".

9 · New Problems

The fact that we had no documents whatsoever increasingly troubled us. Michael's behaviour became ever more erratic; he had no regard for the people around him. He used to rush out on the stairs to check who was coming up, positioned himself in hiding by the window, resisted all my attempts to drag him out of the house. At times he stayed in bed for the entire day, sometimes for two days, staring fixedly at the ceiling without uttering a single word. Our finances sank below the danger line. After selling my suit, I began selling my remaining underclothes. Michael had lost almost all of his money in the Alosha business. I had a little cash left, but not enough by far. I didn't want to think what would happen to us if nothing came up. I needed a new *Ausweis*, but the problem was that on my walks I encountered nobody whom I knew. So my nerves, too, were on edge. Fortunately, my faith in destiny kept my spirits up. I believed that if my destiny so decreed, an opportunity to escape the entanglement would come my way.

A few days after the hangings, panic seized the neighbourhood. The Germans, acting in concert with the local police, cordoned off a large area and began a systematic house-to-house search. They were hunting able-bodied men for forced labour in the Reich. Michael's overstretched nerves gave way. He found a hiding place in the attic and told me to join him there. I didn't want to: the place looked too obvious to me and, besides, by holing up we would surrender the remaining shreds of our prestige. The simple people among whom we lived would draw the most fantastic conclusions from our behaviour. That would make it impossible to remain in the apartment even if nobody turned us in.

When Michael heard me refuse his suggestion, he almost succumbed to an attack of hysteria. He began with entreaties and ended up weeping; the tears ran down his face which was contorted by fear. Finally, I agreed to join him, out of pity. Luckily, the search party skipped our house for some unfathomable reason. We returned to the apartment after hiding in the attic for an hour-and-a-half.

I decided then and there to do everything in my power to obtain documents. I cound no longer bear living with a perpetual threat looming over me. As for fear-ridden Michael, our ways would have to part.

My anxieties about our landlady's attitude were unfortunately proven right almost immediately. There was an imperceptible change in her conduct; nothing explicit, just a mixture of disrespect and of something else which I did not dare to define. I believed at first that the reason was our miserable financial situation, but after devoting a great deal of thought to the subject, I came to the conclusion that her behaviour had to be caused by something else; after all, the landlady knew how we felt about the Germans and she should rather commiserate with us. The fact that we were selling all our belongings should not be a cause of wonder where unemployed workers were concerned. No, there had to be another reason.

I recalled a multitude of details to which we had attached no significance but which looked different under the spotlight of a concrete suspicion. I remembered the seemingly innocent questioning of one of the students at the surveyors' course, who inquired about the conditions in Poland, especially as far as Jews were concerned. I had not paid any special attention to that, nor to whispered conversations which would be cut off when one of us approached, nor to strange glances directed at us. It seems that all these signs had been imprinted in my unconscious as on a photographic film. Now the film was being developed, uncovering an unbroken chain of logically impeccable assumptions and proofs ... all pointing to the unmistakable conclusion: our landlady and all the people around us knew that we were Jews.

The realization jolted me like an electric shock. I was stupefied with terror. Unwilling to believe my own reasoning, I again checked all the minute details in the chain of evidence. It all hung together very nicely. There could be no further doubt: they had long suspected us, and our hiding in the attic served as final proof. They knew! There was no point in waiting – we should leave and obliterate the traces behind us as carefully as possible. Perhaps it was just as well that circumstances were forcing my hand; otherwise God knows how long we would have gone on vegetating. I decided to undertake a systematic search for our companions in the escape from Lvov – perhaps one of them had succeeded in finding a useful contact. I would sell the remainder of my possessions in order to raise some cash. In the morning I would go out to look for ... to look for what? Oh, yes, for pie in the sky!

I left the room in the morning. I forced myself to choose a different route than usual. Today I had to walk through the main streets. I had to summon up a real physical effort to overcome my fear of full exposure. It was necessary, I argued with myself, but nevertheless an instinctive quiver ran through my body when I emerged onto the busy main street.

My eyes swivelled from side to side so as not to miss a familiar face and in order to catch the first glimpse of impending danger. My search prolonged itself endlessly. I passed and repassed the market and the area near the City

Governor's office, and tramped through most of the town, without encountering anybody who was at all familiar. I didn't know where to turn and didn't have any addresses – addresses were, of course, the most carefully kept secret. I turned to go back home.

The unknown lies in wait behind every corner and can always spring out to surprise you. I walked along, less frightened now but still very uneasy because of the failure of my search. Suddenly I heard shouts of "Hello, you there!". I felt that the shouts were directed at me, but deluded myself that somebody else was meant and did not turn around. What rotten luck to be caught when I was just a stride or two away, from the refuge of the labyrinth of alleyways.

The shouts are repeated. I hear hurried steps behind me. Another moment … No, it's no use pretending … I'm the target. I turn around. I am relieved when I don't see a German or a Polish blackmailer behind me. It's Victor, my companion on the journey from Lvov who had disappeared from sight a long time ago. I'm overjoyed and grab his outstretched hand. My handshake is so warm and my happiness in meeting a man who shared a few days' journey with me, is so evident that Victor is surprised. After a second or two I feel ashamed of my uncontrolled gush of emotion.

After exchanging a few standard questions about our doings, I regain sufficient control of myself to make the inquiries which are of real importance.

"How is work?"

"Only idiots work. Goddamn sons-of-bitches!"

"Right you are. But the *Ausweis*, isn't it difficult to get along without it?"

"That's another matter, bud. My brother-in-law works in a company, and he arranged *Ausweis*-papers for us. The main thing is to get around the fucking Germans. You don't have an *Ausweis*, right? Aha! Well, we'll get you one. How about your cash?"

"What cash?"

"You're trying to fool me? Nobody risks his head for nothing. I can arrange an *Ausweis* for you, but only for ready money. Not much … 500 pieces."

"Where? How? Who?"

"It's none of your business! Give me the cash, I'll give you the *Ausweis* rubles … well, so long." An expressive shrug.

Unexpectedly, after so many disappointments, the sought-for opportunity was presenting itself. I agreed to the price and ordered two *Ausweis*, for myself and for Michael. I did not settle immediately because that would have roused suspicion and raised the price. So I bargained and enjoyed listening to a few harangues delivered in the wonderful juicy Lvov argot. In the end, Victor agreed to deliver the papers within two days, and even revealed his address, as an exceptional gesture of goodwill.

I returned in a rosy mood. Michael realized immediately that I had good news. I told him that I had ordered two *Ausweis* documents and that our run of bad luck was perhaps coming to an end. I also explained why, we should move to another apartment. Michael showed so much fear when I told him why I was convinced that our cover was blown, that I almost regretted being frank with him. There was the risk that he would do something crazy, but on the other hand I had to tell him, so that I could coach him how to behave in our new lodging – provided we found one. He promised with tears in his eyes to behave exactly as I instructed him.

My high spirits sank a little when I set out to count our cash. The two of us, after selling almost all our belongings, had a little over 1,500 rubles. After paying for the documents we would have barely enough to live on for two or three days. A gloomy prospect, but we would manage somehow. In the meantime, I directed our landlady to buy sixty glasses of corn grain, to serve as our "iron rations". The pale phantom of hunger was staring us in the face, but that was the least of my worries – I could always handle that problem.

I received the papers from Victor on the appointed day. After paying him I felt much better although my pocket was a lot lighter. A piece of stamped cardboard and a photograph, a piece of rubbish, yet it makes me feel so much better. It's a typical, senseless illusion of security (there is really no security); as a matter of fact the *Ausweis* won't save me from real danger. Unconsciously, I know all that, yet I feel better with it than without it. I can't explain this rationally, but that's how it is.

As we all know, when it rains it really pours. More unpleasant news awaited me when I got home: the landlady asked for a loan of 200 rubles. We knew what such requests for loans meant. We should be thankful that the sum was so modest, but now we were left with less than a hundred rubles and 60 glasses of corn grain. Well, it was better than nothing.

We sat down to dinner. We had to pay respect to the food; there was sure to be a longish period of waiting for the next half-decent meal. The bean soup was marvellously thick. Each spoonful spread heavenly warmth through our innards. The second dish was fried potatoes and bread. The crust was days old but who cared? It was genuine bread and I grudged every bite taken out of it. Michael observed me, somewhat puzzled, because usually I ate rather quickly and did not toy with the food. I explained that from the next day on, we were limited to a diet of corn meal until our cash flow improved. His face fell. When he got it through his head, that he was eating the last of our bread (price of a loaf: 100 rubles), the despair reflected in his eyes could have melted stones – in times gone past, of course, when feelings were still important.

Well, life is not a bed of roses. The happiness which had warmed our hearts when we got the *Ausweis* had gone completely cold. Michael was ever a worrier and now he had a good reason to worry. The tragic mask over his face did not dissolve even with the appearance of the last meal of the day – coffee and bread. He was certainly considering what he was going to eat the next day after the last of the bread had gone. I didn't worry overmuch – it was pointless. Tomorrow I intended to start looking for new lodgings.

10 · Vladek Shows me how to Falsify Documents

While wandering around the town, I had noticed with approval a neighbourhood called "the factory" which consisted of workers' houses. The next morning I set out to search for a room. My empty stomach growled mildly but I ignored it. I went from house to house inquiring about vacancies. I garnered odd bits of information, but no news about rooms to let. I did not despair, however. It was just a matter of having enough patience. Anyway, I enjoyed being able to move freely the whole day in the pursuit of a worthwhile objective. It was evening before I returned.

Fortunately our landlady did not pay too much attention to our affairs. She had stopped inquiring when we would start work, and now that we prepared our own food, she was quite happy and did not stick her nose into our pots and pans. We went to sleep early – a wise move for people who had no light, had nothing to do, and in addition now had to find some way to still the pangs of a hungry stomach. A sleeping person needs no food.

The sense of emptiness inside was unpleasant but did not trouble me too much. I was reminded of the hungry days in prison. Perhaps I had been more exhausted then, because of my stay in camp, yet the turmoil of other emotions was so intense that the lack of food was forgotten. Anyway, in comparison to the thirst which had tortured me then, all other matters paled. I tried to get rid of these unpleasant memories which overcame me and did not let me escape into sleep. So I began to concentrate on the evening bombing raid which had begun as usual. In the end I fell asleep to the sound of explosions.

I spent the mornings of the second and third day of our enforced diet in search of lodgings. In the end luck came my way. I found a room in the working-class neighbourhood, far away from any nosy Poles – I felt that this consideration was of paramount importance. The landlady was decidedly anti-German: she was the wife of a Communist Party member who had been evacuated when the German army drew near. She was happy to offer us a room. It had no heat and no bedclothes, but it boasted a separate entrance. She demanded an official quartering order, a so-called "*Beschlagnahme*". A week before, this would have been impossible. However, I had an *Ausweis*. I showed the room to Michael the same day. We arranged with the landlady that

I would take out a quartering order the next day and we would move into her room within three days.

The following morning I visited Victor to ask his advice on how to obtain an official notice of quartering order. Victor accompanied me willingly, perhaps less because of an altruistic desire to help me than from an urge to show his mettle. He talked non-stop, telling stories about his escape from the prison on Lecki street, how ten Ukrainian policemen tried to detain him, how he broke away, how he defended himself against armed assault, and how he succeeded in getting away (though wounded eight times by bayonets) by jumping from a first floor window. I didn't know if he was telling the truth or only expressing boastful fantasies. I realized that it wasn't the first time he was recounting these tales, and as we would certainly meet again and again, I would hear them several times and have the opportunity to come to my own conclusions. For the moment, I was wholly absorbed by the thought that in a minute I would enter a German office of my own free will and beard the lion in his den.

It was too late to draw back. Victor was quite sure of himself – he had done this before. We passed the sentry at the entrance. My heart skipped a beat, quite unnecessarily, as the man hardly noticed us. The next sentry was posted inside the hall. This one was watching us, but I was a little calmer and was aware how superficial this inspection was. Victor next tackled the doorman, speaking to him in German to explain the purpose of our visit.

My legs have no strength, they feel stuffed with cotton wool. Victor is not impressed at all by the fact that we are in the lion's mouth. He pokes gentle fun at my evident fear. A terrifying door ... we knock and find ourselves in a room. A German is sitting at one table and two young Ukrainian women at another. Victor tries out his broken German again. The German points to one of the women. We station ourselves at the other table. The clerk knows very little German and is uncertain about her ability to write in that terrible language. Now I regain my confidence and explain what we want. She takes out a blank form and obediently fills it in, according to my instructions. It's just a question of minutes – the wished-for document is safely in my pocket.

"Heil Hitler!" We leave.

My importuning stomach drew me back to reality. The quartering order in my packet pointed to the future, but meanwhile I wanted real food and couldn't pay for it. Michael was waiting at home. Nervous as a cat, because of my trip to the Governor's office, he had prepared the unappetizing meal all by himself and it was sitting on the table. The prospect of sudden manna from heaven was slim in our prosaic era, so I sat down to eat. A fugitive thought darted through my mind: these were far from prosaic times – the events around us could bear comparison with the worst description of Hell or of the

Apocalypse. However, it really was not worth meditating on that subject – first I had to survive. So I forgot about everything else and started to consider how to carry out a project whose outline had flashed into my brain a short while back: how to obtain blank forms, official stamps, and other paraphernalia which would enable me to thumb my nose at death.

In the evening I informed the landlady that we had received new instructions, and had to leave town the next day. Next morning we took our leave and moved to the new lodgings. We received the red-carpet treatment. The official quartering order made the proper impression – it was affixed to the door with considerable satisfaction and some pride, and stirred up quite a bit of envy in the hearts of our new landlady's female neighbours on the street. It did not take us long to place our pitifully few belongings in the room. Then it was time for me to go and see Vladek.

During the first few minutes of our meeting we spoke feelingly about our acquaintanceship in Lvov, about my being senior to him in years, and other such trivia. Then Vladek broached a subject which, only the previous day, seemed to bc food for fantasy. I was so surprised I almost laughed.

Vladek happened to obtain work (as a non-Jew, needless to say) in the office of a construction firm in Lvov. As the only conscientious worker there, he gained the confidence of the boss. He was transferred to the Ukraine with the rest of the firm's personnel. When the Russian advance had begun, the boss fled and instructed Vladek to evacuate the firm. Trifles like rubber stamps and such were "left behind". Their appropriation had opened dazzling opportunities before my old-new friend. I learned in passing that the *Ausweis* I had purchased from him was 100 per cent fake ...

Vladek had already discovered the truths, which were only becoming clear to me in the last few days and which I treated like revelations. He was determined to return to Lvov to rescue the remnants of his family. He had provided himself with various needed documents, some of them faked and some genuine, which had been obtained by the judicious display of the false ones. Some of the documents were only partly false – a female name changed into a male name, and so on. I was transported by delight at the sight of this arsenal of false documents and rubber stamps.

Vladek told me that even before being sent to the Ukraine he had met a prewar acquaintance who had often captained a volleyball team. Vladek had been a passionate volleyball player. The reader may have guessed that this acquaintance was the legendary Salek Meisner, whose name I mentioned in the first chapter of this book.

Meisner had been dressed in clothes which closely resembled a German army uniform. He revealed to Vladek the secret of fabricating Wehrmacht marching orders. Vladek found the whole business very much to his liking. While still in Lvov, he began to fabricate documents, he prepared blanks, ID cards, and so on. He acquired a partner, who had invented a wonderful method of faking official stamps with the help of india ink and a certain kind of paper used by engineers and draughtsmen. A few sheets would be of great help here if he could only manage to fetch them from Lvov.

Vladek confided that he was about to take a leaf from Meisner's book and go to Lvov wearing an army overcoat. He had learned that workers for the Wehrmacht were being issued old army uniforms, which had been withdrawn from use in the German army. Vladek was of the opinion that an army coat would serve as the best means of protection.

After my initial shock at the very idea of using the "sacred" uniform of the master race, I was delighted with the absurd character and undoubted practicality of the whole daring enterprise. Vladek planned to take his friend Kola with him and to shepherd from Lvov ten people or so, including four or five paying passengers. Vladek's gang was also short of cash.

I did not mention my own money problems – assistance was unlikely and I didn't want to appear as an object of pity. I let Vladek understand that a "trip" of the kind he planned appealed to me. He seized on the idea and promised that very soon after his return he would provide me with the means of fabricating documents, in return for a share of my profits, from smuggling people out of Lvov. Well, we would see how things turned out. He thought that his trip would take ten or twelve days. Unfortunately we could not communicate while Vladek was away on his trip.

So I became a new member of the racket – I hardly know what to call our partnership. Perhaps the best definition would be to call it an association of gangsters. As a matter of fact, that was the term we employed later; it made the desired impression and best expressed the adventurous spirit of our pack of young men.

Now all that remained was to wait on events – there was nothing else we could do.

11 · Counterfeiting

After Vladek left I finally took the opportunity to accustom myself to our new lodgings. During the two days before his departure I was too busy and too excited to do so. After all, the maelstrom of practical preparations and mental stress attendant on a guerrilla expedition which was intended to snatch several Jews from the jaws of death was a very sharp and sudden change from the winter's stagnation planning for the uncertain future. While waiting for Vladek's return, I became friendly with his associates Misku and Victor.

Reaching Turkey was the acme of our desires. I myself had not dared to think of getting so far. My plans for winning freedom, when I made bold to think beyond my immediate circumstances, lacked any definite shape. My present companions thought in terms of definite actions, heartened by the holes they had already knocked through the imprisoning wall erected by the Germans. One who possessed a marching order and the appropriate stamps could journey throughout Nazi-occupied Europe, from the White Sea to the Black Sea. The overwhelming obstacle was how to board a ship, leaving the territory under German rule. Odessa seemed a likely port for embarkation. The problem was to get aboard a ship.

The ghetto constituted a sombre background to our memories. But we did not like to prod still fresh wounds and our tendency, like that of all young people, was to think about the future. Still, we touched on the ghetto period again and again, almost against our better judgement. I learned that the parents of Vladek and Misku had been killed in the *Aktion* of August 1942. Vladek had realized that working for the Germans was the riskiest course of all, but he had to earn his bread, so he continued working for them but had been on the look-out for any opportunity to leave Lvov. He devoted his energies to the couterfeiting of documents. In the beginning, rubber stamps and metal stamps could be counterfeited only with great difficulty. But a partner of his, named Precel (now living in Australia as a graphic artist), had invented a way to copy a stamp which was already affixed to a genuine document. It was an invention of a genius, very easy to implement. It required a special kind of paper used by engineers and draughtsmen for their plans, and also a pencil, a pen, india ink, a comb and some artistic talent.*

* I don't describe the exact method here because some of my readers may be tempted to employ it for purposes of personal profit.

I was dazzled by the simplicity of this method. It did not require the physical paraphernalia of real stamps, inks, etc. We could carry all we needed in a small bag. Our method produced much more convincing stamps than those copied with the help of a hardboiled egg, and other similar primitive methods. But the best news of all was that even a police expert armed with modern tools would have been unable to distinguish between the original genuine stamp and its copy. Before the war I would have been repelled by the whole business, but now my life often depended on a stupid stamp. So I enthusiastically took my first steps in the noble art of counterfeiting, and did my best to become as proficient as possible.

The Germans had no idea what was happening. They could not believe that the harried, persecuted Jews could invent on their own such a promising device which transformed a person in hostile territory into a self-sufficient individual. Later, when some of our gang were captured, with their forged documents, the Germans searched diligently for our ties with a foreign intelligence organization. They simply could not bring themselves to believe the truth, that a group of Jewish youths, completely on their own, travelled freely near the front lines, entered military installations, gathered restricted information and subsisted on army stores to the tune of hundreds of thousands of marks. Even today, the whole enterprise seems a miracle even to me, who participated in it.

Malnutrition now began to make inroads into my organism. I became fatigued after a walk. Spells of dizziness bothered me. The stomach contractions ceased. The landlady wondered at my drawn and pale face. She cursed the Germans who drove people to hard labour without providing sufficient nourishment. She was of the opinion that ground corn was not enough of a meal for supper. If she had only known, that it was our only meal! Still that would not have changed matters – she would not have shared her food with us.

12 · Preparations to go to Lvov

According to our calculations, Vladek should have returned about fourteen days after his departure for Lvov. Twenty days passed, and various doubts began to creep into our minds regarding a successful conclusion to our first attempt at a sortie inside the jail walls. Anything could have happened; he could have been caught at the railway station in Dniepropetrovsk (on second thoughts, that was unlikely, we would have heard about it); on the train in the course of a chance inspection (very likely), in Lvov at the station or on the streets; or during the night in an apartment. In a word, the chances for his capture were legion, especially on the way back, burdened with people unaccustomed to bold risks. It was all too terrible for words. Nothing should happen to him … nothing had happened … my galloping imagination was playing tricks on me. The main thing was to keep calm, undoubtedly something had come up to detain him. Even solitaire no longer interested me.

Michael and I were in the midst of a conversation about the chances of Vladek being caught. Then, there was the agreed-upon knock on the window shutter. I ran out into the yard, happy to hear news about Vladek. The news was excellent – Vladek in person. We embraced, like the best of friends. So the whole idea was right, after all: the new "method" had been tested and found effective. Now we could make a start.

Vladek asked whether my landlady was trustworthy, as he wanted to find accommodation in our house for two people. I put his mind at rest, and he returned after a few minutes with two companions. I knew one of them from Lvov. I succeeded in persuading the landlady to take in the two, with the help of a little charm and some inspired storytelling.

It was nine o'clock, which was then considered late at night in Dniepropetrovsk, so we could not go out and get some food, but our guests had the *Verpflegung* which they had collected on the way. I sat down to a meal with them. There was bread on the table for the first time in three weeks, not to speak of butter and sausage, and my hands almost trembled with anticipation. I ate very slowly so as to savour in full the heavenly taste of day-old bread from an army bakery. It was delectable. It was proof that a new period was beginning.

Vladek said that everything had gone much more smoothly than expected. There had been no hitches on the train to Lvov. Obtaining a place to stay for the first night had posed some difficulty but they had managed. Vladek and Kola had brought their wives, together with six other Lvov Jews. One of Vladek's sisters had been sick with typhoid and could not come. The other one had stayed behind to care for her. He was planning to go to Lvov again to get them out.

I offered to accompany him. Vladek agreed immediately but pointed out the danger in an escapade of that sort. I realized the risks perfectly well, but did not see any alternative if I wanted to survive. Vladek promised to provide me with anything I might need. In the meanwhile I would take out new credentials.

Our guests, newly arrived from Lvov, wished to learn everything possible about the situation in Dniepropetrovsk, and rained questions on us. They inquired about lodgings, regulations about registering new tenants with the authorities, the food situation, the attitude of the local population to Poles. Naturally, nobody mentioned Jews. We did not paint a flattering picture of the city, but even so, Dniepropetrovsk must have seemed an earthly paradise to the new arrivals as it would to anyone who had succeeded in breaking out of the hell of Lvov.

My acquaintance from Lvov did not have much money but the other, confided Vladek, was "loaded". He was a likeable fellow, black-haired and rather short. He was a businessman in the positive sense of the word, smooth in manner, and full of understanding for those who were temporarily down on their luck. Because of these qualities he bore the nickname "Sweetie". He put together some of the remarks we let fall, realized the state of our finances and made a sweeping offer to underwrite the household expenses. He wanted to hand me the money for the next day's shopping. I appreciated his attitude very much but did not agree to mortgage my independence. We could discuss arrangements regarding our upkeep later on.

Understandably, I did not sleep much that night – new plans and projects churned in my brain. Now that I had decided to go to Lvov I remembered the commercial proposition of Vanya, our landlady's son. Dyes or caustic soda would bring in enough profit for me not to have to worry where my next dinner was going to come from. Then I would be able to forget about money matters for a while and devote my whole energy to the search for a safe route into the wide world.

Vladek advised me that his army coat had served him admirably; nobody had bothered him. So I'd better get something similar for myself. A complete uniform was the best solution, but barring that, I could make do with a soldier's coat and cap.

The next day I managed to take Vladek aside to arrange the details. We would depart in seven to ten days. Vladek planned to bring back ten or eleven people, and documents had to be arranged for them. He offered to lend me his coat which was too big for him. I made out a travel *Ausweis* for myself, took the coat, and borrowed Sweetie's army cap. I decided to test my new disguise by visiting one of the army canteens. Dinner there cost next to nothing, the food was reputed to be of good quality, and I would be obliged to nobody besides Hitler, with whom I had accounts to settle.

I selected the first army mess for noncoms that I saw. My heart was pounding, but not as intensely as before. That fact encouraged me. The gendarme at the door demanded to see my papers. I showed him my travel warrant. He glanced at it and let me in. At the office inside I purchased a chit for 1.5 marks, a trifling sum – and seated myself at the smallest table.

My intention was to talk to as few people as possible. One of the waitresses took my chit and a moment later a plate of steaming soup rested in front of me. It was excellent. Then a big portion of meat and potatoes, a dessert of a cake from cream of wheat, and black coffee. After a long diet of ground corn, these dishes were in some measure wasted on me; I had forgotten how to savour normal food.

There was a surprise inspection during the course of the meal, which, luckily, I passed with flying colours. When I noticed the gendarmes my knees shook but there was nothing I could do except put my trust in luck. When they reached my table I showed them my travel warrant with a confident flourish and calmly continued eating. After a moment I heard one of them say. "This one is a civilian worker attached to the army". I almost sighed aloud with relief. "Everything in order". "Heil Hitler!" It was the first time I had pronounced the accursed words of this salutation. I would grow used to it in the future.

In the meanwhile, I felt on top of the world. Even the food tasted better. I drank two black coffees in order to prolong my enjoyment of the situation to the utmost.

I came home proud as a peacock. As was my habit, I analysed the circumstances in the light of what the gendarme had said. It seems that in the eyes of a military policeman I was a civilian, in spite of my uniform, and thus of no special interest. He had not checked my documents thoroughly because his task was to search for deserters. Checking the document of "the civilian riffraff" was a task for the regular police. What about them? Why, that was the point: a policeman would not dare approach me because I looked every inch a respectable soldier of the Wehrmacht. The very thought dazzled me like lightning. New and glorious perspectives opened up before us. We had to complete our soldier's outfits, obtain parts of uniforms, army boots, and so on, salute officers on the streets, and in general behave like perfect soldiers. We all had worn parts of uniforms, so wearing a full uniform would only be the final step.

Vladek and the others agreed completely. We decided to purchase all the army clothing we needed from German soldiers who were selling anything for which they could find takers. Kola proposed that we use the Nazi salute instead of the standard military one – the officers would avoid us because they wanted to have as little contact as possible with Nazi Party members. Yes, it wasn't a bad idea at all. We only had to say "Heil Hitler" convincingly, which meant to garble the words casually: haihitla, hiettla, hitla, eehtla, hhh-tla and the like.

Michael was frightened by my escapade but at the same time he felt very important because of my success and my impending trip to Lvov. It's difficult to realize nowadays the meaning of a return to a place associated with such nighmarish experiences. It was even more significant than coming back, of one's own will, to the mouth of hell from which one had escaped by a hairsbreath; it meant dancing on the teeth of the trap which had held us captive a short while ago.

Sweetie, having heard of my intentions, came out with a very interesting proposition. He knew that I wished to import from Lvov various items that were in short supply on the market in the Ukraine, and also that I was short of cash. He offered to lend me 500 or 1000 marks to this end, provided I agreed to escort his sister from Lvov. He would pay me separately for this service. I did not quite know at first how to react; I needed money, but how could I honestly promise to smuggle someone back with me in view of the fact that it was my first trip? He, however, urged me earnestly to agree.

I went to Vladek to ask for advice. He said that as far as he was concerned, I could attempt to bring back a number of people. He promised to provide me with all the imformation I needed for the forging of documents, and even offered me a share of the take. After considering the matter for a short while, I accepted. After all, I would not be doing any harm; on the contrary, I would be offering someone a chance to get out. There was no harm in accepting payment for my services – the people concerned seemed to have the wherewithal. Vladek had to pay for the upkeep of the family he brought from Lvov but he had no cash, just as I had none. Our only asset was the courage to risk our lives. What's more, I was sick and tired of fasting.

In the evening I told Sweetie I agreed to his proposition, and the following morning began preparations for the trip. There was no difficulty in obtaining paper for the documents. We would merely go to a store reserved for German personnel and demand what we needed in a suitably arrogant tone, in German. The Ukrainian clerk would not dare to question us.

The texts of the documents evolved by degrees. We began with a modest *Urlaubschein* (furlough pass) and ended up with printed special permits – *Sonderausweis*. I manufactured *urlaubschein* for ten people, together with a special permit for collecting rations etc. along the way to Lvov. At every train station I intended to collect these supplies as well as an authentic stamp on my permit. The people accompanying me from Lvov back to Dniepropetrovsk would be issued "100 per cent genuine documents" attesting to their coming back from a furlough. The process of authenticating the manufactured papers in the appropriate office went smoothly. There was a branch of the construction firm Daniel Kuzyk in Dniepropetrovsk – we forged a stamp for the non-existent Stefan Kuzyk firm. Soon the fictitious firm became better known throughout the offices in the city than the genuine one. Nobody noticed the difference in the name! Were we to meet somebody who worked in the Kuzyk enterprise, or anybody who was familiar with it, we had a ready answer: we were employed by an entirely different firm, which had never been located in Dniepropetrovsk.

Filling out the appropriate document forms took two hours. At the end I was handed a bill to be paid by the Kuzyk firm, collected the documents, signed a receipt for the blanks according to the rules, and paid. Next we had to affix photographs to the documents which, by the way, had been printed in Lvov. We collected pictures of all our acquaintances, living and dead, and affixed them to the documents. The plan was to destroy these documents when we reached Lvov, and make out new ones with photographs of our "passengers". The names and dates would remain the same, of course. We had a stamp and could make out all the documents we liked.

Inventing names was not as simple as one might think; it took quite an effort. It was not advisable to have a middle-class Polish name so all the names ending in "... ski" and "... icz" were out – especially because I myself had a name ending in "... ski". The family names had to be simple and common ones of the peasant or worker type, so as not to arouse any attention. First names were also a problem. If none were repeated among the group, the fact was liable to draw attention but we also had to avoid too many repetitions. We also had to be careful not to write many women's names, because there were not too many women workers in the Ukraine. However, since we planned to take out about five women eventually, we picked convenient names, such as Stefan which could easily be changed into a female name, Stefania. The documents listed the age of the holder, which was a bothersome detail, as the photographs we chose had to fit the approximate age of the person we hoped would ultimately possess the document.

After prolonged debates, these difficulties were solved. All the unused materials were disposed of without leaving a trace, and the "official" papers were repeatedly checked until pronounced satisfactory. Last of all, we had to obtain the *Durchlasscheins*. These documents were issued by the police department at the City Governor's Building. I had passed my test of fire already during my earlier visit to the office in that building, but at the thought of a visit to the police department I broke out in goose pimples. Vladek and Kola explained meticulously where, how, and with whom I was to transact what they knew from their own experience to be an anxiety arousing business. To calm my fears, they explained that the man in charge in the office I was to visit was a certain Count Modl, who was known to be a courteous gentleman, who did not attach too much importance to his official duties. I was to go there the next day. Fine. I didn't have a uniform yet, and perhaps it would have seemed out of place, so I chose to dress up in the *Volksdeutsche* fashion, My British overcoat fitted my role, and I borrowed a hat with a feather, the "hunting hat" beloved by German civilians and by the *Volksdeutsche* who aped them slavishly. I also shined my boots to the required mirror finish.

I can't say that I slept soundly that night. Nevertheless, the following morning I set out resolutely, ready for anything. I decided to speak only German. In an unexpected encounter with my dear Poles, I would avoid any conversation, play the irritated German and, if strictly necessary, slap them in the face without arguing. On the tram, I entered the compartment reserved for Germans. Usually the trip took about 40 minutes, but as my bad luck would have it, the engine broke down. After a wait of half an hour the motorman announced that we were stuck and that a special tram was on its way to take on the passengers. The precious minutes were ticking by, and I was nervous as a cat. The lunch hour was approaching, and I was thinking about giving up for the day. Finally the relief tram came. I got off at the Governor's Building and found my way unerringly to the Police Department following to the letter my friends' instructions. My knees shook a little but I could not hesitate too long – twelve o'clock was approaching fast.

I opened the door, clicked my heels in the military fashion, flung out my arm in the official salute:

"Hei-tla!"

I was pulling the lion's whiskers, and the lion ... did not roar. I approached the desk and again did the business of Hei-tla. I explained my requirements to the count. His Honour was terribly sorry, but his office hours ended at five to twelve, and it was Saturday on top of it all. I had completely forgotten about Saturday. Still, the count was the soul of courtesy. When he saw the look of dismay on my face (caused partly by genuine regret and in part by a natural feeling of fear, a fact which he did not realize at all) he hesitated a second, and then graciously offered to return to the office after lunch so as to enable our group to leave as quickly as possible for our furlough. In the meantime the documents would remain at the office.

After a round of courtesies in German, I found myself on the street again, considering how to spend an entire hour. In the centre of town, I did not intend to eat at the canteen for German employed personnel; there was no point in looking for additional trouble. I could not enter a military canteen because I wasn't wearing army clothes. Then I noticed a large barber shop nearby. I could surely spend a peaceful hour there. I entered, quite ready for a longish wait, as several customers were waiting their turn. However, I had forgotten that I was a German, and waiting in line was not meant for the likes of me. One of the barbers almost threw a native out of the barber chair in the middle of his haircut, so as not to make me wait. I calmed him down with a patronizing gesture, indicating that I preferred to wait and read a newspaper in the meanwhile.

I read happily; I hadn't read a newspaper for quite a while (although the rags on sale, which pandered assiduously to the Nazis, hardly deserved to be called newspapers). Their pages were filled with descriptions of the heroic deeds of the Wehrmacht. Were it not for the fact that we, who lived near the front, were privy to a myriad uncensored items of information, I would be sure from the printed news that the Germans were nearing Vladivostok, and that Russia had ceased to exist.

At about twenty to one I settled in a barber's chair. The poor fellow had lots of trouble with my haircut: I ordered constant changes, to fill the minutes until one o'clock.

Sharp on the hour I stood outside the door to the office. Perhaps he had prepared a trap for me? No, surely not, I knocked. "Come in!" "Heil Hitler!" "Heitla!"

My documents were already being prepared. The ceremony of making out the necessary papers and signing them took about a quarter of an hour. Finally, I expressed my thanks for the special effort my case had necessitated, and was free to scoot out. Damn it, it all went off so smoothly! I wonder at my former self who feared German offices so. A short while ago my whole comportment today would have seemed a heroic enterprise, but today I am in the know. I am a tried and tested member of our band, that's to say, our pack of gangsters.

The others awaited me impatiently; this was my debut in a new role, the role of an aggressor. They worried that something had happened to me because I was so long in returning. It was easy to make a mis-step in these adventures.

They were very happy at my success. I was the first among us to obtain a large number of the *Durchlasscheins*.

Now the time had come to agree on the people we were to bring back from Lvov. We settled on the ways and means of communicating with the ghetto, and established the date of my departure. We agreed that I would board the train in four days, dressed in as complete a uniform as possible.

I tried on Michael's boots. They almost fitted me; they were a bit too tight but that was a trifle. I had no idea that the trifle would cost me dearly. I already had an overcoat and cap, and had bought army pants on the market for a few marks. But I couldn't find a proper shirt – they were all too small or too worn. After a thorough search, I had no choice other than to purchase a canvas army shirt worn on work details. It was not exactly the proper uniform for wintertime, but I had my coat.

When everything was ready, I put on my new clothes at Vladek's apartment. My landlady was unpleasantly surprised by my clothes but I explained that they were my official worker's uniform. I also notified her that my furlough was due in a week, that I would bring back textile dyes and perhaps strike a deal with Vanya. That news pleased her so much that she bore me no ill-will because of the uniform. I still had a day and a half left until my departure, so I decided to stroll in the centre of the city in order to accustom myself to the uniform and to try out my salute. Everything went smoothly. First of all, I visited Sweetie's apartment. They had never seen me in my uniform before, so at first they took alarm when they saw a German coming in. Their joy at recognizing me was correspondingly all the greater.

Sweetie lent me the required sum for purchasing dyes. He explained meticulously how I should contact his sister. Replete with their wishes of "good luck", I walked on.

The several Poles who came my way did not even glance at a German. I saluted each officer, laughing inwardly until my insides ached. Each passing moment increased my confidence. Suddenly I saw my erstwhile landlady. My heart sank. She looked at me but it was clear she didn't recognize me. She passed by like a complete stranger, she who had lived with me under the same roof for two months. I almost jumped for joy: the uniform had so altered the way I looked that even people who had good reason to remember me would not recognize me.

The next day I went to the office which issued railway passes. A line of soldiers stretched for 200–300 yards in front of the entrance. Naturally, I joined the line at first, but after half and hour's wait I realized that the chances of getting to the head of the line that day were non-existent. I asked the "comrade" standing in front of me to hold my place in line, and went to look for the exit from the building. The door was at the back of the building; nobody was around. I decided to take a risk – the worst that could happen would be to be thrown out. When I entered, nobody took the slightest notice.

I approached one of the six tables which stood inside, looked for a soldier whose face seemed good-natured, and inquired whether he was the person who dealt with passes. He said that unfortunately he wasn't the right person but as I had lost my place in line by going to the wrong table, he himself would take care of me. We went to a sergeant who checked my travel warrant, okayed it with the proper stamp, and issued me three chits for the train. We were two, but had decided to obtain three, just in case. It all took just a few minutes.

Vladek was waiting in line in a different spot, for safety's sake. I was proud as a peacock when I called him aside and said that everything was arranged! Vladek laughed till he felt dizzy when I told him how I had slipped in by the back entrance. Our entire road to survival was really a kind of "back entrance"! So I was merely compounding the procedure. Back entrance squared – that sounded not bad at all.

In the evening we stood at the entrance to the railroad station amidst a mass of soldiers. I felt completely safe in that crowd. The gate opened. The chits were checked, and we were aboard the train in a matter of minutes. The darkness was Stygian – a wartime blackout. We setted down as comfortably as we could for the two-day trip.

13 · The Trip to Lvov

"EEinsteigen! (ALLL aboard!) Close the doors!"

I first heard this monotonous cry of the train guards on my journey from Lvov to Dniepropetrovsk. This time the announcement refers to us, too, as we are members of the Wehrmacht in good standing. We have succeeded in getting good places next to the window, Vladek on the seat opposite me. The benches are too short for lying down but a place by the window confers an undoubted advantage. All the seats are heaped with luggage; we sit amidst mountains of suitcases, backpacks, bags and packages. I never guessed that soldiers carry so much luggage.

I learned later that the contents were mostly food. Each soldier going on furlough carried along all the provisions he could obtain in exchange for blankets, uniforms, etc., destined for his famished family in the *Vaterland*. There were almost no weapons – nobody wished to be burdened by unnecessary military equipment. On the other hand, stolen army provisions, such as lard, sausages or cigarettes, were deemed essential.

After a while, when everybody had settled down, conversation began, but mainly about family matters. Each soldier told where he was going, spoke about his mother, wife and so on reported how much time had passed since his last home visit, and listed the goodies he was bringing to his near and dear ones who had forgotten the taste of such items. One soldier boasted that he was carrying 3,000 cigarettes "confiscated" during the evacuation of army stores near the Volga.

Neither Vladek nor I took part in the discussion but this was hardly noticed as each traveller was absorbed in himself and his plans for the furlough. The talk quietened down gradually and our companions began to nod off. I saw a living illustration of the oft-heard saying that a soldier is able to sleep no matter what his circumstances are. Snoring heavily, they slumbered on rucksacks, suitcases and boxes, their bodies contorted to confirm to the available space.

The close air, the snores, and the monotonous clacking of the wheels lulled me to sleep, too, though I really had lots to think about and a thousand and one plans to make for the duration of my "furlough". Today I often wonder at the ease with which I adjusted to the fact of riding a train dressed in a German uniform. Somehow it seemed natural to me, despite being an erstwhile denizen of the ghetto, an inmate of a concentration camp, and escapee from a train bound for the gas chambers. It is fortunate that human nature is such that we forget the near past so easily, or rather that we accommodate ourselves so rapidly to changing circumstances. Perhaps the process is not easy, but it is, none the less, possible.

I was one of the first to awaken at dawn. Soon the others, too, began to stretch their cramped limbs. The train pulled into a large station for a stop of fifteen minutes or so. To my surprise almost all the soldiers hastened to the well and the washroom erected from planks, although the temperature was about ten degrees below freezing. Naturally, I also washed myself rapidly, so as not to stand out, though I was well aware of danger if I exposed myself too much. Then I ran to obtain the famed *Verpflegung*.

An incomparable emotion of pride and contentment filled me when I returned to the railroad car loaded down with food; I drew my rations on the basis of a travel warrant issued for a number of persons. I felt a blissful sense of mastery over the Master-Race, the feeling of duping, by means of a stupid forged signature, that mass of would-be lords and masters into parting with stores destined for their use, for the benefit of those whom they considered "our courageous warriors". My cup ran over when I savoured the biting irony of the circumstances; these rations were issued to a damned Jew, an "inhuman beast", destined to serve either as soap or as fertilizer, depending on the chance location of the particular gas chambers to which he was sent.

During the period when our gang roamed the Ukraine, we used to draw as many supplies as we could, because from time to time we needed money and food was the easiest merchandise to market. By rough calculation, we obtained army supplies sufficient for some 1200–1500 persons for a period of 200 days each! We had everything we needed, and we also were the source of livelihood for dozens of people who depended on our largesse and, together with us, were provided with sustenance by Hitler!

After returning from my first "raid" on a supply depot I stored the food in the knapsack and suitcase. The huge quantities of bread were impossibly bulky, but cigarettes were both compact and valuable. I was ashamed how rapidly an erstwhile starveling like me learned to treat good food with disdain. Success had turned our heads a little. Though we were on our guard against an excess of enthusiasm, such a crazy turnabout as the one we had experienced was bound to endow us with a good measure of impudence. Destiny had toyed with me. Packed into a short span of time I had experienced the ghetto, the camp, prison, starvation in Dniepropetrovsk, and then, all at once, here I was a "100 per cent German" accorded special privileges as a "frontline worker".

The fact that I had drawn supplies for ten people, thus enjoying more privileges than the most privileged Germans around me, also played its part in our general high humour.

The journey passed uneventfully, and there was no friction whatsoever between me and Vladek. He, as the more experienced, gave me the benefit of some priceless advice on the vulnerable spots in the control system of the different supply depots which could be turned to the advantage of a fast operator.

For me, the trip offered the opportunity to observe the 1,200 kilometre route from Dniepropetrovsk to Lvov. I had been too nervous riding the other way to notice and assimilate what I had seen. Now, I reconnoitred even the stations where I did not draw rations, in order to check out the lie of the land for possible use in the future. Znamienka – Kamienna – Biala Tserkiev, Fastov, Kasatin – Shepetovka. Finally Zdolbunow, the border of former Poland. We have two more hours to go until Lvov.

I feel some nervousness as we approach this city which had been turned by the Germans into a veritable hell. Perhaps I'll meet someone I know? I'll be discovered ... who knows. Well, whatever will be, will be! Vladek is jumpy, too. We arrange our meeting for the next day. Today, Vladek will sleep at the apartment where his sick sister is hidden, while I will have to find a lodging for the night through my own efforts.

I did not have a clear idea how I would go about finding a place, but did not worry too much. An acquaintance of mine in Dniepro had given me the address of a Polish office in the centre of Lvov. The manager was his friend he would surely arrange a bed for me somewhere. That office would serve as my temporary harbour. Vladek did not give me any detail about his hiding place, so as not to tempt me into following him there.

The Krasne station. Thirty minutes to Lvov. We will get off at the suburban station Podzamcze. It's best to avoid the main one. My thoughts are spinning: what will happen, how it will go. Memories attack me like a pack of mad dogs, exciting me so much that I have to exercise strenuous control so as not to betray anything to the outside world. Here's the Baczynski factory! The station now, any minute! Look out! The train slows down, the rails glide ever more slowly under my nervous gaze. The platforms. We're really here! The train stops. Lvov.

The train guards announce that all of us are to get off and report at the delousing station. The announcement is very convenient because it means we don't have to try to slip away unofficially. We have no intention, needless to say, of going to the delousing station (and strip naked ... ugh!) but we leave the train amidst a whole crowd of soldiers. Nobody, but nobody, takes any notice of the two of us. We leave the station, of course, by way of the special exit for soldiers. Everything goes off smoothly, and here we are, on the street.

14 · Back in Lvov

The streets of Lvov. Memories, memories again. How many happy moments I had spent in this once-beloved city, how many youthful dreams I had woven walking around these well-known city walls which now are so alien to me. How many memories of despair and losses endured in the last few years awaken at these sights. I must not think about all that now. I drag myself back to reality. Why, I am a member of the Wehrmacht. Well, that is an exaggeration, but at least I am an Aryan, and those usually look at the world through rosier spectacles than we.

A tram. That's a chapter by itself in the story of my life. As a child I used to steal a ride on that very tram. Later I had a monthly student's ticket and lorded it on the front platform near the motorman; that was the favourite location for the city's students. Still later, the tram was transformed into a magic carpet of legend, forbidden to Jews like me, carrying non-Jews effortlessly and miraculously from one end of the town to another. The only tram left to Jews was the platform formerly used for transporting coal and now burdened with heaps of corpses on their way to "the sand" for burial. Enough, get rid of these ghosts from the past!

I entered the compartment reserved "for Germans only", settled down comfortably and looked patronizingly at the members of the "slavefolk" (the Germans liked to play on the words "slav" and "slave") crowded in the rear of the tram. I tried to drive back tears and look haughtily at the slavish horde. No, they were not worth even a glance from my privileged eyes. The tram passed near the border of the ghetto. I pretended to look at the tragic sight with a mixture of curiosity and indifference. I couldn't let myself look for too long, lest I become an object of attention. I observed with an aching heart deserted streets, silent witness to 180,000 innocent men, women, children and old people, healthy and sick, who had been bestially murdered for the sin of being born Jewish. That was a sin which could not be expiated in our modern world. The ghetto disappeared rapidly from sight. We were passing the Sobieski school, site of the March *Aktion* – more than 20,000 victims. We rolled on. The former military prison – 3,000 killed immediately after the arrival of the Germans. Ah, on this street corner an uncle of mine had been brutally beaten. He had died on the street. Yes, here it stood. Why, here is where the Temple stood, a synagogue that was the pride of the Jews of Lvov, now a heap of rubble ... When would it end, this journey among the nightmares of the past!

I get off at the street once called Karol Ludovic, now Legionow. What the devil! This should be the "1st of May Boulevard". But now it's Hitler-Ring, so named on the occasion of the first anniversary of the German occupation of the city by the instigators of the "New Order". It's a pity that the symbols of the new regime are lacking; the hangman's noose, a bunch of whips, and a bonfire for burning books. Hitler-Ring! Ugh!

The office I was looking for was located on the street formerly named "The 3rd of May". I pulled myself together and rang the bell. A young man opened the door. "Where is Mr. X?" I inquired. The man invited me inside, oozing courtesy. He was probably expecting a lucrative business deal with a German who spoke Polish. Unfortunately, X was not in Lvov; he had gone on a trip to Warsaw the previous day. My host outdid himself in offers of assistance. What was my business, perhaps he could ... this ... and that ...? But his face did not inspire trust. I said that it was a personal matter, and left.

It was around six in the evening, a relatively late hour. It was getting dark, and I had no idea where to turn. I thought about all the non-Jews I knew in Lvov, considered whom I could trust enough to ask for shelter, perhaps risking everything. Nobody came to mind, I didn't want to admit any thought of despair. A thousand ideas and stratagems flitted through my brain, as was usual with me in moments of danger. A solution was bound to come up. I walked mechanically towards Legionow, when I was passing Passage Haussman I recalled that during my walks around the city I had visited a Jewish acquaintance employed by a Ukrainian engineer in one of those business offices which in that period sprang up and vanished like mushrooms. The engineer had made a very good impression on me. My acquaintance had praised him as a man whom you could trust absolutely.

I mounted the steps to his apartment at a run, without a moment's hesitation. Face to face with the door though, I decided to come back as near 8 o'clock (the police curfew hour for natives) as possible. So I wandered about the city for nearly two hours more. It was a town of ghosts for me, but it was better not to think about that. I had more pressing problems. The hours crawled along very slowly, but finally it was time for my dive into the unknown.

I pressed the bell. "Ich möchte sprechen mit Herrn S." I spoke German as a matter of course. Then I received a jolt – he still had not come home. His wife and daughter, with the help of the maidservant, attempted to explain, in rudimentary German, that Herr Engineer S. should be back shortly because the hour was late, and would I agree to wait for him? I consented out of the goodness of my benevolent heart. I sat there waiting on pins and needles. I sensed the shock of the inhabitants in the entire apartment house as they wondered what a uniformed German was doing in their building.

Finally, Mr S. returned. He did not recognize me, of course, and treated me in a very formal manner mixed with ill-disguised fear. Then I explained who I really was, and why I dared to invade his apartment. At that, his countenance cleared. He did not believe his own eyes. What? A Jew in a uniform? Impossible. After I had explained what I was doing in Lvov, he asked me to repeat my explanation. Naturally, I told him only part of the truth; I did not want to reveal secrets unnecessarily. Basically, I told him enough for him to imagine that was the whole truth.

Mr S. was delighted, overwhelmed by the whole business, and very enthusiastic, about my achievements. Luckily for me, he took a sportsman's view and came down on my side. Of course, I could spend the night at his home. He would help me insofar as he could, it would be an unforgettable experience for him. He had always sided with the Jews, and so on. His good intentions were obvious to me. Thank you, Almighty Providence! "An ounce of luck is worth a pound of brains."

I made it clear that I would pay for everything, but Mr S. would not hear of it. So I offered my provisions, provoking a smile of thinly disguised ridicule. However, when I unpacked my suitcase and spread my goodies on the table (a two-pound jar of butter, three cans of excellent meat pies), and offered him German cigarettes, Mr S. was flabbergasted. To complete my triumph, I stressed the fact that we were guzzling these delicacies by courtesy of Hitler, that they hadn't cost me one pfennig and were, so to say, a trophy of war, He was completely bedazzled by the concrete proof of my success in the unequal fight against our common foe.

During this evening repast everybody licked their fingers over the long-forgotten delicacies, and they could not have enough of my stories about various adventures. Luckily, I have a good capacity for drink – otherwise I could not have lasted through the innumerable toasts in honour of my future success, luck, continued good health, the coming defeat of the Germans, and so on. Finally I went to bed, tired out by the train journey, the nervous strain, the dinner and the heavy drinking. I fell asleep immediately, almost as safe and sound as a babe in its mother's arms.

I felt as if nothing could threaten me, though I was dancing on the razor's edge. I knew that betrayal was an everyday occurrence and lay in ambush everywhere I turned, that chance could turn malicious and let loose on me a random house search. Still, it was all a calculated risk, and I had to live with it. It was not worth worrying overmuch – I fell asleep and slept like a king.

Although I was quite happy in my lodgings, I thanked my hosts in the morning and left them all my supplies. These were an unnecessary encumbrance for me but manna from heaven for them. The engineer invited me warmly to sleep freely at his place in future if I remained in Lvov but I had no intention of endangering his freedom and my life by sleeping twice in the same apartment.

I left the house, yesterday's nightmares had fortunately departed, but the city seemed only a shadow of its forner self. The traffic on the streets was minimal and consisted mainly of soldiers. The civilians seemed to be slinking along, probably afraid of being caught in a round-up, kidnapped for compulsory labour in Germany, and the like. The shops were not even a shadow of the past. The majority were closed and the rest gaped frighteningly with empty show-windows. Unfamiliar names adorned the shopfronts. The gay Lvov of old had died and did not exist any more.

The time for my meeting with Vladek arrived. We were both punctual and even if we were not, a short wait at the tram stop chosen for our rendezvous would not have awakened suspicion. We conversed in German. It was a great pleasure to walk freely along the streets where a short time ago we had been driven along like mad dogs. We saluted officers, feeling amused contempt. Our objective was the OKW (the High Command of the Wehrmacht) office where Sweetie's sister worked, among numerous other Jews. Relations with the non-Jews were not bad at all: anybody who needed to be bribed had been taken care of so that the Jewish workers felt almost at liberty.

The department of the OKW where the Jews were employed had diverse functions. It dealt with the posting of entertainment items to the fighting units: periodicals, gramophones, games, etc. There were also a number of workshops, mostly employed in manufacturing articles for the private consumption of the German personnel who worked in the High Command. The management especially prized the gold workshop. A close acquaintance of Sweetie worked there as a goldsmith. Entrance to the workshop was forbidden except to a select group of Germans. As a result it was the best meeting place for Jews who were looking for a discreet place where they could talk over important affairs. The goldsmith cultivated good relations with the Germans. So he was the logical person to be a go-between in any matter which concerned them – bribes, gifts, "teaching the ropes" to new personnel, and the like.

Sweetie had described to us precisely where the goldsmith worked, so we found him without having to make inquiries. Naturally, nobody paid attention to two soldiers walking through the building. The goldsmith was very pleased when we explained who we were and the purpose of our visit. We were in the middle of an intense discussion about how to establish contact with the people we wanted in the ghetto, who could leave with us and which papers were necessary when someone entered the room, of course without knocking first.

The goldsmith and Vladek saw the unbidden guest first. Noticing the expression on Vladek's face, I turned about, and found myself face to face with a *Feldebel* – a senior noncom. I came to attention. Though I knew that we were found out, I felt no fear – it was too late for that. Later, when recalling the occasion, I was always surprised at the many insignificant details which had embedded themselves in my memory, although I was gazing at the vision of Death in a uniform. I remember my unbuttoned jacket, Vladek's nervous movements, the unnatural calm of the goldsmith, some compromising documents scattered on the table.

The German cut through the moment of nervous tension with a curt "Heil Hitler", and addressed a question on some unimportant topic to the goldsmith. Then he asked us if we were also commissioning some gold objects for ourselves, and without waiting for an answer added: "It seems you fellows are coming here from the front. Heil Hitler", and he wasn't there.

We were so dumbfounded by the incident that we did not even ask the goldsmith who this angel from heaven was. Then the goldsmith broke the silence, and explained that the man was Staff-Sergeant Saupe, the real boss of the OKW in Lvov. His relations with the Jews were ideal. He used to intervene whenever he could help them and when unable to do so, he advised them who could assist them.

Staupe, said the goldsmith, had undoubtedly realized at first sight who we were; the workshop was out of bounds, and our "uniforms" suffered from various defects, obvious to an experienced staff sergeant though invisible to people who were not experts in the dress code of the German army. Still, he had pretended that everything was O.K. People said that he had advised the Jews to leave Lvov as rapidly as possible, using Aryan papers. By the way, I later learned that Staupe had taken Sweetie's sister to the train in his own car and practically bundled her into the carriage himself. She maintained contact with him by letter for a long time after she had arrived safely in Dniepropetrovsk.

It all sounded very nice. Still, the memory of the moment when I had suddenly seen the German and thought ourselves lost before we had even spread our wings, continued to send chills down my spine for a long time.

The conversation with the goldsmith had eminently satisfactory results. Our contact with the ghetto was assured. The next day we were to receive concrete information about the people in question. The friend of the goldsmith, a certain Casick, would serve as a go-between, because it was inadvisable to visit the workshop too often. Casick left the OKW building frequently on confidential business which enriched various Germans who were in cahoots with him. He gave us the address of one A. Soltiss, a non-Jew, who would agree to take us in. We could trust him completely, because he lived (for some unclear reason) under-cover, using forged documents, and subsisted on illegal trading along the Lvov–Warsaw route. It later transpired that the address was as good as gold.

Casick promised he would meet Soltiss in the afternoon and Vladek left to visit his sister again. I walked around the town for a while and then set out to try my luck with Soltiss. Fortunately, Soltiss lived opposite the *Soldatenheim*, so the street was filled with soldiers all day long, and my presence went completely unnoticed.

A woman opened the door. She said that Mr Soltiss was in, and could speak with me. I spoke German to begin with, then put my cards on the table and told him who I was and who had sent me. At first his face reflected disbelief; he probably thought it was some kind of a trap. After a few moments of conversation I succeeded in allaying his suspicions towards me, and my explanation was accepted as genuine. He was delighted with such a capital story and invited his wife and his business partner, Karol, to hear it, assuring me that they could be trusted absolutely. He told them about the unheard-of fact – a Jew in a German uniform, roaming about as free as a bird. The atmosphere mellowed. I was invited to partake of their meal. Hors d'oeuvres, vodka, all the works! And then stories, in an unending stream. I learned from them that my hosts did not enjoy much peace and quiet. We Jews had even more serious troubles, true, but any troubles are unpleasant business.

Soltiss had come to the attention of the police through some "business" deals, and was forced to flee and assume a different name. Flushed with vodka and excited by rivalry with a Jew in tales of dangerous living, he displayed an assortment of blank official forms of inestimable value for me: a regional railway pass, the passport of *Volksdeutsche*, a blank form for an ID card and so on. One could obtain everything for cash, he asserted, even the passport of a Reich citizen.

Karol did not lag behind. He told me how he had almost been caught in Krakow, and escaped, trading shots with the German police. Unfortunately trading supplies had been sized, but they wouldn't catch him so easily, though official letters with his description had been circulated to the police.

The visit of an acquaintance cut short our exchange of reminiscences. In the evening, they promised, we would have a good time if I was not afraid to stay at their place. I agreed, of course, noblesse oblige. I told Soltiss that Casick was due at 5 o'clock. He responded with an invitation to stay in the apartment till then, and proposed a meeting with a businessman who could offer me some interesting deals. Making the most of the opportunity, I said that textile dyes interested me very much. Soltiss agreed to a deal on the spot, provided he could make a profit. We loved each other like brothers, but let's count the coins too.

I was served lunch in a separate room, to keep my presence secret, because some guests came for the noonday meal. In the afternoon Soltiss produced the businessman he had promised to introduce to me. He was a nondescript character dressed in a railwaymen's uniform. A second or two after he had opened his mouth to speak, I recognized the unmistakable Jewish accent. It was a wonder he could survive even a day.

This character introduced himself as Kunzio. His personal history was incredible even in that miraculous period so replete with unlikely occurrences. He had applied for a job with the railway system, brandishing a faked ID card, and had been taken on. He explained away his singsong Polish speech by claiming that he had been born and brought up in Volhynia, where people spoke a special kind of Polish. Nevertheless, it seems people had caught on and informed on him more than once, probably because they were indignant that a Jew dared to besmirch the uniform of a railwayman. Each time this had happened, he got away with his story, either by luck or ingenuity. Once, when he was sent to a doctor to check his "credentials", he bribed the physician with a watch at the critical moment of exposure. Still, his pals on the railway hadn't quite overcome their suspicions. It was only after he passed a medical check-up by the military commission that they began to believe him. Seeing my puzzled expression, Kunzio recounted an unsurpassed story.

He had a close acquaintance, a non-Jew. Kunzio accompanied him when many railwaymen were called up for a military check-up, preparatory to possible service in Germany. He took off his clothes like all the others and walked around in the main hall in his underwear. When his number was called he sent his non-Jewish friend and remained in the hall. None of his mates could know for sure whether he had already had his check-up or if his number had not yet come up. People were occupied with their own troubles and did not check his movements. What's more, the very fact that he had waited calmly before the check-up was sufficient evidence of his "innocence". Nowadays, said Kunzio, when anyone dared to question his antecedents, the others would shush him, telling him not to be stupid, the guy had been stripped naked in front of a medical commission.

Kunzio's main source of money came by trading in anything he could. His expenses went beyond personal needs, because to survive he had to keep on good terms with the "bosses". He did this by inviting them to wild parties at his expense … In addition, he was paying for a number of his relatives who were in hiding with non-Jews. He also sheltered in his apartment in a clothes closet a woman who had jumped off a train bound for the Belzec death camp, and had unfortunately broken her hand. Yes, life wasn't a fairy tale for Kunzio, but rather a detective thriller or a fantastic story out of the Wild West.

I needed a knapsack. That was a trifle, he said; the knapsack would be delivered the next day. The reader should know that articles of that kind were not to be found; the stores were generally empty, if they hadn't closed down. "Exotic" items like knapsacks had been sold out during the German invasion of Poland in 1939. The surviving knapsacks had been "secured" during the Russian occupation. But Kunzio had a solution to every problem. Not to worry, the knapsack would be mine the next day. I did not inquire about the price – it was an unimportant detail.

Kunzio also offered his assistance in the departure from Lvov. He advised me to use the same suburban station we had used on arrival, where he knew some people. He would guarantee a safe exit naturally for a consideration. This proposition was not to be lightly disregarded. I would consider it with due gravity at the proper time. In the meantime Soltiss began negotiating with Kunzio about astonishing quantities of gold. A deal was struck, and Kunzio departed.

Casick came at 5 p.m., closely followed by Vladek. We arranged the schedule of our departure with Casick and discussed various important details: how many women could accompany us, the preparations we should make for the trip, and most important of all how to arrange for the photographs and personal data needed the next day. If the papers were ready the next day, we could leave within three days at the most. Vladek's sister was sick with typhoid but the crisis of the illness had already passed. She might be able to come with us; if not, he would have to return to Lvov and collect her another time. Casick had to leave at 6 p.m and Vladek left soon after.

I had the address of a place where I could spend the night in safety, so I started to take my leave but the Soltiss couple didn't want to hear of it. I had promised to stay, hadn't I? We would talk a while, down a few drinks, and have some fun if we were in the mood for it. After all, these were difficult times, and we needed to relax. They urged me to remain so warmly, that I assented in the end.

Soltiss then began to recount incredibly interesting stories about his crazy escapades on the route to Warsaw. Searches, road blocks, tricks, bribes – he drew the picture of a Poland under the German rule that was quite new to me. Each of his trips afforded sufficient material for a sensational novel. Trading in gold was no joke; the penalty was death. But under German occupation one lived cheek by jowl with death all the time, so people got used to it and developed an almost familiar relationship with the figure who wielded a scythe.

Karol told me that in spite of the warrant of arrest he kept on travelling, giving the Germans the slip. He used to visit his fiancée in Cracow (her mama was the queen of a well-known neighbourhood where vice and crime flourished), regardless of the risk to himself.

I contributed my part to the fund of anecdotes, which followed each other endlessly. Our purpose was perhaps not so much to boast as to ridicule the arrogant Germans, to show them up as dumb jerks who could be tricked and foiled at every step. In spite of their boot on our necks, we managed to move around freely and even more, we broke their laws time and again, thumbing our noses at the Master Race. True, there were narrow limits to what we could do, but things looked much rosier seen through the fumes of alcohol, and we felt very content. I offered the remains of my German-issued victuals to Mrs. Soltiss. She received them unwillingly, persuaded only by the argument that provisions looted from the enemy were an obligatory adornment to any feast worthy of its name.

We sat down to the evening meal. Even in prewar times a supper of this kind would have been deemed a feast. Sausages, ham, herring, cold meat, a pie, rolls, bread, and decent drink in great quantities. We were in excellent humour right from the start, excited by our reminiscences and by drink. Our spirits rose further after we had emptied a few additional bottles. We laughed at nothing, shouted, interrupted each other, sang – a veritable pandemonium. Soltiss amused himself with his wife's sister-in-law; his brother-in-law flirted with the teenage daughter of the hosts. Karol "wooed" me: "Adam, I love you, come with me to Krakow. We'll make a heap of money. My Zosia has a friend, a real peach, just for you. Nothing doing with these kike friends of yours, you won't earn much with them. A clever one like you is too good for the poor bastards. Give me a kiss, Adam, you're pulling my leg when you claim you're a Jew. Anyway, no matter. We'll make a million, and slip away to Turkey ...".

I sobered up suddenly. What was I doing here? I was condemned, was less than a beast. I, a Jew, among these *goyim* at a crazy drinking party, while my people were perishing, were being beaten, murdered, tortured by the Nazi hooligans? Perhaps a new frenzied *Aktion* was even now being let loose in the ghetto; perhaps hundreds of innocents were being slaughtered in the labour camps, thousands being gassed according to plan. Perhaps the Angel of Death was waiting for me across the threshold. No, much closer, he was sitting on my shoulder and touching my hair, so that I shouldn't forget him even for a moment ... Damn it, more vodka! Whatever I enjoy now is mine for ever.

The fumes of alcohol enveloped me once more. I talked shouted and sang with the others, exchanged kisses with one, comforted another who was sobbing on my shoulder. The room spun before my eyes like a crazy merry-go-around. Someone turned on the gramophone – oh! the daughter. She wanted to dance with me, why not? The rest of them staggered on unsteady feet, pretending to dance, feeling up their female partners. A real bacchanale!

A knocking on the adjoing wall of the next apartment introduced a jarring note into the drunken harmony. Soltiss explained that it was their neighbour, a German. What, a German wants to put a stop to our party? I'll show him. My brain, although soggy with drink, tries to hold me back, but in vain. I open the window and at the top of my voice pour out all my accumulated anger at the German. Whatsa matter, you damn so and so! How dare you interrupt a holiday party! Don't we decent Catholics have the right to enjoy ourselves once a year, on Easter? Why do you have to stick your nose in our affairs? And much more of the same kind.

I don't know to this very day why the whole row did not end badly for all of us – God knows I didn't mince my words. Perhaps the neighbour chose golden silence at the sight of a uniformed German; maybe he gave up on the incoherent reproaches of a drunk. I don't care what his motives were. At the time, I didn't even care what would happen next. Perhaps that was the reason why the German drew back and didn't utter another word.

Nevertheless, the party had passed its climax. Soltiss lay in a drunken stupor, but his wife kept her wits to the end, and she even managed to hold the erotic impulses of her daughter in check. My chivalrous defence of the girl's maidenly honour had been countered by Karol who forcefully rammed his head into my stomach in the best tradition of the slum neighbourhoods of Krakow, or perhaps Warsaw. I fell down heavily, next to the wall but after a minute or two Karol bent over me, kissing me and asking my forgiveness, the tears steaming down his round face. We just had to down another glass to cement our reconciliation. That did for us. We fell asleep against the wall, muttering promises of eternal friendship.

At night's end I awoke from a heavy slumber and immediately remembered the quarrel with the German. He would surely try to show us what's what. Time to fade away! In the meantime, Karol rose and immediately began searching for liquid refreshment. I washed up. A cold shower sobered me completely. At the same time Soltiss prodded his wife awake and told her to fix breakfast. What's bound to happen will, I reflected, and remained for breakfast. The meal was very tasty, nothing happened – fortunately.

At leave-taking, the Soltisses invited me with genuine warmth to visit them again. I had to promise Karol that I would not depart without saying goodbye to him. I also managed at the last moment to make a deal with the brother-in-law; he would purchase dyes and a knapsack for me.

I went out into the street, to look for Vladek. It was early morning, the streets were almost deserted. I did not hurry and could not walk rapidly anyway, because Michael's boots hurt my feet terribly. Both my heels were blistered and I could hardly take a step. Along my route I found a cobbler who inserted cork insteps, but they didn't help much. There was nothing to do ... I would have to drag myself to Dniepro by hook or by crook. I found Vladek in the hideout we had settled upon. We visited the OKW building to ascertain who would accompany us on the trip back. Vladek's sister was convalescing but did not have enough strength for a route of 1,200 kilometres, so it would be necessary to return to Lvov for her. The people in the OKW were waiting for us. We decided to separate for the trip. Vladek would leave towards morning and I would take a night passenger train.

Casick had collected the candidates and the photos. There were eighteen people in all, including four women. We took down all the personal data, and promised to let them know when we would leave. We warned that each passenger should be ready to leave immediately after being notified.

Vladek left to visit his sister again, and I wanted to look for a few friends who lived in Lvov. We arranged to meet at the Soltisses at 3 p.m. I took a walk through the town – my home town. Here I had been born, gone to school, fallen in love for the first time. It was the town of my youthful years, the once – beloved town of youthful fancies, fun and games, crazy parties.

Now the city only stirred up hate on my part. Here I had gone through hell on earth. My experiences, as if extracted directly from the feverish fantasies of a sick mind and made real, had swept away the memories of youth which are so dear to a person. The parks of Lvov, the first dates, it had all disappeared ... I only remembered that Polish students had tormented Jews here, and the Germans had later completed an enterprise begun so well. I had better not remind anyone of those things, nor even let myself recall them; they were much too vivid in my mind. I hated the city, the battlements, the parks, the bars and cafés, the thronging memories which added their sharp bitterness to a loathsome reality. No, I didn't want to see my once-beloved Lvov any more. It was a chapter of my life which should be closed. The proverbial bitter dregs at the bottom of the wine glass had swollen and were filling the glass to overflowing.

The sight of an officer striding in my direction restored me to reality. I saluted according to regulations and realized that it was not the right time for sentimental reflections. I decided to leave Lvov as soon as possible.

I entered the first restaurant I saw. It took me a lot of effort to overcome the distrust the manager displayed at the sight of the uniform, but I was served in the end. On my way home, I had an urge for some coffee. I was just passing the *pâtisserie* of Wonhout. I entered without hesitating too much in the doorway, remembering that before leaving for Warsaw this *pâtisserie* had been almost a home from home in the afternoons, a place where I drank coffee and read the papers. I knew it was foolish, but bravado won out, and I went in.

There were three or four plates on the counter, with the remains of unappetizing cakes, and bottles of imitation essence of tea. I sat by a table and ordered coffee, resigned to being served a wartime *ersatz* brew. I looked around the room. If one took into account the fact that it was only noon, and there was a war going on, the *pâtisserie* was quite full. I saw to my surprise that a customer at a neighbouring table was enthusiastically tackling a large slice of a magnificent-looking *torte*. I called the waitress and instructed her to serve me with the same pastry as that man. She went pale and started drivelling about rationing. I cut her short and told her curtly to cut out the crap and do as I told her. A moment later Mr Wonhout himself presented himself at my table. He was a *Volksdeutsch* who spoke German perfectly. He also began an involved explanation about his problems with the rationing authorities, so he was sorry but ... I cut him off in the middle of a sentence and spoke in the domineering tones of a member of the *Herrenvolk*: "All right, all right. But I don't care a shit. Please let me have the same cake as over there".

He realised that there was nothing doing, and perhaps he wanted to smooth my ruffled feathers. Anyway, he delivered the *torte* personally and, miracle of miracles, a cup of real coffee. He seated himself at my table and struck up a sociable conversation. I told him that the rigours of rationing were familiar to me, that I commiserated with all my heart with his difficulties, that the pastry was excellent, and similar courtesies aimed at pacifying him. He asked me out of the blue if I had ever visited Lvov, for my face looked familiar. Of course I denied this heatedly. The importance of a uniform! It changes a person completely. Besides, there was the matter of the unbridgeable chasm between a member of the Master Race and a Jew: the normal mental processes served as an unconscious barrier to any attempt to connect a one who was at the bottom of the abyss into which the Jews had been pushed with a uniformed German, who belonged at the top of the social ladder. Such an attempt would have been a crime of *lèse majesté*!

When I was leaving, I purchased, for a steep price, some slices of the superior pastry for the Soltisses. By that time, Wonhout was probably quite sure that I was really a black marketeer, he had no objections to the deal, and was not afraid I would inform on him.

At about 2 p.m. I presented myself at the Soltiss apartment, armed with a package of pastry of almost pre-war quality. Mr Soltiss was delighted with my gift and greeted me with overflowing hospitality. The dyes and knapsack were ready and waiting. There was no sign of yesterday's party. Fortunately, the German neighbour hadn't been heard from, and after the preceding night's revelry I was considered a member of the household. The paradoxical humour of the situation amused me mightily.

Vladek came in shortly thereafter. Experience had taught all of us that while fun was fun, business always came first. The Soltisses left the two of us alone to discuss our affairs. We came to the conclusion. that we had everything we needed to fabricate the documents. If we could do this immediately, we were free to depart that very day.

We set to work. The Gestapo would have admired our handiwork: affixing the photographs, altering the stamps, filling out the forms. One last check, and we were ready. We're leaving today! The Soltisses tried to detain me but naturally I did not treat this seriously. We contacted our clients, told them to which of the two groups each belonged, when and where to gather at the rendezvous, and how to conduct themselves. Kunzio undertook to escort my group through the railway station and buy their train tickets. Vladek didn't need his services. His group numbered eight people, mine nine, including Sweetie's sister. Everything was arranged. Thank God, we were going.

My train was due to leave at 8 p.m. I took leave of the Soltiss household at a light supper. Obviously we couldn't forgo a last toast. I took my modest luggage – a suitcase with the textile dyes and a knapsack – and set out.

My heart beat a bit rapidly, but basically I felt absolutely sure of myself, almost peaceful. I moved freely through the station. Nobody even thought to notice a soldier, one of the thousands passing through each day. I noticed Kunzio on the platform but gave no sign of familiarity. I looked restlessly for my people. They were scattered in various inconspicuous corners of the station. Luckily there were only a few police spies around; one could spot them at first glance.

It was almost 8:30. Damn it all! The last moments were stretching out with agonizing slowness. Kunzio came up to me to get a match for his cigarette. He said without moving his lips that I should pay special attention to Sweetie's sister and one other client; he would get the others on the train. What the hell was happening with the time – it had slowed down to a crawl. A signal? Yes, the train is coming. Here it is.

The train was quite crowded but the passengers on the platform managed to push their way in. There were a few civilians bound for Tarnopol; the rest were army personnel going to the East. I was allowed into a railway car reserved for soldiers but my people were pushed into the civilian cars.

The train remained at our station for five minutes only. Soon the gendarmes escorting our train took up the cry: "Tarnopol – Zhemerinka – Fastov – Dniepropetrovsk! All aboard!! Shut the doors!" We were moving.

The worst was behind me. The only problem still ahead was the border check on the frontier run.

My companions in the compartment were going to the front and, unlike me, were not very lighthearted. I in contrast, was returning from the front to the rear. We talked for a while and then, it being rather late, they all lay down to sleep as comfortably as the crowded conditions permitted. I visited my protégés and then settled down to sleep as well.

I slept until morning and awoke only when we reached the Zhemerinka station. Here we were to switch trains. My people were already on the platform. Their nervous expressions could be seen from a distance. Fortunately, nobody was watching them, or we could certainly have been caught. I approached them to calm them down. They all moved together, and I followed them all of us lost in the crowd.

Passkontrolle! Now we were in the hands of Lady Luck. I passed the control point first without any trouble. Then I sent my group through, one at a time. Everything worked like a charm. The documents were first-class – I had manufactured and checked them personally.

It was harder to secure seats on this train. The soldiers did not want to let in the "civilian baggage". Only when I explained that these were workers bound for the front zone did they unbend a little. If truth be told, they could not understand why people should be in a hurry to reach the front line, if they were not forced to go there.

15 · Back to Dniepropetrovsk

It took an entire day for the train to crawl the distance to Zhemerinka. When we arrived, I had to draw our rations to avoid raising suspicions among the passengers. But my boots increasingly bothered me, and I sensed that my feet were swelling. I could not walk even a few steps without limping painfully.

Nevertheless, the mission was carried out. At the cost of considerable pain, my knapsack was filled with sausage, butter, cigarettes, cheese and bread. I distributed this largesse among the members of my convoy and there was still plenty left. My feet hurt like the devil!

At Znamienka we went with ease through a surprise check of documents. I couldn't react to that success with the joy it deserved because my feet were killing me. At Vinnitsa I couldn't stand the pain any more and visited the local infirmary. A medic pulled off my boots with an effort. My feet were so swollen that they looked like two wooden blocks. The medic said with a malicious smile that it would now be impossible to put on the boots again – as if I couldn't see that myself! My pleas for treatment elicited a length of bandage, some ointment (which I was assured, wouldn't help), and pain-killing pills. My travel warrant was adorned with a note saying that I had been treated at military infirmary number so-and-do, and was to present myself for further treatment at the next infirmary along my route.

I returned to my compartment on bare feet. There I met with a surprise which, in contrast to other surprises of that kind, had a happy outcome. An employee of the railroad system who was seated in our compartment had taken a fancy to Sweetie's sister. In view of my unwelcoming expression he had not dared to speak to her, thinking her to be my girlfriend. When I left the train, however, he had struck up a conversation, and soon learned that I had no sexual claims on my ward. When I returned, he wanted to get on my good side, deluged me with useless advice – and offered me the loan of his slippers, a princely offer in the circumstances. I could not and did not refuse this gift from Heaven, which at least enabled me to move though my feet still hurt.

At Fastov, Vladek joined us with his group. We felt we were safe for the time being. We were to leave Fastov only in the evening, for the railway line was out of order. I paraded the platform in my slippers and then visited the infirmary where they took care of me as "a brave fighter". "Our soldiers, who hasten to the front in spite of ill health are real heroes!" I received special rations calculated to raise the morale of the sick. I did not need my morale raised but the chocolate was excellent.

The trainman brought confidential news which gladdened my heart. The Soviet partisans had destroyed a large segment of the railway. Departure from Fastov before the next morning was out of the question, but he assured us that the Wehrmacht would take care of the bandits, we shouldn't worry. In the meanwhile, he suggested, why not go to town and have some fun.

So I visited *Soldatenheim* ("Soldiers' Home") – a kind of a club where accommodation could also be had. It was a boring place to spend time but it was worth my while to file away that institution for future reference. Our documents were accepted as genuine without any reservations. A soldier guided us to a peasant's cottage where vodka was illegally sold. We had a few drinks, then entered a cinema, naturally bearing a sign "For Germans Only." The film was third-rate, like all the pictures produced in Germany in those years, but the visit itself was good for our morale.

Our trainman was a priceless find. At the time I did not appreciate how much he contributed to the construction of my "house of cards" – the confidence born of wearing a uniform. He guided my first steps in the world of special privileges obtainable by Germans as a matter of course. That knowledge proved fantastically useful to me and my colleagues in the course of our masquerade in German uniforms. Only the first step was difficult, and even then it was not so hard in itself; but the company of my guide certainly saved a lot of wear-and-tear on my nerves. Besides, his matter-of-course confidence, which was quite natural in "the genuine article", reduced to a minimum any risk to me.

The trainman's information proved correct. We left Fastov late in the morning. I did not lose any opportunity to promenade on the platform at each major station and draw my special rations for sick soldiers. The trainman besieged Sweetie's sister with increasing ardour, but in view of the absolute failure of his wooing, he continued to suspect that I was having an affair on the side with my "book-keeper", as I introduced her. He was stationed in Dniepropetrovsk, and that is where he arranged a meeting with us in the near future, no doubt in the hope that it would be easier to get me away from her in the city, and that he would have better luck there.

I met with Vladek and with our entire group only at the stations, so as not to attract anyone's attention. Vladek was escorting his younger sister, and was anxious to get back safely. I was fatigued by the constant need to supervise my female companion's every word and gesture, to prevent self-betrayal. We had only 200 kilometres more to go, very little after traversing 1000 kilometres.

At times I realized delightedly how different this train ride to the Ukraine was from the first one. The fear, restless uncertainty about the future had vanished like smoke. Instead, there was a strange cheerfulness and even a luxuriant self-confidence. Dniepropetrovsk, which was approaching, did not fill me with anxiety. I had a place to live in. I was at home there. Considering the surrounding circumstances, it was really quite amusing, wasn't it?

16 · Life in Dniepropetrovsk

Michael was enormously pleased to see me return in one piece, in good health and – last but not least – in possession of a fat billfold. Sweetie was delighted by his sister's arrival. She told him about our journey which had been – she thought – packed with adventure, and how I had conscientiously taken care of her. Sweetie could not thank me enough. He knew that my financial resources needed a transfusion, and he paid me royally for bringing his sister. I felt a little embarrassed to be collecting money for rescuing people, but he stressed that he had enough, while my pockets were empty. There was really no adequate reward for what I had done for him and his sister, because no one else had agreed to do it. It was only fair to share his cash reserves with me. Anyway, money was not important.

My return from the breakneck expedition to Lvov left me feeling like a Roman commander celebrating a triumph. Vladek and the people we had brought competed in describing my courageous behaviour and told everybody how I had cared personally for each person in our convoy. They swore that they had arrived safely thanks solely to my bravery and audacity. I myself was of the opinion that the main reason for my success were Michael's boots which did not fit my pampered feet. Necessity was to blame for most of my bluffing and audacity.

Fortunately, the ballooning popularity and hullaboo centred on my person did not go to my head. I realized very well that my popularity, resulting from the stories about the trip, reflected the fact that the less those around me were able to summon enough energy to display bravery (or rather to overcome fear), the more they praised my courage. That courage seemed to me rather problematical. I knew quite well that I had almost died of fright several times, but I was not free to reveal my feelings.

My landlady and her son Vanya could not contain their joy when the learned that I had brought the dyes. It was not just a business deal for them but deliverance itself, because while neither of them worked, they had to eat.

Dyes were a most sought-after commodity on the market – second only to food. The German soldiers who returned from the front line used to sell anything they could. The most logical thing to do was to sell their spare uniform which only burdened them. The Russians bought up everything, paying in moonshine vodka manufactured from potatoes and other inferior ingredients. The moonshine liquor was in great demand though it was laced with amounts of fuel.

The uniforms were obviously useless to the Russians as long as they retained their original colour. But a shirt or pair of trousers that was dyed could be valuable. A small packet of dye worth 30 pfennigs in Lvov could bring up to 10 marks in the Ukraine. Even after I had paid a considerable commission to the salesmen, I still amassed a large sum.

I stowed the notes in suitcase and knapsack because there was no other place for them. Dniepropetrovsk had no banks, and even if there were a bank it would be out of bounds for me. There were no shops, either. Only by a lucky chance could one get hold of a Russian who had a few "piglets" (the common term for 5-ruble gold coins from the times of the Tsars) and was ready to sell them. I couldn't spend much money on food, either; for there were no luxuries to be found anywhere. Our everyday food was potato soup; occasionally, if the landlady was especially lucky, we had an emaciated chicken. By the way, I cannot resist the urge to note that now that I had plenty of food to eat, I found it difficult to reach my apartment at lunch hour because each acquaintance had become a "friend" and would invite me *ad nauseam* to stay for a meal. Cynicism was the inevitable outcome.

At the time I was an inveterate smoker, to the tune of about thirty cigarettes a day. This meant that I had to draw *Verpflegung* for at least five people in order to obtain my normal daily number of cigarettes. Today I think I must have been crazy to demand an increase in my official ration of six cigarettes a day, on the strength of my working in the tense war zone, instead of forging an additional travel warrant. Evidently craziness of that sort pays off in wartime. I myself could hardly believe it when the noncom behind the desk in the City Governor's Office perused the documents testifying to my serving as a master builder detailed to the construction of fortifications (forgeries all, from A to Z), and approved an increased ration of 15 cigarettes for the duration of my stay in Dniepropetrovsk. I didn't care so much about the cigarettes themselves – perhaps my real purpose was to challenge fate, to prove to myself again that I was superior to the dumb Fritzes. I was "bearding the lion in its den" – and I succeeded.

I learned through the grapevine that, in the light of my popularity, Marjan and Jurek, my original guides to the Ukraine, were eager to contact me. I was not so eager for a meeting because the memories of our parting were not good ones. But in our "gangsterish" milieu an encounter was unavoidable. Marjan was superfriendly, in contrast to his disagreeable arrogance on our voyage from Lvov.

The conversation soon turned to the subject of our prospects for the future.

Marjan claimed that while in Lvov he had met Meisner. Meisner had told him that he had been in Romania but had returned because there one had to pay for everything and the cost of living was terribly high. We talked about the possibility of fleeing to Turkey. We would have to go to the port city of Odessa on the Black Sea; there was a chance we could purchase a boat there or find some other means of transportation.

I stated that first of all I had to visit Lvov once more and take on another convoy. Marjan and Jurek had similar projects. We arranged to meet again after the trip to Lvov so as to flesh out our plans.

In the meantime, my roommate, Michael, decided that he, too, would go to Lvov to fetch his wife and his sister-in-law. He turned to me for assistance in the forging of documents. Naturally I provided him with all he needed and bade him good luck when he departed.

The Jewish colony in Dniepropetrovsk was growing day by day, and I was afraid that something would have to give before long. It was a large city, true enough, but in the circumstances in which we were forced to operate each of us activists had to be a first-class "cowboy". We were not very numerous – perhaps ten, or fifteen – the rest were people who were, so to speak, riding on our backs. In the meantime, however, I didn't like to worry too much about our situation. We lived from day to day, but nevertheless we lived and wanted to go on living.

Our days were passed in card games and drinking parties. Sometimes our partners in these pastimes were Germans – civilian workers employed by the military. Bombing raids were a nightly feature. Our gang did not pay them much attention, but the Germans had a panicky fear of bombs and raids; the first wail on the siren would send them headlong to the nearest cellar or makeshift shelter. They would not stay above ground for anything. The drinking would resume after the all-clear and continue till late at night.

A Jew who came into town from Kiev told us that a band or two, similar to ours, were operating there. Everyone was looking for a way out of the Nazi stranglehold. Various trips undertaken for reconnaissance did not, however yield any results – other than the pleasure of going on a trip.

For instance, somebody told us that the Red Cross infirmary at a certain railway station issued a very tasty fruit soup instead of the usual mushroom – and barley soup. The station was quite close – a matter of one or two hundred kilometres – it was worth visiting. Urged by a lunatic, daredevil whim, I went there, accompanied by two others. The fruit soup was truly first-class. The trip was worthwhile! The Red Cross nurses were in a very flirtatious mood and made bold advances to us.

As the only man over thirty in our "gang" which comprised mostly youngsters of twenty or so – I understood thoroughly the specifics of our situation. A side "adventure" of that kind could end in a disaster. None of us could allow himself to have sexual relations which would, so to speak, bare the truth about him. If was only with great difficulty that I managed to tame the wolf-like appetites of my mates – for I have to admit that the nurses were much more appetizing than even their excellent fruit soup! We returned to Dniepropetrovsk the following day, and lapped up the admiration of the members of our circle.

Still, the trip was just a diversionary thrust from the point of view of a grand strategy. It was necessary to devote serious thought to the future. I had to go to Lvov again and fetch eight people in fulfilment of promises I had made to them or their relatives on my first trip there.

The preparation of forged documents had already become a practised routine. My uniform looked even more convincing for I had corrected various defects and omissions. I sold off my entire stock of dyes and acquired a small fortune in rubles. Now I faced the problem of how to exchange my cash for the marks which were the legal tender in Lvov. Misku, among whose many contacts were some individuals with unusual qualifications, found a German civilian who agreed to exchange rubles for marks in return for a fat commission.

This time Victor would go to Lvov with me.

17 · Back to Lvov – and Warsaw

The journey to Lvov went off almost without a hitch, apart from the fact that at the Znamienka station the train was surrounded by a cordon of military police who were checking documents. Several soldiers with questionable papers were taken off the train. Perhaps they were deserters. We were not questioned – our documents were perfectly in order, weren't they?

Lvov again. The ghetto was in the last stage of liquidation. I contacted my "passengers". One of them urged me to include his brother, who was living in Warsaw, in our convoy. He was very stubborn and I understood his concern very well. Although an extra trip was not to my liking at all, I agreed.

Lodging with the Soltisses had became a problem because envious neighbours had begun prying into the affairs of the prospering family. I arranged through them the purchase of another shipment of dyes, as insurance for whatever might occur but I sensed that my presence in the apartment was a burden, a situation that I did not like at all.

The next day, when I told Karol that I wished to change my accommodation, he offered to put me in contact with a friend of his who possessed an absolutely secure "den". I also needed to make some "investments" namely, to exchange my marks for items of value even outside the borders of German-occupied territory. I exchanged all my marks for gold and two watches. The "source" was naturally contacted through Karol.

In the evening Karol led me to a dive in the Kleparow suburb and introduced me to an acquaintance of his, who went by the name of Stefan. His expression turned sour when he saw a guy in a German uniform, but after Karol took him aside for a short whispered conversation Stefan sent me a more welcoming look.

We talked briefly, then Stefan sent Karol away and invited me to accompany him to the "den". We ambled down a few lanes, jumped a fence, crossed two courtyards and entered a building by way of a hole in the wall. When the flame of a candle illuminated the interior, I felt extremely uneasy. It was a cellar whose walls dripped with moisture. The furniture consisted of two makeshift plank beds and a wardrobe which lacked a leg. But the source for my shock was something entirely different. The walls of the cellar were covered with Torah scrolls whose parchment served as wallpaper.

I could not let slip the slightest sign that I recognized the origin of the wallpaper. I probably had been described by Karol as a German or a *Volksdeutsche*, and as such I should be ignorant of such things. Whatever Karol had told Stefan, he had certainly not betrayed the fact that I was a Jew.

My host took out a flask of vodka and I supplied an assortment of edible goodies from my knapsack, although in my mood I had not the slightest desire to eat or drink. I gave thanks to the Lord when the dawn came at last, and the infernal sleepless night was over, I could throw off the damp blankets. I wanted to forget about my host who had revealed his despicable character through the manner in which he had desecrated our holy religious scrolls, thank him for an "excellent night's sleep", and leave as fast as I could.

I arranged with Victor that I would return within three days. In the meantime he would prepare everything for our departure. I took a military transport train to Warsaw. It was much less comfortable that an ordinary passenger train but I did not want to risk an encounter with pre-war acquaintances or with police agents at the station who might remember my face. The soldiers wondered aloud why I was going to Warsaw, where "*Kämpfe mit Partisanen*" were taking place at that very moment. I invented a plausible-sounding story about a shipment of building material for the construction of fortifications in the front zone. The journey to Warsaw lasted the entire night. The fellows around me cut short the usual conversations and fell asleep in the cramped space. I reached Warsaw in the late morning without any advertures on the way.

The "'battles with the partisans" the soldiers had mentioned referred to the uprising of the Warsaw Ghetto. The battle was in full swing. The ghetto was in flames. The unmistakable stench of burning blanketed the entire city. The mood on the streets was one of dejection. People went about with bowed heads.

I tried to find my " 'passenger" as quickly as possible and leave the inferno. Finally I managed to contact him. He wanted to postpone his departure till the next day in order to settle urgent personal matters. I did not agree to this and announced my resolute intention to leave at 9 p.m. that night at the latest, without him if necessary. He had to give in, naturally. We arranged a meeting for 8 p.m. near one of the restaurants on Nowy Swiat.

I took a tram to see what remained of my former apartment on Poznańska street. Through the tram windows I observed many houses in ruins. There was apparently no chance of meeting a former acquaintance. The conversations in the tram were rather restrained. Still, one overheard sentence stuck in my memory: "It's a pity our cattle don't eat meat, otherwise we could furnish them with very cheap feed". The smell of fire and of scorched flesh, the remnants of the ghetto rebels, hung over the city in a grim cloud – and those characters had time for macabre wisecracks. My last hour in Warsaw stretched out endlessly.

Finally I met my passenger and we set out. Again I picked a military train as our means of transport. I explained at the railway station that I was the foreman of a construction crew going to the front zone with a worker, to deal with the building of fortifications. As we were travelling so far, all the way to Dniepropetrovsk, we were assigned a very comfortable carriage on the train and sent off with a "bon voyage".

We reached Lvov the next day without a hindrance. Although my passenger had been given papers of a *Frontarbeiter* (a worker in the front zone), he followed me everywhere like a shadow. I had difficulty in contacting Victor, for I had arrived a day early. I delivered my passenger to his brother and told them we were going to the front the next day. We would have a difficult trip, because Victor intended to take his mother along.

I arranged to purchase the last of my provisions through the Soltisses, because I had decided that this would be my last trip to Lvov. I had the irrational feeling that I should not press my luck. Victor told me that Michael had left for Dniepro the previous day with his wife, her sister, and two other passengers. These journeys were taking on too much of a mass character.

Michael had surely shared his plans with his friends and acquaintances, just I had done. I wasn't too thrilled by the turn things were taking because – as I had repeatedly stated – not everybody had the needed courage and audacity and most important, the character of a fighter and fluency in German to make a go of it. I was afraid of betrayal because of any one of many unknown and uncontrollable factors. Were the German authorities to institute tighter surveillance, our chivalrous escapades would come to on end.

The greatest advantage of our masquerading in German uniforms lay in the assumption that an ordinary policeman would not dare to investigate soldiers, while an MP, even if he checked our documents, would regard us as *civilbande*. But that advantage would evaporate if ever one of us betrayed uncertainty or fear when the circumstances required reckless confidence. During my months in uniform it happened only twice that a gendarme demanded to see my papers. The careless confidence which I displayed when I drew them from my pocket convinced him that he had guessed wrong and was unnecessarily troubling both himself and me. My documents were not even cursorily examined. But now I felt that I should put an end to the masquerade – it was becoming too much of a good thing.

On the following day I collected the dyes from the Soltiss family and took my leave. In the evening we held a rendezvous on St. Martin street near the railway station, the same place we had used on our last trip. Our group was rather unwieldy – Victor and I were taking 14 people in all, including three women – but we were processed through the station without a hitch. We took our seats in two carriages, I reassured our people; after crossing the frontier into the Ukraine we would have more room on the train and would be able to stick together.

A gendarme accosted me at the frontier. "Was hast Du hier in diesen Rucksack?" I answered jocularly that I was carrying textile dyes. He advised me smilingly not to try out my wisecracks on him, and moved on. I should add that even a genuine German soldier caught smuggling dyes of that kind was condemned on the spot to service at the front in a penal unit, where death was sure to come within a short time.

We stopped off for a day in Kasatin so that I could acquaint myself with a "den" rumoured to be part of Meisner's "legacy". The "den" was perfect. It was a cottage with a garden standing by itself in a large orchard. It was the property of a family of deaf-mutes; only the grandmother could speak. The rest of them communicated in sign language. They put a spacious room with five beds at our disposal after we had paid them handsomely, chiefly in foodstuffs.

The filth there was incredible. For the first time in my life I saw white lice crawling on the bedclothes. The pots and pans were caked with a layer of embedded grease half a centimetre thick. But all this was unimportant compared to the potential value of an excellent hiding place. I slept very well on the floor and we continued to Dniepro in the morning.

In Dniepropetrovsk we delivered our passengers to their friends, relations or to makeshift hiding places. More permanent arrangements would be made the following day. As for myself, I planned to have a short period of rest and then redouble my efforts to find a breach in the Nazi cordon surrounding me.

Michael told me that, unfortunately, his passengers had been discovered. He had taken them to the main station, told them where to board the train, and taken his leave. He had observed from a distance that some police agents accosted them. His people, so he told me, had managed to shake them off and run away. He himself had boarded the train to Dniepro with his wife and her sister as if nothing had happened.

Michael's tale served to confirm my fears. The cloth was wearing thin and beginning to tear! Marjan and Jurek were of the same opinion. I learned that they had been looking for me during my absence and urgently wished to meet with me as soon as possible.

The following days were spent in various business matters, such as the sale of the dyes through my landlady, and their exchange for rubles. Vladek and I settled our accounts. He said that his family had a prior claim on his finances. Anyway, continuation of our partnership would have meant unloading his family responsibilities on my shoulders. But we would keep in touch and inform each other of anything which could affect our plans for the future.

18 · My Cover is Blown

I met with Marjan and Jurek a number of times. We discussed various possibilities of breaking out of the stranglehold of German rule. Our schemes were imaginative and compared favourably with the brainchildren of a writer of adventure stories. Unfortunately, most of them were quite unrealistic. In the end we agreed on a number of further reconnaissance trips. We would try out a few new ideas. If any plan seemed practical, we would act upon it, and take with us our relations, friends and colleagues. We agreed to pool our resources and become partners. They had a treasury of stamps and forms for a variety of documents. I had a notebook filled with copies of stamps and a large number of forms, too. Moreover, Marjan knew exactly two words of German and Jurek, who spoke some German, had a terrible Jewish accent, I would be contributing my first-class knowledge of German to our enterprise.

We settled on our initial step: I would visit the City Governor's office (mainly in order to obtain a stamp of theirs) and ask for a furlough pass to Proskurov. We decided that our destination would be Zhemerinka, a town on the border with Romania, because according to various reports it was the best jumping-of place for leaving the Ukraine. However, since it was a border town, it could not serve as our declared objective. This we had to have a travel warrant for a different destination, and when we arrived at Zhemerinka we would say that we were just passing through.

I went to the Governor's Office. After I had spun them a likely tale and displayed the recommendation for a furlough from my imaginary firm, I received a permit for me "*und zwei Mann*" to go by train to Proskurov and back between 30 May and 20 July 1943. The stamp was a lulu.

The three of us set off for Zhemerinka, a small Romanian town in the district of Transnistria. It was then governed jointly by the Romanians and the German military authorities. Because of its location on the border everybody, even German soldiers, were obliged to obey the curfew hour, 8 p.m.

We, former ghetto dwellers, had forgotten that anything could be purchased in normal shops. The shops and restaurants of Zhemerinka, accessible to any paying customer, seemed to us the gateway to paradise. We took advantage of the opportunity, entered the first restaurant we saw, and gorged ourselves on a pound of ham per person washed down, naturally, with plenty of vodka.

Jurek and I managed to keep our heads following the feast, but Marjan lost his wits completely. He began tossing the oranges he had bought on to the sloping roof of a cabin. When the oranges rolled down the slope he called to the people who had gathered that these were gift oranges from heaven – they were free to join us and catch them. We dragged him from there with great difficulty, but not very far, he halted suddenly in front of a horse and began an involved ritual of greetings because (he claimed) it was an old friend of his who hailed from Lvov. We pulled him away by main force because we wanted to avoid any intervention by the gendarmes.

As chance would have it, Marjan's dumb, irresponsible stunt had a positive side to it, too. One of the local citizens attached himself to us and began to "court" us, with the clear intention of establishing contact. He was a tall fellow, with brown hair and a full moustache. It turned out that he was a Pole (possibliy even a Polish Jew) who had heard Marjan speaking Polish loudly and had determined to approach us and talk. He owned a sizeable one-family house, where he let rooms to passing strangers. I gathered that he was chiefly engaged in black market activities.

Naturally, I was full of suspicions but in the circumstances felt that I had to go along with this fellow's overtures. He said that his name was Laskowski, that he was originally from Poland, but after marrying a Romanian girl had settled in Zhemerinka. He told us he was ready to help us however he could.

At first I told him an ingenious fairy tale about us but later, when I saw I could trust him a little, I admitted that we were political refugees from Poland. We were looking, I said, for a way to escape from the German-dominated areas and to join our army which was fighting with the Western Allies.

Laskowski gave us some advice – whether it was good or not, we did not know. In any event, he suggested that we should try to break out through the town of Nicolaiev on the shore of the Dniester River. The best route would be through Odessa, but it was very difficult. A special permit to cross the border into Romania was needed. In Laskowski's opinion, it was nearly unobtainable. He then invited us to an early supper at an inn, and soon afterwards we had to part as the curfew hour was approaching. I told him we were going to Tarnopol since I did not want to leave too specific an address.

We walked to the station. The train to Nicolaiev was due in two or three hours ... we filed the information for possible use in the future. We had decided to go back to Kasatin. En route to the station we purchased toilet soap – it was of poor quality but in Russia it was considered a real find.

In Kasatin we received bad news from Dniepropetrovsk from a fellow who had just come from there to try to stop a convoy on the way from Lvov.

Dniepro was now out as a destination, as a large-scale round-up of Jews had taken place there. Nobody knew, of course, what was the cause of the disaster – nobody could ever know for sure. What I had feared for some time had now come to pass. The unknown beast crouched in the corner had pounced.

According to one version, a Russian girlfriend of one of our boys learned that he was married and wanted to fetch his wife from Poland. She went to the Gestapo and turned him in together with his friends. Another version blamed two Gentiles from Poland, Szyjka (who had tried to blackmail me) and Palinski, who felt envious of our exploits. They too tried to smuggle people out of Lvov and were discovered because of some foolish oversight. To save their skin they spilled the beans and added plenty on their own initiative.

The Germans were conducting daily raids in the various neighbourhoods of the city. The fellow said that many people had fallen into the hands of the Germans. Once they were in the hands of the Gestapo thugs, they had to say something for nobody could long resist the bestial beatings and the tortures. So they said that their papers were supplied by Adam Rolski (my alias), that he had smuggled them and probably the majority of the others across the border to Dniepropetrovsk, and so on and so forth.

Now the Germans were looking for Rolski – me – and making inquiries about him.

The chickens had come home to roost; that was the deferred payment for my exaggerated renown. A large number of our people in Dniepro knew that I was out of the city – it was easiest, and relatively safe, to make a scapegoat of an absent person. None the less I made light of the whole business. I lived in the shadow of death in any case, and the additional risk was not such a heavy burden relative to the ones that I already bore. You cannot die twice.

I later learned from people who had eluded the Gestapo that the Germans thought I was the ringleader of an espionage organization which had at its disposal a printing press, dies of stamps, etc ... That was their explanation for the extent of our activities; they could not imagine that a Jewboy from the ghetto was, on his own, able to acquire blank forms, manufacture the appropriate stamps, and supply military documents which were flawless copies of those used in accordance with army regulations. They could not permit themselves to recognize that an anonymous Jew, an *Untermensch*, could by himself fool the mighty *Herrenvolk*. No, that was an impossibility. Yet that was the truth!

Before leaving Dniepro I had put aside a supply of blank forms for travel warrants, so we didn't worry about our friends. After a "council of war" we decided that Marjan and Jurek would go to Dniepropetrovsk while I would remain for the time being in Kasatin – it was too risky to show my face in

Dniepro. They would fetch their families and those of our friends who were free to leave. Immediately after their return to Kasatin the three of us would go to Nicolaiev. The house of the deaf-mutes in Kasatin was the best hide-out known to us, so we would use it as our staging point. Marjan and Jurek departed, and I began a period of waiting.

I knew that I had to spend five or six days in Kasatin so I decided to register at the town commandant's office. I presented myself to the officer-of-the-day, Oberleutnant Egloff. I told him I was awaiting my boss, from Dniepropetrovsk, an engineer, who was due in a few days. Obviously I needed some rations as well as pocket money to be deducted from my future salary. Egloff shrank from the notion of paying out cash, but when I did not press my claims for pay, he gave me a document which entitled me to draw special travel rations for three people, for a four-day period. The orderly at the warehouse told me with a laugh that I needed a small cart for the provisions. I took him at his word, hired a cart (the driver was promised two loaves of bread), and was issued a sizeable load of provisions. Together with the rations I had drawn as usual at the railway station, they constituted a precious supply of foodstuffs. The quantity of bread was a problem – in those days I did not touch bread because I wanted to leave room in my stomach for more tasty food.

While I was talking to the owner of the cart, a young local woman appeared and helped me to explain to him what it was I required. She seemed one of "ours". I could not ask her outright, of course, or even mention the subject, so I arranged a meeting with her that afternoon, purportedly to inquire about the conditions in the locality where I was planning to stay for a number of days.

When we met, she told me that her employer was a German, but that her insides churned at the thought of having to work for him in order to save her life. She inquired several times what I was going to do with the quantity of bread in my possession, until I asked her outright whether she would like a loaf or two. She did not answer, and the subject remained open. On the spur of the moment I told her that I did not trust her and suspected that she was probably in touch with illegal elements. Evidently I didn't look too "kosher", to her, either, because she blurted out that the Russians in Kasatin were boycotting her for they thought she was collaborating with the German in whose household she was working. She would pay a price for the bread, whatever I demanded. She asked me to leave the sack with the bread in a yard. Either she or her messenger would fetch it at night. In the end she confessed that she was a Jewess and that the bread was destined for the partisan fighters.

I didn't take a pfennig from her, naturally. I left the sack in the yard – it vanished in the course of the night. We met a few more times. I gave her a few blank forms for *Frontarbeiters* so that her needy friends could fill them in and use them to draw rations from the Germans. I then disappeared from her sight.

I lived almost like a king. I idled the whole day long, and had plenty to eat. In the morning I guzzled a quart of whipped cream with a liberal sprinkling of sugar and did not even touch bread, for the reason I have mentioned. Nevertheless, the waiting was gnawing at my nerve ends and I could not really enjoy the pleasures of my day-to-day existence.

In the meanwhile a group of Jews from Lvov arrived in town. My neighbour and friend Dr I. Wittlin was among them. They could not continue their journey because of the disaster in Dniepro. Ater they had stayed in Kasatin for two days, I succeeded in persuading their guide to move on to Kiev, where calm reigned at the moment. I did not want to endanger the hide-out of the deaf-mute family.

I was left alone with my thoughts, waiting without the end in sight. The days stretched out, eleven days, until the second half of June. Then Marjan, Jurek, Roma, Mure and two other men arrived from Dniepro. They had emptied everything out of my apartment there and informed me that the Germans were undertaking an intensive search for "Adam Rolski".

The following day Casick Reifer, son of a well-known Lvov merchant, arrived with two teenage girls in tow. They had been in the care of Marjan in Dniepro and were told to come to Kasatin. Unfortunately there was an error in their travel warrant and they had left the train at the wrong station. They didn't know what to do and almost turned to the Gestapo in their despair. Luckily Casick had noticed them, added the formula "*und zwei Mann*" to his warrant, and brought them along. They were Anna and Hela – who is now my wife. We talked things over and shared the feeling that the rug was being pulled slowly but surely from under our feet.

I argued for a speedy departure but Marjan was waiting for news from his mother, so we had to indulge him. It was spring, the weather was beautiful, a flowering orchard, our youth and spirits bloomed – and Hela. The romantic intermezzo lasted three days. Memorable hours!

When Marjan received the information that all was well with his mother, he, Jurek, Roma, Hela, and I decided to go to Zhemerinka and perhaps further on. The others remained in Kasatin. I repeatedly drummed into their heads the strict prohibition: not to show their faces on the street; this was a source of danger! Finally I was persuaded that they would heed my warnings, and we left.

19 · Odessa

We arrived in Zhemerinka in the midday hours. First of all we took our ladies to lunch at the restaurant where we had eaten on our previous visit. During the meal I struck up a conversation with the proprietor and the waiter, the better to inform myself about the local conditions. We were all Germans, of course, and spoke German only. The proprietor offered to let us rooms if we meant to stay a number of days. This meant that others, too, used to pass through and remain in town for a short time.

In the afternoon we scouted the small town. We conferred and decided to stay together one more day. Then we, the men, would leave for Nicolaiev, a small-sized port town on the Black Sea, about 700 kilometres distant from Zhemerinka. Roma and Hela would stay and wait for us. The women would register with the Romanian police according to regulations. We reckoned our trip to Nicolaiev and back would take about six days. We rented two rooms for a week, with an option for another week.

The following day we accompanied Hela and Roma to the police station. I ordered the policeman at the desk to keep an eye on our ladies and help them with anything they needed. I spoke German, naturally; the policeman, I saw, did not understand a word, but my commanding tone was more persuasive than mere words. He stammered out just one reservation: they should present themselves at the police every two or three days.

We had a difficult trip because on the way to Nicolaiev and had to switch trains a number of times. We had plenty of opportunity to test the credibility of our new identities. Here I should explain that while I was staying by myself in Kasatin I had thoroughly examined our new circumstances and had come to the conclusion we should change our status. Until then we had always pretended to be *Frontarbeiter* – Polish workers hired by German enterprises for the purpose of constructing fortifications in the battle zone. If someone mistook us for German soldiers because we wore discarded Wehrmacht uniforms – so much the better. It seemed to me that in our present circumstances we would do better to present ourselves as *Volksdeutsche*, who spoke German only. As for our credentials, it would be best to add to them the all-purpose formulation, *Vermachtgefolge*. Nobody (including me!) knew what was meant by the word. The German sphere of occupation was awash with various units, which were paramilitary, pseudomilitary, and auxiliary to the armed forces, The nonsense word *Vermacht* smacked irresistibly of the Wehrmacht while *gefolge* (roughly "following") could be construed as meaning a unit attached to the regular army. Later, I added the legend *mit Uniform* which legitimized our use of Wehrmacht uniforms. Marjan and Jurek were very pleased with my idea. Marjan, who knew almost no German, had a tendency to poke fun at the language we were using. He claimed that German was not a language at all but a chaotic babble, and tried to persuade us that he was right by means of a lunatic experiment. At one of the stations our train stood alongside one pointed in the opposite direction. Marjan stationed himself at the window and started to babble persuasively at a soldier in the train opposite him: le blah, blah, bluh, bam ... and so on. He concluded with an emphatic. "Och! Du Buschneger!" (Ah, you're a Negro from the bush"). The soldier couldn't understand what Marjan was babbling, of course. He seemed to think that it was an exotic local dialect of German, and tried to respond. We were sitting out of his sight in the compartment and roared with laughter, I wept real tears of merriment. Marjan pretended that he was all ears, nodded his head and grimaced. Luckily; our train started to move. Marjan had time to shout *"Siewas"*! ("Howdy" – one of the few German words he could speak) at his partner in dialogue, turned to us and said: "Well, wasn't I right?"

After two days of very slow progress we reached Nicolaiev. Here I stumbled for the first time. The experience was like being drenched by a bucketful of icy water.

We drifted around the town to get some information learned nothing useful. Then I entered the gendarmerie station to register. The senior noncom who received me looked at our travel warrant as if examining an exotic animal and inquired: "Who made this out?"

I realized that something was out of order so I responded cheekily: "God knows, it wasn't me, for sure": He retreated immediately, said he didn't hold me personally responsible, but I should know that a civilian firm, even if it was working for the Wehrmacht, had no right to issue travel warrants, that my boss had clearly transgressed army regulations. The noncom stressed the fact that he had nothing against me personally, and he even gave me an official chit that empowered me to spend the night at a *Soldatenheim*. Still, when I came back the following day to register at the office, he said, his superior would take the matter up.

Bad luck! I had encountered a veteran, a prewar noncom of the regular army, who knew all the military regulations by heart. As may be imagined, I wished only to find myself on the other side of the door.

The success of our bluff depended overwhelmingly on the obedience of each and every German to the existing rules and regulations. The Germans had a blind respect for any official document, anything written in official language, stamped and signed. It seemed that they were incapable of independent thought, or that they preferred to be guided by written instructions so as to avoid any inner conflict about what to do.

The Soviet writer llya Ehrenburg remarks in *Julio Jurenito* that it is very difficult to carry out a revolution in Germany; if the demonstrators or the rebels had to cross a park on their way to their objective they would run only along the public paths because of the signs "keep off the grass". This characteristic of the Germans – perhaps the outcome of education since early childhood – undoubtedly was the chief reason for our long reign of insolent piracy.

Obviously we had no intention of going to the *Soldatenheim*. The atmosphere of Nicolaiev had become too oppressive. We hurried to the railway station. A goods train was about the depart to the north. In the station toilet I rapidly filled out a new travel warrant, and we boarded the train. After a hundred kilometres or so we switched trains at a station whose name had escaped my memory. A few stations further on we changed the travel warrant and switched trains again. We repeated the procedure several times. After two days devoted to confusing any would-be pursuer, we arrived in Uman, I think and spent the night at a *Soldatenheim*.

The journey back to Zhemerinka was long but time did not drag for we were immersed in preparing detailed plans for the trip to Odessa. It was now our only chance of breaking out.

Marjan, who usually proposed various harebrained schemes, came up for once with a good idea. We should make the acquaintance of somebody stationed at the German gendarmerie post. I was nominated for the mission on the strength of my proficiency in German. Yes, but how should we prepare the ground so that the German would be well-disposed to me from the start?

Marjan proposed that he and Jurek would register at the post after the arrival of the morning train from Dniepropetrovsk, and announce to the noncom on duty that *Bauleiter* (construction foreman) Adam Rolski was due to arrive from Kiev the same day. They were holding an important letter with urgent instructions for him, they would tell the duty noncom, and should be contacted as soon as Rolski registered at the gendarmerie post. They would be waiting in the restaurant near the railway station. Marjan judged that after an introduction of this kind, I would no longer appear as just another soldier but as a person with a familiar name. That should enable me to befriend the hypothetical noncom. I could stand him to a beer, chat him up – who knows.

Jurek and I liked the idea, especially because we did not have a better one. We agreed to implement the plan, and thought it out in detail. The trip to Zhemerinka ended without any further adventures. Apparently the too-smart noncom in Nicolaiev had forgotten about me, for nobody displayed any interest in us.

Our ladies were quite apprehensive by the time we arrived, we were two days late. We announced that we were going to Odessa within two days. They told us that they had obediently registered twice with the Romanian police, as agreed. On one occasion a Jew was brought from a nearby camp, to serve as a translator. When Hela had held out her hand at the end of the meeting, he was afraid to clasp the hand of a German woman. Hela had calmed his misgivings; the fact of his being Jew was immaterial. The poor man probably told the inmates of the camp on his return that there were still decent Germans in the world.

The following day we carried out our little scheme. Marjan and Jurek registered at the gendarmerie post. Then they returned to our room and we played cards till noon, when the train from Kiev was due. They seated themselves in the restaurant while I mixed on the platform with the crowd of soldiers getting off the train. Then I walked phlegmatically to register according to regulation.

I presented myself to the noncom on duty. He jumped up like a jack-in-the-box as soon as I had given my name.

"Ja, Kamerad. you have an urgent message. Drop everything. come back later. All the rest can wait".

He didn't want to listen to any explanations, urged me toward the door, and ordered me to collect the urgent letter immediately. He did not reply to my phlegmatic inquiries – first of all I was to collect the important instructions which had come from my headquarters. I managed to set up a meeting in the afternoon. He assured me again that he would arrange for all my needs when I returned, but now I'd better hurry.

Marjan's idea seemed to be bearing fruit. In the afternoon I visited my noncom again and told him I had received a new travel warrant – this time to Odessa. I invited him to have a beer with me. He was not at all surprised about my going to Odessa, and I took this to be a favourable portent. During our friendly chat over a couple of beers I confided in him. I really had no desire to go on a long inconvenient trip to Odessa, but orders were orders, so there was nothing to be done. He expressed sympathy for the onerous task ahead of me, and promised to issue a reservation for a special railway car "*nur für Deutsche*" (for Germans only), which also entitled me to free entrance to the restaurant car. Unfortunately the train was due to depart very early in the morning; at 5 a.m. Secretly I was delighted; I was in a greater hurry to leave then he imagined! I thanked him, and we returned to the office. He wrote out the official directives himself and said goodbye with great warmth.

We were at the station early next morning. My noncom proved to be as good as his word: he had left instructions with the guard detachment at the station to take me and my people under their wing. This enabled us to omit the obligatory muster on the platform, where all the passengers for Odessa were required to give a satisfactory account about their mission in that city.

We were directed to the special car reserved for Germans. Roma and Hela travelled on a separate travel warrant – Roma as a Red Cross nurse and Hela as a secretary. As soon as the train left the station, I invited Hela to breakfast in the restaurant car. At this point the reader should take note of a number of important facts. It was a time of war, with its attendant myriad restrictions. Just a few months earlier we had been living in the ghetto. Hela was so young that she had not yet had the opportunity to experience the luxury of restaurant cars on passenger trains. We were still overwhelmed by the mood engendered by our short romantic interlude in Kasatin. The headlong leap from the abyss of the ghetto to the luxurious restaurant reserved for German officers alone acted like heady wine. It should be added that the assortment of dishes was exceptionally rich, the quality first class, the brandy was French cognac, and the atmosphere elegant. The tables were covered with snowy linen and the tableware was crystal and silver.

We talked in German, of course, engrossed in each other, as God intended all young couples in love to be. We paid no attention to anyone else; but a young and pretty woman was quite a rare passenger during wartime, especially so close to the fighting area.

Soon a young officer asked for permission to join our table. Another joined us almost immediately. Weren't we all comrades in the struggle against the enemies of the Third Reich? One glass of cognac followed another. Within the hour, half the people in the restaurant were gathered around our table. Our mood, mellowed by alcohol, was excellent. The gay party continued past the noonday meal. We succeeded with difficulty in extricating ourselves so we could take a rest. The journey lasted, if I am not mistaken, two days, so the "party" in the restaurant car was repeated the following day. We were in a gay mood and the trip passed quickly. Hela and I were inundated with invitations to further meetings in Odessa, which we had no intention of honouring.

After our arrival in Odessa we paid a visit to the German army headquarters, according to the rules of the game we played. The army clerk in charge of living quarters directed us to the local *Soldatenheim*. The two rooms assigned us were very nice and well furnished. The house, surely confiscated from its previous residents, had large, high-ceilinged, old-fashioned rooms. The room where we now lodged even boasted a piano.

We went out in the morning, to survey the town. Odessa was a handsome city, with broad and well-lit streets. The greenery of parks and public gardens struck the eye. The destruction of war was not too apparent, but there were almost no stores apart from a few inns and restaurants.

For appearances sake I visited the appropriate office to obtain a chit for *Verpflegung*. I also inquired where the offices dealing with appropriations of construction materials were situated. Then I visited two of these offices, supposedly in a search of an engineer named Krause from the firm Wilhelm Lenz Strassenbau. I stressed the final "'e"' in the name of the fictitious Krause, so as to engrave my (rather ridiculous) search in the memory of those concerned.

During our wanderings we encountered one of "ours" (my name for the gangs similar to our ring in Dniepro), a fellow named Janek Fuchs, familiar to Marjan from Lvov. I took a liking to this Fuchs almost immediately. He was only 19 or 20 years old, proudly wore a sem-iuniform, sported riding breeches, and was shod in gleaming tall boots. He had come to Odessa with a friend, on a scouting expedition from Kiev.

A large group of "ours" lived in Kiev together with numerous "'passengers" smuggled from Poland. They were all looking for a way out, at least to Bucharest. In Bucharest, the capital of Romania, so people said, Jews were not persecuted as terribly as in German-held territory. A Jew could survive there. True, Germans also lived there, but only as guests of their allies the Romanians. The Jews in Kiev, said Fuchs, had learned through various unconventional channels of information that the conditions in Bucharest were not so bad.

He, for his part, knew for a certainty that to get to Romania one had to display a special *Ausweis* (*Sonderausweis*) and a permit to cross the frontier. For soldiers this permit was waived – a military railway pass would suffice. He claimed, with typical youthful irresponsibility, that the Germans were not really well versed in the documents required. Any document which bore a nice clear stamp of an army field unit would do. Perhaps there was some validity for this view – even the systematic Germans must have been influenced by the chaos of war. Besides, the rules must have been relaxed to some extent, what with the deteriorating military situation after the defeat at Stalingrad and the demoralization incurred by the continuing German withdrawal.

Fuchs advised us to start looking for the appropriate forms, stamps etc. In the meantime, it being the end of June, we should sample the many pleasures of the beach. He also recommended a restaurant on one of the main streets. It was called "Deutsche Ecke" and served officers and men of the SS – the waitresses were *Volksdeutsche*. Lunch there would cost us just 2.20 marks, compared with about 30 marks in an ordinary restaurant. There was one rule: those entering the dining room were obliged to give the Nazi salute and the SS man senior in rank had to return the salute. This sounded very interesting, we had to try it out.

On parting, Fuchs went off in the direction of "Deutsche Ecke". He looked a perfect Gentile and every inch a fighter. If there were more like him among "ours", the break-out must succeed in the end. We continued to stroll about, hoping to meet somebody interesting. Perhaps a lucky coincidence would occur, perhaps we would catch a glimpse of the light at the end of the tunnel. We had lunch in an inn and returned to our *Soldatenheim*.

I decided to repeat the successful experiment we had carried out in Zhemerinka. Striking up an acquaintance with a noncom at the headquarters of the gendarmerie in Odessa would surely be very useful. The noncom on duty, named Karol, accepted with pleasure an invitation to have beer with me. We had a long conversation, but I could not learn anything of interest to "ours". Karol advised me to visit the cinema which was featuring a good movie. I collected the rest of our group and went to the cinema. The film was mediocre, the usual propaganda drivel.

The next day we took advantage of the fabulous weather and went to the beach – we hadn't anything better to do. During our walks, Jurek always carried our stamps, blanks and forms in a knapsack, but it would be stupid and risky to take them along to the seashore. We would always have to leave somebody on guard when we entered the water, a procedure which might give rise to suspicion. If left alone, the knapsack's contents could fall into the hands of some petty thief who might then lose his cool and deliver them into the hands of the German gendarmes.

I thought it best to hide our incriminating stuff somewhere in the room – but where? Somebody suggested the piano, but it seemed too prominent a piece of furniture to serve as a hiding place.

In the end I hit on the idea of putting the parcel containing the stuff in the ceiling light fixture which consisted of a platter of some transparent material hanging from three ropes fixed in the ceiling. It was unlikely anybody would look inside the platter, which was difficult to reach even with the help of a chair. It also seemed improbable that someone would turn on the lamp in broad daylight. My idea was happily accepted. Marjan climbed on my shoulder and placed our valuables in the platter of the ceiling fixture.

Being at the seashore was a wonderful experience. We enormously enjoyed the sun and the dip in the sea in our rented bathing suits, and then had lunch in town. For some reason I separated from my companions and returned to the *Soldatenheim* after paying a short visit to the *Quartieramt* – the army department which dealt with the assignment of lodgings to military personnel.

As I was leaving the *Quartieramt* I was accosted by a *Gefreiter* (a junior noncom) who seemed to be at a loose end. He struck up a conversation which mainly consisted of endless idle questions such as: Where are you from? Where will you be going back? What are you doing in Odessa? In the beginning I answered civilly enough but after a few questions, which I deemed enough to satisfy normal curiosity, I told him off. I liked my peace and quiet, I said with an edge to my voice. It wasn't his business to know who I was looking for and what I was doing. Then I muttered "Eil Hitla", and strode away. The *Gefreiter* seemed to retreat at my stringent tone, and hastily said goodbye.

My group was already in the *Soldatenheim* when I arrived. The landlady told us, while we were still in the corridor, that she had been visited by three gentlemen from the police who asked about us, searched our room and even looked inside the piano. They did not stay long. The first thing we did was to turn on the light in the room. The parcel in the lamp was untouched. We breathed more easily.

It is my rule not to wait for an attack. I prefer to assume the role of the attacker and take the bull by the horns. I decided on the spot to go to my noncom, Karol, and inquire about the search and the investigation. I realized perfectly well that escape was out of the question because I was in a blind alley. If the Germans had something on us and wished to arrest us, they might do it soon, but it was more probable that they would come at night, as was customary in totalitarian countries. It was better to beard the lion in his den – a course which might sow confusion in their ranks.

The three of us went to see Karol. The noncom said he knew nothing about the affair – it was certainly not initiated by him or his headquarters. When Karol directed his words at Marjan, who stood by my side, I always answered, naturally, for Marjan did not understand a word. Karol did not catch on. We said goodbye as if perfectly satisfied, though our hearts were in our throats.

When we were in the corridor, Karol suddenly ran out and drew me aside. He told me that to his thinking the investigation was probably conducted by the GFP ("*geheime Feldpolizei*" – the Intelligence Department of the Military police). The *Gefreiter* whom I had encountered, had later talked to Karol about me. He had said almost plaintively that I had brushed him off rudely. The GFP were looking for three soldiers who had deserted from their unit at the front line but it seemed we were all right because he, the *Gefreiter*, had heard by chance in the *Quartieramt* that someone from the front had inquired about an engineer by the name of Krause who was supposed to meet him in Odessa on army business.

Karol's parting warning sounded ominous: "That fellow is no *Gefreiter*. He is a GFP agent. The guy is dangerous. "A cold shiver passed through me. The Unknown may leap at you from ambush in a completely unexpected guise.

It was clear that we were in for a night of hell. Nothing was sure. If they wished to make an arrest they would surely come at night. But if the night passed quietly, it would be a sign that we had made it again. We took turns standing watch, four hours each. I had the watch between midnight and 4 a.m. We had decided to defend ourselves if the need arose – slavish surrender would mean certain death one way or another. Our only handgun was to be used by the man standing watch. I didn't shut my eyes throughout the night. When morning dawned, in spite of fatigue, I felt as if born anew.

We went to the beach again. We were having a great time, so we decided to continue with lunch at the "Deutsche Ecke". Fuchs was right. I performed my "Eil Hitla!" act and an SS officer hailed in return. That was true happiness! Real pleasure! The scoundrel would have had a heart attack for sure if he had known that his courteous bow had been aimed at a common Jew, who had lived in the ghetto just a few months previously. But it was inconceivable, of course, that such an *Untermensch* would have the audacity to enter a restaurant reserved for the Aryan elite. He didn't know that it was possible, but I did. It was a delight to be able to jeer inwardly at him and his *Herrenvolk* pretensions – it was worth everything.

We had a good lunch, paid 2.20 marks each, visited a pastry shop ten yards away and paid 5 marks for a cake. The disproportion in prices served to remind us of our *chutzpah* in taking advantage of the economic privileges accorded us on the strength of our forged credentials. That, too, inspired a pleasant feeling of achievement.

But that was just a small achievement. More to the point, in spite of thoroughly investigating various possibilities and endless conversations with various people, we had not achieved anything concrete. Janek Fuchs' information was proved correct but I still didn't know who issued the magic *Sonderausweis* and to whom – in a word, how to obtain such a document.

The days passed fruitlessly, apart from one minor incident. I continued to enter any office which displayed a sign showing it was connected with construction business, and inquire after my engineer, Krause. I always checked whether they had heard the name correctly: not Kraus, mind you, but Krause. I also inquired about the possibility of reaching Bucharest, without result. One day, as I walked along, sunk in thought, I suddenly realized that I had passed a *Feldwebel* (staff sergent) without saluting him. True enough, a moment later I heard a loud "Halt!" I stood at attention and suffered through a hectoring in the best barracks tradition. How dare I omit the salute; this wasn't the front zone, and so on, I reacted to each admonition with a rousing "Ja, Herr Feldwebel", which was followed by another piece of his mind, and then again "Ja, Herr Feldwebel", and all the while I laughed inwardly. Here I was, cheating and deluding him and his like, and he, instead of placing me under arrest or shooting me on the spot, was putting me on the carpet for omitting a salute. A real idiot! After returning to the *Soldatenheim* I recounted the incident in detail, and we all enjoyed a hearty laugh.

Almost a week had passed, and the period allotted to our furlough was coming to an end. Though we were having a great time, we could not remain in Odessa. We decided to cut short our fruitless efforts and try our luck in Zhemerinka; if the need arose, we would even go to Lvov, where, we had various contacts which might prove useful. Karol said we should present ourselves at the *Quartieramt* and tell the officer there we were leaving, so he could cross us off his register.

The train for Kiev was due to depart at 10 a.m. Early in the morning, at 7 a.m., Jurek and I presented ourselves to the officer-of-the day at the *Quartieramt*. He questioned me in detail what our kind of work was, what I had done in Odessa, and the like. Finally, he stamped our collective travel warrant with the day's date. He noted something in his register, and I had my "Eil Hitla!" ready.

Then I had a lunatic idea. I didn't hesitate, begged his pardon, and inquired whether I might ask for a personal favour. He assented naturally. I told him that I had a girlfriend in Kiev who was pressing me to obtain silk stockings for her. I had looked for stockings in Odessa but had no luck. People had told me this article could only be obtained in Bucharest. How could I get there?

Jurek thought I had gone crazy. He pulled at my shirt in an effort to bring me back to earth. The officer heard me out patiently, stood up, suddenly approached me, patted my arm and said; "This is the first time that I've heard the truth in this room. You'll get a *Sonderausweis* from me." He pointed at a whole packet of blank forms which lay on his desk.

At that moment he was interrupted by the ring of a telephone. He turned away and stood there, listening intently to the voice on the phone and answering in a half-whisper. I took advantage of the fact that his face was partly turned away, and unhesitatingly pulled out a few sheets from the pile on the desk, as well as a number of smaller blanks which were heaped alongside. I hid them under my shirt in one swift motion.

We waited patiently for the officer to finish his conversation. It took a few minutes, and then he continued with the business in hand. He promised to write in the official register that I, Adam Rolski, should be issued a "*Sonderausweis nach Bucharest*" the next time I got to Odessa. I need not doubt his word – the document would await me.

I thanked him, "Eil Hitla!", and I was outside, inebriated by the unexpected development. Jurek was similarly bursting with joy. Marjan was waiting on the lawn in front of the *Quartieramt* building. We told him about the miracle, interrupting each other. We all felt drunk. We couldn't restrain ourselves dancing about like Indian braves, to celebrate our joy and triumph, laughing like madmen all the while. Our ladies didn't know how to contain their happiness when they learned how Fate had smiled at us. This lucky turn heralded at long last a breach in the Nazi wall that confined us.

20 · Preparations for Escape

We boarded the train to Kiev and began to make our plans for the future. Hela and I would remain in Zhemerinka. Marjan with Jurek and Roma would go to Kasatin or further on. They would collect the members of their families and notify our friends how to reach Bucharest.

We didn't have enough of the stolen *Sonderausweis* forms but I was convinced that the trip was possible even with an ordinary travel warrant and a *Wehrmachtfarschein* (a military train pass). Janek Fuchs was undoubtedly correct: nobody knew for certain what was permitted and what was not; the demoralization he counted on could be sensed in the air. In short, audacity would reap its reward. I, together with another three or four people, would go to Bucharest first. Then Marjan could follow with his family in two parties; and then Jurek with his friends. I was of the opinion that as many people as possible should have the benefit of the information we had collected.

I did not like Marjan's exploitative attitude; he attempted to push me to the forefront, so that I would serve as kind of a shield. And if my luck didn't hold he and his dear family would try something else. I am not very restrained in my language by nature. After a heated exchange of words we arrived at the conclusion that we didn't have to stick together. Each of us could act independently. This was not at all to the liking of Jurek, or even Roma. In the end I agreed to carry out the plan as outlined. That meant I would go first and beat a path through the jungle. Naturally, Hela would accompany me. We would wait for two or three more people whom they would direct to me from Kasatin. In the meanwhile I sent word to Dniepropetrovsk that it was possible to go to Bucharest, and how to get there.

After reaching Zhemerinka, I rented two rooms from Laskovski because it was clear that we would have to stay in the town for a week or two. Since a civilian woman was more conspicuous than a soldier in that place and time, Hela again registered with the Romanian police. The days passed lazily, but our nerves were stretched taut. After a few days Ania and Casick joined us. I rented rooms for them nearby without any difficulty.

One day two men appeared and said rather vaguely that they had been directed to me from Kiev. Today I still have to laugh when I recall the conversation. They naturally did not want to divulge who they were, what they were told, or who had sent them to me; if I proved to be somebody other than the person they were directed to find, they did not want to disclose confidential information which might do harm. On my side, I feared they might be agents-provocateurs. In a word, we were all actors in a spy thriller.

When I mull over these matters today, I realize that a large number of my moves, fears, reservations, and precautions were influenced by detective stories and thrillers I had read. From such sources I had a ready fund of knowledge about the various possibilities of discovery, of betrayal and capture in circumstances very similar to those we encountered in our real life later on. Still, I may be forgiven if I hold that more than once our real-life adventures outdid anything the writers had invented.

But back to my uninvited guests. When we overcame our mutual suspicion, I learned that they were Rysiek, (surname Pfau) formerly of Lvov, and his colleague, nicknamed Sobota. They already knew that a breakout to Bucharest was within the realm of possibility, and that I intended to try it shortly. I can't understand to this very day how news of this kind spread with such rapidity, though we had neither the postal service nor the telegraph at our disposal. I shared my information with them as a matter of course.

Rysiek and Sobota had planned to stay in Zhemerinka for one day only, and then return to Kiev and fetch the rest of their band. However, something completely unexpected occurred: Ania and Rysiek fell in love at first sight. They couldn't keep their eyes off each other. In the end he took her to Kiev.

They left behind a very valuable piece of information: two addresses in Bucharest, which had reached them by an unlikely route. They were said to be addresses of very trustworthy people. Such an address was truly priceless; it ensured a place where one could stay and perhaps get rid of the German uniform when the opportunity arose.

Before Rysiek, Sobota and Ania left, we arranged a rendezvous in Bucharest, again following a tried-and-true spy thriller prescription – the central post office in the city. Bucharest would surely have such a building, and people loitering there would not attract attention.

After a week's wait, a friend visited us with the news that Marjan and Jurek were ready to leave within two or three days. I was now free to set out on my trip.

21 · Bucharest – and New Dangers

The muster on the station platform in Zhemerinka went off smoothly after I had displayed the group *Sonderausweis* issued to "Adam Rolski und 3 Mann" (these were Hela, Casick and one Joseph Koral).

The train journey was also devoid of any adventures. This time I didn't want to risk any escapades in the restaurant car, especially since I had to keep an eye on Casick all the time. He had "bad looks". Each of us, and surely each Pole, would recognize him as a Jew at first sight. The best course was to tell him to sleep, which he did for most of the trip. Still, I had to remain close to him so I could cover for him if needed. The trip somehow ended without any mishap.

In Odessa we had to wait two hours for the train to Bucharest. On boarding, we were asked about our Wehrmacht train pass, which I had ready for inspection. The noncom in charge of the station guards assigned us seats. This trip also went off painlessly, and it was much shorter than the train ride to Odessa.

At the frontier I exchanged some of my marks for lei, the Romanian currency. I took advantage of the fact that Romanian passengers boarded the train to question them extensively about life in Bucharest. One Romanian (for all I know, he could have been a Jew) was ready to talk to my heart's desire. Perhaps he wished to display his knowledge of German, or, perhaps to do business. He said that life was all right, one could obtain all the necessities, food was plentiful but much more expensive than before the war. There were crowds of aliens in Romania, chiefly in Bucharest. There were very many refugees from Poland. The YMCA and their own special bureaus took care of their needs. The *refugiat polonais* usually gathered in a café in the centre of Bucharest.

When I asked whether they were free to do so, and what was the name of the café, he replied that Romania was a free country, and that the café was called "Transnistria". The last bit of information was very important: undoubtedly I would find acquaintances there and learn how one could get settled in Bucharest.

At ten o'clock in the morning we rolled into the Bucharest railway station. The disembarking passengers were greeted by a giant sign which instructed all Wehrmacht personnel to register at the office on the right. I had absolutely no intention of doing so at that moment.

We left the station and went into the city to look for the addresses Rysiek had left me. Casick and I wanted to take off our uniforms and become civilians as soon as possible. Hela didn't wear a uniform, of course, while Joseph was wearing the clothes of an ordinary workingman. Unfortunately, both addresses proved to be useless. There was nobody at home at the first one while at the second, the man in the apartment took one look through the window at German uniforms, pretended not to understand what I said, and refused even to open the door.

Various dodges (such as leaving the uniform in the dressing cabin of a swiming pool) seemed too dangerous. The person who found the abandoned uniform might think someone had been murdered, and set in motion a police investigation. In the end, I concluded that I would once more attempt a tried and true tactic – the frontal attack. We would register at the Wehrmacht office at the station and demand that we be assigned rooms at a hotel.

We went back to to the station, I left my group in the station compound, and went ahead to the *Urlaubüberwachung* (an office supervising military personnel on leave). This department of the German military was situated in a small house with a picket fence around it. A gendarme (from the German military police) stood at the entrance and handed out small numbered metal tokens which were to be given to the duty clerk who assigned rooms, together with personal credentials, proving that one was entitled to quarters at the expense of the Wehrmacht.

When I approached the gendarme, he had run out of numbers tokens. However, when he heard that I had just come in from Odessa after a night-long journey, he said he would not keep me waiting until he was resupplied with tokens; he would bear in mind that he had let me into the building without one.

Nobody knows, nobody *can* know, what trifle may decide one's fate. I can't say that I am especially favoured with luck, but it's certain that I am not a *schlemazel* – the butt of fate's bad jokes. My mother stated categorically that I would be lucky. that I was "born with a cap on my head" as the Polish saying goes. I know from experience that often enough things go my way without my having to put up a fight. Still, there is always the lurking fear that something will go wrong at the last possible moment and then I will have to apply all my reserves of energy, audacity and ingenuity so as to overcome the contrariness of fate. In any event, at that moment, I recalled that not so long before, when I was trying to escape from the labour camp, the Germans had liquidated the camp on the very night before the date I had fixed for my escape attempt. They had then thrown me into jail together with the remnant of the inmates. Thus my heart beat more rapidly than it should when I handed my papers to the clerk on duty.

He collected my *Sonderausweis*, the personal *Ausweis*, and the military train pass. Upon his inqury about the metal to ken, I told him that the supply had been temporarily exhausted. He accepted my explanation without much interest. After ten minutes or so, I asked him about my papers and my hotel. He replied that my papers were with the captain, and that I would get them in a moment. As a matter of fact he did call me soon after, and said the captain wished to speak with me.

I went in; "Eil Hitla". The captain showed me to a chair and inquired who had sent me to Bucharest, and why. I recounted my fairy tale, that I had been awarded a furlough, but also that I was to meet here with my engineer, Krause, and so on.

While telling my story, I watched his face and eyes. It was obvious that he was a well-educated person, perhaps an officer of counter-intelligence. His eyes revealed that he did not believe me. Once more, this seemed the very last moment before capture. I pretended naiveté, asked to have my papers back, because I was fatigued by my prolonged journey. He answered that it would just take a few minutes more. Would I wait outside?

I left his room and stood by the window near the clerk who was supposed to return my documents. Through the next window, I could overhear the replies of the telephone operator: "Ja, Herr Hauptmann". The patrol should come at once? … when? Jawohl, Herr Hauptmann, four men immediately …"

I needed nothing more. I walked slowly in the direction of the gate. The gendarme there remembered me and let me out without a further check. I continued in the direction of the station.

Bravo! The providential absence of a metal token. At the station I dispatched Joseph and Hela to the café "Transdnistria". They should seek acquaintances from Poland; if unsuccessful they would find help at the YMCA I would manage somehow. If I didn't make it to the café in time, I told Hela, she should wait for me each day at noon at the main entrance to the post office.

Together with Casick, we jumped on the steps of the first tram to appear. From the rear platform of the tram I observed a patrol of German gendarmerie approaching the entrance to the railway station.

Casick had the address of a relative of his father's, Engler by name, a stonemason who carved monuments for graves. We switched trams twice before we reached the address. When we entered the office, the two gentlemen sitting there displayed considerable fear which they seemed to be controlling only with great difficulty. Casick immediately attempted to reassure them. He revealed his real name, said he was from Lvov, and explained that the uniform was a temporary disguise. It was obvious that they didn't wholly believe him, and feared a provocation or God knows what.

I joined the conversation and said soothingly that we were in a fix ourselves because we had just escaped from the railway station. Casick. then volunteered a few particulars about the family which calmed their anxiety and convinced then, finally that we were not provocateurs. Engler's partner in the stonecutting shop was an engineer named Spinndel.

I find it difficult to find appropriate words of praise for the gracious kindness of these men who undertook to shelter two strangers, risking consequences that at best would be very unpleasant.

We remained with them for three days. Later, Engler told me that he had been extremely afraid, and had prepared a million and a half lei in cash to buy his life and ours in case of a surprise search or a raid. It was a revelation to me that it was possible to ransom oneself in such a situation. Afterwards I came to the conclusion that in this respect Romania was a "golden country" for refugees; one could extricate oneself from almost any predicament by means of an appropriate bribe.

The next day I sent Casick to the post office to meet Hela at noon and tell her where I was staying, that I was O.K., and also that I could not show my face in town for the moment, for my *Ausweis*, with my picture, was in the hands of the Germans. In all probability the police and the gendarmerie were looking for me. So my private war had perhaps ended with a minor defeat or perhaps a draw. But no!! It was a full-scale victory for me because I hadn't been murdered, I LIVED.

22 · Life in Bucharest

World War Two was roaring along full steam, yet its impact on Romania was relatively slight. The Romanians led quite normal lives, food was plentiful, there were no shortages of essentials. Still, prices had gone up, and this hit the population hard. We, on the other hand, considered the marketplace a real paradise. The prices seemed modest in comparison to the black-market prices we had been forced to pay in the Ukraine. As I have written, my private war had come to a temporary close. Nevertheless, the adventures of my odyssey still had not ended.

Hela had met plenty of acquaintances in the café Transnistria, among them her classmate W.F., who had come from Kiev a few days before us with her husband, sister and brother-in-law. Hela spent the night with her. The next day she met Casick near the post office and learned how I was doing. I decided to change my name and to alter as far as I could, the way I looked. I let my moustache grow and took to wearing sunglasses. My name was now George L. Sulawa (vide the certificate of baptism with a photograph, attested by the local authorities of Zaleszczyki). I took leave of the Englers with heartfelt thanks for their hospitable shelter.

One of my acquaintances introduced me to a certain Dzwonkowski who was said to have very good contacts. He had come to Bucharest years before, knew the city, and could help me in my dealings with the authorities.

Finding living quarters did not present any difficulty. I rented a room in a *pensione* recommended by Dzwonkowski, in the very centre of Bucharest. Hela and I introduced ourselves as Gentiles of course – the only ones (as I later learned) in the place! The others were all Jews, in hiding for obvious reasons. The landlady was also a Jewess who was protected from searchers and spot checks by the fixed sum, with which she bribed the police. When I got the picture I decided to find another place: I did not at all like to live in a location which was known to the police as a refuge for Jews. It was a case of guilt by association.

My most pressing concern was to establish contact with my brother, who had escaped from Zaleszczyki to Romania. I knew that he lived in a small town called Slatina, in the Oltenia district. I asked Dzwonknowski what I should do and he immediately advised me to phone. He rang up Slatina and spoke at length in Romanian. I didn't understand a word. At the end of the conversation he told me we should phone again in two hours, when my brother would be called to the telephone. After hours had passed, we phoned again. This time my brother, Poldek, was on the line.

Poldek was so amazed to hear my voice that his first reaction was one of suspicion; someone was misleading him on purpose. We agreed that he would come to Bucharest in two or three days. He needed the time to arrange a permit to leave Slatina.

Two days later Poldek came to the *Pensione*. We talked about the Russian occupation and then about the Nazi period. For two and a half days I kept telling him the full story. I told him about the tragic death of our parents, answered his questions, explained the whys, the whens and the wheres of the various events. We accounted for our whole family, which was quite numerous – there had been 93 guests at my Bar-Mitzvah, all close relatives, aunts, uncles, cousins, their husbands and children. I was certain I had given a full account to my brother of what had happened.

Among other details, I told him that in the so-called 'small ghetto' in Lvov there were 45,000 people whose food supplies had been completely cut off. My brother jumped up in protest, the better to express his doubt: "You're exaggerating! That's impossible! Why, that would mean mass murder!" I was struck dumb. I did not tell any more stories. I had only been giving him some facts about the "small ghetto" and not the most cruel ones at that.

At that moment I realized that a normal person, brought up in ordered conditions, could not grasp what the Germans had done. The mind boggles at the thought of deeds which exceed in brutality and cruelty anything we could ever imagine, actions compared with which even the loathsome exploits of Genghis Khan pale into insignificance. Our education and our reading create certain patterns into which we fit our life experience. I think that even the most extreme individualist, who is entirely free of preconceptions, would not be able to accept the factual truth of the German schemes and actions against the Jews. The enormity of it by far exceeded normal human understanding. Only a person who had had direct experience could understand what had happened.

Poldek told me parenthetically how my phone call had reached him. He was on the beach when a policeman on a motorcycle appeared. He had instructions to take my brother to the town hall, for a VIP from Bucharest was due to phone him in an hour.

That cheeky character, Dzwonkowski, had placed a call to the chief-of-police in Slatina, and had masqueraded as God knows who. His authoritative tone of voice had convinced the chief that he was talking to a personage.

Poldek said that conditions in Romania were satisfactory, there were no persecutions, nobody insulted or boycotted Jews. All the Jewish refugees from

Poland lived in peace. They even received financial assistance from the Joint Distribution committee in the United States, throught the intermediary of the YMCA. The war went on far away, it seemed; it reached Romania solely by means of radio communiqués or short news items in the press.

What sufferings I could have avoided by a flight to Romania. Poldek tried to persuade me to move now to Slatina. His permit for Bucharest was valid only for three days. He and others like him lived perfectly legally and had to respect the regulations.

However, I decided to remain in Bucharest. I found a room on Vasile Lascar Street. Dzwonkowski said he could arrange a residency permit for me and provide credentials as a political refugee in Romania. He demanded a horrendous sum of money in return. I conferred with the man who had recommended Dzwonkowski to me. He advised me in no uncertain terms to accept the offer – it was worth all my money.

I paid up, and obtained an identity card as a political refugee. Not long thereafter it became clear that the card was a worthless scrap of paper forged on a stolen blank form. A cursory inspection would reveal this fact; nobody would honour the document. At the same time I discovered that my "adviser" had received a sizeable cut from the sum I had paid to Dzwonkowski on his recommendation.

It is worth recounting the circumstances that misled me into being victimized. Dzwonkowski said that I had to present myself at the headquarters of the secret police, the Siguranca, to have my document stamped for approval. He accompanied me, of course. We entered a roomy hall where seven or eight office workers where seated. Dzwonkowski took me to one of them, greeted him and spoke with him in Romanian. A sign in Romanian and in German hung on a wall by the clerk's desk. "The office worker receives a salary in recompense for his functions – there is no need to pay anything extra". I must admit the sign had a positive effect on my morale.

The clerk spoke to me directly in German, wishing to display his proficiency in a foreign language. He demanded 500 lei for a stamp tax. I asked Dzwonkowski what to do. He nodded affirmatively. The clerk took the 500 banknote I held out, and with boundless effrontery put it nonchalantly in his pocket. Then he motioned to a desk in the corner of the hall and said that the clerk there would sell me the desired stamp. My skin crawled. An open bribe under the eyes of several office personnel! I would be arrested in a matter of minutes ... But nobody reacted at all; it was none of their business. Dzwonkowski told me in Polish to fetch the stamps.

When we exited from the building, he invited me to have a bite and drink with him, in honour of the successful outcome of the business of the document. Indeed, for him personally, it was a great success! He took me to a high-class place on the Calea Victoria. At the entrance to the dining room there was a buffet table crowded with various hors d'oeuvres – olives, herring, sandwiches with salmon and caviar. A barman served drinks. We each had a vodka and chose our hors d'oeuvres, together with a crowd of other customers. Dzwonkowski urged me, as a connoisseur to sample widely – the buffet was famous for its variety and quality. We had another vodka and ate on. After some time he asked whether I had had enough. When I nodded yes, expecting we would now enter the dining room, he led me to a side exit and thence into the street. We didn't pay. I wasn't too surprised at his brazenness, but the cynical invitation to the stolen meal – I had been practically made an accessory to larceny! – shocked me and nearly made me sick.

Hela and I went to the YMCA where we registered. When asked whether we needed accommodation, I replied that we were living for the time being with friends but that we might possibly ask for relocation to the provinces, to a centre for refugees from Poland.

We were sucked into the current of refugee life. No – the previous sentence is a lie, except for the unlovely expression "sucked into". We were immersed (without any volition, out of mere inertia) – not into a current but rather into a bog – for there is no movement for any kind in the life of refugees. One "sits on suitcases" as the saying goes. One waits passively for what tomorrow will bring in its wake, and nothing happens. It's not 'life', either, but dreary existence.

Of course, in comparison with ghetto existence, this vegetative life is quite pleasant. Good coffee for breakfast with fresh rolls. Then a walk to kill the time – and, ah! it's already noon. It's time to visit the café, meet the refugee crowd and learn what's new – which means gossip, and more gossip. A bit of politics, a short discussion about the situation on the various fronts. The war was so far away; it did not affect us directly.

So the day passed, punctuated for variety's sake by the appearance of new escapees who had succeeded in reaching Bucharest by fantastic routes. One of my friends B. Feller, a veterinary doctor by profession, came to Romania as a cattle herder, driving a herd of cows from a God-forsaken hamlet in the Ukraine on the instructions of the German authorities. Quite a number of people came from Dniepropetrovsk and Kiev.

It was clear to me that the exodus must cease within a short time because it was taking on mass proportions. In fact, two or three people were arrested at the border crossing. It was difficult to learn the circumstances of the arrest, but rumours immediately spread about raids, manhunt, and the like that would begin in Bucharest.

Unfortunately, the rumours proved correct. I met a man who had escaped from his guards at the railway station in Bucharest. He had been arrested in Kiev and the police had found many travel warrants on him, including one to Bucharest. He had been brought to Bucharest so that he could identify other escapees. So the rumours about raids were entirely correct.

23 · Slatina

Hela and I decided to move to Slatina, where my brother lived. I went to the YMCA. to ask for the appropriate reference. They were eager to oblige with the desired document and with train tickets thrown in. We collected our meagre belongings and took the train to Slatina the next day.

I have written about the dreary existence in Bucharest, but that was a vibrant way of life compared with the emptiness of life in Slatina. We met many well-educated people from Poland, yet boredom and aimlessness suffocated all of us and controlled our conduct and our thoughts. The greatest problem was how to kill time.

Still, owing to the stay in Slatina I accomplished two important (or perhaps not so important) things. First, I learned shoemaking, especially how to make slippers with rope soles. Second, Adam Weinsberg from Krakow persuaded me to put into writing my wartime experiences, beginning with the escape from Warsaw the first days of September 1939, when the war broke out.

Organizing the notes I had made over the years, most of them couched in cryptic language and stenographically short, blocking out the plan of the book, and then the writing itself, occupied me for days on end and during very many sleepless nights. When I recalled the details of my escape from Warsaw, the Russian occupation, the German-Russian war, the ghetto, I lived once again in the hell which I thought I had left behind.

Still, putting my experiences on paper had positive aspects. First, it occupied the best part of the day. I struggled hard to find words which would help the reader understand the nightmare I was trying to describe. The reader, I knew, had not experienced all these things and would frequently be unable to grasp events which have no equal in human history in the immensity of their cruelty and the degree of brutality employed in the implementation of the cruel design (this inability may be one of the givens of human personality).

The task is surely beyond my powers. One would need the pen of a Dante to call up from the imagination of the reader a picture of what happened to the Jews in Poland. I have attempted to furnish dry facts, to describe them as objectively as I can, but sometimes a violent upsurge of emotion overwhelms the pen and the words may seem too exaggerated or out of place.

On the other hand, reliving the hell of the ghetto helped me to overcome the trauma of the radical transition from the ghetto and my risky disguise as a member of the Wehrmacht – that dance on the edge of the sword – to the peaceful vegetative life among a small group of Polish refugees in Slatina.

Life here is like living in a glass retort. The quiet is so absolute that a wife caught *in flagrante* with one's friend becomes an exciting event of the first magnitude, and provides a subject of conversation for several weeks. The question of what the YMCA will serve for dinner becomes a source of concern and anticipation. The peace and quiet, which have come so abruptly after the stress of the last months, are disorienting.

We are cheered by the news that the war is not going well for the Germans. But it all happens at such a remove that there is no direct influence on our tranquil existence as refugees.

24 · Back to Bucharest

The situation on the Eastern front was fluid and the war began to come worrisomely closer to us. In March, April and May 1944, the Russian armies took back from the Germans a large part of the Ukraine, including the regions which had been assigned to the Romanians in the wake of the German conquests in Russia: Transnistria, Bukovina and Bessarabia. The Russians entered Galicia, the region in which Lvov was situated. They were quite close to us. The approaching defeat of the Germans was evident.

The time was coming for decisions: where to go, how to ensure relative freedom of movement. In the light of my wartime experiences, I didn't even wish to think about going back to Poland. There was some talk about the possibility of a passage to Palestine. I decided to go to Bucharest to inquire about this.

As I have repeatedly written, Romania was truly a "*Goldene Medine*" (Golden Country) for those who were forced to live in the shadows. I took a train to Bucharest – naturally without requesting a permit. In return for a modest bribe, the train conductor found a seat for me in a first-class compartment and forgot about the ticket.

In Bucharest I learned that the Jewish committee in Romania was making arrangements for people to go to Palestine. I moved Hela to Bucharest and began searching for some way to be assigned to one of the boats. In spite of strenuous efforts I could not obtain places although I was coopted onto the committee which organized the sailings.

We did not go to Palestine. Instead, we were caught in one of the infernal maelstroms of the war unknown to us till then – the mass bombardment of a city. While we were still in Slatina in May soaking in the sun on the beach, we had observed in clear daylight the overflight of such an armada, headed for Bucharest or for the oil wells in Ploesti. There were 300 to 500 B-17 planes, called "Flying Fortresses". The entire sky was darkened with countless dots. Though the planes were passing at the height of at least 3,000 metres (about 10,000 feet), the roar of their engines was loud enough to squeeze our skulls as in a vice. It seemed as though several train engines were rolling directly over my head. The horrendous experience of the overflight is indescribable. One feels a helpless grain of dust in face of an overwhelming power similar to the forces of nature – earthquakes, hurricanes and the like.

We lived through two months of mass bombardments in Bucharest while trying to be assigned places aboard a ship to Palestine. In July 1944 the ship *Kazbek* departed at the beginning of August three additional ships: *Mefkur, Bulbul* and *Morina.* Friends who witnessed their departure from Constanza told the rest of us that they had observed German officers in the port area grinning ironically at the sight of Jews pushing their way aboard so as to leave at all cost.

Some of my friends and colleagues were on those ships: Muna Hoch, Janek Wachtel, Casick Reifer, and others. After a few days tragic news reached us: the Germans had torpedoed the boats on the open sea. They had sunk *Mefkur* with 400 passengers on board and shot at those who attempted to escape by swimming from the sinking ship. Only five people had miraculously survived. Muna Hoch and his wife were among the victims. Janek Wachtel reached the Greek shore by a stroke of luck. After many days of wandering in the wild hills of Greece, he reached the coast of the Ionian Sea, and from there he got to Palestine.

In spite of my superstitious fears of "missing the boat", when the clock face shows almost twelve, this time Lady Luck had been good to me – I didn't succeed in getting a berth on one of those ships. Now it was entirely clear why the Germans had grinned when the ships were steaming away.

Not long afterwards, on 24 August 1944, Romania capitulated and surrendered to the Russians. The Germans left Bucharest in great haste. It may be said that they were gone from one day to the next, even within hours. As one of their last acts, the Germans, evidently out for revenge, decided to bomb the palace of the king, who had "betrayed" them.

In those days I had found a room in the immediate vicinity of the royal palace, so I had the doubtful pleasure of living through this bombing raid. The anti-aircraft defences of the city had been entirely in the hands of the Germans, and after their departure there weren't even air-raid warning sirens left. The small house where we lived was cut in half by a bomb. Our room suddenly had just one wall left, and the remnants of two side walls. I am not able to describe the enormity of the horrors which befell us during the five or six hours the raid lasted. We rushed to an air-raid shelter located in the cellar of building under construction. It had five concrete floors, but no walls. A bomb fell on the building, penetrated all the floors, and exploded on the ground floor, immediately above our cellar.

The hundreds of people in the cellar were overcome by blind panic. I was fortunate enough not to lose my head, and moved to the back exit. Very few people had the courage to leave by that route, for the wooden scaffolding had caught fire. Hela and I rushed through burning planks and emerged at a run into the street.

I will always remember our flight through the entire length of the Calea Victoria. Bombed-out houses, burning houses, people jumping out of the windows of houses in flames. A green chestnut tree was burning like a torch.

We reached the neighbourhood around King Carol Boulevard, covered with dust and soot. For two days and two nights we stayed in the first shelter where we were admitted, until we had sufficiently recovered from our appalling experience, and were able to go out into the street and search for accommodation.

25 · Through Bulgaria to Palestine

In October 1944 the Jewish Agency, which was based in Jerusalem, began to organize train passages to Palestine through Bulgaria (which had been liberated by the Russians) and Turkey. At first only small groups of ten to fifteen people were dispatched. I succeeded in placing my brother and wife in one of the first groups. Only after several small groups had got through were two large ones organized, about 300 persons each. I was included in the first one under the name of Hoch. The original Hoch had perished on a torpedoed ship, and it would be a sin to waste the immigration certificate to Palestine, which had been issued in his name by the British.

I rather think that I'm not a *"schlemazel"*. On the contrary, I may claim that luck decidedly favours me – hadn't I found way and means to save my life amidst the mass murder of three and a half million Polish Jews? Still, I have to say that I always have to struggle hard in order to succeed in the face of encroaching danger. In all the difficult moments I have experienced – and I've lived through plenty of them – I had to break through the barriers facing me by myself. Still, I must have been born lucky, because until now, my tendency to fight my way out of difficulties had been crowned by success. I have faith in the aura around me, the aura of combat.

Our group left Bucharest on 19 November 1944, in the morning. The train compartments were a little crowded, but that was unimportant. We crossed tha Bulgarian border without a hitch. Around noon the train reached a locality named Stara Zagora. The chief of the railway station there demanded to see our passports. The majority of us were travelling under a so-called collective passport, but about fifty possessed individual passports. These became apprehensive, suspecting a trap. It was a perfectly natural reaction, considering our experience under Russian occupation and in the ghetto. In a conversation the Bulgarian station chief, told me that the Russian military commander had demanded to examine our passports, but they would be returned by 2 p.m. We delivered our passport with the exception of several passengers who refused to part with them.

Unfortunately all the misgivings proved correct. The Russian commander did not return the passports. When I intervened personally, he announced that the matter would take a number of days. He had to ask for directions from higher authorities, as there was a possibility that among us were Polish officers who had not registered with the Russian authorities as required.

Our group did not lack people who were "veterans" of the fight for survival. After a prolonged council-of-war it was decided to notify various world figures about our plight and mobilize the high-and-mighty of the Western world to deliver us, this time from the Russian grip. The same day telegrams were sent to the Jewish and non-Jewish personalities in Europe and the USA who were known to us, such as President Roosevelt, Winston Churchill, Generals Eisenhower and Patton, and many others. At noon the following day, the telegraph clerk in the post office refused to send any more wires abroad. Instructions from the Russian military command, he said.

Our main concern after passports was the supply of food for about 350 people. There was a Jewish community in Stara Zagora, but it only numbered nine families. They did what they could to help us, but the food situation left much to be desired; it was difficult to purchase food even for a high price. I went to the commander's headquarters almost every day, only to return without achieving anything. The reply did not vary: "There is no answer yet. It will come tomorrow, for sure".

About thirty days passed in this manner. Then I was invited to spend the night with the head of the Jewish community and his family. The Jewish families used to invite a few of us, from time to time, "to sleep in a real bed" – a genuine treat for us.

Around 9 o'clock in the evening, after the curfew went into effect, there was a sudden knocking at the door. It was the Russian secret police, the NKVD. They had come for me. "Take a blanket" they told me. I knew this phrase from the period of the Russian occupation in Lvov. It signified a long stay in a cell, and it was used to apply psychological pressure on the person being arrested. Hela urged the NKVD to let her accompany me. The son of the head of the family graciously offered to join us as interpreter. The NKVD people finally agreed to this.

The three of us were led through deserted, deathly-still streets to the NKVD quarters and seated us in a dimly lit corridor. We were told to wait for the officer in charge and were forbidden to converse. A guard was posted every five paces. I waited … and waited … endlessly. It was a well-tried method, meant to wear down the nerves of the prisoner, destroy his powers of resistance, and wipe out the last shred of his self-confidence. They wished to transform me into a bundle of nerves filled with anxiety. What did they really want of me?

At last, around midnight, a guard called us to enter the room of the officer.

The conversation started in innocent vein. He wanted to know who I was, where I came from, what my occupation was, how I knew Russian so well, etc. Then, he abruptly cut short the seemingly friendly exchange of information, and stated that we were really a hostile element, for we were running away from the Soviet authorities who had done so much for the Jews!

His words caused me to go off the deep end. All my irritation at the endless procrastinations, the helpless anger, the ruined dreams of freedom turning into dust – all these found expression in an attack of blind rage – just the opposite of the expected reaction. Later, Hela told me that I turned pale and began to shout, foaming at the mouth, that "... they do nothing to help us" "... news from Poland speak of attacks on Jews", "... the Poles throw Jews off moving trains".

"We are being murdered and robbed, in the very same places where the cobblestones were soaked with the blood of my parents, sisters, brothers, and friends, whom they had openly murdered, jointly with the Germans, just a short time ago. There is no peace for us Jews in Poland. The Soviet authorities are doing nothing to help us". I yelled for so long that I had no breath left. Hela was pulling at my jacket, but I didn't know that.

The room filled with a sudden silence. After a few moments, the officer broke the stillness. "*Vy pravy* (you're right)," he said "Go home".

I couldn't believe my ears. He called a guard and ordered him to escort us to our house. About ten days later I was called to the headquarters and all the passports were returned to us. We could go on.

It was the second half of December when we reached Tzvillingrad railway station on the Bulgarian–Turkish border, in the middle of a violent snowstorm. We had prepared ourselves for a journey to Palestine, to warmer climes, so we suffered terribly from the cold. But that was almost of no importance, in comparison with the news we received on the spot. Turkey did not want to let our train in. Great Britain had published new regulations which forbade any immigration of Jews to Palestine, beginning on 1 January 1945. The Turks were afraid that, as a result, we would be forced to remain in Turkey. On no account did they wish to permit this.

Bulgaria, however, did not need "homeless people" either. For the moment, the trains were shunted to a rail siding on the "no-man's land" between the borders of Bulgaria and Turkey.

Tzvillingrad was a small village and there was almost no possibility of feeding the 700 stomachs of the two groups who were being delayed there. On the advice of the station chief, we sent out people to purchase provisions. They returned almost empty-handed except for three sacks of beans.

It was terribly cold. We had no food. There was no water, either. Out of pity, the man in charge of the two refugee trains which were standing in two feet of snow, turned on the heat and offered a glass of water per person, so that we could wash. Thirst could be quenched by eating the all too plentiful snow. Each person received twelve beans per day, which were cooked in the homes of peasants who took pity on us.

Again we began to bombard the world with pleas for help. The suspenseful wait lasted for about eight days, if my memory does not mislead me, but the result was what counted. After we had tearfully drunk to a happy New Year in the office of the station chief on the last evening of 1944, we were notified on 1 January 1945 that we were free to move on to Turkey and from there to Palestine.

(This account was written in the spring of 1944 in Slatina/Bucharest. The last two chapters were written in February 1945, in Tel-Aviv.)